SECOND EDITION

EGO PSYCHOLOGY
and
SOCIAL WORK
PRACTICE

Eda G. Goldstein

 THE FREE PRESS

The Free Press
A Division of Simon & Schuster Inc.
866 Third Avenue, New York, N.Y. 10022

Printed in the United States of America

printing number
     5 6 7 8 9 10

Library of Congress Cataloging-in-Publication Data

Goldstein, Eda G.
    Ego psychology and social work practice / Eda Goldstein.—2nd ed.
      p.   cm.
    Includes bibliographical references and index.
    ISBN 0-02-912150-7
    1. Psychiatric social work.   2. Ego (Psychology)   I. Title.
HV689.G58   1995
362.2'0425—dc20   94–41130
                                                           CIP

To Pat
With Gratitude and Appreciation

CONTENTS

Acknowledgments   vii
Introduction   ix

PART I   HISTORICAL DEVELOPMENTS
Chapter 1   The Scope and Evolution of Ego Psychology   3
Chapter 2   The Emergence and Assimilation of Ego
             Psychology into Social Work Practice   29

PART II   THEORETICAL UNDERPINNINGS
Chapter 3   The Ego and Its Functions   53
Chapter 4   The Ego and Its Defenses   72
Chapter 5   Ego Mastery and the Processes of
             Coping and Adaptation   86
Chapter 6   Object Relations and Ego Development   113

PART III   PRACTICE APPLICATIONS
Chapter 7   The Nature of Ego-Oriented Assessment   143
Chapter 8   The Nature of Ego-Oriented Intervention   166
Chapter 9   The Nature of the Client–Worker
             Relationship   200
Chapter 10   Ego-Oriented Intervention with Diverse
             and Oppressed Populations   230
Chapter 11   Ego-Oriented Intervention with Special
             Populations   257

Chapter 12   The Diagnosis and Treatment of
                  the Borderline Client   289

Bibliography   321
Author Index   351
Subject Index   357

ACKNOWLEDGMENTS

When I wrote the first edition of *Ego Psychology and Social Work Practice* over a decade ago, my professional development was at a different point than it is today. Largely because of the book's success, I have had the rewarding opportunity to meet practitioners, trainees, and supervisors in diverse agency settings in addition to students and faculty at schools of social work in many regions of the United States. I have been touched by the warm response and encouragement that I have received from this varied audience. A major impetus for this second edition comes from the questions raised and interests expressed by the many individuals whom I have met.

My early interest in ego psychology began when I was a student at the School of Social Service Administration of the University of Chicago in the mid-1960s. There I was inspired by the humanity and spirit of Helen Harris Perlman, one of the true shining lights of the social work profession. Some gifted and generous mentors have played a significant role in shaping my intellectual life and clinical pursuits since that time. When I was engaged in doctoral studies at the Columbia University School of Social Work, Carol Meyer and Carel Germain, each in her own distinctive way, helped me to broaden my thinking. I shall always be grateful to Dr. Otto Kernberg, with whom I was privileged to work at both the New York State Psychiatric Institute and the New York Hospital, Cornell Medical Center, Westchester Division, for his confidence in my abilities. During my seven-year association with him, my professional activities expanded to encompass research and teaching and I gained a deeper understanding of ego psychology and object relations theory and their application to the diagnosis and treatment of borderline and narcissistic pathology. Before and after my departure from New York Hospital in 1981, the social work department, under the able direction of my friend, Norma Hakusa Counts, was an important support system. My later work with Dr. Marjorie Taggart White helped me to grasp the significance of self psychology and marked an important turning point in my professional interests. I shall always be grateful for her encouragement and vision and for sharing in my struggle to understand conflicting theoretical and clinical models.

As chairperson of the social work practice curriculum area at the New York University Shirley M. Ehrenkranz School of Social Work over the past decade, I have had the good fortune to work with an intellectually stimulating and talented faculty. I am appreciative of the ongoing collegiality I enjoy with Associate Dean Eleanore Korman, George Frank, Jeffrey Seinfeld, Barbara Dane, Judith Siegel, Judith Mishne, Lala Straussner, and Martha Gabriel. I could not have asked for a more congenial atmosphere. I shall always remember the personal support that I received from Dean Shirley Ehrenkranz and her passionate commitment to the School.

I am happy to have renewed my association with the Free Press and extend my thanks to Susan Arellano, senior editor, for strongly urging me to undertake the second edition of *Ego Psychology and Social Work Practice* and for expertly guiding me in the writing process. I could not have completed this task without the help of Richard Lenert, my administrative assistant at New York University. My friends and colleagues Enid Ain and Lucille Spira have been staunch supporters during the preparation of this edition, and Patricia Petrocelli deserves special appreciation for her encouragement and technical assistance. Lastly, I am indebted to my students and clients, who have taught me about the creativity, resilience, and fragility of the ego and about the environmental and therapeutic nutriments that restore, maintain, and enhance ego functioning.

INTRODUCTION

The original aims of *Ego Psychology and Social Work Practice* were to provide the social work student, practitioner, and educator with a general ego psychological framework for understanding human behavior and to demonstrate the linkages between ego psychological concepts and social work practice. When the first edition was published in 1984, it appeared to fill a gap in the social work literature. It became a widely used text in schools of social work and a popular resource for trainees, practitioners, and supervisors in the practice arena. At the present time, ego psychology still occupies a central place in social workers' knowledge base. A large representative study of practitioners found it to be the major theory guiding clinical work (Mackey, Urek, and Charkoudian, 1987). Courses in human behavior, psychopathology, social work practice, and intervention with special populations, which are offered in academic settings, training institutes, and agency staff development programs, draw on ego psychology.

While the concepts that make up the core of *Ego Psychology and Social Work Practice* are still current a decade after the book's publication, there are many factors that point to the need for a second, revised edition. First, there have been numerous developments that have enriched and modified ego psychological theory. These include new perspectives on women, gays and lesbians, and the impact of trauma; greater appreciation of cultural, ethnic, and racial diversity and the effects of oppression on personality development; and increasing research on human behavior throughout the life cycle. Second, alternative formulations such as object relations theory, self psychology, and cognitive theory have linkages to, as well as important differences from, ego psychology. They offer new and often complementary dimensions to our understanding of developmental processes and fresh approaches to intervention. Third, changes in the problems that practitioners confront have led to the application of ego psychological treatment principles to special populations. For example, AIDS, rape and other forms of violent assault, substance abuse, homelessness, sexual abuse, and domestic violence have had staggering effects and necessitate a vast array of programs and creative interventions. Further, increased understanding of women, people of color, and gays and lesbians has generated more sensitive and affirmative treatment approaches. Greater numbers of clients are presenting with severe ego deficits such as those associated with borderline disorders, and practitioners are eager to experiment with different treatment strategies in their work with such individuals. Finally, social agencies and hospitals have undergone dramatic shifts. Despite the compelling need for comprehensive and differential treatment, intervention has become increasingly short-term. Individuals trained in business and corporations are administering human service settings and large managed care organizations are determining the nature of service.

In trying to respond to these changes, I have attempted to preserve in this revised edition the core of *Ego Psychology and Social Work Practice*, while enriching it by adding material that addresses newer theoretical and practice developments. It is my hope that this expanded volume will maintain the overall appeal of the first edition and make it more relevant to today's practice needs.

THE SIGNIFICANCE OF EGO PSYCHOLOGY

When ego psychological concepts emerged in Europe and the United States in the late 1930s, they highlighted the importance of an individual's adaptive capacity and linked individuals to their social environment. "Here at last was the happy synthesis between the social order and the psychological depths—the ego, which bridged these two worlds" (Briar and Miller, 1971:19). Ego psychology offered social work a theoretical base that has had far-reaching practice implications to be discussed throughout this book. Many practice models draw on ego psychological concepts to some extent (Turner, 1986).

Ego psychology embodies a more optimistic and growth-oriented view of human functioning and potential than do earlier theoretical formulations. It generated changes in the study and assessment process and led to an expansion and systematization of interventive strategies with individuals. It fostered a reconceptualization of the client-worker relationship, of change mechanisms, and of the phases of the interventive process. It helped to refocus the importance of work with the social environment. Moreover, it has important implications for work with families and groups and for the design of service delivery, large-scale social programs, and social policy.

Ego psychological concepts have been refined and extended greatly, however, since their assimilation into social work in the late 1930s, the 1940s, and the 1950s. Further, more recent theoretical and research developments within ego psychology point to new practice directions and offer additional understanding of the human growth process and the nature of maladaptation. Extensions and modifications of ego psychology have shed light on women's development, the adult life cycle, survivors of trauma, and the experiences and strengths of people of color and gays and lesbians. The application of ego psychological interventions is far-reaching and has significance for work with some of the most pressing problems and difficult populations that practitioners encounter.

WHAT IS EGO PSYCHOLOGY?

Ego psychology comprises a related set of theoretical concepts about human behavior that focus on the origins, development, structure, and functioning of the executive arm of the personality—the ego—and its relationship to other aspects of the personality and to the external environment. The ego is considered to be a mental structure of the personality that is responsible for negotiating between the internal needs of the individual and the outside world.

The following seven propositions characterize ego psychology's view of human functioning.

1. Ego psychology views people as born with an innate capacity to function adaptively. Individuals engage in a lifelong biopsychosocial developmental process in which the ego is an active, dynamic force for coping with, adapting to, and shaping the external environment.

2. The ego is part of the personality that contains the basic functions essential to the individual's successful adaptation to the environment. Ego functions are innate and develop through maturation and the interaction among biopsychosocial factors. Crucial among these are hereditary and constitutional endowment; the drives; the quality of interpersonal relationships, particularly in early childhood; and the impact of immediate environment, sociocultural values and mores, socioeconomic conditions, social and cultural change, and social institutions.

3. Ego development occurs sequentially as a result of the meeting of basic needs, identification with others, learning, mastery of developmental tasks, effective problem-solving, and successful coping with internal needs and environmental conditions, expectations, stresses, and crises.

4. While the ego has the capacity for functioning autonomously, it is only one part of the personality and must be understood in relation to internal needs and drives and to the internalized characteristics, expectations, mores, and values of others.

5. The ego not only mediates between the individual and the environment but also mediates internal conflict among various aspects of the personality. It can elicit defenses that protect the individual from anxiety and conflict and that serve adaptive or maladaptive purposes.

6. The social environment shapes the personality and provides the conditions that foster or obstruct successful coping. The nature of cultural, racial, and ethnic diversity as well as differences related to gender, age, and sexual orientation must be understood in the assessment of ego functioning.

7. Problems in social functioning must be viewed in relation

to both possible deficits in coping capacity and the fit among needs, capacities, and environmental conditions and resources.

Many theorists have contributed to the development of ego psychology, and the concepts are not unified. Two major streams within the evolution of ego psychology have had an impact on social work practice. One stream flows out of classical Freudian psychoanalytic theory, with its emphasis on unconscious and instinctual forces in personality development. While embodying revisions that expanded and altered Freud's views substantially, psychoanalytic ego psychology focuses on the ego's defensive function; on its role in mediating between the inner life and external reality; on the development of autonomous ego functions and the inner world of object relations; and on the interplay of innate temperament and capacities and the caretaking environment. The concepts that have evolved permit an appreciation not only of normal development but also of the precursors to certain types of pathological conditions in children and in adults that were not well conceptualized by classical psychoanalytic theory.

Psychoanalytic ego psychology is associated with a clinical and psychotherapeutic orientation within the social work profession. The concepts are well formulated, have enormous explanatory power, and seem to bear close resemblance to many aspects of clinical reality in work with troubled individuals. A reliance on the theory as an underpinning to social work practice has been attacked vigorously by those who feel that ego psychology is too narrowly focused on individual pathology; that it does not deal sufficiently with the impact of the social environment on human behavior; that it minimizes work with the family, group, and social environment; and that it has failed to generate a social work practice model distinct from psychotherapy. Such critiques equate ego psychological theory with a monolithic and narrow practice model rather than a valid frame of reference for understanding human behavior that can lead to diverse types of intervention with the person and his or her social environment.

A second theoretical stream within ego psychology emanates from an interest in the more rational and problem-solving capacities of the ego; the individual's drives for mastery and self-actualization; the acquisition, development, and expansion of coping capacities all through the human life cycle; and the individual's relationship to society and culture. It focuses on the ego's capacity to cope with, adapt to, and shape the environment as well as on the impact of the environment and culture on ego development and in fostering adaptive behavior. Proponents of this view often minimize the significance of the unconscious and instinctual forces in personality, the defenses, the inner life, and the childhood past. They focus more on the rational and adaptive ego as it enters into life transactions.

This theoretical stream has been associated with social work practice approaches that focus on improving the more rational, cognitive, problem-solving capacities of people; on enhancing their adaptive capacities; on modifying aspects of environment that are not conducive to effective coping; and on improving the fit between the individual and the environment. This emphasis has been criticized by those who seek more "in-depth" understanding of human behavior for ignoring the unconscious and instinctual determinants of behavior, for underrating the significance of entrenched inner pathology and ego deficits, and for its simplistic view of the interventive process. Practitioners complain that the concepts are either too general and abstract on the one hand or too concretely focused on behavior on the other. Social work theorists committed to this thrust are struggling to make the concepts operational in ways that can be used effectively by practitioners (Germain, 1979; Germain and Gitterman, 1980). Important questions have surfaced as a result of this theoretical thrust. What is effective coping? In which situations and to what degree does one need to understand the "inner man" in order to enhance social functioning in particular person-environment situations? So far these questions are answered only partially.

While these two currents within ego psychology overlap to some extent, they tend to have different proponents, and at times one view is used to negate the importance of the other. The following chapters will deal with both trends within ego psychology. Each addresses crucial although somewhat different aspects of human functioning. Each is necessary to encompass the complexity of human behavior and to guide intervention. Nevertheless, there is no simple theoretical integration of these views. While each has led to different emphases in practice, the concepts jointly help the practitioner to find the optimal ways of helping clients who seek social work services. Perhaps it is only in the practice arena with each individual client that the true integration of these concepts can take place.

THE PLAN OF THE BOOK

This book is divided into three parts as follows:

Part I summarizes the historical evolution of ego psychology and its extensions, as well as related theoretical developments. It also traces the introduction and assimilation of ego psychological concepts into social work practice and discusses current professional issues.

Part II describes core ego psychological concepts that provide the underpinnings for social work practice and selected newer ideas that have expanded our understanding of biopsychosocial development and maladaptive behavior.

Part III discusses the principles and techniques of ego-oriented practices generally and their specific application to work with women, people of color, gays and lesbians, and special client populations including adult survivors of incest, substance abusers, persons with AIDS, the chronically mentally ill, and individuals with severe developmental arrests.

Writing the second edition of *Ego Psychology and Social Work Practice* seems an equally if not a more compelling task today than it did when I first conceived the book in the early 1980s. There is continuing ferment within social work over the need to identify the core body of knowledge that underlies practice (Goldstein, 1980; Mishne, 1982; Simon, 1977; Strean, 1993). More than twenty years ago, Carol Meyer (1970:27) observed that "there are hardly any boundaries to the knowledge that social workers need to get through the working day." This condition has heightened as the knowledge base necessary to an informed practice has grown and become increasingly specialized. Social work's historical tendency to polarize knowledge of people and knowledge of environments still exists. In my view, ego psychology transcends this unfortunate dichotomy. It is my hope that this book will contribute in some way to the important and challenging task of articulating the knowledge base of professional practice and helping practitioners in their quest for competence.

PART I

HISTORICAL DEVELOPMENTS

CHAPTER 1

THE SCOPE AND EVOLUTION OF EGO PSYCHOLOGY

It is customary to view ego psychology as evolving from and extending classical psychoanalytic theory.[1] Sigmund Freud laid the foundation for the contemporary study of the ego. His daughter Anna extended his ideas, and Heinz Hartmann, along with Ernst Kris and Alfred Lowenstein, made the theoretical leap that initiated current views of ego functioning and development. David Rapaport, Erik Erikson, René Spitz, John Bowlby, Margaret Mahler, Edith Jacobson, and others made seminal contributions to ego psychology. The writings of all these theorists do not constitute an integrated and distinct theory but are bound loosely together and often referred to as "psychoanalytic ego psychology."

From a historical perspective, others who represented different intellectual traditions also contributed to the understanding of ego functioning and development. Interpersonal theorists such as Alfred Adler, Karen Horney, Erich Fromm, and Harry Stack Sullivan focused on the social and cultural determinants of personality. Otto Rank, Abraham Maslow, Carl Rogers, and Henry Murray emphasized a more holistic, humanistic, and growth-oriented view of human development. Jean Piaget and others focused on cognition, one of the building blocks of ego functioning, as central in personality development; more recently, others have refined cognitive theory and utilized its principles in understanding and treating many types of emotional disorder. The study of stress and crisis and the adult life cycle has added to our understanding of human behavior and maladaptation and has generated more focused treatment approaches.

Contemporary feminist writers such as Jessica Benjamin, Nancy Chodorow, Dorothy Dinnerstein, Carol Gilligan, and Jean Baker Miller and her colleagues at the Stone Center for Developmental Services and Studies at Wellesley College in Massachusetts have proposed new perspectives on women's development. Likewise, more affirmative views of gays and lesbians, increased awareness of the impact of childhood trauma, and greater understanding of populations that are culturally diverse and oppressed have modified and enriched ego psychology and resulted in more sensitive interventions.

Personality theories that have linkages to, but also some important differences from, ego psychology have become popular. For example, the work of Melanie Klein, W. R. D. Fairbairn, D. W. Winnicott, and Harry Guntrip—British object relations theorists—and the contributions of Heinz Kohut, who originated self psychology, have complemented and in some instances modified our understanding of the developmental process, human problems, and their treatment. Finally, Daniel Stern's research has shed new light on self development in infancy and challenged prevailing views.

From a broader perspective, an appreciation of the impact of environmental systems and social change sheds light on the complexity of factors that shape ego development and foster or obstruct effective coping and adaptation.

A comprehensive study of the field of ego psychology requires consideration of selected theoretical contributions both within and outside of psychoanalytic ego psychology. This chapter will trace the historical evolution of various theoretical developments that make up this body of knowledge.

PSYCHOANALYTIC EGO PSYCHOLOGY

FREUD'S STRUCTURAL THEORY

In the 1923 publication *The Ego and the Id*, Sigmund Freud presented a radical revision of his earlier topographic theory of mental functioning in which he described the unconscious, preconscious, and conscious regions of the mind (Freud, 1900). The view he proposed in 1923 and in later publications (Freud, 1926,

1933, 1940) became known as structural theory and marked the beginning of an ego psychology.

In order to understand the significance of structural theory, it is important to consider the basic thrust of Freud's earlier writings. Freud's hypotheses about personality functioning stemmed from his clinical work with adult patients. He reconstructed their early life experiences based on what they reported during psychoanalytic treatment. Freud believed in psychic determinism, in the power of the unconscious mind, and in the strength of the instincts. In his view nothing occurred by chance; all behavior was motivated by unconscious conflicts stemming from early childhood and centering on the expression of aggressive and sexual instincts. Freud identified the psychosexual stages (oral, anal, phallic, Oedipal) that were central in the origination of anxiety, conflicts, defenses, adult character traits, and neurotic symptoms. Psychoanalysis attempted to relieve adult symptoms by releasing unconscious fantasies and conflicts (lifting repressions) so that they would become conscious. In the process their power would be dissipated. The individual's energy would be freed to be used more positively, and his or her behavior would come under conscious control.

Freud was thought by many to be pessimistic about human growth potential. In a critique of classical psychoanalysis, Horney (1945:19) wrote that "Freud's pessimism as regards neuroses and their treatment arose from his disbelief in human goodness and human growth. Man, he postulated, is doomed to suffer or to destroy. The instincts which drive him can only be controlled or at best 'sublimated.'" It was said of Freud that he "dethroned rational man," since he considered even the highest forms of individual creativity to be derived ultimately from unconscious, instinctual forces. While many do not agree with Horney's portrait of Freud, it is true that classical psychoanalytic theory did not focus on the adaptive, rational, problem-solving, and self-actualizing capacities of people. Further, by focusing on intrapsychic phenomena, it minimized the impact of external reality itself, that is, the environment and interpersonal relationships, on human behavior.

With the publication of *The Ego and the Id* (1923), Freud himself shifted his emphasis. Structural theory described the ego as one of three structures of the mental apparatus of the personality along with the id (the seat of the instincts) and the superego (the conscience and ego-ideal). He defined the ego by its functions: mediating between the drives (id) and external reality; moderating conflict between the drives (id) and internalized prohibitions against their expression (superego); instituting mechanisms (defenses) to protect the ego from the painful experience of anxiety; and playing a crucial role in development through its capacity for identification with external objects.

Structural theory permitted greater understanding of the individual's negotiations with the external world and led to an appreciation of the impact of the environment and interpersonal relationships on behavior. The therapeutic task was articulated in Freud's (1933:57–80) statement, "Where id was there shall ego be." This referred to the individual's being helped to develop a greater capacity to engage in rational behavior, that is, to mediate successfully between his or her needs and external reality.

Structural theory nevertheless reflected Freud's earlier instinctual emphasis. The ego was seen as drawing its power or energy from the id and developing as a result of frustration and conflict. Thus ego capacities were not viewed as innate, adaptive, or autonomous from the drives, nor did Freud discuss the development of ego functions systematically. Further, "the psychosocial implications of reality and object relations remained unexplored theoretically" (Rapaport, 1959:11).

THE EGO AND ITS DEFENSES

Freud died in 1939. The first important extension of structural theory was initiated in Anna Freud's 1936 publication, *Ego and the Mechanisms of Defense.* She gave an expanded role to defense, identified a greater repertoire of defenses, and linked the origin of defenses to specific developmental phases. Many behavioral manifestations that previously were thought of as direct expressions of instinct could now be viewed as defenses against anxiety. For example, anger might be viewed as serving defensive purposes in a particular situation rather than indicating aggression *per se.*

Anna Freud also drew attention to the idea that defenses may serve other purposes than merely protecting the individual from anxiety and conflict. She identified the importance of the adaptiveness of so-called defensive behavior. For example, regression (a return to an earlier developmental phase, behavior, or level of functioning in order to avoid anxiety) can be a way station prior to the individual's engaging in more adaptive, reality-oriented behavior. Anna Freud systematically delineated and traced the evolution of different developmental lines that constitute personality formation, for example, from suckling to rational eating, from wetting and soiling to bladder and bowel control, from irresponsibility to responsibility in body management, from egocentricity to companionship, and from dependency to emotional self-reliance. Her diagnostic profile is still used today to give a complete picture of a child's structural development (Freud, 1965). Considered to be the primary originator of child psychoanalysis, Anna Freud also made seminal contributions to the treatment of children.[2]

Building upon an enlarged understanding of the role of defense, Wilhelm Reich (1949) helped to explain further how individuals developed habitual patterns of behavior (character defenses and character traits) in early childhood. His writings led to an expansion of the goals of psychoanalysis from symptom removal to modification of the ego's characterological defensive structure (character armor), which interfered with optimal functioning.

AUTONOMOUS EGO FUNCTIONS AND A THEORY OF ADAPTATION

A second important development in ego psychology and the first significant revision in the theory was introduced by Heinz Hartmann in *Ego Psychology and the Problem of Adaptation* (1939). Hartmann argued that psychoanalytic theory required expansion in order for it to become a more general psychological theory of human behavior. Hartmann, both independently and then with his collaborators (Hartmann and Kris, 1945; Hartmann, Kris, and Lowenstein, 1946) developed and refined the concept of the autonomy of the ego. He postulated that ego apparatuses were innate and that they arose during the evolution of the species in the service of survival, hence in the process of adaptation.

Hartmann proposed that both the ego and the id originated in an "undifferentiated matrix" at birth out of which each, having its own energy source, developed independently. The individual is born "preadapted" to an "average expectable environment" for the species, and the ego matures independently of the vicissitudes of the instincts of conflict. Ego functions such as perception, memory, intelligence, thought processes, motor activity, and reality testing, for example, are "conflict-free" and have a "primary autonomy" from the drives. The exercise of these functions gives pleasure in its own right. Other ego functions can arise or lose their autonomy by their connection to conflict. If this occurs, however, they also can undergo a "change of function" by being neutralized and divested of such conflict. Once neutralized, they develop "a secondary autonomy" and serve adaptive purposes.

Hartmann also discussed the importance of the ego's organizing capacity in his description of the synthetic function of the ego, following Nunberg's (1931) description of the ego's tendencies to unite, bind, integrate, and create. Further, Hartmann proposed that in addition to man's capacity to change outside reality to suit himself (alloplastic adaptation) or to change himself to comply with the demands of reality (autoplastic adaptation), man could search for an environment that might best suit his psychological potential.

In emphasizing the ego's role in adaptation, Hartmann also provided an important link to reality and to the interpersonal relationships viewed as essential in creating the optimal conditions for ego development. Thus Hartmann added a new dimension to psychoanalytic theory by focusing on the individual's innate ego apparatuses and their conflict-free development and on his or her more active, adaptive relationship to external reality.

Hartmann's concepts led to an appreciation of the positive power of the ego's energy and capacities in neutralizing conflict and in fostering improved adaptation during the treatment process. Areas of intact ego functioning could be supported and enhanced. Measures could be taken to build ego where deficits existed.

Since Hartmann many authors such as Bellak, Hurvich, and Gediman (1973) and Beres (1956) have described the various types of ego functions, their development, and their role in adaptation. David Rapaport (1951, 1958, 1960) was a seminal theorist who synthesized the new ego psychological concepts with Freud's earlier contributions. He identified the importance of considering personality generally and each individual specifically from six points of view: the topographic (conscious, preconscious, unconscious), the structural (id, ego, superego), the genetic-developmental (historical), the dynamic (the drives), the economic (distribution of energy), and the adaptive (relationship to reality).

PSYCHOSOCIAL INFLUENCES AND THE HUMAN LIFE CYCLE

A third crucial development in ego psychology is reflected in the writings of Erik Erikson. Erikson reacted to what he felt to be Freud's lack of attention to the importance of interpersonal, environmental, and cultural factors in development and to his lack of appreciation of lifelong developmental processes.[3]

In *Childhood and Society* (1950) and *Identity and the Life Cycle* (1959), Erikson described ego development as psychosocial in nature, involving progressive mastery of developmental tasks in each of eight successive stages of the human life cycle. At the beginning of each stage there is a normal developmental crisis, a temporary state of disequilibrium resulting from new coping demands on the individual. Successful crisis resolution is contingent upon the mastery of biopsychosocial tasks inherent in each stage.

Erikson, in conceiving of development as a lifelong process, was the first to deal with adult growth and to see the importance of the ameliorating or compensatory effects of later crisis resolution. While adhering to the importance of biological factors in development, Erikson called attention to the influences of the interpersonal field, the environment, the society, and the culture on the childrearing process and on ego development.

Erikson also viewed the individual as more than the sum of his or her ego functions and defenses. The outcome of each of the eight successive developmental phases contributes to identity formation. Successful negotiation of each stage results in the individual's developing the strengths of trust, autonomy, initiative, industry, ego identity, intimacy, generativity, and ego integrity in contrast to a sense of mistrust, shame and doubt, guilt, inferiority, role confusion, isolation, stagnation, and despair.

Erikson's ideas provided the rationale for therapeutic approaches that address the dynamic interplay between current life cycle needs and the inner and outer resources available to meet them and that involve interventions directed beyond the individual psyche.[4] If psychosocial factors in the here and now are causal, then it follows that intervention must encompass the current psychosocial field. Erikson's theories paved the way to notions of primary prevention through interventions aimed at improving adaptive fits between caretakers and children as well as between individuals and environmental resources.

OBJECT RELATIONS AND EGO DEVELOPMENT

In Freudian and early ego psychological parlance, the term "object relations" referred to the child's growing libidinal investment in others and to the quality of an individual's *actual* interpersonal relationships. Later object relations theorists used the term to encompass the nature of a person's *internal* images or representations of the self and the object world and their relationships with one another. Object relations theories focus on how the external world is taken in and how the resultant internalizations influence psychic structure and later personality functioning. While Hartmann and Erikson drew attention to the individual's relationship to the external environment and paved the way to a theory of object relations, other theorists concentrated on the nature of early attachment and built an object relations perspective more firmly into ego psychological theory.

René Spitz (1945, 1946a, b, and c, 1959, 1965), a seminal attachment theorist, believed that social stimulation was necessary for infants' growth.[5] He actually observed a condition, which he called marasmus, in which infants languished and sometimes died for lack of touch and other forms of nurture. Spitz's observations about the harmful effects on children of hospitalization and separation from the maternal object led to more systematic understanding of the fundamental connection between successful and faulty ego development and the interpersonal field. Spitz's early work shed light on the nature of the particular type of depressive reactions experienced by children when separated from their mothers. His later studies of the mother-child relationship produced a wealth of data on the specific effects of maternal attitudes and behavior on the child's normal ego development and on the importance of the mother's ability to regulate herself in accordance with the child's needs. He identified the significance of critical periods in early childhood during which the failure to meet certain needs at the right time leads to developmental deficiencies that cannot be corrected later. The "organizers of the psyche" that form as a result of adequate caretaking are important building blocks of optimal personality functioning.

Other contributors to attachment theory were M. D. S. Ainsworth (1973), Ainsworth and S. Bell (1969), and John Bowlby (1969, 1973). Ainsworth (1973:1–94) delineated four sequential stages in the development of social attachment, the process by which the infant acquires a specific positive emotional connection to his or her mother or primary caretaker. Successful interpersonal relationships depend on the establishment of such a bond. The failure to achieve this developmental milestone, as a result of maternal deprivation, for example, is a significant factor in the genesis of severe ego and interpersonal pathology.

Bowlby's work (1969, 1973) added to the evidence for the importance of the infant's early attachment to the mother and identified the negative effects of separation and loss on ego development. His description of different types of attachment, that is, secure, avoidant, ambivalent, and disorganized, have helped to explain both the child's and the adult's relationship patterns (Biringen, 1994). Bowlby's discovery of the grief reactions of very young children when separated from their mothers, characterized by the three stages of protest, despair, and detachment, enlarged our understanding of the impact of children's early caretaking experiences.

Like Spitz, Margaret Mahler (1951, 1968, 1972; Mahler, Pine, and Bergman, 1975) generated crucial data and theory from studying children. From her observations of their autistic and symbiotic psychoses, which she related to profound deficits in mother-child interaction, Mahler moved into the study of normal development.

Using systematic observations of children playing alone and with their mothers in a nursery setting as well as when separated from their mothers, Mahler established the phases by which the child develops the capacity for attachment, separation, and individuation. In minute detail Mahler traced the normal child's transition from nonrelatedness (autism) to fused or merged self-object relatedness (symbiosis). She then described the first separation-individuation phase in which the child begins to differentiate from the object (differentiation and practicing subphases) while developing his or her autonomous ego functions. She traced the buildup of the child's stable and integrated internal representation of the caretaker (the object), which culminates during the next subphase (rapprochement) with the development of object constancy. A second separation-individuation phase in adolescence that results in the consolidation of ego identity also has been noted in line with Mahler's ideas.[6]

In close collaboration with Mahler, influencing her research and theory on the one hand and building upon it on the other, Edith Jacobson (1964) proposed a theoretical developmental model that integrates the findings concerning the child's evolving relations with others into ego psychology. She described the child's acquisition of a sense of self and showed how intrapsychic structure develops in association with the child's interactions with significant others. Interested in certain pathological conditions such as depression and manic-depressive conditions Jacobson linked these conditions to early disturbances in object relations.

Mahler and Jacobson, both American object relations theorists, adhered to Freud's structural model and to the revisions and extensions of Anna Freud, Hartmann, and others. In contrast, the British object relations group, which will be discussed later in the chapter, constituted a distinct theoretical line that also has contributed to our understanding of development, psychopathology, and the treatment process.[7]

NEW PERSPECTIVES ON PSYCHOPATHOLOGY

Psychoanalytic ego psychology and object relations theory have shed light on the origins and nature of many pathological conditions and have resulted in new treatment approaches to individuals with severe developmental arrests. Robert Knight (1953) was the first to apply ego psychological understanding systematically to the diagnosis and treatment of borderline disorders. Since Knight, other theorists such as Gerald Adler (1985), Gertrude and Rubin Blanck (1974, 1979), James Masterson (1972, 1976), and Otto Kernberg (1975, 1976) have utilized this body of knowledge to understand and treat the special problems of borderline individuals, as Chapter 12 will discuss. Likewise, applications of ego psychological theory led to new ways of viewing the etiology, symptomatology, and treatment of other conditions such as depressive disorders (Jacobson, 1971) and schizophrenia (Arieti, 1974; Bellak, Hurvich, and Gediman, 1973; Federn, 1952).

OTHER THEORETICAL CONTRIBUTIONS AND EXTENSIONS

Intellectual currents that differed from those described thus far also focused on ego functioning and development. Theories that emphasized the social determinants of behavior evolved along with those that stressed growth motivation and the individual's striving for competence. Cognitive and learning theory, stress and crisis theory, and the study of adult developmental processes yielded new insights into human behavior.

THE SOCIAL DETERMINANTS OF BEHAVIOR

Numerous theorists emphasized the crucial role of social determinants in development. Prominent among these were Alfred Adler (1951), Karen Horney (1937), Erich Fromm (1941), and

Harry Stack Sullivan (1953). While each developed a distinctive theory, as a group they focused on several common issues. They foreshadowed Erikson's work but, unlike him, rejected the importance given to the biological and instinctual bases of behavior. They viewed personality as intrinsically interpersonal and social rather than biological in nature. Neuroses and neurotic character traits were seen as resulting from conflicts between individual needs and societal or environmental conditions. "Neuroses thus present a peculiar kind of struggle for life under difficult conditions" (Horney, 1939:11). While accepting the importance of the unconscious, these theorists focused on the present meaning of behavior. A review of these theories is beyond the scope of this chapter.[8]

SELF-ACTUALIZATION AND GROWTH MOTIVATION

Adler, Horney, and Fromm also viewed individuals as striving toward self-realization or self-actualization. They emphasized the more holistic, humanistic, and creative aspects of human behavior as well as the conscious strivings and rational capacities of the individual. This view is summed up in a statement by Horney: "My own view is that man has the capacity to grow and change as well as the desire to develop his potentialities and become a decent human being, and that these deteriorate if his relationship to others and hence to himself is, and continues to be disturbed. I believe that man can change and grow and go on changing as long as he lives" (1945:19).

Likewise Otto Rank (1929, 1945, 1952) evolved the concept of the will, which he viewed as more than the ego, a mere structure of the mind. The will is all that is active in the individual. It is the integrative force in the personality as a whole. Rank viewed man as born with an innate push toward assertion and creativity. The core of his being is his active relationship with the world. Man has choice and dignity. He is not bound by the past, and there are no limits to his ultimate capability. Individuals grow through asserting their wills against those of others.

Writing later, Abraham Maslow (1954) and Carl Rogers (1951) built their work around the individual's striving toward growth and self-actualization. Maslow described two different but equally crucial sets of innate needs: basic needs such as food, security, and self-esteem, and growth needs such as justice, beauty, and order. As the individual matures with the help of a benign environment that meets his or her basic needs, growth needs become more operative.

In a similar vein Henry Murray (Murray and Kluckhohn, 1953) viewed the ego as the central organizer of behavior, promoting the expression of positive as well as negative impulses. Among the basic needs Murray described are autonomy, achievement, affiliation, and understanding, as well as aggression, dominance, and exhibitionism. Murray linked his conception of individual need to that of specific environmental conditions that foster or satisfy basic strivings.

AN EMPHASIS ON COMPETENCE

Robert White (1959, 1963) postulated that the individual is born with not only innate and autonomous ego functions that give pleasure in their own right but also a drive toward mastery and competence. Thus, according to White, the ego actively seeks opportunities in the environment in which the individual can be "effective." In turn the ego is strengthened by successful transactions with the environment. Thus an individual's behavior can elicit a reaction from the environment that will reinforce or promote ego functioning, self-esteem, and a sense of competence.

While White stressed personal attributes such as self-confidence and decision-making ability as reflecting a sense of competence, other authors suggested that competence occurs in an interpersonal (Foote and Cottrell, 1965) and social (Gladwin, 1967) context. Smith (1968) emphasized both personal abilities and social role performance in his conception of competence. Allport (1961) suggested that while it was erroneous to say that a need for competence is the only motive of life, nevertheless it comes as close as any need to characterizing the life process.

AN EMPHASIS ON COGNITION AND LEARNING
IN EGO DEVELOPMENT

Many theorists (e.g., White, 1974) have suggested that cognitive functioning is central to adaptive behavior, and Jean Piaget's theory of intelligence (1951, 1952, 1955) offers concepts that complement those of ego psychology. Piaget evolved a general theory of intellectual development in which he identified a series of sequential stages. What is important is that the child's thinking, view of the world, and ability to assimilate and accommodate to it are shaped by the particular stage he or she is in. There are four main stages: the sensory-motor stage from birth to age two, in which the child learns to construct and reconstruct objects; the preoperational stage from two to seven, in which the child develops the capacity for symbolization; the stage of concrete operations from seven to eleven, in which the child is able to perform acts in his or her mind what previously had to be performed in actuality; and the stage of formal operations from eleven to fifteen years of age, in which the adolescent develops more abstract thinking capacities and can understand and use metaphor, think about his or her thoughts, reason in terms of the future, and think in terms of values and ideals.[9]

Building on Piaget's formulations, Lawrence Kohlberg (1966) proposed a theory of moral development. He described six stages beginning with a fear of punishment and an obedience orientation at the least developed or premoral stage, and ending with a morality of individual principles or conscience orientation at the most advanced stage. Since these early writings, numerous individuals have contributed to the development of cognitive theory and its use in treating certain emotional disorders, particularly anxiety states, panic attacks, phobias, and depression (Beck *et al.*, 1979; Beck, Freeman, and Associates, 1990). Since cognitive theory views faulty thinking as central in personality dysfunction, intervention aims to help individuals to recognize their unique thinking style; to identify the distortions that enter into their perceptions, emotions, and actions; and to learn new ways of thinking, feeling, and acting (Werner, 1986). The cognitive model relies on a different set of assumptions about personality development, human problems, and their treatment than does ego psychology; nevertheless, selected aspects of it can be integrated into ego-oriented approaches.

COPING WITH STRESS AND LIFE EVENTS

The impact of interpersonal relationships, environmental factors, developmental and role transitions, and traumatic events focused attention on the outer stresses with which individuals must cope and to which they must adapt. Efforts to characterize various types of environmental stresses and the individual coping mechanisms that develop in order to deal with them have led to important contributions. Coping mechanisms called forth to deal with environmental stress can be viewed in terms of their adaptive or maladaptive features. While there is evidence that coping capacity and vulnerability may have some constitutional underpinnings, an individual's ability to cope with stress reflects not only his or her characteristic strategies of adaptation but also the impact of interpersonal relationships and the nature of environmental supports and resources (Birns, 1985:1–19; Bowlby, 1988; Escalona, 1968; Murphy and Moriarity, 1976).

There is a vast literature on stress theory that ranges from studies of the performance of individuals under various types of biological, physiological, and psychological stress (Selye, 1956; Lazarus, 1966) to those of the impact of war conditions (Grinker and Spiegel, 1945) and of other large-scale disasters (Tyhurst, 1957). Lindemann's work on grief reactions (1944) after an extensive fire made a seminal contribution to the stress literature by tracing the stages by which individuals cope with the loss of loved ones. The impact on the ego of stress resulting from catastrophic illness or surgery has been addressed by many authors (Janis, 1958). Still others have focused on the impact of natural life events on individual and family coping (Hill, 1958; Le Masters, 1957; Rapoport, 1962). All these developments led to the systemization of crisis theory (Kaplan, 1962; Golan, 1978; Parad, 1965; Parad and Parad, 1990).

A major contribution of crisis theory is the description of the ego's capacity to restore equilibrium through a characteristic use of coping mechanisms that lead to the mastery of stress and to crisis resolution. A significant feature of this capacity is the individual's problem-solving skills, which, while shaken by the crisis, gradually reassert themselves if certain conditions are present (White, 1974).

More recent applications of crisis theory have extended to many life events such as AIDS (Lopez and Getzel, 1984) and rape, violent assault, physical and sexual abuse, and domestic violence (Abarbanel and Richman, 1990; Bowker, 1983; Brekke, 1990; Lee and Rosenthal, 1983; Liles and O'Brien, 1990).

THE ADULT LIFE CYCLE

While Erikson was one of the first major theorists to describe stages in adult life and to suggest that ego development continues throughout adulthood, others have since studied the adult life cycle more systematically. This body of work has focused on: understanding the evolution of identity, defenses, and character traits over time (Benedek, 1970; Butler, 1963; Elson, 1984; Goldstein, 1992a and 1992b; Neugarten and Associates, 1964; White, 1966; identifying the coping demands and developmental tasks of life-cycle stages and role transitions (Gould, 1978; Le Masters, 1965; Levinson, 1978; Peck, 1975; Vaillant, 1977); and identifying the positive and negative effects of life crises (Coehlo, Hamburg, and Adams, 1974; Tabachnick, 1990).

NEWER AREAS OF INQUIRY

Despite ego psychology's biopsychosocial perspective and its broader focus in comparison to Freudian theory, it too came under attack for viewing difference as deviance, "pathologizing" the behavior of those individuals who were not part of the dominant culture, and emphasizing their ego weakness or deficits rather than their unique patterns of development and strengths. Further, it appeared that many psychodynamically oriented clinicians focused mainly on their clients' internal worlds and ego capacities or lack thereof, while neglecting the impact on personality development of society and of overwhelming life experiences such as childhood sexual abuse, domestic violence, racism, and poverty. Consequently, many individuals admonished proponents of ego psychology for "blaming the victim." More recently, however, ego-oriented practitioners have made significant efforts to correct for a sometimes narrow and biased focus as they gradually integrate newer areas of inquiry into their work. Some of the more significant of these currents will be discussed below.

WOMEN

Early ego psychological writing remained rooted in Freud's belief that women were anatomically inferior to men and that penis envy developed as a consequence of women's biologically based sense of inadequacy. Freud viewed the act of bearing a child, particularly a son, as enabling women to compensate for their deficiency. He further argued that the successful resolution of the Oedipal period led to a sound sense of gender identity, heterosexual object choice, and superego formation, but he described even so-called mature women as less ethical and having less of a sense of social justice, and as more envious, weaker in social interest, more vain, narcissistic, secretive, insincere, masochistic, childlike, and incomplete (Freud, 1933). Helene Deutsch (1925, 1930), a leading European psychoanalyst during Freud's time, subscribed to the belief that women showed inborn tendencies toward passivity, narcissism, and masochism. An important and longstanding consequence of these early views was the equation of mental health with male traits such as assertiveness, independence, and ambition, while women who manifested these more desirable characteristics were viewed as pathological.

Karen Horney (1939) and Clara Thompson (1942) were the first major psychoanalysts to criticize the biological determinism in the prevailing view of women. They argued that women's envy of men and sense of inadequacy were culturally based, but their ideas were not integrated into mainstream psychoanalytic thought. In contrast to Freud, Erikson was less disparaging of women, but he also saw their biological makeup as determining their psychological development. Further, his theory of the life cycle embodies a traditional view of women, as will be discussed further in Chapter 5.

As a result of the second wave of feminism and the contemporary women's liberation movement, which began in the 1960s, a new wave of popular and professional literature that disputed conventional views of women emerged. For example, Betty Friedan's book, *A Feminine Mystique,* criticized Freudian theory, calling it obsolete, a major obstacle for women, and a cause of distorted views of their role in society (Friedan, 1963:95–96). Others joined in, drawing attention to the masculine bias in society, expressed through its values, institutions, and policies. They challenged the rigidity of gender arrangements, pointing out vigorously that established theories of personality, professional attitudes, and treatment services reflected sex-role stereotyping, a disparaging view of women, and other forms of gender bias; that is, they applied a male perspective and masculine standards to observations of and theories about women (Brodsky and Holroyd, 1981; Broverman *et al.,* 1981).

This era ushered in women's support networks, collectives, consciousness-raising groups, crisis intervention services, and a health movement (Valentich, 1986). Programs on women's studies were created in colleges and universities. Critiques and revisions of psychodynamic theory began to appear both inside and outside of feminist circles (Benjamin, 1988; Blum, 1977; Chodorow, 1978; Dinnerstein, 1977; Gilligan, 1982; Jordan, 1990; Kaplan and Surrey, 1984; Miller, 1977; Schafer, 1974). An important emphasis of many of these writings is that women's need for relatedness is central to their self-development.

The literature on women has also drawn attention to the powerlessness, dependence, and helplessness that women experience and to women's victimization in society as reflected in sexual abuse, rape, domestic violence, poverty, and other forms of violence against women (Abarbanel and Richman, 1990; Berlin, 1981; Faria and Belohlavek, 1984; Simon, 1988; Star *et al.,* 1981). Many writers have linked women's socialization to their propensity to develop emotional disorders such as depression, hysteria, phobias, alcoholism, and eating disorders (Boskind-Lodahl, 1981; Collins, 1993; Lerner, 1981; Pape, 1993; Symonds, 1981; Turnbull, 1989; Weissman and Klerman, 1981).

Finally, more gender-sensitive, affirmative, and empowering interventive perspectives have also been put forth (Bricker-Jenkins, Hooyman, and Gottlieb, 1991; Collins, 1986; Greenspan, 1983; Howell and Bayes, 1981; Norman and Mancuso, 1980; Valentich, 1986).

DIVERSITY AND OPPRESSION

Until recently even ego psychology's conception of normal development was based largely on observations of white Anglo-Saxon, middle-class, heterosexual individuals and tended to equate difference with deviance. Thus, the unique experiences, characteristics, strengths, and coping strategies of populations that are ethnically and racially diverse or that have a gay or lesbian sexual orientation were not fully appreciated. As this tendency began to shift, much of the early literature on ethnic minorities—African Americans, Latinos, Asians, and other people of color—focused on their vulnerability to the negative effects of immigration, biculturism, stigmatization, discrimination, and poverty (Boyd-Franklin, 1989; Chestang, 1972; Comas-Diaz and Minrath, 1985; Espin, 1987; Pinderhughes, 1983). More recent contributions have described the special attributes, development, and strengths of culturally diverse groups (de la Cancela, 1986; Ghali, 1982; Ryan, 1985; Wilson, 1989) and more culturally sensitive interventive approaches have emerged (Chestang, 1987; Devore, 1983; Gutierrez, 1990; Hirayama and Cetingok, 1988; Jones, 1979; Montijo, 1985; Robinson, 1989; Schlossberg and Kagan, 1988; Solomon, 1976).

Likewise, the gay and lesbian liberation movement that was energized after the Stonewall rebellion in New York City in 1969 helped to focus attention on homosexuals as a stigmatized and oppressed population and on the need for according them their full measure of civil liberties. It also challenged traditional views of homosexuality and gradually led to a reexamination of strongly held attitudes toward and knowledge about gays and lesbians.

Followers of Freud viewed homosexuality as a failure to successfully resolve the Oedipal stage. Even early ego psychological writings continued to regard homosexuality as deviant development and all homosexuals as suffering from developmental arrests (Friedman, 1986; Prozan, 1992:295–307). Some writers still adhere to this outdated view despite the fact that most studies comparing homosexuals and heterosexuals cannot differentiate their personality characteristics and show that gays and lesbians, like heterosexuals, display a full range of personality functioning, strengths, psychopathology, and problems in living (Falco, 1991:22–26; Gonsiorek, 1982b:9–20). A significant development occurred in 1973, however, when the American Psychiatric Association decided to remove homosexuality *per se* from its *Diagnostic and Statistical Manual of Mental Disorders* (APA, 1980), although it created a category termed ego-dystonic homosexuality (homosexual feelings or behavior about which one is uncomfortable). This later diagnosis was eliminated, however, in 1988. Nevertheless, some clinicians continue to view gays and lesbians as deviant and pathological (DeCrescenzo, 1984:115–36).

A new awareness and emerging research findings have identified the widespread nature and debilitating effects of homophobia at the individual and the societal level and have supported more affirmative perspectives on gays and lesbians. Even within psychoanalytic circles, there have been critiques and revisions of traditional views (Burch, 1993; Friedman, 1986: 483–519; Friedman, 1988; Isay, 1989; Spaulding, 1993; Weille, 1993). Studies of the positive coping of gays and lesbians over the life cycle have emerged (Berger, 1992; Coleman, 1982; Colgan, 1988; Hetrick and Martin, 1988; Lewis, 1984; Tully, 1992). Some writers have focused attention on homophobia in the professional community and on the indiscriminate use of diagnostic labels and other negative treatment practices (DeCrescenzo, 1984:115–36; Gonsiorek, 1982b:9–20). An important development has been the evolution of more affirmative treatment models in work with gay and lesbian clients (Falco, 1991; Gonsiorek, 1982a; Malyon, 1982; Martin, 1982; Schwartz, 1989). Finally, the incidence of AIDS in male homosexuals and the gay and lesbian community's response to this catastrophic epidemic has also generated new understanding of the needs, struggles, and strengths of homosexual men and women (Dane and Miller, 1992).

TRAUMA AND ITS IMPACT

While Freud originally believed that neurotic individuals suffered from repressed traumatic memories of childhood sexual seduction by important adults, he later emphasized the child's wishes for and fears of such experiences in the causes of neurosis. Consequently, classical Freudian theory emphasized the impact of fantasy rather than real-life events in causing later symptoms and personality difficulties. While ego psychology led to a renewed focus on the impact of reality, it neglected the study of childhood trauma (Miller, 1984).

In mental health circles, there has been a longstanding interest in the effects of certain types of harrowing events such as combat experiences, brainwashing and torture, the Holocaust, and natural disasters such as fires, floods, and earthquakes. More recently, attention has expanded to encompass the special problems faced by victims of violent crimes, sexual abuse, and domestic violence (Courtois, 1988; Davies and Frawley, 1994; Herman, 1992; Van der Kolk, 1987).

The diagnosis of post-traumatic stress disorder (PTSD) was included in the third edition of the *Diagnostic and Statistical Manual* of the American Psychiatric Association in 1980 (APA, 1980) because of the growing awareness of the long-term disabling effects of traumatic experiences and their role in causing certain emotional disorders and addictions. Moreover, a growing literature exists on the optimal treatment of trauma survivors (Abarbanel and Richman, 1990; Bowker, 1983; Courtois, 1988; Davies and Frawley, 1994; Herman, 1992; Lee and Rosenthal, 1983; McFarlane, 1990; Patten *et al.*, 1989; Turner and Shapiro, 1986). Further, questions about whether certain clinical diagnoses are being applied incorrectly to what are really survivor syndromes have been raised. For example, the incidence of sexual abuse in the histories of so-called borderline women, substance abusers, and in those diagnosed with multiple personality or other types of dissociative disorders is staggering (Blake-White and Kline, 1985; Herman and Van der Kolk, 1987; Kilgore, 1988; Kroll, 1993; Wheeler and Walton, 1987).

NEW DIRECTIONS IN PERSONALITY THEORY

Personality theories that have linkages to, but important differences from, ego psychology complement and in some instances modify ego psychology's view of development, psychopathology, and the treatment process.

BRITISH OBJECT RELATIONS THEORY

An extremely important set of ideas comes from the work of the British object relations theorists (Mishne, 1993; Greenberg and Mitchell, 1983). Members of the British group such as Melanie Klein (1948), W. R. D. Fairbairn (1952), D. W. Winnicott (1965), Harry Guntrip (1968, 1971), and others focused on the development of internalized object relations in the earliest stages of life. American psychoanalysts, who were loyal to Anna Freud, originally considered the theories of the British School as anathema. Their writings are receiving considerable attention of late in some circles and offer significant insights into the entrenched problems of individuals who show severe developmental difficulties, for example, borderline, narcissistic, and schizoid individuals as well as those who have had histories of neglect, abuse, and other forms of trauma (Seinfeld, 1990, 1991, 1993).

The British object relations theories suggest treatment strategies that reflect foci differing from, although not altogether incompatible with, those advocated by ego psychologists. The provision of a therapeutic holding environment, the modification of pathological internalized object relations that are interfering with optimal functioning, and the building of more positive internalizations are central concepts. Otto Kernberg (1975, 1976), who drew heavily on the work of Melanie Klein, is a seminal theorist who tried to integrate British and American object relations theories. Others have begun to apply the writings of the British group to work with couples and families (Scharff and Scharff, 1987, 1991).

SELF PSYCHOLOGY

Originally identified with classical Freudian psychoanalysis and ego psychology, Heinz Kohut (1971, 1977, 1984) originated self psychology based on his experiences treating narcissistic disorders. Relegating the drives and the structural model of the mind (id, ego, and superego) to the background, Kohut argued that the individual is born with an innate sense of self that is the central organizing and motivating force in the personality. He described the nature of self development in the context of an empathic caretaking environment that is responsive to an individual's life-long need for selfobjects. He argued that traumatic or severe and protracted empathic failures with respect to the child's emerging needs produce deficiencies in the structuring of the self and are responsible for later self disorders. Kohut's emphasis on the role of the therapist's empathy with the subjective experiences and selfobject needs of the client or patient gave his treatment model a distinctive character (Wolf, 1988).

STERN'S RESEARCH ON SELF DEVELOPMENT

Supporting many of Kohut's views regarding self development, Daniel Stern's (1985) recent study of the evolution of the self, based on his systematic observations of infant-caretaker interaction, offers a new perspective on the developmental process. Stern gives evidence that the infant is born with an innate sense of self and awareness of separateness from others, and that the child's self evolves as a consequence of complex and recurrent interpersonal transactions. Stern's findings with respect to the innate and ongoing nature of what he calls the four senses of the self provide an alternative to Mahler's conception of discrete separation-individuation stages.

THE IMPACT OF ENVIRONMENTAL SYSTEMS

The study of the impact of the family, small groups, organizations, social structure, and social change also have increased our understanding of the complex factors that influence individual coping. The utilization of knowledge of these larger systems alongside the use of an ego psychological framework leads to a greater use of interventions that address person-environmental transactions rather than only the individual.

THE FAMILY, THE GROUP, AND THE ORGANIZATION

Individuals spend a large proportion of their time in families, small groups, and organizational structures. Each of these environmental systems has its own unique characteristics and rules that influence individual coping. Thus family systems theories, theories of small group behavior, and organizational theories all contribute to understanding the context in which individual development occurs all through the life cycle.

At the same time theories of family and group processes in particular have benefited from extensions of ego psychology. Concepts such as defense, adaptation and coping, the life cycle, identity, ego mastery and competence, coping with stress and crisis, problem-solving capacities, and person-environment mutuality have been useful in reconceptualizing the family as a dynamic system that changes over time in response to inner needs and outer demands and conditions. They have focused attention on the progressive and adaptive processes in families and the conditions that foster or obstruct them. Similar extensions have been applied to group processes.

SOCIAL STRUCTURE AND SOCIAL CHANGE

It has been pointed out that "the ability of persons to maintain psychological comfort will depend not only on their intrapsychic resources, but also—and perhaps more importantly—on the social supports available or absent in the environment" (Mechanic, 1974:33). This dimension of individual coping has been neglected to a great extent in theories of human behavior. Yet it is a major factor in successful social adaptation. Newer practice models (Germain and Gitterman, 1980) recognize that the institutions of the society provide the individual with the preparation needed to cope effectively with the environment. The institutions themselves also must change, and what constitutes effective coping itself must change, as the culture undergoes transformation. This view links any study of individual coping and adaptation to the social and institutional context in which it occurs.

Over two decades ago, Alvin Toffler wrote *Future Shock* (Toffler, 1970), which warned that the rapidity of cultural change was outstripping humanity's coping capacities. Toffler cautioned that unless people learn to control the rate of change in their personal affairs and in society, they will suffer adaptational breakdowns. But not even Toffler could have fully envisioned the staggering changes in our computerized society that have occurred since that time: the capacity for instantaneous communications via satellites and facsimile machines; the rise and fall of Reaganomics; the collapse of the Berlin Wall and the Soviet Union; high-technology warfare seen on television in the comfort of our homes; the altered roles of men and women; the quest for equal opportunity and full civil liberties by many oppressed groups; mounting domestic and unpredictable and unprovoked violence; the prevalence of substance abuse; the scourge of AIDS; rampant child maltreatment; increased homelessness and the deterioration of the cities; escalating racial polarization; and the wanton exploitation and abuse of the physical environment. It seems clear that the stresses induced by cultural change and the discrepancies that exist between new demands and the paucity of essential social supports have had a major impact on our ability as individuals to manage in today's world. While we know so much about ego development and the conditions that foster or obstruct successful adaptation, as a society we seem to have neglected using this knowledge to provide the resources, policies, and strategies to help us cope more optimally with our ever-changing environment.

NOTES

1. For a review of the significant concepts of psychoanalytic theory see Charles Brenner, *An Elementary Textbook of Psychoanalysis* (New York: International Universities Press, 1965).
2. For example, see Anna Freud, *Normality and Pathology in Childhood* (New York: International Universities Press, 1965).

3. For an excellent discussion of Erikson's ideas see Henry W. Maier, *Three Theories of Child Development* (New York: Harper & Row, 1969).
4. In this connection Erikson's work bridges psychoanalytic ego psychology with those theories that give more credence to the impact of social and cultural factors on personality and that focus on the ego's more active role in coping and adaptation.
5. For an excellent discussion of the work of Spitz and Mahler see Gertrude Blanck and Rubin Blanck, *Ego Psychology in Theory and Practice* (New York: Columbia University Press, 1974).
6. See Peter Blos, "The Second Individuation Process of Adolescence," in Aaron Esman, ed., *The Psychology of Adolescence: Essential Readings* (New York: International Universities Press, 1975), pp. 156–177.
7. For a review of the theories of Winnicott, Fairbairn, and Klein see Harry Guntrip, *Psychoanalytic Theory, Therapy, and the Self* (New York: Basic Books, 1971; paperback, 1973).
8. This group of theorists has been labeled "neo-Freudians," the "social psychologists," or the "nonlibido" school of psychoanalysis. For an in-depth discussion of the theories see Ruth Munro, *Schools of Psychoanalytic Thought* (New York: Holt, Rinehart & Winston, 1955).
9. For an excellent discussion of Piaget's concepts see Henry W. Maier, *Three Theories of Child Development* (New York: Harper & Row, 1969).

CHAPTER 2

THE EMERGENCE AND ASSIMILATION OF EGO PSYCHOLOGY INTO SOCIAL WORK PRACTICE

E go psychology was assimilated into social work in the late
1930s and throughout the 1940s and 1950s. It quickly became
a major underpinning to all of social work practice during those
years. At the time it provided social workers with "a connecting
link between concepts about instinctual drives and unconscious
conflict and concepts about social role and its ties to the structure
and functioning of institutions" (Stamm, 1959:87–88). In this regard ego psychology for a time helped to bridge the polarization
that the social work profession has struggled with over its history: the dispute over whether to direct its efforts toward "people-helping" or "society-changing."

In order to understand the impact of ego psychological concepts on social work practice, it is important to consider the antecedents of ego psychology in the theoretical base of social work.

HISTORICAL PERSPECTIVES

THE IMPACT OF MORAL, RELIGIOUS, AND POLITICAL VALUES

When the social work profession evolved in the late nineteenth
and early twentieth centuries, "the truth was simply that the
causes of behavior were little understood. The culture imposed
its morals and values on social work, as well as on all the hu-

manistic professions" (Hamilton, 1958:13). In an effort to make charity "scientific," the early social workers were preoccupied with separating people into those with "good" or "bad" character or into those who were "worthy" or "unworthy" as a rational basis for making decisions about help-giving (Woodroofe, 1971:77–100; Lubove, 1971:1–21; Hollis, 1963:7–23; Briar and Miller, 1971:4–41).

The Charity Organization Society (COS), which gave birth to social casework, viewed individuals rather than social conditions as the main focus of helping efforts. In contrast, the settlement movement put more emphasis on society's responsibility for the conditions in which people lived. Many social workers advocated social legislative action, social reform, and broad preventive programs (Siporin, 1970:13).

Thus two somewhat antagonistic trends existed in the early history of the profession, and there was no unifying theory or broad agreement guiding social work practice. As social casework consolidated in the years after World War I, the focus on the individual took precedence over an emphasis on the society.

THE "SCIENCE" OF FACT-GATHERING

As social casework developed into an activity requiring paid, trained workers, there was an emphasis on developing the methodology for making judgments about whether and how to give help (Woodroofe, 1971:101–17; Lubove, 1971:22–54). Mary Richmond's *Social Diagnosis* (1917) put forth study, diagnosis, and treatment as the principles underlying social casework. While Richmond viewed environmental conditions as crucial in affecting individuals, nevertheless she viewed each person as unique in the way he or she dealt with these social factors (Woodroofe, 1971:105–107). While Richmond did not see people as "morally responsible for their plight" (Meyer, 1970:39), she viewed the individual as the proper focus of casework efforts. The techniques suggested were more rational and also included environmental manipulation.

Richmond did not develop a conceptual framework about the social environment (Mailick, 1977:403). Richmond drew on the prevailing knowledge available in many fields, but sociology, psychology, and psychiatry were not well developed. No major theoretical perspective on human behavior commanded attention.

PSYCHOANALYTIC THEORY AND SOCIAL CASEWORK

The shell-shock casualties of World War I, the adjustment of soldiers returning to civilian life, and the child guidance movement in the early 1920s brought social workers in hospitals and clinics into greater contact with psychiatric principles and practices. According to most social work historians, the impact of these ideas on social work practice was so dramatic and widespread that the period has been labeled "the Psychiatric Deluge" (Woodroofe, 1971:118–51).[1] Further, it has been argued that the psychiatric deluge contributed to the eclipsing of concerns about the social order and led to a greater focus on the individual (Woodroofe, 1971:121). During this period Freud's theories gained acceptance within some segments of the social work profession.[2] The implications of psychoanalytic theory for those social workers who were exposed to it were enormous. "Into this era of moral conformity Freud's theory of personality burst like the atom, and the 'fall-out' from the explosion proved extremely frightening to many people both in and outside the profession" (Hamilton, 1958:14).

Psychoanalytic theory stressed the impact of unconscious, irrational, instinctual forces in early childhood and the significance of subjective and fantasied reality in shaping behavior. It postulated fixation points in early childhood that determine later behavior. It explained the role of defenses (as protections against anxiety) and the individual's tendency to repeat early childhood conflicts in adult life and even in the client-worker relationship itself.

Psychoanalytic theory provided a rationale for the failure of clients to make changes in their lives and for their refusal of help altogether (Hollis, 1963:7–23). The unrelenting problems that clients presented and their uncooperativeness were explained by their unconscious childhood conflicts and could be treated by helping efforts aimed at uncovering these conflicts. Uncooperativeness was seen as resistance to change.

Many social workers, particularly those who were supervised and even analyzed by psychiatrists and psychoanalysts, emulated their medical colleagues, used psychoanalytic techniques in their practice, and passed along what they learned to those they supervised or with whom they consulted.

Among the techniques adopted from psychoanalysis were those that aimed at bringing early childhood memories and unconscious impulses and conflicts to the surface; at helping the client understand their manifestations in the therapeutic relationship and in other areas of the client's life; at modifying defenses and lessening resistance to change; and at modifying the conflicts themselves. These techniques included free association; interpretation of dreams; the use of the social worker-therapist as a blank screen onto which the client could project his or her characteristic attitudes and conflicts toward significant others (transference); interpretation of the presence of unconscious conflict and its connection to past events and people in the client's life; and the interpretation of resistance to change or to the therapeutic process itself.[3]

Casework practice, particularly on the East Coast, which was a major intellectual center of the social work profession, became infused with psychoanalytic theory and techniques. This may have been less true for casework in other parts of the United States (Field, 1980:499–501). This led to what many have termed excesses (Hamilton, 1958:11–37) and to what others (Meyer, 1970:36–53) have called "wrong turns" in the profession, because they sidetracked social workers from their fundamental concern with the development of a helping method that would enhance their clients' social functioning. The theme underlying these criticisms was that psychoanalytically oriented casework narrowly addressed the inner person rather than his or her environmental transactions. "It was one of the aberrant features of the attempt to carry psychoanalytic principles and techniques, primarily concerned with the neurotic, into casework that treatment became so preoccupied with the inner life as almost to lose touch with outer reality and the social factors with which social workers were most familiar" (Hamilton, 1958:23).

Other criticisms of the use of psychoanalytic theory in social work pointed to its pessimistic and deterministic view of people and its reliance on a medical or disease model in viewing human problems.[4] It was attacked for leading to a process that robbed the individual of responsibility for moving his or her life forward, created undue dependency, and opened an unrealistic, never-ending process of exploration of the past (Yelaja, 1974: 151–52).

These criticisms were pivotal in a schism that arose within social work. Functional casework, developed initially by Taft (1937, 1950) and Robinson (1930, 1950), rejected Freudian theory and the casework approach adopted by the diagnostic group. They drew instead on the theories of Otto Rank, who viewed individuals as more active and creative in seeking health, capable of changing themselves and their environment within the limits of their capacities, and able to use relationships to move toward their life goals (Smalley, 1970:90–91).

The widening of this schism between diagnostic and functional caseworkers occurred during the severe economic depression of the 1930s, when greater and greater numbers of "worthy" people of "good character" found themselves in desperate financial circumstances and required economic assistance. For the first time government-sponsored public agencies employed social workers who had previously worked in mental health and family agencies. These workers struggled with how to give help to their new clients—through psychological counseling or through supplying necessary services.

Functional casework adopted an approach to clients that offered them a relationship, irrespective of need, in which they could learn to assert their will and to fulfill their uniqueness. The use of the relationship came to be linked to the function of the agency. Thus the client seeking assistance could be helped by means of the casework relationship to accept or reject the agency's service, and in the process emerge more fully.

The functional approach was criticized for leading to its own excesses. The stress on client self-determination, individual responsibility, and the casework relationship as an end in itself at times seemed to result in the deprivation of needed services and in what has been described as punishing and withholding techniques to evoke a supposedly necessary will struggle.

Another current also existed at this time within the social

work profession; it emphasized the social determinants of behavior and pointed to social treatment, that is, interventions directed at improving environmental conditions. Those who held
this view, however, "were out of tune with the prevailing
Freudian ethic and the preoccupation with personality change
through psychological procedures" (Siporin, 1970:16).

THE EMERGENCE OF EGO PSYCHOLOGY

Beginning in the late 1930s, though more significantly in the
post–World War II period, ego psychology gained recognition in
the United States. Anna Freud, Hartmann, and Kris and Lowenstein, Rapaport, and Erikson emphasized the ego's innate, conscious, rational, and adaptive capacities, the autonomous or
conflict-free areas of ego functioning, the adaptive role of defense, the importance of interpersonal and environmental factors, and the capacity for growth and change all through the life
cycle. Social workers readily adopted the new concepts. Hamilton (1958:22) wrote of the climate:

> When ego psychology began to permeate psychoanalytic theory
> caseworkers would no doubt have grasped its importance even
> if they had not been harrowed in a literal sense by reality stresses
> of the depression years. The experience of this period helped
> them to rediscover those inner resources of character to which
> casework itself had always been attuned. It is part of man's her-
> itage that under the greatest pressure he seems to attain his
> greatest stature. Perhaps the renewed emphasis on ego strength
> was a desperate last stand in a world that was crumbling to
> pieces; perhaps it was part of the vision of man's strength and
> sturdiness under adversity.

In the 1940s and 1950s numerous individuals became associated with attempts to assimilate ego psychological concepts into
social casework and with efforts to define the goals and techniques
of social casework as differentiated from psychotherapy. Prominent among these were Lucille Austin (1948, 1956), Louise Bandler
(1963), Eleanor Cockerill and colleagues (1953), Annette Garrett
(1958), Gordon Hamilton (1940, 1951), Florence Hollis (1949,
1964), Isabel Stamm (1959), and Charlotte Towle (1948, 1954).

A fundamental aspect of ego psychology is its conception of people. Ego psychology embodied a more optimistic and humanistic view of human functioning and potential than that reflected in classical psychoanalytic theory. As described by Lutz (unpublished):

> All of those aspects of ego theory tend to alter the older view that the client who is faced with problems is necessarily sick, or that his behavior is pathological or deviant. He is seen rather as responding dynamically to his life situation, at times coping with his situation and mastering it. He is seen to have potentialities for higher orders of functioning which can be called into play to help him deal with his problems. Pathological degrees of impairment of ego development or of regression under stress are recognized, but even in these circumstances, emphasis is placed on helping the ego to develop, retain, or regain as much autonomy in its functioning as possible through strategic, convergent, sustaining alterations of his environment by means of therapy, education, and the provision of resources and services.

Ego psychology viewed environmental and sociocultural factors as important in shaping behavior and in providing opportunities for the development, enhancement, and sustainment of ego functioning. Thus it overcame the splitting off of the intrapsychic world of the individual from the social context in which he or she lived.

Ego psychological concepts were used to refocus the study and assessment process on (1) the client's person-environment transactions in the here and now, particularly the degree to which he or she is coping effectively with major life roles and tasks; (2) the client's adaptive, autonomous, and conflict-free areas of ego functioning, as well as his or her ego deficits and maladaptive defenses and patterns; (3) the key developmental issues affecting the client's current reactions; and (4) the degree to which the external environment is creating obstacles to successful coping.

Ego psychology provided the rationale for interventive approaches that were directed at improving or sustaining adaptive ego functioning by means of work with both the individual and the environment. A repertoire of techniques for working with the ego was systematized, and numerous efforts to classify ego-oriented casework were attempted.[5] Ego psychological concepts also provided a bridge to work with families and groups that could be used to enhance and modify individual and family functioning.

Ego psychological concepts recognized the reality of the client-worker relationship in contrast to an exclusive focus on its transference or distorted aspects. The relationship was seen as embodying more positive potential as a tool for enhancement of client functioning. Further, it was important for the worker to use him- or herself in other ways outside of the client-worker relationship to help the client, for example by assuming the role of mediator or advocate for the client.

Ego psychological concepts moved beyond an exclusive emphasis on insight into unconscious past conflicts and their current manifestations as the mechanism for individual change. Ego psychology led to a focus on (1) freeing and enhancing innate ego capacities without necessarily altering underlying personality conflicts; (2) providing experiences in the caseworker-client relationship that would correct for past developmental failures or deprivations; (3) providing learning opportunities in the casework relationship and in real life in which new behavior could be exercised and reinforced with resultant enhancement of competence and self-esteem; and (4) creating environmental supports that would permit more effective exercise of specific ego functions.

Ego psychological concepts helped to transform the casework process from a never-ending, unfocused exploration of personality difficulties to a more deliberate and focused use of the phases of the casework process. Ego psychological concepts underscored the importance of engaging the client in a helping relationship in which he or she could exercise innate ego capacities and take more responsibility for directing his or her own treatment and life. This led to more active and focused goal-setting. The middle phase of the casework process required more selective and circumscribed exploration, intervention, and monitoring of progress. The termination phase was viewed as "therapeutic" in its own right—a time for the client to test how well he or she can manage life. Further, because of the importance of the sustaining environment, the post-termination phase became more critical. It was necessary to ensure continued environmental support for enhanced ego functioning after the formal end of the treatment process.

Ego psychological concepts are applicable not only to direct practice with individuals, families, and groups but also to the design of service delivery, large-scale social programs, and social policy. By providing a theoretical understanding of the dynamic interplay among biopsychosocial factors during a lifelong growth process, ego psychology helps to identify individual needs and the kind of environmental conditions and resources essential to meeting human needs and fostering growth. Such knowledge can serve as a guide to the design of preventive, developmental, and rehabilitative services all through the life cycle.[6]

EGO PSYCHOLOGY AND THE PROBLEM-SOLVING MODEL

Efforts to incorporate ego psychology and related behavioral and social science theories also led to a distinctive problem-solving casework model developed by Helen Perlman (1957). She attempted to bridge the lingering dispute between diagnostic and functional caseworkers as well as to offer correctives for practices that she viewed as dysfunctional for the client. Significant among these were long waiting lists, high dropout rates associated with a lengthy diagnostic process, and the practice of engaging in a relationship with the client that had no purpose with respect to the client's request for help.

Drawing heavily on the writings of Hartmann and Erikson, Perlman was the first to incorporate the theories of White and Piaget into social work. She also drew on practice-based research.[7] Perlman evolved a casework model that was based on the premise that all human living is effective problem-solving. Her model emphasized the rational, flexible, and growth-oriented aspects of individuals. Client difficulties were viewed as stemming from disruptions of normal problem-solving capacities in relation to specific situations and deficiencies in some combination of client motivation, capacity, and opportunity (Ripple, Alexander, and Polemis, 1964).

Through a real relationship that began as soon as worker and client met, and embodying an assessment process specifically focused on the problematic situation and on the client's motivation, internal capacity, and external resources, the goals of casework were (1) to release, energize, and give direction to the client's motivation; (2) to release and then repeatedly exercise the client's mental, emotional, and action capacities for coping with his or her problems; (3) to find and make accessible to the client the opportunities and resources necessary to the solution or mitigation of the problem; and (4) to help individuals in families cope with whatever they are currently finding insurmountable in a way that will make maximum use of their conscious efforts, choices, and competencies.

At the time of its emergence the problem-solving model was unsuccessful in bridging the dispute between the diagnostic and functional caseworkers. The former viewed it as altering the diagnostic process too radically and minimizing the significance of psychoanalytic theory. While it shared common features with functional casework, it was viewed as too different. Nevertheless, Perlman made an important contribution that has enjoyed wide acceptance.

ISSUES IN THE UTILIZATION OF EGO PSYCHOLOGY IN CASEWORK PRACTICE

Despite ego psychology's potential to bridge person and environment in theory and practice, and irrespective of the massive efforts to define casework practice as psychosocial in nature, casework practice often was criticized for its focus on the inner life of the individual at the apparent expense of attention to the environmental component in intervention. It was also accused of abandoning the poor in favor of the middle class. Moreover, despite extensive efforts to distinguish social casework from psychotherapy, such a distinction seemed elusive. Even though the casework method embodied the conception of environmental intervention, there were those who believed that ego-oriented casework was misguided in that it minimized the society-changing pole of social work's dual mission. This criticism gained more adherents as clients appeared at the doors of social agencies who were "harder to reach" and "multiproblemed" and as economic pressures again began to plague all sectors of society.

Ego psychology came under attack as casework itself increasingly became the focus of the frustrations of society and certain segments of the profession, who viewed it as too closely connected to psychoanalytic theory and the medical model and too narrowly conceived, expensive, and lengthy (Wasserman, 1974:48). Ego psychology was accused of being another form of blaming the individual and making him or her responsible for the social conditions causing his or her difficulties. In this view, assessing what constituted ego strength and ego weakness was seen as merely another way of determining whether people were "worthy" or "unworthy" and of "therapizing" rather than helping them.

Finally, as has been true generally of practice theory during the history of social work, the concepts and associated practices stemming from ego psychology were not made operational and researched, so evidence supporting their efficacy was not forthcoming. This became increasingly important as the research that did begin to accumulate on casework effectiveness was negative or equivocal and as casework came under attack.[8]

CHANGING VIEWS OF SOCIETY AND SOCIAL WORK PRACTICE

Beginning in the 1960s and throughout the 1970s multiple factors within society and within the social work profession converged and radically altered the role of ego psychology within the theoretical base of social work practice, and that radically changed practice itself.

A FOCUS ON MACROSYSTEMS INTERVENTION

The 1962 presidential election ushered in the Kennedy and Johnson years and the War on Poverty. The country's leaders believed that the federal government should take a major role in ameliorating if not eradicating social problems and instilled a new sense of hope that positive changes were possible. Large-scale programs financed by the federal government were mounted.

The social work profession turned its attention away from case-work to community organization, social program and policy design, and social action. "Macrosystems" rather than "micro-systems" intervention achieved more status and many schools of social work modified their programs accordingly, reducing the amount of curriculum space allocated to personality theory and direct practice. Believing that increased manpower would promote the profession's ability to reform social policies and programs and serve the poor, undergraduate programs in social work proliferated and large numbers of trained social workers with B.S.W. degrees soon entered the field.

RESEARCH ON THE EFFECTIVENESS OF CASEWORK

Another important influence on the social work profession at this time was the accumulation of disheartening research findings on the effectiveness of casework (Mullen, Dumpson, and Associates, 1972; Fischer, 1976). The studies were utilized by the critics of casework to argue against its widespread use and to withdraw funding from longstanding more individualized services. Similar problems permeated the field of psychotherapy (Parloff, 1979). Many practitioners who were committed to case-work felt demoralized, while others tried to reaffirm traditional practices.[9]

THE CIVIL RIGHTS, WOMEN'S, AND GAY
LIBERATION MOVEMENTS

The push toward equality, social justice, and freedom from oppression on the part of people of color, women, and gays and lesbians also contributed to a challenge of psychodynamic theory and individual treatment. A general distrust of the medical model and its view that people who encountered difficulties in coping were afflicted with diseases that could be diagnosed and treated gathered momentum. As discussed in Chapter 1, followers of ego psychology were criticized for blaming the victim rather than the effects of oppression, poverty, and trauma and for "pathologizing" the behavior of women, gays and lesbians, and those who are culturally diverse rather than respecting their unique characteristics and strengths. An anti-labeling and anti-treatment atmosphere prevailed. Alternative services such as consciousness-raising, rap, and other types of self-help groups began to flourish.

THE KNOWLEDGE EXPLOSION AND THE PROLIFERATION OF PRACTICE MODELS

The accretion of knowledge in the behavioral and social sciences fostered the development of new practice models. Theories from the fields of sociology, social psychology, economics, and political science enriched the "macro-level" of practice as they illuminated the structure, functioning, and change mechanisms of large social systems. On the "micro-level," this period witnessed a resurgence of interest in and further development of crisis theory and cognitive theory—both closely allied with ego psychology—and a rekindling of interest in learning and behavioral modification theories. Further, small group theory, family system theory, communication theory, and general systems theory all came into their own (Kammerman *et al.,* 1969).

Group work which advanced in the 1950s, and community organization both consolidated around their distinctive knowledge bases. Within casework practice models proliferated, so that by the end of the 1960s one text (Roberts and Nee, 1970) added behavioral modification, crisis intervention, family-centered casework, and the socialization approach to the psychosocial, functional, and problem-solving models. Turner's *Social Work Treatment* (1986) cites over twenty treatment frameworks.

While ego psychology informed a variety of these approaches, its significance as a unifying theory for social work waned as competing theories and practice models commanded attention and as attention turned away from an exclusive reliance on psychodynamic approaches.

PROFESSIONAL POLARIZATION AND UNIFICATION

The developments discussed above renewed the perennial debate over which aspect of the social work profession's dual mission—"society-changing" and "people-changing"—was to take precedence (Goldstein, 1980:173–78). While the emphasis on "society-changing" in the 1960s restored the "social" to social work, it did so at the expense of alienating many practitioners who felt abandoned by the profession's national organization, which seemed to neglect their interests and expertise.[10] This sense of alienation was symbolized by the formation in 1971 of a new professional organization, the Federation of Societies for Clinical Social Work, which had somewhat different aims from those of the broader-based National Association of Social Workers. The use of the term "clinical" became controversial because of its association with the medical model and psychotherapy. The stated aim of the Federation, however, was to meet the needs of practitioners and consumers of direct practice and to correct for the perceived lack of attention to direct practice on the part of the larger profession (Strean, 1993:15).

In the 1970s and 1980s the development of a unifying definition of social work practice that encompassed intervention with both people and environments received attention in the writings of Bartlett (1970), Gordon (1969:5–11), Germain (1979), Meyer (1970, 1976), and others.[11] The ecological perspective or life model, for example (Germain, 1979; Germain and Gitterman, 1980), stresses the locus of social work intervention as the interface between people and environments. It sees the goal of social work as maintaining, restoring, and enhancing social functioning through improving individual coping and adaptation and through environmental amelioration. The ecological perspective draws on ego psychological concepts, particularly those that depart from the more traditional psychoanalytic ego psychological base. It emphasizes coping and adaptation; the rational, cognitive, problem-solving capacities of people; the need and quest for personal and social competence; and the importance of creating better fits between an individual's phase-specific needs and environmental resources. It gives a prominent role to restructuring the environment as well as to improving individual capacities. While the life model has achieved an important niche in the practice arena and still is undergoing refinements, it lacks appeal to certain segments of the direct practice community who argue that it minimizes understanding of personality and that its concepts are amorphous and difficult to utilize in the real world (Goldstein, 1983:21; Lang, 1982; Mishne, 1982; Strean, 1993:15).

RECENT TRENDS IN SOCIETY AND SOCIAL WORK PRACTICE

The decade of the 1980s brought Ronald Reagan and George Bush to the presidency of the United States. A conservative economic and political philosophy that reflected a marked contrast to the prevailing views of the previous two decades dominated the scene. During this period some significant trends within the social work profession occurred that have continued into the 1990s.

THE RESURGENCE OF DIRECT PRACTICE

Direct practice reasserted its importance during the 1980s and 1990s for numerous reasons. General disillusionment with government as a consequence of political assassinations, the intense struggle over the Vietnam War, and the failure of the Great Society programs to wipe out social problems set in. In the face of economic cutbacks and a government that did not believe its role was to bear responsibility to help those who were economically disadvantaged or otherwise suffering, social work professionals were among those who experienced feelings of powerlessness about influencing the development of responsive social programs and policies. Thus, a sense of demoralization and pessimism about social change prevailed for a time.

Concurrently, the awareness of the pressing needs of clients for individualized services has led to renewed attention to microsystems intervention and has generated creative approaches in work with special populations. These include Vietnam veterans, substance abusers, the victims of sexual and physical abuse, rape, and domestic violence, and persons with AIDS and their caregivers. There has been more experimentation with emerging interventive models (Turner, 1986). As a profession, social work has pressed for more status through licensing. Over two-thirds of the states have licensing statutes and some also have vendorship laws, that is, the right to third-party reimbursement for services to social workers in private practice.

Along with the resurgence of direct practice, ego psychology has enjoyed a renaissance of interest. Its emphasis on ego functioning and defenses, normal coping strategies, the need for mastery and competence, cognitive processes, person-environmental transactions, biopsychosocial factors in development, growth in adulthood, and stress and crisis addresses the needs of a broad range of clients. Refinements and extensions of psychoanalytic ego psychology that address internalized object relations and self development provide an "in-depth" dimension to understanding human behavior, maladaptation, and severe personality difficulties. The integration of knowledge regarding cultural diversity, female development, trauma, and the impact of oppression on certain populations has broadened the applicability of the theory. Ego-oriented intervention is applicable to many diverse populations, provides the conceptual underpinnings to a variety of practice models, and has linkages to family and group approaches.

The revival and expansion of direct practice in the past two decades have not escaped criticism or problems. While enriching the practice repertoire, the abundance of interventive models and varied interests has led to specialization and professional fragmentation. There is considerable controversy about whether certain approaches are consistent with social work practice and about the knowledge and skills that constitute their core. Certain segments of the profession voice concern about the numbers of practitioners who have attempted to elevate their status by calling themselves "clinical" social workers or psychotherapists and who work with middle-class clients outside of social agencies. Likewise they express dismay about the seemingly large numbers of students entering social work training who want preparation for private practice. Both groups are seen by some as elitist and as having abandoned their identification with social work and its historical commitment to serving the poor, to agency practice, to client advocacy, and to other forms of social activism (Walz and Groze, 1991). In rebuttal, it is argued that such stereotyping is self-serving, polarizing, and a form of scapegoating (Strean, 1993:15).

While some social work practitioners may not identify with the broader mission of the profession, it is erroneous to equate clinical social work with a narrow view of practice. The definition of clinical social work put forth by a task force of the National Association of Social Workers reaffirmed its person-in-situation perspective, its inclusion of a range of approaches, and the fact that psychotherapy is a part but not the whole (Ewalt, 1980:23). Thus clinical social work, in itself, is consistent with a broad psychosocial focus. Despite the increase in the percentage in private practice, most social work practitioners are so engaged on a part-time rather than a full-time basis and continue to be identified with social work as a profession. The vast majority of social workers are employed in social agencies where clinical knowledge and skills, broadly defined, as well as advocacy and linkage to necessary resources are necessary to help clients. In this connection, a recent national study of graduate social work students shows that beliefs about "students' flight from traditional social work values into entrepreneurial, private practice orientations have been overestimated." It presents evidence that "students, now as in the past, are predominantly entering social work to advance their professional skills and potential and are highly committed to the concept of involvement with the disadvantaged" (Abell and McDonnell, 1990:63–64).

Of more serious concern are the variety of constraints in the practice arena that stem from shrinking budgets, the widening gap between clients' needs and available resources, the increasing emphasis on crisis intervention and very brief treatment, a business rather than human relations ethos in the administration of social agencies, the growth of managed care with its often bureaucratic and mechanical application, and society's lack of commitment to addressing many social problems. Further, low salaries, inadequate staffing, diminished supervision, the erosion of practice standards, and the use of vast numbers of poorly trained personnel have contributed to low morale and poorer-quality services.

THE IMPORTANCE OF PRACTICE RESEARCH

Research has greatly enriched ego psychological theory by providing empirical support for many of its concepts and expanding our understanding of child and adult development and the ways in which people cope with stress, crisis, and life events. In contrast to these advances, systematic research on intervention has lagged, although important strides are being made.

While the practice studies that were cited in the 1970s did not support the efficacy of social casework (Mullen, Dumpson and Associates, 1972), they were seriously flawed. The interventive goals, processes, and outcomes studied were not well-selected, defined, operationalized, and measured (Perlman, 1972:194). More rigorous research methodology was advocated (Bloom, 1983; Blythe and Briar, 1985; Fischer and Hudson, 1983; Levy, 1983; Reid, 1983). In the years since these early studies, findings on the outcomes of intervention have yielded more positive results (Rubin, 1985; Thomlison, 1984). Yet the problem of operationally defining psychodynamic and psychosocial variables and interventive processes remains, and research on this type of practice still is at an early stage. More attention has been devoted to studying behavioral, cognitive, and task-centered therapies, the goals, techniques, and outcomes of which are more easily specified and measured than those of ego-oriented or psychosocial intervention. A further problem is that methodologically rigorous, quantitative research designs have been applied mechanically to poorly conceptualized practice or have produced trivial results.

Outcome evaluation alone is not sufficient to advance the development and application of ego psychology to social work practice (Goldstein, 1983a:17–21). While systematic studies of the effectiveness of ego-oriented practice with specific target problems and populations are needed, qualitative and other research strategies that move beyond the current preoccupation with large experimental or single-case designs are equally necessary. Further, those involved in clinical practice must become involved in the formulation, design, and implementation of such studies either by acquiring practice research expertise themselves or by collaborating with researchers interested in and challenged by the problems inherent in conducting clinical studies.

IMPLICATIONS FOR SERVICE DELIVERY AND SOCIAL POLICY

While ego psychology makes its greatest contribution to understanding human behavior and shaping social work direct practice models, it has important implications for service delivery and social policy.

Ego psychology can be particularly useful in directing service delivery toward primary prevention rather than only remediation (Roskin, 1980). Its emphasis on the importance of developmental stages, role and life transitions, stress and crisis, and trauma to human functioning suggests the need for social work services to be positioned in people's lives where and when they are likely to need and use help (Meyer, 1970, 1976). Ego psychology alerts us to when and under what conditions during the human life cycle such help might be needed. As suggested by Meyer (1976:75), hospitals, clinics, schools, recreational facilities, and child welfare agencies are common places where people congregate. Day-care centers, nurseries, factories, corporations, unemployment centers, and legal-aid offices can be added to this list. Likewise, there are certain events and times in people's lives that trigger the need for help, and when its availability can prevent more serious breakdowns in social functioning. Separation, divorce, illness, death, pregnancy, job loss, marriage, parenthood, and retirement are examples. The identification of high-risk populations or individuals who can be offered services before problems develop or escalate is another important measure.

Ego psychology's assimilation of knowledge regarding the negative effects of oppression on people of color, women, and gays and lesbians, as well as of the strengths and attributes of diverse populations is resulting in more sensitive practices and programs.

At the same time ego psychology's view of the significance of chronic or stable impairments to the ego capacities that some individuals bring to their life transactions points to the need for a range of remedial, rehabilitative, or sustaining interventive services, many of which need to be offered on more than a short-term basis. Short-term or crisis intervention, while helpful in many instances, is not suited to addressing long-term suffering or longstanding maladaptation. In this regard current social policy and financial constraints present serious, if not insurmountable, obstacles to meeting the needs of many individuals in society, particularly those who are poor.

Ego psychology's appreciation of the significance of an individual's needs for mastery, decision-making, and autonomy suggests the importance of services that are structured to promote clients' active participation in matters affecting them (Germain, 1977; Goldstein, 1981).

Ego psychology's conception of the importance of social and environmental factors in promoting adaptive functioning points to the role of environmental intervention in direct practice efforts. Equally important, however, is the role of social workers in contributing to social policies more conducive to promoting human growth and preventing maladaptation. The aim of ego-oriented practice is not to help an individual adjust to a disturbed society (although we all have to come to terms with the constraints and conditions under which we live, to some degree). Ego-oriented practice views the social and environmental context as a proper locus of interventive efforts if it is creating obstacles to the individual's growth and functioning. Clearly the goal of making the social environment and social policy more responsive to many clients' needs requires that social workers actively engage in social and political action. In this respect the goals of "people-helping" and "society-changing" are reciprocal and to some extent inseparable.

This is a critical issue as we face the devastating effects of social policies that are inimical to meeting the needs of the underprivileged and less-privileged members of society. While the direct practitioner works to alleviate and minimize some of the tragic effects of these policies on the individuals served, collective intra- and interprofessional action to obtain needed services and to influence social welfare policy is essential.

NOTES

1. For a different perspective on this topic see Martha Heineman Field, "Social Casework Practice During the Psychiatric Deluge," *Social Service Review*, 54 (December 1980):483–507. The author argues persuasively that the psychiatric deluge was not as dramatic or as widespread as believed and that psychodynamic theory was assimilated slowly and unevenly into social work practice.
2. Social workers who were most immediately and directly affected by Freudian theory were those in psychiatric clinics or hospitals and child guidance clinics, particularly on the East Coast.
3. For a more detailed discussion of these techniques in social casework see Katherine M. Wood, "The Contributions of Psychoanalysis and Ego Psychology to Social Casework," in Herbert Strean, ed., *Social Casework: Theories in Action* (Metuchen, N.J.: Scarecrow Press, 1971), pp. 76–107.
4. For a discussion of social work's preoccupation with the medical model and its consequences for the profession, see Carel B. Germain, "Casework and Science: A Historical Encounter," in Robert W. Roberts and Robert H. Nee, eds., *Theories of Social Casework* (Chicago: University of Chicago Press, 1970), pp. 3–32.
5. For a detailed discussion of these general techniques see Florence Hollis, *Casework: A Psychosocial Therapy* (New York: Random House, 1964).
6. For an interesting elaboration of this idea see Carol H. Meyer, *Social Work Practice: A Response to the Urban Crisis* (New York: Free Press, 1970), pp. 82–104.
7. See Lillian Ripple, Ernestina Alexander, and Bernice Polemis, *Motivation, Capacity and Opportunity*, Social Science Monographs (Chicago: University of Chicago Press, 1964).
8. For an interesting discussion of the issue see Helen Harris Perlman, "Once More with Feeling," in Edward J. Mullen and James R. Dumpson and Associates, eds., *Evaluation of Social Intervention* (San Francisco: Jossey-Bass, 1972), pp. 191–209.
9. For example, see Helen Harris Perlman, *Perspectives on Social Casework* (Philadelphia: Temple University Press, 1971). This work contains several articles dealing with the issue that appeared earlier, among them "Casework Is Dead," "Can Casework Work?" and "Casework and the Diminished Man."
10. For a discussion of this issue see Margaret G. Frank, "Clinical Social Work: Past, Present, and Future Challenges and Dilemmas," in Patricia L. Ewalt, ed., *Toward A Definition of Clinical Social Work* (Washington, D.C.: National Association of Social Workers, 1980), pp. 13–21.

11. Two issues of *Social Work* have been devoted to identifying the core of social work's base of knowledge and skills: "Special Issue on Conceptual Frameworks," *Social Work,* 22 (September 1977), and "Conceptual Frameworks II," *Social Work,* 26 (January 1981).

PART II

THEORETICAL UNDERPINNINGS

CHAPTER 3

THE EGO AND ITS FUNCTIONS

F reud described the ego as an organization or substructure of the mental apparatus defined by its functions in *The Ego and the Id* (1923), as well as in later publications (1926, 1933, 1940). A difficulty arises, however, when one tries to delimit the concept of the ego precisely, because (1) conceptions of the number, nature, and development of ego functions have changed since Freud's time and (2) the ego not only has been described as a group of functions, but also as both a complex self-regulating structural organization and a motivational system (Klein, 1970:511–25). This chapter will discuss the major functions of the ego in order to provide a framework that guides the assessment of an individual's ego strength and adaptive capacity.

THE CONCEPT

Ego functions are the essential means by which an individual adapts to the external world.[1] Whereas Freud thought that the ego derived its power from the id and developed as a result of frustration and conflict, both of which prompted the individual to action, Hartmann was the first to suggest that while all "ego apparatuses" undergo maturation during the developmental process and are affected by the environment, some nevertheless are initially independent of, and have a "primary autonomy" from, the id.

Since Hartmann's seminal contribution many authors have advanced their views regarding the number of significant ego functions. Some identify several discrete, simple functions, while others group these discrete functions under a few overarching and more complex ego functions. For example, while perception, memory, intelligence, and thought processes can be considered separately, they also can be subsumed under the more complex ego function of reality testing.

The most comprehensive and systematic effort to describe and study ego functions can be found in the work of Bellak and colleagues (1973). They identified the following twelve major ego functions, each of which is dependent upon more discrete mechanisms:

1. Reality testing
2. Judgment
3. Sense of reality of the world and of the self
4. Regulation and control of drives, affects, and impulses
5. Object relations
6. Thought processes
7. Adaptive regression in the service of the ego
8. Defensive functioning
9. Stimulus barrier
10. Autonomous functioning
11. Mastery–competence
12. Synthetic–integrative functioning

REALITY TESTING

The accurate perception of the external environment, of one's internal world, and of the differences between them is a complex ego function that is essential to all adaptive behavior. It develops as a result of the interaction between innate ego capacities (such as perception, memory, intelligence, and thought processes) and psychosocial factors (such as interpersonal relationships and environmental influences) during the developmental process.

An important distinction exists between the ability to perceive stimuli and the capacity to test reality. The latter refers to the ability to differentiate between one's own fantasy life or subjective experience and the objective world and to determine whether the source of stimuli is inside or outside the self. Further, one must be able to appraise and interpret stimuli accurately and understand cause-and-effect relationships. Thus, the child's cognitive capacities and degree of differentiation from others affect his or her capacity to test reality. For example, a young boy who is not yet able to understand causal relationships and who engages in magical thinking may interpret his mother's increased sensitivity and affection in a time of need as a capacity to read his mind. Accurate in the perception that his mother meets his needs, the child misinterprets the reasons and the complex verbal and nonverbal communicative process underlying the mother's behavior. The belief that wishes and fantasies control events constitutes a normal or phase-appropriate thinking process at a certain point in the early years. The continuation of such beliefs beyond their phase-appropriate point will lead to serious impairments in the capacity to test reality and in social functioning. Thus, a sixteen-year-old adolescent male who has the conviction that all of his teachers call on him in class in order to humiliate him because their special powers make them aware that he has not studied shows serious disturbances in reality testing that affect his school performance. Similarly, a twenty-three-year-old woman who believes that her fantasies of becoming an artist will lead to success without her having to work will neglect to develop the ability necessary to achieve her goals.

Likewise, in early childhood the child goes through a normal phase of not being aware that the image reflected in a mirror emanates from his or her own body. An adolescent male who is conflicted about his homosexual impulses and hears voices calling him a "queer" and telling him he would be better off dead shows a serious impairment in his ability to test reality. Unable to experience the internal nature of his struggle, he projects his guilt onto external objects whom he then views as attacking him.

Not all distortions in the evaluation of internal and external reality imply a loss of the capacity to test reality. Individuals engage in a variety of defenses (as will be discussed in Chapter 4) that limit accurate interpretations of reality to some extent. Two important factors usually distinguish the distortions due to defense formation from faulty reality testing. First, the distortions imposed by defenses are more subject to correction. For example, an individual who experiences a friend as angry at him because he projects his own unwanted, unconscious anger onto his friend may be able to correct his perception if the friend flatly denies being angry. Second, while the distortions resulting from a defense that arises to ward off anxiety or unconscious conflict may limit accurate interpretations of events and motives, they generally are less extreme and do not have a bizarre quality. For example, an individual may not acknowledge the malevolent motivation of another who hurts him and may continue in a relationship in which he is hurt easily. The distortion imposed by the denial of his friend's aggression may result from unconscious taboos regarding thinking "bad" angry thoughts about others. Thus he denies or rationalizes the meaning of the behavior, so that he does not experience conflict. These defenses, however, do have a price. Reality testing is not severely impaired, but the inability to perceive motivation accurately has negative consequences for his interpersonal relationships. In contrast, a depressed woman who is convinced that she is worthless, that she has hurt others by her actions and deserves to be punished in spite of all evidence to the contrary, has such an extensive and extreme denial of reality that it constitutes a severe failure of reality testing.

The most severe manifestations of the loss of the capacity to test reality are seen in delusions (false beliefs that are adhered to and that cannot be validated) and hallucinations (false perceptions that are adhered to and that cannot be validated). Such severe impairments generally are common among individuals thought to have schizophrenic or other types of psychotic conditions.

In order to evaluate reality, as experienced by a client, the practitioner must have a full understanding of the sociocultural background and support system of the individual, since there is a need to know if there are culturally sanctioned beliefs that, while seeming strange, nevertheless are shared phenomena within a subculture.

JUDGMENT

An individual must develop the capacity not only to test reality accurately but also to act upon the outside world. His or her actions involve decisions as to what behaviors are appropriate in

certain circumstances. Judgment involves the capacity to identify possible courses of action and to anticipate and weigh the
implications or consequences of behavior in order to engage in
appropriate action, that is, behavior directed to achieving desired goals with minimal negative consequences.

Good judgment is dependent on accurate perception and testing of reality and is essential to effective problem-solving. Good
or bad judgment may be specific to certain situations or may be a
general quality. Thus, a person may demonstrate good judgment
in the way he or she deals with a particular set of circumstances
but may show variability in his or her overall ability to cope with
situations appropriately. An adolescent member of a football
team may be tempted to skip football practice in order to socialize with members of his peer group who are not on the team and
who make demands on his time. If he gives in to peer pressure
without anticipating its consequences, he may be dropped from
the team. This would show poor judgment in this instance. If the
same adolescent persistently fails to anticipate the consequences
of his actions, he gives evidence of a more serious impairment of
judgment generally.

Good judgment, like good reality testing, evolves during the
developmental process and is dependent upon the maturation of
complex cognitive processes and repeated experiences within
the realm of interpersonal relations and person–environment
transactions. Practice in anticipating the consequences of behavior, in planning and taking appropriate actions, and in getting accurate feedback from the environment is crucial. Deficits in
judgment may stem from deficiencies in innate cognitive equipment or from failures in the developmental process. The exercise
of good judgment may lead to the control of or a delay in the expression of impulses. The ability to control one's impulses, however, is essential to good judgment. One may feel extremely and
justifiably angry at an employer who criticizes one unfairly but
refrain from an angry outburst because of the realistic appraisal
that one may be fired if one gives in to a burst of temper.

Because the appropriateness of behavior is contingent upon
cultural and societal norms, it is important to understand the
context in which behavior occurs. Similarly, because of its link to
the achievement of individual goals, one must understand what

a person is trying to achieve by his or her actions when evaluating his or her judgment.

SENSE OF REALITY OF THE WORLD AND OF THE SELF

It is possible to *perceive* inner and outer reality accurately but to *experience* the world and the self in distorted ways. A good sense of reality involves the ability to feel or to be aware of the world and one's connection to it as real, to experience one's own body as intact and belonging to oneself, to feel a sense of self, and to experience the separation or boundaries between oneself and others as distinct organisms.

This complex ego function provides the basis for the core experience of one's physical and psychological identity and relation to others. The developmental process by which an infant moves from a state of nonawareness of the world to one in which he or she becomes a separate and unique person in transaction with distinct others is inextricably connected to the development of a sense of reality.

A good sense of outer and inner reality is most apparent by its absence. An individual may experience himself or herself as estranged from the surrounding world (derealization) as if there is an invisible screen between him- or herself and others. Often there is a sense of walking in a dream. Depersonalization is the most common form of disturbance in the sense of reality. One feels estranged from one's own body as if one were apart from it and looking at it, as if it were a distinct object. Another variant of this is to feel that parts of oneself or one's body are disconnected and do not belong to oneself. Certain distortions of body image also involve disturbances in the sense of reality. An individual may feel that a particular part of his or her body is extremely ugly, although knowing that this is not a valid perception. One may look in the mirror and experience the contours of one's face changing and yet know this is not possible. The loss of a sense of boundary between the self and others is evident in the experience of literally merging with another in intense relationships. In a psychological sense one may feel as if one has no identity of one's own, that parts of one's own inner experience are strange, or that one has an inner emptiness. Problems in self-esteem are often experienced.

While a poor sense of reality may be evident in those with poor reality testing, the converse is not true. There are those who retain the capacity to test reality but show a disturbed sense of reality. They feel alienated from themselves or others. They know that what they experience is not objectively so but nevertheless undergo a distortion of their experience. The combination of good capacity for reality testing and poor sense of reality is common among those individuals who are thought to have borderline conditions.

REGULATION AND CONTROL OF DRIVES, AFFECTS, AND IMPULSES

The ability to modulate, delay, inhibit, or control the expression of impulses and affects (feelings) in accord with reality is the hallmark of adaptive functioning and is essential to living among others. To develop this capacity without overcontrolling or undercontrolling one's impulses and feelings is a major developmental task. Similarly, the ability to tolerate anxiety, frustration, and unpleasant emotions such as anger and depression without becoming overwhelmed, impulsive, or symptomatic is necessary to optimal functioning.

While the maintenance, regulation, and control of impulses and affects rest with the ego, they are affected by the amount and intensity of impulses and unpleasant emotions (id) within a given individual. They also depend upon the nature of internalized constraints against the expression of impulses (superego) and the impact of frustrating, dangerous, or unpleasant life circumstances (reality). Thus it is important to understand the relative strength of impulses, prohibitions, and reality pressures in evaluating this ego function.

Almost everyone can become overwhelmed at times and may act impulsively, yet retain good impulse control generally. A reasonably well-functioning woman who begins to abuse alcohol after a separation from husband and children or the death of a parent, or during the pressures of relocation, may show a serious and selected loss of impulse control. Such behavior, however, may not signify as severe and pervasive an impairment in impulse control as that of a woman who takes tranquilizers chronically to shield herself from all tension associated with job pressures, chores, and interpersonal and childrearing demands. At the same time a selected loss of impulse control as evidenced by a serious suicide attempt by a person who tightly controls the expression of feelings and impulses may have tragic consequences.

Disorders of overregulation of impulses and affects also can have serious consequences for an individual's well-being, as exemplified by a woman who cannot permit herself any sexual pleasure or by those unable to experience angry feelings directly who turn anger against themselves instead.

The capacity to tolerate affects or feeling states such as sadness, anxiety, depression, or elation is another aspect of this ego function. Such feelings are a normal part of life. For example, a man may fear that any woman he becomes attached to will reject him. His anxiety may be so intolerable as he enters a new relationship with a woman that he distances himself from her by constant demanding behavior that has the effect of driving the woman away. Likewise a woman anticipating a change in her relationship with her best friend resulting from geographic relocation may be unable to tolerate the intense feelings of sadness and loss. She may minimize the significance of the change to herself and consequently act toward her friend as if the relationship is unimportant to her.

OBJECT (OR INTERPERSONAL) RELATIONS

Within contemporary ego psychology the concept of object relations has assumed a more central position than it held previously. It refers to both the development of one's internalized sense of self and others and the evolution of the capacity for mature interpersonal relationships. Many theorists (Jacobson, 1964; Mahler, Pine, and Bergman, 1975) view object relations as central to the development of all other ego functions. It is hypothesized that the evolution of one's internalized sense of self and others and the evolution of one's external relations with others occur simultaneously and provide the context for personality development. The emphasis on object relations complements Freud's original focus on the drives as the motivators of human behavior and is more in keeping with current conceptions of the ego. Because of the significance of this concept and its complex developmental sequence it will be discussed in more detail in Chapter 6. What follows are some general considerations.

The optimal development of internalized object relations requires that an individual perceive him- or herself as a separate person with three-dimensional qualities and be able to view others in a similar fashion. This capacity is crucial to identity as well as to mature, loving relations with others. Its development begins at birth and is dependent upon the child's experiences with others. Object relations are significantly shaped during the critical stages in the first several years of life, although development continues throughout adolescence and adulthood. The child's ability to achieve object constancy around the age of three is accompanied by the development of an inner, separate, stable, and integrated sense of self and of the object (primary caretaker) as distinct from the self. Determining whether or not an individual has achieved such integration in childhood and has consolidated his or her identity in adolescence is a crucial task in assessing overall ego functioning. It is likely that an individual lacking such integration will show impairments in other more discrete ego functions. Such individuals, depending on the nature and degree of the impairment of object relations, may show a fragmented, diffuse, or split identity as well as chaotic, infantile, withdrawn, self-centered or antisocial relations with others. For example, a 23-year-old woman who clings to her friendships with female friends may react with intense anger, feelings of rejection, and devastation if a friend develops a close relationship with another person. Such a reaction may signify that she views her friend as an extension of herself rather than as a separate person, and that she needs her friend in order to feel whole and good. The friend's interest in another frustrates the young woman's need for total possession and also engenders feelings of rage, unworthiness, or badness.

Severe impairments in internalized object relations and in the quality of interpersonal relationships are common in individuals who are thought to have borderline, narcissistic, and schizophrenic conditions.

Individuals who have achieved a separate and integrated sense of self and others may still reflect selected difficulties in maintenance of self-esteem and identity as well as problems in interpersonal relations. To the degree that unconscious conflict may affect one's sense of identity and interpersonal relations, various difficulties emerge. For example, a man who has unresolved conflicts stemming from his anger at his stern, disciplinarian father may tend to relate to all authority figures as he did to his father. He becomes fearful and antagonistic to his boss when the latter offers constructive criticism. Such an individual carries over past relationships into the present inappropriately.

One does not assess the quality of internalized object relations and interpersonal relationships on the basis of single instances in a person's life. What is important is the patterning of these qualities as they are reflected in past and current functioning.

THOUGHT PROCESSES

Mature thinking generally is taken for granted in that most individuals can perceive and attend to stimuli, concentrate, anticipate, symbolize, remember, and reason. Most individuals are able to communicate their thought processes clearly through language. Thinking and speaking usually are organized, logical, and oriented to reality rather than fragmented, irrational, and oriented toward fantasy. The physiologically normal infant has the innate biological equipment to develop the capacity for mature thinking, and this ego function is thought to begin as part of the autonomous, conflict-free sector of the ego. Nevertheless, the infant's thought processes are underdeveloped (primitive) and must undergo a maturational sequence.

An important development in the maturation of thought processes is the individual's shift from primary process thinking to secondary process thinking. Primary process thinking follows the pleasure principle in that it is characterized by wish-fulfilling fantasies and the need for immediate instinctual discharge irrespective of its appropriateness. Wishes and thoughts are equated with action so that action upon the outside world is not necessary in order to obtain gratification in a psychological sense. Primary process thinking has other important characteristics: (1) it disregards logical connections among ideas; (2) it permits contradictions to exist simultaneously; (3) it has no conception of time, so that past, present, and future are confused; (4) wishes are represented as actual fulfillments; and (5) it utilizes the mechanisms of displacement (exchanging the original goal for another) and condensation (combining two or more ideas into one). In contrast, secondary process thinking follows the reality principle. It is characterized by the ability to postpone instinctual gratification or discharge until reality conditions are appropriate and available and replaces wish-fulfillment with appropriate action upon the outside world. Wishes and thoughts alone are not sufficient in order to obtain gratification. Secondary process thinking is goal-directed, organized, and oriented to reality.

Mature thought processes are essential to optimal adaptation. The individual who is dominated by autistic thinking, that is, by his or her inner preoccupations without reference to others or to reality, cannot relate to the surrounding world. The person who is unable to organize his or her thoughts in a logical, goal-directed way cannot communicate with others. The individual who is unable to symbolize cannot speak coherently or reason. The person who responds to stressful situations with diminished capacity to concentrate, remember, and anticipate will lack essential elements for effective problem-solving. The individual whose affects or emotions are disconnected from his or her thoughts and behavior, or whose impulses and feelings are expressed in a chaotic way, cannot communicate the truth about what he or she thinks and feels to others.

As with other ego functions, thought processes fluctuate and are affected by extreme stress. It is important to determine whether impairments in thinking are chronic or whether they represent an acute disorganization. Severe impairments in thought processes are common among individuals with schizophrenic conditions.

ADAPTIVE REGRESSION IN THE SERVICE OF THE EGO

The concept of regression originated in Freud's writings as a defense in which an individual literally goes backward, returning to a previous phase of development. He or she engages in behavior that has been given up or is considered to be part of an earlier (more primitive) era in order to avoid anxiety or conflict. The idea that regression can serve adaptive ends was an important contribution to ego psychology. Adaptive regression in the service of the ego connotes an ability to permit oneself to relax the hold on, and relationship to, reality; to experience aspects of the self that are ordinarily inaccessible when one is engaged in concentrated attention to reality; and to emerge with increased adaptive capacity as a result of creative integrations. A boy working on a term paper that is due the next day may become increasingly fatigued and, try as he may, unable to draw the conclusions necessary to finish the assignment. He decides to take a nap from which he emerges with the "brainstorm" that permits the completion of the task. A mother permits herself to give up temporarily her adherence to logical, organized speech and thinking and talks baby talk to her infant. She empathizes with the child's urgent needs, which can be communicated only nonverbally, even though these needs are not part of her adult experience. A psychotherapist relaxes his or her attention to a client's words and becomes aware of the fantasies, feelings, and thoughts that they evoke, using this awareness to tune in to the complex meaning of the client's communication.

It can be seen that adaptive regression in the service of the ego is an important ego function that enables the individual to move forward, to cope more effectively, or to exercise creativity. Often it is said that artists use this particular ego function extensively; they are able to touch the more deep-seated or primitive aspects of their personality in the service of their art.

A crucial factor in assessing regressive behavior is whether it serves adaptive or maladaptive ends. At times of increased work stress, for example, it may be helpful to withdraw from stress-producing stimuli by going to sleep early in order to recoup and refresh oneself. An individual who withdraws into sleep during all leisure time with his wife in order to protect himself from conflicts associated with intimacy shows more maladaptive behavior.

DEFENSIVE FUNCTIONING

Because of the significance of defenses in normal and abnormal development, Chapter 4 will discuss this topic in detail. What follows are general considerations.

According to most psychodynamically oriented theories, the individual develops unconscious, internal mechanisms called defenses to protect him- or herself from the painful experience of anxiety or from fear-inducing situations. Defenses can be adaptive or maladaptive. Adaptive defenses protect the individual from anxiety while simultaneously fostering optimal functioning. For example, denial of mortality may serve adaptive ends if it allows the individual to function well by protecting him or her from constantly living with a heightened awareness of all the illnesses, accidents, and destructive acts that occur every day. Maladaptive defenses also protect the individual from anxiety, but often at the expense of optimal functioning. For example, denial that results in putting oneself in a dangerous situation or refraining from seeking necessary medical attention may protect one from experiencing the discomfort associated with danger or illness but does not lead to adaptive behavior.

There are a large number of defenses, and most authors have suggested that they differ with respect to when they emerge developmentally. Similarly, many believe that personalities organized around a certain constellation of defenses (those of a higher level or of a later developmental phase) are more mature than those organized around defenses arising from earlier periods.[2] It is important also in personality assessment to determine whether an individual utilizes defenses flexibly or rigidly, selectively or pervasively.

STIMULUS BARRIER

All living organisms are responsive to internal and external stimuli as a result of their sensorimotor apparatus. All individuals develop a mechanism by which they regulate the amount of stimulation received so that it is optimal—neither too little nor too great. Each individual appears to have a different threshold for stimulation. Thus some people seek out what may appear to others as excessive stimuli. In contrast, there are those individuals who become overstimulated by what seems to be minimal excitation. While children appear to be born with some innate capacity to deal with stimuli, this capacity is influenced greatly by the nature of the child's environment. Children who are exposed to excessive environmental or internal stimulation resulting from frustration may have their circuits overloaded and fail to develop the appropriate self-regulating mechanisms, or may withdraw into themselves as a means of coping. Some children may suffer from sensory deprivation, and this may result in a craving or hunger for stimulation, as exemplified by the individual who perpetually seeks excitement and surrounds himself with loud music.

An important aspect of the stimulus barrier is the degree to which an individual is able to maintain his or her level of functioning or comfort amid increases or decreases in the surrounding level of stimulation. There are individuals who can tolerate additional stimulus loads such as noise or work demands without its affecting their work performance or emotional state. Other individuals experience considerable stress when there is any alteration in the level of stimulation. In certain situations people may resort to sleep or withdrawal to avoid this stress. When one is fatigued or physically weak or ill one's threshold for stimulation may be lowered considerably. In some instances extreme sensory deprivation or bombardment may result in personality breakdown.

AUTONOMOUS FUNCTIONS

Hartmann originally proposed that certain ego functions such as attention, concentration, memory, learning, perception, motor functions, and intention have a primary autonomy from the drives and thus are conflict-free, that is, they do not arise in response to frustration and conflict as Freud suggested. They are innate, have their own energy source apart from the drives, and develop and mature given the average expectable environment.

At the same time, these ego functions can lose their autonomy by becoming associated with conflict in the course of early childhood development. For example, the capacity to remember, while innate, may be adversely affected by painful, anxiety-provoking, or traumatic events. Likewise, the capacity to learn may be influenced negatively as a result of the withdrawal of parental love or the presence of negative attitudes when a child shows curiosity.

The concept of secondary autonomy refers to other capacities of the individual that originally develop in association with frustration and conflict but later undergo a "change of function" and acquire autonomy from the conflict with which they were associated. Thus certain interests originally may develop as a way of coping with stress but later are pursued in their own right. For example, a child may learn to build model airplanes as a way of controlling a chaotic environment. This activity and those related to it may become divorced from the original motivation that led to their development and may then be pursued because they give pleasure.

In adulthood an individual becomes vulnerable to the temporary loss of autonomy in certain areas as a result of upsurges of anxiety and conflict. The degree to which individuals are able to maintain and to regain areas of primary and secondary autonomy is a crucial factor in assessment. There are individuals who, while suffering from extreme stress or conflict, nevertheless maintain a high level of functioning at work, for example. Thus work remains conflict-free or an autonomous area. Other individuals, who function well under usual circumstances, may show severe impairments (regression) in their ability to engage in certain activities when they experience stress. Their autonomous functioning may be restored, however, through helping efforts or when the stress is reduced.

It is hypothesized that one of the main reasons for disturbances in primary or secondary autonomy is the fact that selected behavior acquires aggressive or libidinal energy or becomes associated with a conflict that must be defended against. A young lawyer may show an inability to concentrate on his legal briefs in preparation for court appearances because his success in court is equated with a destructive competitive urge that he guards against. A young writer finds herself unable to work at a particularly challenging assignment that may lead to the recognition she seeks because she fears that success will lead to independence, which is equated with abandonment.

The fact that individuals who show severe disturbances in their functioning or serious problems in selected aspects of their lives nevertheless demonstrate intact and autonomous functioning in other areas is a crucial point of leverage in the interventive process. One can support and enhance areas of strength and marshal them to help the client cope more effectively. A woman with a poor self-concept who has difficulty making friends and asserting herself on the job may be talented and show excellent work skills. She may be helped to focus on building her career, which enhances her self-esteem and enables her to begin to take more risks in other areas. A young schizophrenic man with good intelligence and ability to observe himself may have poor relationships with others because of his demanding behavior. Through his intelligence he may be helped to consider the impact of his behavior on others and to learn more effective ways of dealing with people.

MASTERY—COMPETENCE

The degree to which one is and feels competent originates early in childhood as a function of one's innate abilities, one's mastery of developmental tasks, and the appropriate feedback of significant others in the environment. It affects the way one experiences and deals with the world. At the same time the quest for competence may be an important force in human motivation (to be discussed in more detail in Chapter 5).

Freud himself proposed that the ego had motivational properties when he identified the ego's self-preservation instincts. He abandoned this view, however, when he emphasized the role of sexual and aggressive instincts as the propelling forces within the personality. Psychoanalytic instinct theory saw all behavior, including creativity, curiosity, and knowledge-seeking, as rooted in sexual or aggressive instincts. While mastery experiences were identified as important in the personality, a drive toward mastery was not postulated.

The view that even infants engage in active attempts at adaptation (Hartmann, 1939; Erikson, 1950, 1959) gave rise to the idea that the organism experiences pleasure not merely through the reduction of tension or need but also through exercising autonomous ego apparatuses in the service of adaptation. This led to the postulation of the presence of a mastery drive or instinct (Hendrick, 1942, 1943; White, 1959, 1963) by authors who hypothesized an inborn, active striving toward interaction with the environment leading to the individual's experiencing a sense of competence or effectiveness. Both Hendrick and White differentiated the striving toward competence from the vicissitudes of sexual and aggressive instincts. For example, during the anal period of development the child needs to learn how to control the impulse to defecate, but the ability to bring that impulse under control leads to a sense of mastery over the body. The gradual accrual of a sense of mastery or competence becomes a crucial part of self-confidence in dealing with the world and thus becomes an important aspect of identity or sense of self.

Closely related to the concept of mastery is that of coping capacity. While the former usually refers to an individual's ability to meet new challenges, the latter generally refers to the capacity to handle stressful situations. Coping ability involves mastery but implies the individual's capacity to use basic internal resources and available external resources to develop novel solutions.

SYNTHETIC–INTEGRATIVE FUNCTION

Many authors, including Freud, have emphasized the ego's organizing role in addition to its more discrete functions.[3] Child development research (Spitz, 1959; Mahler, Pine, and Bergman, 1975) has provided important data pertaining to this conception of the ego. In this view, a primary feature of the ego is its capacity to "organize mental processes into a coherent form" (Blanck and Blanck, 1979: 23). The synthetic function is responsible for binding or fitting all the disparate aspects of the personality into a unified structure that acts upon the external world. The synthetic function is responsible for personality integration, the resolution of splits, fragmentations, and conflicting tendencies within the personality. In this respect there are individuals who may show good ego functioning on selected characteristics but whose overall personality integration is deficient. Thus the person may act in contradictory, fragmented, inconsistent, unpredictable, or chaotic ways, which reflects an internal lack of coherence as well.

EGO STRENGTH VERSUS EGO WEAKNESS

The term "ego strength" implies a composite picture of the internal psychological equipment or capacities that an individual brings to his or her interactions with others and with the social environment. The term "ego weakness" reflects deficiencies in an individual's internal equipment that may lead to maladaptive transactions with the social environment.

Important to the assessment of ego strength are the concepts of stability, regression, variability, and situational context. Within the same individual certain ego functions may be better developed than others and may show more stability. That is, they tend to fluctuate less from situation to situation, or over time, and are less prone to regression or disorganization under stress. Further, even in individuals who manifest ego strength, regression in selected areas of ego functioning may be normal in certain types of situations, for example, illness, social upheavals, crises, and role transitions, and do not necessarily imply ego deficiencies. It is important to note that it is possible for the same individual to have highly variable ego functioning, although in cases of the most severe psychopathology ego functions may be impaired generally.[4] Finally, the situational context is a key variable in evaluating ego functioning, because some aspects of the social environment may evoke better or worse functioning. Thus not all difficulties in functioning stem from impairments in ego functioning. It is crucial to evaluate the stresses, conditions, resources, and supports in the social environment in relation to the needs and capacities of the individual.

SUMMARY

This chapter has discussed the concept of ego functions and has described twelve of the major ego functions in detail. From this review it can be seen that while the individual is born with innate ego capacities that mature over time, the impact of interpersonal and environmental factors is crucial to the evolution of mature ego functions during the developmental process. The assessment of ego functioning permits an evaluation of the internal capacities that the individual brings to his or her life transactions. But such an assessment always must consider the nature of the individual's needs and capacities in relation to the conditions of the surrounding environment.

NOTES

1. For a discussion of this topic see Leopold Bellak, Marvin Hurvich, and Helen Gediman, *Ego Functions in Schizophrenics, Neurotics, and Normals* (New York: John Wiley & Sons, 1973), pp. 51-79.
2. It is hypothesized, for example, that borderline patients show more primitive or lower-level defenses than do neurotic patients.
3. Gertrude and Rubin Blanck have traced the development of this view in *Ego Psychology II: Psychoanalytic Developmental Psychology* (New York: Columbia University Press, 1979), pp. 15–30.
4. For example, in Bellak's work the schizophrenic population studied was impaired generally in ego functions. See Bellak, Hurvich, and Gediman, *Ego Functions*.

CHAPTER 4

THE EGO AND ITS DEFENSES

The concept of defense is rooted in classical psychoanalytic theory, although it acquired more significance with the emergence of Freud's structural theory and through the work of Anna Freud. As noted in Chapter 3, defenses are a crucial ego function. This chapter will consider the concept of defense and then will describe the common types of defense mechanisms in more detail.

THE CONCEPT OF DEFENSE

In *Inhibitions, Symptoms, and Anxiety* (1926), Freud proposed that defenses arise to mediate between the pressures of the instincts and those of the internalized values and prohibitions of the superego. When conflict develops between id and superego, anxiety emerges and acts as a signal to the ego to institute some type of action to eliminate the anxiety. Defenses are part of the ego's repertoire of mechanisms for protecting the individual from such anxiety by keeping intolerable or unacceptable impulses or threats from conscious awareness. Defenses operate unconsciously. For example, a sexual urge in a woman might stimulate anxiety if it conflicts with an unconscious prohibition against the expression of such an impulse that stems from the woman's earlier sexualized relationship with her father. Such an individual may develop the defense of reaction formation when she experiences sexual feelings toward other men. Instead of becoming consciously aware of her sexual feelings, she may convert them (unconsciously) into feelings of revulsion. In this way she not only protects herself from anxiety but also keeps the childhood conflict buried.

All people use defenses, but their exact type and extent vary from individual to individual. Generally a given person favors some defenses over others. Better-functioning individuals tend to use defenses flexibly and selectively rather than rigidly and pervasively.

All defenses falsify or distort reality to some extent, although in individuals who function more effectively such distortions are minimal or transient and do not impair the person's ability to test reality. To the degree that such defenses enable the person to function optimally without undue anxiety, they are said to be effective. In many instances, however, depending on the intensity of the conflict, the nature of the current stimuli evoking it, or the fragility or pervasiveness of the defense itself, such mechanisms may prove to be ineffective or maladaptive. They may (1) prevent the individual from gaining needed satisfaction; (2) be insufficient to contain the anxiety or conflict so that the person becomes overwhelmed, symptomatic, or disorganized; or (3) distort reality to such a degree that overall ego functioning is impaired. Thus a woman may deny (not face emotionally) the prospect of her husband's possible sudden death after an acute heart attack while she functions smoothly and makes all the medical and practical arrangements essential to his receiving appropriate care. The denial protects her from anxiety while fostering her ability to cope effectively. Were she to fail to recognize the seriousness of her husband's medical condition to such an extent that she refrained from trying to get medical attention, her use of denial, while protecting her from anxiety, would hamper her ability to cope effectively. It is not always easy to distinguish between adaptive and maladaptive defenses. A complicating factor in evaluating defenses is that they can have both effects within the same individual. For example, a recovered alcoholic's ability to defend against experiencing certain emotions that might weaken his or her ability to remain sober may be adaptive. Such a defense, however, also may limit the degree to which he or she can experience and verbalize anger or participate in and enjoy intimacy with a spouse.

Characteristic defenses are thought to originate in specific developmental phases.[1] Within psychoanalytic ego psychology defenses are linked closely to the maturity and level of personality or character development generally. A person's predominant defenses and character traits are viewed as evolving from the same developmental fixation points.[2] While individuals may employ defenses arising from both early and later developmental phases, should the earlier, lower-level, or immature defenses predominate, the personality of the individual will appear more infantile. For example, the defenses of projection and denial are thought to be associated with earlier phases of development than are the defenses of repression and sublimation. Thus an individual who uses denial and projection extensively often will exhibit less maturity in his or her overall personality functioning than will the person who relies on repression and sublimation.

Efforts directed at modifying defenses create anxiety and often are resisted by the individual. Resistance also operates unconsciously. The person does not seek deliberately to maintain his or her defenses. Resistance, however, creates obstacles to achieving the very changes that are desired. A shy individual who wants to improve his relations with others by becoming more assertive and outgoing may change the subject when it is suggested that there are social activities in which he might engage in order to meet new friends. Such an individual may seem uncooperative or uninterested, when in actuality the topic makes him quite anxious, as it threatens his characteristic mode of defense.

While it may seem desirable to try to lessen or modify certain maladaptive defenses in a given individual because they interfere with effective coping, such mechanisms also serve an important protective function. In many cases they should be respected, approached with caution, and at times strengthened, such as when the individual begins to become disorganized. In instances in which the person's ego is weak, the anxiety aroused by efforts to confront or modify defenses may lead to their rigidification or to more explosive, withdrawn, or bizarre behavior. Consequently, it is crucial to undertake a full evaluation of a person's ego functioning before undertaking any type of therapeutic intervention attempting to alter defensive functioning.

Under acute or unremitting stress, illness, or fatigue the ego's defenses, along with the other ego functions, may become impaired. This alteration often is reflected in the defense's failing, that is, it is not able to protect the individual from intense anxiety. Or, on the contrary, the defense rigidifies, that is, it becomes more extreme. When there is massive defensive failure the person becomes flooded with anxiety. This can result in a severe and rapid deterioration of ego functioning, and in some cases the personality becomes fragmented and chaotic, just as in psychotic episodes. When there is an extensive rigidification of defenses, an individual may appear exceedingly brittle, taut, and driven; his or her behavior may seem increasingly mechanical, withdrawn, or peculiar. Measures must be taken to restore or strengthen the defenses and to reduce the stress.

DEFENSE MECHANISMS VERSUS COPING MECHANISMS

Since defenses operate outside of conscious awareness, the individual cannot try to use a defense deliberately in coping with anxiety-producing situations. Further, "since the term defense mechanism was appropriated for intrapsychic maneuvers, transformations, and other operations dealing with affects and instincts, another term is needed to refer to the ego's dealing with the actual or objective situation itself" (Murphy, 1970: 67). Thus a child may deal with a fearful event in the external world through avoidance without having the avoidance transformed into an unconscious defense. Likewise an adult troubled by a problem at work consciously may try not to think about it over a weekend that is to be spent out of town visiting friends. In both instances the individuals show an active coping strategy rather than a defense *per se*. It maybe useful to distinguish between coping and defense, the former being the broader concept.

Another argument for distinguishing between these two concepts is the confusion in using one term, defense, to refer to both adaptive and maladaptive mechanisms.[3] Kroeber (1963) has proposed "that the mechanisms of the ego be thought of as general mechanisms which may take on either defensive or coping functions." Kroeber distinguishes between defenses and coping functions using six criteria: (1) defenses are rigid, compelled, channeled, and perhaps conditioned, whereas coping mechanisms are flexible, purposive, and involve choice; (2) defenses are pushed by the past rather than pulled by the future; (3) defenses distort the present situation rather than being oriented to reality requirements of the present situation; (4) defenses involve a larger component of primary process thinking and partake of unconscious elements rather than involving secondary process thinking, and coping mechanisms include both conscious and preconscious elements; (5) defenses operate as if it were necessary and possible wholly to remove disturbing affects and may involve magical thinking rather than operate in accordance with reality; and (6) defenses allow impulse gratification only through subterfuge and indirection rather than in an open, ordered, and tempered way.

An example of this distinction between defenses and coping functions can be seen in the ego function of selective awareness described by Kroeber. He suggests that the maladaptive outcome of this particular ego function is the defense of denial, in which the person refuses to face thoughts, perceptions, or feelings that are painful to acknowledge. In contrast, the adaptive outcome is reflected in the coping mechanism of concentration, in which the person is able to set aside recognizably disturbing feelings or thoughts in order to stick to the task at hand.

COMMON DEFENSE MECHANISMS

When Sigmund Freud formulated his ideas about defense, he emphasized one primary mechanism: repression. In *The Ego and the Mechanisms of Defense* (1936), Anna Freud identified nine defenses that were familiar in theoretical writings—regression, repression, reaction formation, isolation, undoing, projection, introjection, turning against the self, and reversal—to which she added a tenth: sublimation. A recent classification of defenses in a review chapter on psychoanalytic theory (Meissner, Mack, and Semrad, 1975) lists twenty-nine distinct mechanisms, grouped according to developmental levels: narcissistic, immature, neurotic, and mature. Such a grouping is misleading, however, since it is not always possible to make such clear distinctions. In a major book that deals systematically with defenses (Laughlin, 1979), twenty-two major and twenty-six minor defenses are enumerated and described.[4] Space will not permit a full treatment of this topic. What follows is a description of defenses that are commonly referred to in the literature and observed in clinical practice.

ANNA FREUD'S ORIGINAL LIST OF DEFENSE MECHANISMS

Repression. A crucial mechanism central in all neurotic behavior, repression is generally regarded as a more advanced or high-level defense. It involves keeping unwanted thoughts and feelings out of awareness, or unconscious. What is repressed once may have been conscious (secondary repression) or may never have reached awareness (primary repression). Repression may involve loss of memory for specific incidents, especially traumatic ones or those associated with painful emotions. A young woman had been told repeatedly of her father's arrest by the Nazis when she was five years old. Despite her love for her father, her presence at the time of the event, and her observable sense of loss afterward, she had no conscious recall of the incident.

There are major repressions, such as the foregoing example or the case of a man who has pushed out of his awareness any angry feelings at his father, who died when the boy was fourteen. Minor repressions often are reflected in evident lapses of memory at significant times, such as when one is going to announce a well-known speaker. These lapses may have symbolic significance and do not reflect a true memory loss *per se.*

Reaction Formation. Like repression, reaction formation involves keeping certain impulses out of awareness. The way of ensuring this, however, is through replacing the impulse in consciousness with its opposite. A husband who censors his unacceptable angry feelings toward his wife may act in a particularly loving way when irritated (at an unconscious level) by her.

Projection. When an individual attributes to others unaccept-able thoughts and feelings that he himself has but that are not conscious, he is using projection. A woman who has difficulty ac-cepting her strong sexual feeling toward men may feel that all men are interested in her only sexually and are constantly de-sirous of her, while she remains unaware of her own impulses. Projection is considered a lower-level defense. While it appears in better-functioning individuals, at an extreme it may involve serious distortions of others' feelings, attitudes, and behavior. Thus it diminishes the capacity to test reality. Delusions may in-volve projections of one's internal feelings onto the outside world.

Isolation. Sometimes the mechanism of isolation is referred to as isolation of affect, for there is a repression of the feelings asso-ciated with particular content or of the ideas connected with certain affects. Often this is accompanied by experiencing the feelings in relationship to a different situation. A young man is unable to be in touch with sad feelings when discussing his fa-ther's death, but he cries bitterly when viewing motion pictures in which a male authority figure dies. Conversely, a young woman may experience strong emotions in talking about her childhood but be unable to connect her feelings to any thoughts she has.

Undoing. This defense has been termed "a psychological era-sure" (Laughlin, 1979), in that it involves nullifying or voiding symbolically an unacceptable or guilt-provoking act, thought, or feeling. Undoing takes many different forms. For example, a man who has found himself to be sexually attracted to his secre-tary may buy his wife an expensive present. A school-age child who has taken money from his mother's purse may volunteer to go to the store or to do other errands for her. A supervisor may offer an employee a day off after failing to recommend her for a promotion. Certain types of confession, expiation, and atone-ment may be undoing mechanisms.

Regression. Regression involves the return to an earlier devel-opmental phase, level of functioning, or type of behavior in order to avoid the anxieties of the present. Behavior that has been given up recurs. Children who have been toilet trained may lose bladder control after the birth of a sibling who becomes the center of attention. A woman who has been jilted by a lover may become clinging and dependent or engage in fantasies about a previous boyfriend. The nature of the regression often is determined by fixation points during the course of development, that is, by places where the person has received too much or too little gratification.

Introjection. The defense of introjection is quite complex. It involves taking another person into the self, psychologically speaking, in order to avoid the direct expression of powerful emotions such as love and hate. When the object (person) of the intense feelings is introjected, the feelings are experienced toward the self, which has now become associated with or a substitute for the object, thus protecting the object. Introjection has been viewed as an important mechanism in the genesis of many depressive reactions, in that hostile or negative feelings toward an external object are redirected toward the self that has introjected the object. Often this occurs when there has been a major disappointment in or loss of the object. The depressed person's self-punishing and self-deprecating attitudes may be viewed as directed (unconsciously) toward the external object.

Introjection is closely connected to three other mechanisms that are mentioned frequently: identification, internalization, and incorporation.[5] Because of their similarity they often are used interchangeably, although they have somewhat different meanings. *Identification* connotes the modeling of oneself after another. One takes on the values, feelings, attitudes, and characteristics of a loved, admired, feared, or hated person. Identification, as well as the other mechanisms discussed here, is crucial to normal personality development.[6] Thus it is natural to model oneself consciously or unconsciously after a loved or admired person. Identification may be used, however, (unconsciously) to ward off anxiety and conflict. A boy may take on the aggressive characteristics of a father whose violence frightens him (identification with the aggressor) in order to deal with the anxiety related to his being victimized by his father. Identification may be accompanied by *internalization*. This mechanism goes beyond identification and involves "taking in" another person and making him or her part of the self rather than merely "taking on" his or her characteristics. Again the process of internalization can be a normal phenomenon. Thus one may internalize parental values so that they become part of the self. It is defensive if it is used to ward off anxiety such as that associated with being judged if having different views from parents. Internalization overlaps with the mechanism of introjection discussed above and also with *incorporation*, both of which involve a more primitive and early type of assimilation of the object or its parts. Internalization is a more general term and is viewed as a higher-level mechanism.

Turning Against the Self. This mechanism involves the turning of unacceptable impulses one has toward others against the self. It is the reverse of projection and is closely related though not identical to the defense of introjection. In turning against the self, however, one does not necessarily "take in" the object. If one has unconscious hostility toward a loved one, it is the hostility itself that is turned inward. This mechanism, like introjection, plays an important role in depressive moods and feelings of worthlessness. As pointed out by Alexander (1963:115–16) "the admission, 'I hate him,' is unacceptable to the ego and is replaced by the statement, 'I hate myself.' The reason for this reversal of sentiment is guilt created by the hostile feelings toward a beloved person. Turning these feelings inward both relieves the guilt and releases the hostility."

Reversal. Reversal involves the alteration of a feeling, attitude, trait, relation, or direction into its opposite. It is difficult to distinguish reversal from reaction formation. In fact, reaction formation involves a reversal of feelings. Reversal, however, is a more general mechanism and encompasses a greater range of behavior. Thus one type of reversal may be seen in a woman who rebels unconsciously against her mother, who was extremely passive and ineffectual, in order to become an extremely assertive and competent person, while at the same time experiencing extreme guilt and anxiety over her successes.

Sublimation. Sublimation is considered to be the highest-level or most mature defense, although its classification as a defense at all may be questioned. It involves converting an impulse from a socially objectionable aim to a socially acceptable one while still retaining the original goal of the impulse. Freud viewed most forms of exceptional creativity as sublimations of sexual or aggressive instincts. Thus, an artist who paints nudes may be channeling his or her sexual preoccupation into a valued activity. Competitive sports in which an individual finds gratification may involve a sublimation of aggressive instinct. Relationships in which there is a strong component of sexual attraction may become characterized by affection and tenderness.

OTHER COMMON DEFENSES

Intellectualization. The warding off of unacceptable affects and impulses by thinking about them rather than experiencing them directly is intellectualization. It is similar to isolation. People who employ intellectualization extensively appear highly cerebral and can talk at length about topics of seemingly great emotional significance without ever feeling the emotions or situations they describe.

Rationalization. The mechanism of rationalization is the use of convincing reasons to justify certain ideas, feelings, or actions so as to avoid recognizing their true underlying motive, which is unacceptable. A mother with little money may rationalize the purchase of a color TV by saying it is important for her children, because she feels guilty about spending money for something she wants but cannot afford.

Displacement. Shifting feelings or conflicts about one person or situation onto another is called displacement. A woman who is very angry (unconsciously) at her husband for not coming home on time for dinner may find herself extremely irritated with the gas station attendant who keeps her waiting for an unusually long time. Her anger has been redirected to another object, which permits expression of the impulse but in an insignificant, nonthreatening situation.

Denial. The denial mechanism involves a negation or nonacceptance of important aspects of reality or of one's own experience that one may actually perceive. A person may deny the significance of an impending loss because it is too painful to contemplate. An individual may refuse to recognize that he or she has a terminal illness because the assimilation of this knowledge is too traumatic. Or an individual may be unable to acknowledge certain characteristics because they conflict with his or her self-image or idealized view of others. Denial may be of varying degrees and may be present in adaptive as well as in severely maladaptive behavior. The more the denial impinges on one's ability to act appropriately in accord with reality, the more serious the denial will be in terms of overall personality functioning.

Somatization. In somatization intolerable impulses or conflicts are converted into physical symptoms. The person may become preoccupied with physical symptoms, which become a substitute for the unacceptable feelings or conflicts.

Idealization. The overvaluing of another person, place, family, or activity beyond what is realistic is idealization. To the degree that idealized figures inspire one or serve as possible models for identification, idealization can be an extremely useful mechanism in personality development and in the helping process. When used defensively, it protects the individual from anxiety associated with aggressive or competitive feelings toward a loved or feared person. The dangers of idealization are great. Idealized objects are not perceived as whom or what they are. They are therefore likely to disappoint or frustrate an individual or may represent goals and expectations that can never be achieved. By creating an ideal for defensive purposes the individual makes him- or herself unaware of the true nature of his or her feelings.

Compensation. A person using compensation tries to make up for what he or she perceives as deficits or deficiencies. A typical example is the man who feels that his small stature may be equated with weakness or a lack of masculinity and who takes up such interests as mountain climbing or car racing. Such an individual may also become exceptionally aggressive and competitive with other men. Often driving ambition in those who become quite successful and powerful may be related to underlying feelings of worthlessness. Similarly a highly competent, independent individual may be compensating for feelings of dependency and helplessness.

Asceticism. Commonly seen in adolescents, this defense involves the moral renunciation of certain pleasures in order to avoid the anxiety and conflict associated with impulse gratification.

Altruism. In altruism one obtains satisfaction through self-sacrificing service to others or through participation in causes. It is defensive when it serves as a way of dealing with unacceptable feelings and conflicts and often is utilized by adolescents.

Splitting. The main defense of borderline individuals, splitting keeps apart two conscious, contradictory feeling states, such as love and anger or admiration and disappointment. Thus an individual who is viewed as all "good" suddenly may be seen as all "bad." By utilizing splitting the individual protects "good" internal and external objects and the self from aggression. Selected personality traits become associated with "goodness" or "badness," so that, for example, one views assertiveness negatively and compliance favorably, or one may acknowledge one's submissiveness and cooperativeness while denying the existence of independent or rebellious thoughts, feelings, or behavior.

Projective Identification. Commonly found in borderline and other individuals who show severe ego weakness, this defense is apparent when a person continues to have an impulse, generally an angry one, that, at the same time, is projected onto another person, who then is feared as an enemy who must be controlled.

Omnipotent Control And Devaluation. When employing these defenses the individual shows an unrealistic, highly inflated sense of self and an exaggerated, depreciated view of others and attempts to control others totally.

SUMMARY

This review of common defense mechanisms has pointed to the necessity of evaluating whether defenses serve adaptive or maladaptive functions in personality functioning and whether they are used flexibly or are rigidly and pervasively held. It also has considered some of the important issues in considering the modification of defenses.

NOTES

1. Anna Freud, who made the first systematic study of the defenses of the ego, elaborated on this point in *The Ego and the Mechanisms of Defense* (New York: International Universities Press, 1946). For an excellent summary of this topic see W. W. Meissner, John E. Mack, and Elvin V. Semrad "Classical Psychoanalysis," in Alfred M. Freedman, Harold I. Kaplan, and Benjamin J. Sadock, eds., *Comprehensive Textbook of Psychiatry*, 2d Ed., Vol. 1 (Baltimore: Williams & Wilkins, 1975), pp. 482-565.
2. For a systematic discussion of the relationship of character and defense formation see Wilhelm Reich, *Character Analysis* (New York: Orgone Institute, 1949). Later ego psychologists such as Erikson and White expanded our conception of personality development beyond that defined by defenses and character traits. For further discussion of defense development see Otto F. Kernberg, *Borderline Conditions and Pathological Narcissism* (New York: Jason Aronson, 1975). Kernberg proposes that there are three levels of personality organization—neurotic, borderline, and psychotic—each characterized by a particular constellation of defenses.
3. For an interesting article that deals with this issue, see Robert F. White, "Strategies of Adaptation: An Attempt at Systematic Description," in George V. Coelho, David A. Hamburg, and John E. Adams, eds., *Coping and Adaptation* (New York: Basic Books, 1974), pp. 47-68.
4. Laughlin, however, gives little emphasis to those defenses that center on splitting, which is viewed by some authors as the central defense in borderline conditions. See Kernberg, *Borderline Conditions and Pathological Narcissism*.
5. For a discussion of these complex distinctions see Meissner, Mack, and Semrad, "Classical Psychoanalysis."
6. Some of the mechanisms described, such as identification, internalization, idealization, sublimation, and altruism, for example, are im-

portant to the normal growth process and to socially creative and productive behavior. They do not necessarily serve to ward off anxiety and conflict. One can question the value of using the same mechanism to describe adaptive versus maladaptive processes. Freud, however, was attempting to draw attention to the powerful influence of unconscious conflict and motivation on behavior, particularly that of people who were symptomatic. Thus he was concerned about underlying motivation and traced all behavior back to instinctual sources and conflicts. There are individuals who do resort to idealization, altruism, and so on to ward off painful anxiety and conflict, and it is important to understand this. Other individuals, however, more in keeping with ego psychological theory, engage in similar behavior as a normal expression of their growth process, as will be discussed in Chapter 5.

EGO MASTERY AND THE PROCESSES OF COPING AND ADAPTATION

W hereas the earlier ego psychological focus emphasized the role of defense, later developments within ego psychology underscored the importance of the ego's role in adaptation to the environment. Hartmann's writings made it possible to consider how the individual learns to deal with external reality under usual circumstances, that is, when the environment is not endangering or threatening the organism. There is a sense in which all behavior can be considered an attempt at adaptation. Even in the smoothest and easiest of times behavior will not be adequate in a purely mechanical or habitual way. Every day raises its little problems:

> What clothes to be put on, how to plan a time-saving and step-saving series of errands, how to schedule the hours to get through the day's work, how to manage the cranky child, appease the short-tempered tradesman and bring the long-winded acquaintance to the end of his communication. It is not advisable to tell a group of college students that they have no problems, nothing to cope with during the happy and uneventful junior year . . . life is tough they will tell you . . . every step of the way demands the solution of problems and every step must therefore be novel and creative [White, 1974].

This chapter will consider some of the main contributions to understanding how the ego performs its crucial role of adaptation.

EGO MASTERY AND ADAPTATION

The term "ego mastery" is a major concept in understanding adaptive behavior. It has somewhat different though related meanings that can be understood more fully in reviewing the work of Robert White and Erik Erikson.

EFFICACY AND COMPETENCE

White (1959) described the ego as having independent energies that propelled the individual to gain pleasure through manipulating, exploring, and acting upon the environment. White called these energies effectance and suggested that feelings of efficacy are the pleasure derived from each interaction with the environment. Thus, the feeling of efficacy implies that one has enjoyed influencing or doing something to the environment. The individual's development of capacities to interact with the environment successfully is his or her actual competence. At the same time the individual has a subjective feeling about such capacities, and this is termed the sense of competence.

In White's view, ego identity results from the degree to which one's effectance and feelings of efficacy have been nurtured. Thus the degree to which they have found expression and the extent to which competence and a sense of competence have developed are crucial components in the development and maintenance of self-esteem. Moreover, they affect present and future behavior, because they reflect basic attitudes such as one's self-confidence, trust in one's own judgment, and belief in one's decision-making capacities, which shape the way one deals with the environment.

Other theorists, such as Inkeles (1966), Gladwin (1967), and Smith (1968), emphasized the social transactional nature of the development of competence.[1] They counted it useful to think of an individual's actual social skills or social role performance in evaluating his or her competence. Attention also has been drawn to the conditions of the social environment, social structure, and culture that may contribute to or obstruct the development of competence.

THE MASTERY OF DEVELOPMENTAL TASKS AND CRISES

Erik Erikson viewed optimal ego development to result from the mastery of stage-specific developmental tasks and crises. He argued that the successful resolution of each crisis from birth to death leads to a sense of ego identity and may be said to constitute the core of one's sense of self. In *Childhood and Society* (1950) and *Identity and the Life Cycle* (1959) Erikson proposed that the human life cycle from birth to death could be conceived of as a series of eight successive stages. In contrast to Freud's exclusive emphasis on the vicissitudes of libidinal or instinctual development during psychosexual stages (oral, anal, phallic, Oedipal, and so on), Erikson emphasized the interplay of instinctual and psychosocial factors in ego development. In his view each stage is a product of the organism's need to adapt its physiological and psychological needs and capacities to the expectations, challenges, opportunities, constraints, and resources of the social environment.

Erikson saw each stage of the life cycle as having a core psychosocial "crisis," the resolution of which is essential to optimal healthy functioning. Erikson focused on the description of these "normal crises" rather than on the systematic elaboration of more specific developmental tasks of each phase.[2] The psychosocial crises and the particular period with which they are associated can be seen below:

ERIKSON'S EIGHT PSYCHOSOCIAL STAGES	
Crisis	**Period**
Basic trust vs. basic mistrust	Infancy
Autonomy vs. shame and doubt	Toddlerhood
Initiative vs. guilt	Early childhood
Industry vs. inferiority	Later childhood
Identity vs. role confusion	Adolescence
Intimacy and distantiation vs. self-absorption	Early adulthood
Generativity vs. stagnation	Middle adulthood
Ego integrity vs. despair	Later adulthood

The term "crisis" reflects the idea that there is a state of tension or disequilibrium at the beginning of each new stage. In fact it may be said that the stage itself arises when the capacities of the individual are no longer sufficient to cope with the new internal and external demands that arise from the biopsychosocial field in the course of normal development. Each crisis is described in terms of extreme positive and negative solutions, although in any individual the resolution of the core developmental crisis may lie anywhere on a continuum from best to worst outcome. It is possible to leave early infancy with sufficient but less than optimal trust to make the mastery of the next phase possible. Clearly, however, this developmental scheme implies that the ideal resolution of later phases will be dependent on early ones.

The resolution of the core psychosocial crisis of each stage is not merely the sum of the mastery of specific developmental tasks. The former involves a basic change in one's attitude or perspective toward oneself, others, and the world. This basic change becomes a part of one's ego identity—one's feeling about who one is. This concept is akin to the notion of the sense of self.

According to Erikson, resolution of each successive crisis depends as much on those with whom the individual interacts as on his or her own innate capacities. Similarly, crisis resolution is dependent upon the impact of culture and environment as it shapes childrearing practices and provides opportunities or obstacles to optimal adaptation. Following Hartmann, Erikson assumed that the individual is innately equipped to deal with an average expectable environment. At the same time the conditions of the interpersonal field, the environment, and the culture must be regulated to meet the specific needs of the individual. Erikson saw a reciprocity between individual and environment in that if the environment meets the basic needs of the individual, the individual will take his or her place in society. While Erikson drew attention to the impact of object relations and the role of culture and environment on ego development, others have dealt with these topics more systematically and will be discussed further in Chapter 6.

Each psychosocial crisis described by Erikson will now be discussed briefly.[3]

Basic Trust Versus Basic Mistrust. According to Erikson, the foundation of all later personality development occurs in the first stage of the life cycle, in which the infant must develop a sense of basic conviction in the predictability of the world and its fulfillment of his or her needs:

> For the first component of a healthy personality I nominate a sense of basic trust, which I think is an attitude toward oneself and the world derived from the experience of the first year of life. By "trust" I mean what is commonly implied in reasonable trustfulness as far as others are concerned and a simple sense of trustworthiness as far as oneself is concerned. . . . In adults the impairment of basic trust is expressed in a basic mistrust. It characterizes individuals who withdraw into themselves in particular ways when at odds with themselves and with others [Erikson, 1959:55–56].

This stage coincides with the oral stage described by Freud. The infant is completely dependent on and interacts with the world through his or her primary caretaker. The child's main mode of dealing with the environment is incorporative and begins with sucking. To this capacity are soon added feeling, seeing, grasping, biting, and exploring. Acquiring a sense of basic trust necessitates a physical and emotional environment that is responsive to the infant's emerging and changing needs. How the child is handled; the surrounding conditions such as noise, temperature, and so forth; and how his or her inevitable frustrations are resolved all affect the development of trust. The main task of the caretaker is to attend to the child's needs in a way that is predictable and dependable. Developing a sense of basic trust includes tolerating the unknown, learning the process of giving and taking without undue anxiety, and being able to explore the immediate environment without fear, dissatisfaction, or trauma. The child who acquires a sense of mistrust later may show apprehensiveness and fearfulness, turn away from or against others, or reveal chronic depression, emptiness, fear of loss, or a sense of inner badness.

The ability of the caretaker to adapt to and meet the needs of the growing infant is a complex task, since both partners in the dyad bring particular and unique characteristics to the interaction. The degree to which the caretaker can respond effectively depends not only on personality traits but also on environmental supports such as family and friends, the conditions of the physical and social environment, and the values of the culture itself.

Autonomy Versus Shame and Doubt. As the child's musculature develops further in the second year, he or she becomes more active in exploring the world and in establishing the ability to act as an independent entity. He or she strives toward autonomous behavior and at the same time is pulled by dependency needs. This phase coincides with the anal stage described by Freud, and Erikson too underscored the importance of the modes of retention and elimination, or of holding on and letting go, that arise around toilet training. Nevertheless, Erikson viewed toilet training as only one example of the will struggle or battle for autonomy that is characteristic of this period:

> This stage, therefore, becomes decisive for the ratio between love and hate, for that between cooperation and willfulness, and for that between the freedom of self-expression and its suppression. From a sense of self-control without loss of self-esteem comes a lasting sense of autonomy and pride; from a sense of muscular and anal impotence, or loss of self-control and of parental over-control comes a lasting sense of doubt and shame [Erikson, 1959:68].

The importance of mutual regulation can be seen as the child attempts to assert his or her will. The caretaker and the society itself, in terms of the childrearing practices it advocates, must support the growing autonomy of the child while providing necessary nutrients and important socialization experiences that infringe to some extent on the child's will:

> To develop autonomy . . . the infant must come to feel that basic faith in himself and in the world . . . will not be jeopardized by the sudden violent wish to have a choice, to appropriate demandingly, and to eliminate stubbornly. Firmness must protect him against the potential anarchy of his yet untrained sense of discrimination, his inability to hold on and let go with circumspection. Yet his environment must back him up in his wish to "stand on his own two feet" lest he be overcome by that sense of having exposed himself prematurely and foolishly which we

call shame, or that secondary mistrust, that "double-take" which
we call doubt [Erikson, 1959:68].

Initiative Versus Guilt. Having attained some degree of mastery
and self-regulation, the child is ready to broaden his or her hori-
zons. The child must become a particular kind of person in his or
her own right and strives to find out the kind of person he or she
wants to be. This stage coincides with what Freud described as
the phallic stage and begins approximately at the end of the third
year of life. Erikson highlighted the significance of the intrusive
mode in the child's interactions with others and with the environment. Children model themselves after their caretakers during this period and search for others with whom to identify. Both
boys and girls actively experiment with the world around them,
and issues of fantasizing about the future, enjoyment of competition, conquest, and attainment of goals become important. Being the best and beating out rivals becomes crucial. The
development of gender identification, appropriate sex-role behavior, and conscience are important in this phase. Sexual curiosity is intense, and the classic Oedipal conflict occurs during
this period.[4]

As is true in all stages, there is an interplay among the supports available in the family and the larger social environment
and the needs of the child. The availability of opportunities, of
support and encouragement from those close to one, of role
models, of alternatives that permit the expression of one's talents
and capacities, and of a value system that permits role diversity
are crucial to the development of initiative in boys and girls.

Industry Versus Inferiority. In characterizing the first four stages
of development, Erikson wrote:

> One might say that personality at the first stage crystallizes
> around the conviction, "I am what I am given," and that of the
> second, "I am what I will." The third can be characterized by "I
> am what I can imagine I will be." We must now approach the
> fourth: "I am what I learn" [Erikson, 1959:82].

While the fourth stage roughly coincides with the latency period described by Freud, Erikson viewed it as an active stage in

which the child begins to apply him- or herself in school and develops the technology essential to getting along in society as an adult. This phase, unlike earlier ones, is not fueled by turbulent inner needs that press for expression or that create new demands, but rather is a period of relative calm.

Along with the acquisition of necessary skills comes the development of an attitude about oneself in relationship to work. The child optimally develops a sense that he or she can be useful and produce things. He or she learns to persevere and complete tasks. These are essential to feelings of ego mastery. The alternative to the development of industry is the emergence of feelings of inadequacy and inferiority.

Clearly the educational system and its practices contribute greatly to fostering a sense of industry or inferiority. Further, the degree to which the child experiences discrepancies between what he or she produces and what is valued by the family or the surrounding society will have an impact on his or her sense of identity. Being the victim of racism or other types of social prejudice and injustice may undercut the value one places on one's sense of productivity.

Identity Versus Role Confusion. Adolescence brings a rapid growth spurt along with dramatic physiological changes that upset the balance that has been achieved and present new coping demands. The adolescent searches for a new sense of continuity and sameness that synthesizes all that he or she has experienced along with his or her endowments and the opportunities for realizing them.

> The sense of ego identity, then, is the accrued confidence that one's ability to maintain inner sameness and continuity (one's ego in the psychological sense) is matched by the sameness in continuity of one's meaning for others. Thus, self-esteem confirmed at the end of each major crisis, grows to be a conviction that one is learning effective steps toward a tangible future, that one is developing a defined personality within a social reality that one understands [Erikson, 1959:89].

Acquiring ego identity involves the integration of one's past, present, and future; consequently it also entails the integration of past identifications with others into a whole that represents one's unique self. Developing an ego identity requires the ability to use one's capacities to take one's place in society. There may be considerable fragmentation in a process of consolidating identity that involves, according to Erikson, the following dimensions: (1) a time perspective, (2) self-certainty, (3) role experimentation, (4) anticipation of achievement, (5) sexual identity, (6) acceptance of leadership, and (7) commitment to basic values.

The problem of role confusion is considerable when internal and external resources are not sufficient to help an individual consolidate his or her identity. The individual who comes into adolescence with little sense of competence and who faces keen competition in his or her academic and vocational life may experience severe frustration and reinforcement of low self-esteem. A positive identity consolidation may become more difficult. In this respect adolescents who suffer from role confusion often may adopt dysfunctional or antisocial behavior as a way of achieving some type of identity, even a negative one, that is, an identity considered undesirable by one's family or by society.

Intimacy and Distantiation Versus Self-absorption. The consolidation of a sense of ego identity permits one to enter into relationships with others in which real intimacy is possible. This requires an ability to be clear about who one is in relationship to others, to see others in three-dimensional terms, and to love people in terms of their unique characteristics. It requires retaining one's own individual identity in a joint relationship. The adult who has not achieved such a sense of self may feel threatened in close relations with others or may avoid them, may cling to others in the hope of finding an identity, or may remain self-absorbed even though seemingly involved with others. The failure to achieve intimacy may lead to isolation or to a chronic sense of yearning that is only sporadically fulfilled. According to Erikson the fullest expression of intimacy occurs within marriage and involves the sharing of mutual trust, the regulation of cycles of work, procreation, recreation, and preparation for the healthy development of potential offspring.

Generativity Versus Stagnation. Generativity and parenting have often been equated, inasmuch as procreation ensures the continuance of life into the next generation. In Erikson's view those who have attained successful intimacy will inevitably feel the urge to join in the production and care of children. At the same time generativity is a broader concept that can involve carrying out responsibility to the next generation through other forms of activity and involvements. The generative person may not have children *per se* but accepts responsibility for supporting others and society in areas relating to the continuance and promotion of values, traditions, education, and well-being. Those who engage in artistic or other pursuits that contribute to the betterment of others and society may be considered generative. "Where such enrichment fails altogether, regression from generativity to an obsessive need for pseudo-intimacy takes place, often with a pervading sense of stagnation and interpersonal impoverishment (Erikson, 1959:97).

Integrity Versus Despair and Disgust. Ego integrity is developed as the culmination of ego identity. It implies an emotional integration and acceptance of all of one's past experiences and brings a readiness to face death. The final phase involves a sense of wisdom and a philosophy of life that often extends beyond the life cycle of the individual and is directly related to the future of new developmental cycles. In contrast, the individual may despair of what he or she has been, what he or she has not become, and what he or she can no longer be.

> Only he who in some way has taken care of things and people and has adapted himself to the triumphs and disappointment of being, by necessity, the originator of others and the generator of things and ideas—only he may gradually grow the fruit of the seven stages [Erikson, 1959:98].

ERIKSON AND WOMEN'S DEVELOPMENT: A FEMINIST CRITIQUE

As noted in Chapter 1, Erikson's views of women's development were rooted in biological determinism and wedded to a traditional view of women. Based on his observations of children at play, he observed that little girls were concerned with building structures that reflected enclosure, protection, and receptivity while little boys developed erectile, projectile, and active designs. Erikson related these patterns to the woman's vagina and uterus and to the male's penis; thus, he saw women's and men's anatomy as leading to their fundamental orientations to inner and outer space, respectively, and to certain female and male characteristics. For women, these involved passivity, receptivity, docility, ability to concentrate on details, tolerance of limitations, compassion, caring, and so on (Erikson, 1964:582–606). While Erikson wrote of the importance of women's development as persons in their own right and of their capacity to contribute to society, he saw an integrated female identity as resulting in a commitment to a husband and children (Erikson, 1968:265).

When traditional theories about women came under attack in the 1960s and 1970s, feminists simultaneously argued against the biological determinism inherent in psychoanalysis and ego psychology and called for more attention to women's unique developmental course. They criticized Erikson for giving too much importance to biological differences in contrast to cultural factors and socialization in explaining personality development. They also pointed out that his theory of the life cycle was based on male experience and male examples and that when Erikson did refer to women, he persistently and exclusively identified woman as mother (Williams, 1977). While Erikson later acknowledged women's special life course and commented on the value of society's providing room for women's modes of experience and permitting greater role flexibility for women, he nevertheless continued to adhere to a biologically based view of women's personality (Erikson, 1974).

Research on development has shed new light on the factors that influence the formation of gender identification and the effects of gender differences on behavior. For example, Robert Stoller's (1977) studies lent support to the view that parental attitudes and behavior in the child's first five years of life are more important in determining gender identity—that is, whether the child regards itself as male or female—than does his or her actual biological sex at birth. Thus, a self-labeling process occurs as a result of environmental influences that organizes later experience.

In summarizing the results of research on gender differences with respect to intellectual abilities, biology and behavior, and socialization processes, Jacklin (1989:236) concludes that tests of intellectual abilities over the past decades generally do not differentiate males and females; that males have been shown to be more vulnerable than women but the relationship between hormones and behavior is complex and still not well understood; and that while social learning occurs with respect to sex-role behavior, there is some evidence that cognitive gender schema may also be influential.

New conclusions about women's attributes have been reached as a result of studies of females in comparison to males. For example, Carol Gilligan (1982) conducted her research in reaction to Lawrence Kohlberg's widely known theory of moral development. Gilligan criticized Kohlberg for basing his theory on a study of men and then evaluating women with his schema, finding that they rarely attain the higher levels of moral judgment and are less mature than men. She also argued that the male bias toward individuation in Kohlberg's work caused him to neglect the importance of attachment and connection in women. Based on her studies of males and females, Gilligan showed that women's capacity for relatedness, emotionality, and nurturing are essential to their identity development. She proposed a different standard for evaluating women's moral development based on the relationship between caring for oneself and caring for others. In her view, women have a different way of thinking in which conflicting responsibilities in the context of relationships are paramount in influencing their judgments. At the earliest stage, women's moral judgments begin at a primarily egocentric or premoral level; they then move to one based mainly on showing concern for others, and then to an advanced stage that balances concern for others and self-concern. Gilligan further noted that given their unique way of reasoning, many women might be at a disadvantage in achieving success, because their morality does not easily permit them to show self-concern. Chapter 6, which discusses object relations theory, will describe newer views of women's development further.

THE EFFECTS OF OPPRESSION AND THE STUDY OF DIVERSITY

That the theories discussed so far in this chapter lacked grounding in the study of diverse populations and the impact of oppression raised questions about their full generalizability. For example, identity development, one of Erikson's main foci, is affected greatly by the impact of social and cultural factors. It has been recognized that the achievement of a stable and integrated identity is more difficult when, at an early age, an individual does not know where he or she belongs culturally or learns early in life that he or she is a member of a group that is stigmatized by and excluded from society. Such experiences engender low self-esteem, self-hatred, negative self-concepts, feelings of powerlessness, and alienation. Attuned parenting and the presence of other familial and environmental supports will cushion some, but not all individuals from the negative impact of discrimination, racism, and homophobia. African-Americans, Latinos, Asians, other people of color, and gays and lesbians are some major examples of groups within society who are vulnerable to identity diffusion resulting from cultural conflict, feelings of dissonance or difference with respect to others, and the taking in of unfavorable societal attitudes.

In discussing the impact of migration on Latinas, Espin (1987:489–503) discusses culture shock and its effect on adaptation, and Comas-Diaz and Minrath (1985:418–19) comment on the strains of biculturalism, which may create or reinforce split images of the self, loss of centrality, confusion, fear of dissolution, and identity diffusion. Chestang (1972:40–50) discusses the "depreciated character," reflected by a sense of worthlessness, inadequacy, and impotence, that forms among many African-Americans as a consequence of extrinsically imposed devaluation. Pinderhughes (1983:331–38) describes the pervasive feelings of powerlessness that African-Americans feel as a result of the impact of poverty, lack of social justice, and threat of violence. Research also has shown that like other high-stress groups, gays and lesbians may be prone to feelings of self-alienation, self-contempt, and depression, and to substance abuse and suicidal behavior as a consequence of their stigmatized identity and oppressed status (Coleman, 1982; Falco, 1991; Hetrick and Martin, 1988).

Greater individualization of culturally diverse populations has contributed to more awareness and respect for their strengths and special characteristics and has enriched our understanding of their coping capacities. For example, in discussing male machismo, de la Cancela (1986:291–96) points out its adaptive significance in the context of the socioeconomic realities of Puerto Ricans and cautions against "blaming the victim." Instead he advocates a more respectful and attuned approach in work with Puerto Rican men and their families. Similarly, Ghali (1982:98–102), in trying to individualize the Puerto Rican family, describes the unique aspects of their parenting styles and gender roles. Wilson (1989:380–85) highlights the socioeconomic reasons for the prevalence of the extended family in the African-American community and its value and positive effects. Likewise, Ryan (1985:333–40) shows how the teachings of Confucius, Laotze, and Buddha continue to influence Chinese-Americans' ways of life, thinking, and communication.

More affirmative views of gay and lesbian life have emerged. In summarizing the results of several decades of research, numerous authors point out that gay men and lesbians cannot be reliably differentiated from heterosexuals in their personality characteristics, family background, gender, identity, defenses, and ego and object relations development (Falco:22–26; Friedman, 1986:483–519; Gonsiorek, 1982a:5). Some researchers have argued that some homosexuality may have a biological basis, but this is a controversial hypothesis for which there is inconclusive documentation.

Since Kinsey's (1948) famous study of sexual behavior there has been increasing evidence that individuals are not purely homosexual or heterosexual and that sexual behavior exists on a continuum. Further, it has been useful to distinguish between gender identity and sexual orientation. Studies show that generally, gays and lesbians have a strong gender identity, that is, a core sense of maleness and femalenese, and have moved away from playing out gender roles such as "butch" and "femme" (Falco, 1991:10). They may view themselves, however, in rigid or flexible ways in terms of their sexual identity, that is, whether they regard themselves as gay, lesbian, or bisexual, and their actual sexual behavior may vary. It also is clear that there is not one type of homosexuality and that while gays and lesbians share some commonalities, there are significant differences between them. For example, in numerous studies, lesbian women tended to show at least two distinct patterns, one in which they have a conscious sense of being lesbian early in life and one in which they identify as lesbians later in life, often after having relationships with men, sometimes marrying and having children (Burch, 1993:19–59).

An important contribution to understanding the special features of gay and lesbian identity formation has been the delineation of the stages of "coming out," that is, the ways in which individuals acknowledge their sexual identity to themselves and others (Cass, 1979; Coleman, 1982; Falco, 1991; Lewis, 1984). Coleman describes these steps as pre-coming out, coming out, exploration, first relationships, and identity integration. Each has its own issues and poses crucial tasks that must be mastered. Not all individuals, however, go through each stage and the process for many is more fluid and complex (Coleman, 1982:32). In the pre-coming out period, the individual may be more or less aware of homosexual feelings but feels alienated, alone, and stigmatized. Denial, repression of sexual feelings, or other defensive reactions, as well as low self-esteem and serious symptoms may result. While the coming out stage is marked by a great deal of confusion, it begins the task of self-acceptance and tolerance. During this period, individuals tend to seek validation from the external environment. In the exploration stage, the individual likely experiments with new behaviors and in the first relationship stage, looks for a more intimate partner. The integration of a gay or lesbian identity, the final stage, often is a lengthy, evolving, and complex development. It goes beyond acceptance and tolerance to include pride and sometimes community involvement and political activism. Clearly, the outcome of all of these stages is affected by the presence or absence of peer, family, and social supports, positive role models, gratifying relationships, and societal attitudes and policies.

Finally, there is greater awareness of how gay men and lesbians function over the life cycle. The view that homosexuals are loners without long-standing committed relationships, children, or close ties to parents and siblings has been challenged. Increasingly, gay and lesbian domestic partners are raising biological, foster, or adopted children and are struggling with both similar and unique issues in comparison to heterosexual couples and families (Baptiste, 1987). Further, studies of aging gay men and women have shown both commonality with and differences from older heterosexuals in their needs and coping styles (Berger, 1992; Tully, 1992).

THE IMPACT OF TRAUMA

Another significant gap in Erikson's theory of the life cycle as well as in other developmental theories is the lack of attention to the impact of early childhood trauma. Traumatic events are overwhelming and undermine security, safety, and connection. They involve violence, danger, threats to the body or to life itself and cause terror, fear, helplessness, and loss of control. It has been observed that long after the traumatic events themselves, survivors may exhibit characteristic symptoms that interfere with their optimal functioning and are extremely debilitating. Moreover, many of these individuals may be diagnosed as having other types of emotional disorder.

Among the more severe trauma that children experience are single or repeated acts of incest and other forms of sexual abuse. In fact, it has been estimated that one-third of all American women have been molested by family members or outsiders before the age of eighteen (Finkelhor, 1984). Further, there is reason to believe that the incidence of males who have been sexually violated in childhood is significant and vastly underreported. While it generally is thought that sexual abuse begins around six years of age, it occurs from infancy through adolescence. There may be greater numbers of small children who are sexually abused than is known because of children's tendency to repress or dissociate traumatic events (Davies and Frawley, 1994:35).

The trauma of sexual abuse affects all aspects of a child's or adolescent's sense of self and personality functioning and leads to characteristic defenses, personality traits, and symptoms in later life. Along with the premature sexualization of experience and stigmatization that is associated with shame, guilt, and feelings of "badness" or of being "damaged goods," children experience a sense of betrayal and powerlessness (Patten, *et al.*, 1989:-198–99). Courtois (1988:101–15) describes the initial effects of sexual abuse as including emotional reactions such as anxiety, guilt, anger, and depression along with loss and grief reactions; self-perceptions that erode a positive sense of self and lead to a negative identity; physical and somatic effects such as regressive behavior and physical symptoms; sexual difficulties including eroticized and compulsive sexual behavior or negative reactions to physical touch; impairments in interpersonal relationships; and problems in social functioning. There are long-term effects in all of these areas as well, often resulting in what has been termed post-traumatic stress disorder, which can manifest itself in adulthood many years after the trauma, and in other forms of emotional disorder. Adult survivors may experience severe apprehension and anxiety attacks, sleep disturbances and nightmares, flashbacks or intrusive thoughts, fears and phobias, chronic depression, suicidal thinking and behavior, low self-esteem and negative views of themselves, physical problems and complaints, hypervigilance and distrust of others and other interpersonal disturbances, compulsive, impulsive, and addictive behavior, problems in social functioning, difficulties in sexual functioning, and a tendency toward revictimization (Courtois, 1988:104–115). It also appears that childhood sexual abuse is common in the backgrounds of those who are diagnosed as having borderline and dissociative disorders (Blake-White and Kline, 1985; Herman and Van der Kolk, 1987; Kilgore, 1988; Kroll, 1993; Wheeler and Walton, 1987).

ADAPTATION IN ADULTHOOD

While Erikson's view of the life cycle encompassed adulthood, which he saw as a dynamic rather than a static time, others since have studied the adult years more systematically.[5] Colarusso and Nemiroff (1981) offer seven hypotheses about the psychodynamic theory of adult development: (1) the nature of the developmental process is basically the same in the adult as in the child; (2) development in adulthood is an ongoing, dynamic process; (3) whereas child development is focused primarily on the formation of psychic structures, adult development is concerned with the continued evolution of existing structures and with their use; (4) the fundamental developmental issues of childhood continue as central aspects of adult life but in altered form; (5) the developmental process in adulthood is influenced by the adult past as well as the childhood past; (6) development in adulthood, as in childhood, is deeply influenced by the body and by physical change; and (7) a central, phase-specific theme of adult development is the normative crisis precipitated by the recognition and acceptance of time and the inevitability of personal death.

Other theorists have made important beginning contributions to the knowledge of adulthood. Their work has focused generally, however, on (1) understanding the evolution of identity, defenses, and character traits over time; (2) identifying the coping demands and developmental tasks of life cycle phases and role transitions; and (3) identifying the coping demands and strategies associated with stress and crisis.

CHANGES IN PERSONALITY IN ADULTHOOD

There is mounting interest in, and evidence for, the idea that personality change occurs in adult life. Adulthood is seen to contain elements of the past as well as its own dynamic processes, which lead to such changes. Colarusso and Nemiroff (1981) cite the example of the continuing process of identification that may occur in a relationship between a young scientist and an older mentor and its potential for shaping the later achievements of the younger adult. While such a relationship may contain an element of past identifications with authority figures, they point out, its current significance influences the individual's future pursuit of his or her career.

Interpersonal relationships, the impact of social roles, the changing environment and society itself, the need for social recognition and acceptance, growth needs, life transitions, stress, and crisis all provide the impetus for change and shape its direction.

White (1966) described five growth trends that occur within the healthy adult: (1) the stabilizing of ego identity in which one's sense of identity becomes richer, based on accumulated experiences involving a sense of competence and self-esteem; (2) the freeing of personal relationships in which the capacity to perceive, accept, and value people in their own right increases, permitting more gratifying and intimate relationships to develop; (3) the deepening of interests, whereby one acquires greater skills, knowledge, and, consequently, competence in selected endeavors, the pursuit of which have meaning and give pleasure for their own sake; (4) affirmation of, and commitment to, a value system that involves social purposes; and (5) the expansion of caring, in which egocentrism is transcended and the welfare of others becomes important.

Neugarten and colleagues (1964), in their studies of adult men and women, suggest that the tendency toward increased self-reflection and introspection increases in middle age. This heightens later in life and leads to a process of "life-review" (Butler, 1963) in which the older adult reminisces about his or her past life. Such a review often is associated with dramatic changes in the adult personality. Other studies suggest that there are many types of adaptive patterns in adulthood that are associated with good coping with the aging process. These patterns are affected by individual personality styles, sex roles, and sociocultural variables.

LIFE STAGES, ROLE TRANSITIONS, AND THE TIMING OF EVENTS

There are various theories of adulthood. Some authors conceive of adulthood as composed of sequential stages, while others view it in terms of adaptation to changing role requirements, some of which occur at times that are out of step with one's "social clock."

In studying ninety-five normal subjects, Vaillant (1977) observed that as men grow older their defenses become more adaptive and their ability to cope with reality becomes more mature. He identified six stages of adult development. Similarly, Gould (1978) conducted numerous studies of large numbers of adult male psychiatric outpatients and normal subjects. He identified seven different age groups from sixteen to sixty and specific issues linked to each time period.[6] He found that adults changed as they grew older. Peck (1975) also observed fundamental shifts in the ways adults who were coping successfully with aging regarded themselves and others.

The most complex grouping of adult stages comes out of Levinson's (1978) studies. Like Erikson, Levinson relied heavily on the concept of developmental crisis in his theory of adult development, and he identified four major "seasons" or eras of a man's life. The early and middle adulthood eras are subdivided further into two relatively stable periods. Other transitional periods bound each of the stable periods and represent points of crisis in which one experiences the discomfort of needing to alter the "life structure" that one has evolved. The transition or crisis period optimally would be resolved through progression into the next phase.

THE SEASONS OF A MAN'S LIFE

Phases	Age
Era I. *Childhood and Adolescence*	0–17
Early adult transition	17–22
Era II. *Entering the Adult World*	22–28
Age 30 transition	28–33
Settling down	33–40
Midlife transition	40–45
Era III. *Entering Middle Adulthood*	45–50
Age 50 transition	50–55
Culmination of middle adulthood	55–60
Era IV. *Late Adulthood*	65+

Similar to Erikson, Levinson saw each of these periods as having particular developmental tasks. Some individuals master these relatively smoothly. Others find the transitional periods extremely difficult. Some are unable to resolve the issues raised and fail to master the crises. The developmental tasks of each period involve two separate though related components. One must evolve a life structure that integrates one's external situation (one's patterns of roles, interests, goals, lifestyle, and so one) with one's internal state (the personal meaning these external factors have, one's identity, values, psychodynamics, capacities, and the like). At any given stage a tension may develop between the external situation and internal needs. These tensions may precipitate the transitional state in which one considers altering one's current life structure in order to achieve a better fit between the internal and the external situation.

A somewhat different way of understanding ego development in adulthood emphasizes the importance of role transitions in altering behavior. Such transitions as moving from single to married status or from being a spouse to a parent, spouse to widow or widower, student to worker, worker to retiree, and so on are thought to constitute another variation of the normal crises of adult life. The successful mastery of these are essential to optimal functioning and to maintaining self-esteem and ego identity.[7] The crisis resides in the discrepancy between one's usual behavior and the new requisite behavior accompanying a major role change.[8] In many cases even the anticipation of the assumption of a new role with its expectations may prompt dramatic changes. In learning that he is to become a parent, a man who has had difficulty committing himself to a career may feel the impetus to become more invested in work and to provide income for his family.

Neugarten (1968) has suggested that adults of different social classes and ethnic groups share expectations as to when significant events in life such as marriage, parenthood, and so on should occur. Such consensus creates social pressure on individuals to assume particular roles. Likewise, when such roles are thrust upon the individual at times that are not in keeping with his or her expectations, role transition crises occur that not only create disequilibrium but offer opportunities for more dramatic personality changes.

An important and distinctive contribution to understanding the impetus for change in adulthood comes from the work of Benedek (1970). In discussing the impact of the parenting role on individuals, she points to the potential for growth inherent in the parenting process. As each parent faces and relives his or her own past conflicts through dealing with offspring, there is the possibility of reworking such childhood conflicts and resolving them, thus leading to intrapsychic changes in the parent. This focus takes Benedek beyond the view that parents, captive to their own developmental conflicts, inevitably transmit these conflicts to their children. Her emphasis underscores instead the normal growth process that can occur as a result of the parents' conscious attempts to help the child achieve his or her developmental goal, with the result that the parents deal with their own conflicts and possibly reach a new level of maturation themselves. A related conception can be found in Elson (1984) in which she describes the transformation of parental narcissism that optimally occurs during the parenting process.

WOMEN AND DIVERSITY IN ADULTHOOD

The criticism of the male bias inherent in Erikson's conception of life cycle stages, which was discussed earlier in this chapter, also applies to other theories of adulthood. Moreover, because those theories arose during a particular historical period, it is not clear whether the men and women who were studied are similar to those born later, since old norms may not apply and the conditions of life may have changed (Rossi, 1980). In this regard, Barnett (1984:342) points out that women today are better educated, more work- and career-oriented, tend to marry later or remain or become single, and have fewer children in comparison to earlier generations. Moreover, because the salient issues in the delineation of women's unique life cycle issues have tended to be described in terms of markers involving marriage and parenting (Brooks-Gunn and Kirsh, 1984:1–30), many important questions can be raised. Are women who do not fit traditional patterns viewed as pathological or do we need to develop greater understanding of the specific issues facing new generations of women? What is the significance for women of greater choices that may bring them into conflict with the ways in which their mothers and other important female figures were reared and have lived their lives? If women need to evolve their own identities without defining themselves only or at all in terms of marriage and parenting, what motivates them and what are the significant factors that shape their development? What are the important issues facing women who never marry or have children over the life cycle? As women who approach middle-age encounter new options, do they reflect a new set of life cycle issues related to their sexuality, autonomy, relationships with other women and men, creativity, work lives, and productivity that previously were not described? How does our understanding of old age change as greater numbers of women and men live longer and have different options than previous generations?

Similar criticisms and questions can be raised with respect to the inclusion of knowledge regarding those who are economically disadvantaged, people of color, or gay or lesbian in current theories of adulthood. For example, does our view of adult life cycle issues do justice to the experiences of poor, minority adults who may be educationally and economically disadvantaged and excluded from well-paying jobs, career advancement, and the like? What is the expectable life course of those minority women who are single parents and grandparents? What are the special issues confronting gays and lesbians who undertake parenting at midlife? Fortunately, there is increasing interest in investigating these questions.

COPING WITH STRESS AND CRISIS

There are situations that occur in adult life that overwhelm the person's ego and cripple his or her usual modes of problem-solving. At such times the individual's external supports and internal resources may not be sufficient to deal with the stresses bombarding him or her. The most dramatic example of this type of situation occurs in traumatic crises such as death, accidents, natural disasters, acute illness, rape, and violent assaults. Other situations, such as long-term disability or wartime, may pose ongoing stress to the individual, who must learn to cope.

While considerable attention has been focused on tracing the reactions to various common events that are generally experienced as crises, there is besides a complex interaction between a stressful event and the significance it has for the individual, his or her state of vulnerability, and the internal and external resources that will determine how the event is experienced and how the individual copes with it.[9]

There is mounting evidence to support the view that defenses are only one mode of dealing with stress and crisis. The versatility with which the individual copes with stress is striking.[10] Further, there is general consensus among crisis theorists that the state of crisis can lead to a higher level of functioning than occurs in the precrisis state. Under optimal conditions a person not only may regain his or her equilibrium but also may resolve old conflicts and alter dysfunctional attitudes and behavior in mastering the current predicament. In this sense the state of crisis is one that contains the potential for growth.[11]

THE EGO AND THE SOCIAL MILIEU

The study of personality and the processes of coping and adaptation tend generally to ignore or minimize the importance of the social environment on individual development. As pointed out by Mechanic (1974), the emphasis on the requisite coping capabilities, motivation, and defenses essential to successful personal adaptation has been complemented more recently by a greater appreciation of the essential fit between individual capacities and environmental demands and resources in optimal coping. The social environment not only meets the basic needs of the individual but also affects his or her values, character, identity, ego functioning, sense of self-esteem, and sense of competence. It also provides opportunities for and obstacles to successful coping. The social environment, which includes, along with physical and social resources and networks, the attitudes, values, social structure, and policies of the society, may provide a benign and nutritive support system for some individuals; for others it stimulates, aggravates, and perpetuates maladaptive behavior or fails to provide the essential conditions for growth. For example, there may be a lack of fit between individual ego capacities on the one hand and the stresses, expectations, conditions, and rewards of external reality on the other. A person who consistently faces situations that demand more than he or she can deliver will experience not only failure but probably an erosion of self-esteem that may have profound effects on his or her overall personality functioning. Similarly, an individual who has little realistic chance of finding meaningful employment or outlets for his or her capacities may become apathetic and dependent. In this regard the effects of poverty, racism, and discrimination against certain groups of individuals in society such as women, the aged, gays and lesbians, the mentally and physically handi-

capped, and the developmentally disabled contribute to disturbances in identity and self-esteem. Furthermore, the lack of social supports for these groups or for those at certain points in the
life cycle can be expected to have serious repercussions on personality functioning.

Simcox-Reiner (1979) has noted the conditions of our increasingly inhuman and depriving social environment and the discrepancies between values and expectations and the realities of
life that lead to difficulties in interpersonal relationships, low
self-esteem, a sense of irrelevance, and feelings of powerlessness.
While she acknowledges that a basic sense of irrelevance may
originate in childhood, she argues that it is intensified in later life
by the struggle to survive in a society that provides few supports
during developmental crises or at other stressful points in life.
Our society's current insensitivity to and attack on the needs of
its underprivileged and less-privileged can be expected not only
to deprive people of essential material resources but to produce
emotional neglect and profound feelings of despair, rage, and
worthlessness. Such a social context is inimical to optimal parenting and individual ego development. The degree to which the
environment or the society fails to support the growth needs of
its members will drastically affect the psychological capacities of
its members.

SUMMARY

This chapter has reviewed the concept of ego mastery and has
discussed the various phases of the human life cycle. It has emphasized the importance of the dynamic interplay among biological, psychological, and environmental or social factors in
fostering coping and adaptation. It also considered feminist critiques of Erikson's formulations, newer views of women's life
cycle issues, the impact of diversity and oppression on development, and more recent findings about trauma.

NOTES

1. For a summary of the work of Inkeles, Gladwin, Smith, and others who have developed a more sociological and transactional view of competence, see Anthony N. Maluccio, *Promoting Competence in Clients: A New/Old Approach to Social Work Practice* (New York: Free Press, 1981), pp. 5–6.
2. Others have dealt more systematically with the developmental tasks *per se*. See Anna Freud, *Normality and Pathology in Childhood* (New York: International Universities Press, 1965), and Theodore Lidz, *The Person* (New York: Basic Books, 1968).
3. For an excellent summary of Erikson's theory, see Henry W. Maier, *Three Theories of Child Development* (New York: Harper & Row, 1969). Erikson's most complete description of his ideas is in "Identity and the Life Cycle," *Psychological Issues*, 1, No. 1(1959): 50–100.
4. It should be noted that many have found both Freud's and Erikson's views quite sexist, and there are other interpretations of the events described here. For example, see Karen Horney, *New Ways in Psychoanalysis* (New York: W. W. Norton, 1939), pp. 101–19 (paperback edition).
5. For example, see Therese Benedek, "Parenthood During the Life Cycle," in James Anthony and Therese Benedek, eds., *Parenthood—Its Psychology and Psychopathology* (Boston: Little, Brown, & Co., 1970), pp. 185–208; Calvin Colarusso and Robert A. Nemiroff, *Adult Development* (New York: Plenum Press, 1981); Roger L. Gould, *Transformations: Growth and Change in Adult Life* (New York: Simon & Schuster, 1978); Daniel J. Levinson, *The Seasons of a Man's Life* (New York: Alfred A. Knopf, 1978); Bernice L. Neugarten, "Adult Personality: Toward a Psychology of the Life Cycle," in W. Edgar Vinacke, ed., *Readings in General Psychology* (Chicago: University of Chicago Press, 1968), pp. 332–43; George E. Vaillant, *Adaptation to Life* (Boston: Little, Brown, 1977); and Robert F. White, *Lives in Progress* (New York: Holt, Rinehart & Winston, 1966).
6. A summary of the studies of Vaillant, Gould, and Levinson appears in Eileen M. Brennan and Ann Weick, "Theories of Adult Development: Creating a Context for Practice," *Social Casework*, 62 (January 1981): 13–19.
7. For a discussion of the crisis aspects of marriage and parenthood, see Rhona Rapoport, "Normal Crisis, Family structure, and Mental Health," and E. E. LeMasters "Parenthood as Crisis," both in Howard J. Parad, ed., *Crisis Intervention: Selected Readings* (New York: Family Service Association of America, 1965), pp. 75–87 and 111–17.

8. A classic example of this is reflected in the work of Erich Linde-
    mann, "Symptomatology and Management of Acute Grief," *Ameri-
    can Journal of Psychiatry*, 101 (September 1944). Reprinted in Parad,
    ed., *Crisis Intervention*, pp. 7–21.
9. There is evidence to suggest that children vary markedly in their
    ability to cope with stress. Early in life some are quite resilient de-
    spite stressful environments, while others are extremely vulnera-
    ble. See Lois Barclay Murphy and Alice E. Moriarity, *Vulnerability,
    Coping and Growth* (New Haven and London: Yale University Press,
    1976).
10. An excellent collection of articles that deal with the processes of
    coping and adaptation can be found in George V. Coehlo, David A.
    Hamburg, and John E. Adams, eds., *Coping and Adaptation* (New
    York: Basic Books, 1979).
11. For an excellent discussion of the theory and practice of crisis inter-
    vention see Naomi Golan, *Treatment in Crisis Situations* (New York:
    Free Press, 1978).

CHAPTER 6

OBJECT RELATIONS AND EGO DEVELOPMENT

A s the formation, evolution, and pathology of ego identity became a focus of ego psychology, the study of the external and internal world of object relations commanded increasing theoretical interest in the United States.[1] While Erikson's work highlighted the importance of interpersonal relationships in shaping personality, his writings tend to address the acquisition of more global characteristics (e.g , a sense of trust, autonomy, and so on) and do not trace systematically the complex impact that the interpersonal field has on development of a sense of self and of others. It also is not clear from his work how the vicissitudes of the development of one's internalized sense of self (and others) affect later relationships. This chapter will consider some of the major contributions to our understanding of the process by which internalized object relations develop and their impact on later personality development and on interpersonal relationships.

THE CONCEPT

The term "object relations" has at least two different meanings in current parlance. The ego's job is to "form friendly and loving bonds with others with a minimum of inappropriate hostility and to sustain relationships over a period of time, with little mutual exchange of hostility" (Bellak, Hurvich, and Gediman, 1973:42). In this sense the term object relations is synonymous with interpersonal relationships. In earlier theoretical writings the phases in the development of the capacity for mature love relations were linked to instinctual development, and thus all love objects were viewed as libidinally invested. For example, if one referred to the early oral (sucking) period, the corresponding phase of object relations was called auto-erotic (without object); if one referred to the later oral (cannibalistic) stages, the corresponding phase of object relations was considered narcissistic (total incorporation of object). Fueled by the drives, the early incorporation of and identification with significant others were viewed as crucial mechanisms in the developmental process but were not understood fully.

A second usage of the term object relations refers to specific intrapsychic structures, an aspect of ego organization, and not to external interpersonal relationships (Horner, 1979:3). In this view the infant is innately object-seeking from birth, and object relations are thought to integrate drives and affects (feelings) rather than being mere repositories of instinct. The nature of the child's early interpersonal relationships is linked inextricably to stages in the evolution of internalized mental representations of others and of the self, both of which constitute the core of one's psychological identity. In other words, the child develops his or her sense of self and of others as a result of experiences with others. The inner representations of self and others, once developed, affect all subsequent interpersonal relations.

> It is helpful to . . . think in terms of the early mental processes by means of which the newborn infant organizes its world into meaningful patterns. One basic pattern is that of the self-representation while another is that of the object representation. The object refers to the primary mothering person or persons in the environment of the infant and the very young child. The structural and dynamic relation between the self-representations and the object representations constitute what we refer to as object relations [Horner, 1979].

Thus, while one's internal object relations are reflected in external relationships, these two concepts are different. Clearly many factors affect the internalization process, and one's inner mental representations of the self and others do not necessarily reflect fully the real objective self or the real external objects.[2]

In contrast to viewing object relations as a single ego function, some authors view object relations as providing the context in which all ego functions develop. For example, while the capacity to test reality depends, in part, on the maturation of innate cognitive apparatuses,[3] it also emanates from the experience of developing ego boundaries in the relationship between the self and the primary caretaker in early life. Even the exercise of autonomous ego functions themselves can be promoted, shaped, or obstructed by the quality of one's interpersonal environment.

DEVELOPMENTAL PERSPECTIVES

The writings of attachment theorists such as Ainsworth, Bowlby, and Spitz, along with those of Jacobson and Mahler, built object relations theory more firmly into ego psychology. Other important contributions to understanding object relations and self development have come from outside ego psychology. These include feminist critiques of Mahlerian theory, new perspectives on women, the writings of the British School, Kernberg's views, Kohut's self psychology, and Stern's research on the evolution of the self.

THE DEVELOPMENT OF SOCIAL ATTACHMENT

Social attachment is the process by which the infant develops a specific emotional connection to his or her mother or primary caretaker. There is some difference of opinion, however, as to whether the capacity for infant–mother bonding is innate and commences at birth or whether it emerges somewhat later in response to the quality of mothering. Ainsworth (1973), for example, described four stages in the development of social attachment that span the first few years of life. In the first stages (birth to three months) the infant's sucking, rooting, grasping, smiling, gazing, cuddling, and visual tracking are viewed as his or her efforts to maintain closeness with the mother. The infant, however, is not fully differentiated from others.

In contrast, during stage two (three to six months) the infant's attachment to mother is more specific. The infant smiles more and in other ways reacts with excitement or upset to the presence or absence of mother. In this connection both Bowlby (1958) and Spitz (1946c) identified the significance of the infant's preferential and differential smiling response to the mother as connoting that the specific bond between mother and child has been established. There is a good deal of evidence to suggest that the infant's individual characteristics (Bowlby, 1969; Escalona, 1968; Murphy and Moriarity, 1976) and the quality of the mother's holding behavior (Ainsworth and Bell, 1969; Spitz, 1965; and Mahler, Pine, and Bergman, 1975) influence the nature of the infant's attachment to the mother.

In Ainsworth's third stage of social attachment (seven months to two years) the infant seeks to be close to the mother. Behavior seems goal-directed. In the fourth stage, however (two years and older), the child engages in a variety of behaviors designed to influence the behavior of the mother in order to satisfy his or her need for closeness. Thus children ask for special treatment, such as being read to, that gratifies attachment needs.

One of the important issues related to the development of social attachment is whether there is a critical period, that is, an optimal time for its development. Presumably if mastery of a particular developmental milestone does not occur before the end of such a period, it is doubtful whether it ever will develop. Such a view assumes a close coordination between the biological capacities of the organism and the conditions of the social environment. According to Spitz (1946c) the preferential smile, which he believes indicates the beginning of attachment, has such a critical period. Ambrose (1963) locates the critical period for attachment at about twenty to thirty weeks after the infant is born. Other authors (Yarrow, 1964) suggest that such a critical period for the development of social attachment exists from six months to two years. While the time before that lays the foundation for attachment, and the child does already show a gradual increase in preference for the mother, the child also can do well with a substitute mother. After six months the child nevertheless begins to show traumatic reactions when separated from his or her primary caretaker. If prolonged, these may result in serious impairment in the capacity for social attachment.

MAHLER'S THEORY OF SEPARATION–INDIVIDUATION

Within the United States Margaret Mahler's seminal work is the most systematic view of the developmental process of the unfolding of object relations within an ego psychological framework. It also has the advantage of being based on naturalistic observations of children and mothers. In Mahler's writings it is clear that the psychological birth of the individual and the development of object relations are intertwined:

> Like any intrapsychic process, this one reverberates throughout the life cycle. It is never finished; it remains always active; new phases of the life cycle see new derivatives of the earliest processes still at work. But the principal psychological achievements of the process take place in the period from about the fourth or fifth month to the thirtieth or thirty-sixth month, a period we refer to as the separation–individuation phase [Mahler, Pine, and Bergman, 1975:3].

The separation–individuation process reflects two complementary aspects: separation, in which the infant emerges from a fused state with the primary love object, and individuation, in which the child's own unique characteristics are asserted and developed The *sine qua non* of the normal separation–individuation process is the mother's (primary caretaker's) emotional availability while the child separates and individuates. While Mahler basically agrees with Erikson that optimally the primary caretaker should accommodate to the child's needs, she draws attention to the fact that the child's "fresh and pliable adaptive capacity" and need for satisfaction put the burden of adaptation onto the child. "The infant takes shape a harmony and counterpoint to the mother's ways and styles—whether she herself provides a healthy or pathological object for such adaptation (Mahler, Pine, and Bergman, 1975:3).

The separation–individuation process described by Mahler comprises a series of chronologically ordered phases, each of which leads to major achievements in the areas of separation, individuation, and internalized object relations.[4]

The Autistic Phase. The newborn infant generally is unresponsive to external stimuli for a number of weeks and is dominated by physiological needs and processes. He or she sleeps most of the time and wakes when need states arouse tension. The infant's primary autonomous ego apparatuses are still somewhat undifferentiated and are not yet called into play to act upon the environment. The infant literally exists in his or her own world or in what has been termed an autistic state, although gradually he or she becomes responsive, if only fleetingly, to external stimuli. In terms of object relations the child is in a preattachment phase, which some have called a phase of primary narcissism. This normal developmental stage should not be confused with the pathological fixation at the autistic phase or a regression to an autistic state seen in many severely disturbed children. In these cases attachment behavior that normally occurs somewhat later has not been operative or it has been met with severe environmental stress.[6]

SEPARATION–INDIVIDUATION PROCESS AND THE CORRESPONDING DEVELOPMENT OF OBJECT RELATIONS[5]

Phase	Age (Approximate)	Object Relations
Autistic	Birth–1 month	There is a state of unrelatedness or primary undifferentiated (objectless) state.
Symbiotic	1–4 or 5 months	The child's image of him- or herself and mother are fused. There is no separate self or object. There is a fused self–object representation in which all "good" or pleasurable experiences consolidate and all "bad" or unpleasurable experiences are expelled.
Separation– Individuation: Differentiation	4 or 5–8 months	There is beginning differentiation of self from object through the differentiation of the child's body image from that of the mother.
Practicing	8–15 months	As the child actively explores the new opportunities of the real world, there is further differentiation of the self-image

Phase	Age (Approximate)	Object Relations
		leading to all "good" self and object representations and all "bad" self and object representations.
Rapprochement	15–24 months	The child turns back to the mother with new demands for her responsiveness to the child's individuation. There is integration of all "good" and all "bad" aspects of the self-representations into an integrated self-concept and a corresponding integration of all "good" and "bad" object images into a total object representation that leads to object constancy.
On the road to object constancy	24–36 months	The child is able to maintain a stable mental representation of the mother whether she is there or not and irrespective of needs or frustrations.

The Symbiotic Phase. Gradually the protective shell gives way, and he or she begins to perceive the "need-satisfying object," but this object is experienced within the infant's ego boundary and lacks a separate identity. The infant and mother are one entity. All pleasurable sensations are encompassed within their joint boundary, and unpleasurable ones are cast out. The infant's nonspecific smiling response is thought to initiate the symbiotic phase, and it is only when the smile becomes preferential to the mother some time later that the specific bond between mother and child is established.[7]

In the symbiotic state the mother's ego functions for the infant, and it is the mother who mediates between the infant and the external world. The sensations the child experiences from the mother form the core of his or her sense of self, and this period marks the beginning of the capacity to invest in another person. The infant perceives more of the world than previously, although he or she does not realize that stimuli clearly emanate from outside him- or herself and the symbiotic orbit.

Separation–Individuation: The Differentiation Subphase. Differentiation begins at about four or five months. When the child is awake more often and for longer periods, his or her attention shifts from being inwardly directed or focused within the symbiosis to being more outwardly directed. Observations of infants reveal that they tend to look more alert, and their behavior seems more goal-directed at this time. "We have taken this look to be a behavioral manifestation of 'hatching' and have loosely said that the infant with this look has 'hatched'" (Mahler, Pine, and Bergman, 1975:54). This initial period is followed by more exploratory and experimental behavior when the infant is about six months old:

> This can be observed in such behavior on the part of the infant as pulling at the mother's hair, ears, or nose, putting food into the mother's mouth, and straining his body away from mother in order to have a better look at her, to scan her and the environment. . . . Six to seven months is the peak of tactile and visual exploration of the mother's face, as well as of the covered (clad) and unclad parts of the mother's body [Mahler, Pine, and Bergman, 1975:54].

The infant literally begins to separate his or her self-representation from the representation of the mother (the object), although this initial differentiation occurs first with respect to the infant's body image. A period in which transitional objects become important, that is, objects that substitute for the mother through their actual association with her (by smell and touch for example), occurs around this time. Often the infant begins to assume the mother's characteristic behavior toward him or her, such as by self-stroking. At about seven or eight months the infant seems to compare the mother visually with unfamiliar objects in what has been called a "checking-back pattern," and the ability to discriminate the particular characteristics of mother becomes more accomplished. According to Mahler's observations, the phenomenon of stranger anxiety, which has been associated with this period, is a highly individual matter and sometimes occurs only minimally. Where there has been an optimal holding environment in the symbiotic phase, the infant's differentiation subphase is more likely to be characterized by an eager curiosity. It is important to note that during this process the infant's autonomous ego functions are stimulated to act upon the environment.

While there are individual differences that affect the timing and nature of the infant's differentiation experience, the conditions of the maternal holding environment in this and all phases are thought to be a crucial factor in shaping the outcome of the separation–individuation process.[8] If the child is forced out of the symbiosis too early or kept in it too long, the consequences for separation–individuation will be negative. Infants who fail to achieve this initial differentiation of the self from the object or who hold it tenuously are destined to remain fixated in their fused self-object representations, a state characteristic of chronic schizophrenic individuals. Alternatively they may be vulnerable to regression to such fusion states under the impact of stress. Crucial ego functions may also be affected negatively. For example, reality testing, which requires the ability to differentiate self from nonself, inner from outer, and fantasy from reality, will be impaired.

Separation–Individuation: The Practicing Subphase. The practicing subphase continues the process of separation of self and object representations and accelerates the individuation process, as the infant's own autonomous ego functions assume more importance. The first part of the practicing period, when the infant is approximately eight to ten or twelve months old, is characterized by the infant's attempts to move away from the mother physically through crawling, for example. In the second part of this period, from ten or twelve to sixteen or eighteen months, the infant is capable of free and upright locomotion. The maturation of motor functions provides an important thrust to the individuation process at this time. The infant thus expands his or her world and capacity to maneuver in it autonomously, optimally always in close proximity to the maternal figure, who is there to provide support and encouragement. The term "practicing" implies a testing out of one's individual capacities and of being on one's own in a limited sense.

In the early practicing subphase the child experiences the simultaneous pull of the outside world and of the mother, and separation anxiety may increase until the child becomes reassured that mother is still there despite his or her moving away from her. One can observe the repeated efforts initially made on the part of the child to keep track of the mother even as he or she may crawl away from her, and then the attempt to find her if she has been lost momentarily. Gradually the child is more able to be on his or her own for longer periods of time.

> The optimal distance in the early practicing sub-phase would seem to be one that allows the moving quadruped child freedom and opportunity for exploration at some physical distance from mother. . . . During the entire practicing sub-phase mother continues to be needed as . . . a "home-base" to fulfill the need for re-fueling through emotional contact. . . . It is easy to observe how the melting and fatigued infant "perks up" in the shortest time following such contact; then he quickly goes on with his exploration and once again becomes absorbed in the pleasures of functioning [Mahler, Pine, and Bergman, 1975:69].

During the second part of the practicing period, the child's ability to get around independently seems to lead to a "love affair with the world."[9] The child directs his or her attention to all the new and exciting features of the external environment and derives enormous satisfaction from the ability to get along in it. It has been observed repeatedly that the child is so absorbed in these new endeavors that he or she seems impervious to knocks or falls that occur. Similarly, at times the child appears oblivious to the mother's temporary absence. The pleasure in his or her rapidly developing ego functions seems to enable the child to sustain the transient object losses inherent in individuation. As the child practices, he or she acquires new skills. Walking becomes a major accomplishment, and at times the child appears elated with his or her own powers and possibly by his or her escape from total dependency. At the same time it is clear that the threat of object loss is present beneath the surface. Further the child also seems to delight in being "swooped up" by the mother, since this seems to reassure him or her that she is still there and wants the child. Again it must be noted that the mother's ability to support the child's growing individuation through her encouragement while she maintains a continued supportive presence when the child needs her is a critical factor in fostering optimal individuation.

The child consolidates his or her separateness during this period and acquires a more stable internal self-representation that is distinct from the object representation. At the same time the child's self- and object representations are said to be "split," that is, all "good" self and object experiences are separated from all "bad" ones. Thus, when mother is frustrating she is experienced as all bad, although the child tries to rid him- or herself of this feeling; when she is experienced as loving she is all good. Similarly, when the child who is punished may experience him- or herself as all bad, although again he or she tries to be rid of this feeling; the child who is loved and rewarded may experience him- or herself as all good. This normal phase of splitting is overcome in the later rapprochement subphase, when the good and bad self and good and bad object each begin to become integrated. Prior to this integration and to the development of object constancy, the self and the world are experienced in polar and fluctuating terms. The failure to overcome this "splitting" because of difficulties in the rapprochement phase (and earlier) leads to fixations or developmental arrests and has been said to characterize individuals with severe character pathology and borderline conditions. With respect to the development of ego functions, the differentiation process fosters the important capacity for reality testing. The child's autonomous functions develop extensively as does the beginning sense of mastery, and his or her negotiations with the environment support the development of other more complex ego functions.

Separation–Individuation: The Rapprochement Subphase. The maturation of the child's motor and cognitive functions and increased individuation and autonomy paradoxically usher in more concern about mother's whereabouts and anxiety about being separate from the mother. While in the practicing subphase the child is content to be away from the mother for increasingly long periods of time, in the rapprochement subphase the child becomes more needful of her presence once again and appears to want her to share everything as well as to provide constant reassurances of her love. This need for closeness while the child continues his or her autonomous existence characterizes the rapprochement period.

During the rapprochement subphase the, child's belief in the mother's omnipotence is shed as he or she realizes the need to act independently. At the same time the child is now frightened of being completely alone and losing the mother's love.

> The toddler's demands for his mother's constant involvement seem contradictory to the mother: while he is not as independent and helpless as he was only a half a year before, and seems eager to become less and less so, nevertheless he even more insistently indicates that he expects the mother to share every aspect of his life. . . . While individuation proceeds very rapidly and the child exercises it to the limit, he also becomes more aware of his separateness and employs all kinds of mechanisms in order to resist his actual separation from mother. The fact, however, that no matter how insistently the toddler tries to coerce the mother, she and he can no longer function effectively as a dual unit—that is to say, the child can no longer maintain his delusion of parental omnipotence, which he still at times expects will restore this symbiotic status quo [Mahler, Pine, and Bergman, 1975:78–79].

The child's capacity for attachment to others expands beyond the exclusive relationship with the mother during this period, and his or her emotional range becomes greater.

The development of language is an important feature of this subphase. As the child discovers the necessity of communicating verbally, he or she is forced to give up the reliance on preverbal empathy. He or she also becomes aware that the mother has needs and interests of her own. Optimally, the child is able to consolidate his or her identification with and internalization of the mother as a three-dimensional person who loves and hates, rewards and punishes, and has unique characteristics. This enables the child to develop an integrated sense of self as well as a more realistic view of the mother. Thus, the positive resolution of the rapprochement crisis begins to enable the child to overcome the splitting of the self and the object world into all "good" and all "bad" and to develop integrated self- and object representations. This process is essential to the achievement and solidification of object constancy and to the development of empathic capacities, both of which are essential to mature object love. This process continues throughout the next subphase in which there is greater consolidation of identity and ego functioning. While rapprochement difficulties, as well as residues from earlier phases, may be present to a less extreme degree in many individuals, in more severe cases where there are rapprochement failures, severe ego pathology and pathology of object relations occurs. It must also be noted that in the rapprochement subphase, as well as in all phases mentioned, other significant developmental processes are occurring and must be viewed in conjunction with those that emanate from the separation–individuation process itself.[10]

Separation–Individuation: On the Road to Object Constancy. Mahler, Pine, and Bergman (1975:110) cite the two main tasks of this subphase as the attainment of individuality and the attainment of object constancy. Gender identity and superego functioning also advance during this period, which lasts through the third year. This end point is somewhat arbitrary, as the process may continue for some time. During this phase the child again seems able to be on his or her own to a greater degree than previously without undue concern about the mother's whereabouts. Only this time, the child seems to convert the mother's external presence to her internal presence. The child's internalization of the mother, which remains fluid for some time, begins to permit the child to pursue the full expression of his or her individuality and to function independently without experiencing or fearing separation, abandonment, or loss of love. The final achievement of object constancy implies the capacity to maintain a positive mental representation of the object in the object's absence or in the face of frustration. Further, it connotes a related development discussed previously:

> It also implies the unifying of the "good" and "bad" object into one whole representation. This fosters the fusion of the aggressive and libidinal drives and tempers the hatred for the object when the aggression is intense. . . . In the state of object con-

stancy, the love object will not be rejected or exchanged for another if it can no longer provide satisfactions; and in that state,
the object is still longed for and not rejected (hated) as unsatisfying simply because it is absent [Mahler, Pine, and Bergman,
1975:110].

With the attainment of object constancy and the achievement of a
greater sense of individual identity during this phase, the struc-
turalization of the ego achieves a high level. While it undergoes
progressive refinement later, this ego structure becomes the core
of healthy functioning.

The Role of the Father. The impact of the father on the child's ego
development and on the process of internalization has not been
studied extensively in general, nor was it a major focus of
Mahler's research. She did regard the child's relationship with
the father as markedly different from that with the mother. She
saw it as a special relationship, not well understood, and neither
fully outside nor a part of the symbiotic orbit (Mahler, Pine, and
Bergman, 1975:91).

In describing the father's role, Cath (1986:165) emphasizes
that husbands and wives both contribute to each other's nurturing capacities and influence each other's relationships with their
children. It is important that husband and wife and same-sex domestic partners enter into an alliance that will enable them to
jointly rear their offspring even if the couple separates or di-
vorces. Further, while women and men may be able to care for
children in similar and equally effective ways, there is some evidence to suggest that each contributes different elements to the
parenting process. For example, in summarizing the results of
numerous studies of parent-child relationships, Cath (1986:166)
concludes that "infants become attached to both parents in different ways, and that fathers offer more playful, physically
arousing experiences." In contrast, he indicates that women tend
to be more soothing.

One view of the father-child relationship has emerged out of
studies of the separation–individuation process. Abelin (1971)
identified (1) the specific relationship with the father as occurring in the child's symbiotic phase, although later than that

which occurs with the mother; (2) the father's role in the development of the child's identifications with and internalized representations of his or her love objects; and (3) the father as serving a different role from the mother. He represents the outer world and attracts the child away from the pull of the symbiosis. In a sense he comes to be equated with difference, excitement, and novelty. Thus he has a positive role in reinforcing both the child's separation from the mother and his or her individuation by "rescuing" the child from the confines of the relationship with the mother and by supporting autonomous ego functioning.

It must be noted that both Mahler's and Abelin's observations were based on mother–child and father–child relationships within particular types of family structures reflecting specific kinds of childrearing patterns in which the mother was the primary caretaker. Neither writer addressed the issue of how the father's functioning in the role of primary caretaker or in a more shared, egalitarian childrearing model affects the separation–individuation process. Similarly, there is little data on the impact of single or multiple caretakers on the separation–individuation process.[11]

THE SECOND SEPARATION–INDIVIDUATION PHASE IN ADOLESCENCE

From the preceding discussion it can be seen that Mahler viewed the major formative periods in the development of identity and a healthy ego structure as occurring in the first three or so years of life. Consistent with her ideas is the view that a major psychological task of adolescence is the reworking and final consolidation of identity.[12] Blos (1975) has suggested a second separation–individuation phase occurring in adolescence. The oscillating behavior (clinging dependency and a need for complete autonomy) of even the normal adolescent is reminiscent of the earlier rapprochement subphase. In adolescence, however, the separation that must occur is of a different order. The healthy adolescent has an internalized sense of self and others but now must disengage from the more infantile aspects of his or her self- and object representations in order to acquire a more realistically based sense of self and of parents. This disengagement also requires the discovery of new love objects outside the orbit of the family. Mature relations require that one perceive and relate to others in terms of one's own unique characteristics.

For the adolescent who has had earlier separation–individuation difficulties, this period will be particularly turbulent because of the complexity of the maturation and psychosocial demands and expectations of this period. It is not unusual for such adolescents to reveal more serious problems in interpersonal and social functioning at this time. It is often difficult, however, to distinguish between adolescents and their families who are reacting to current stresses, and those in which more serious and persistent individual and family difficulties have escalated at this time because of the pressures of adolescence.

While there is no evidence that gay adolescents differ from non-gay adolescents in their biological and cognitive development, Hetrick and Martin (1988:26) point out that their psychological and social development varies and that "the homosexually oriented adolescent must deal with issues different from those of the heterosexually oriented adolescent." They argue that the main concern for the gay adolescent is the awareness that he or she belongs to a stigmatized and oppressed group. This realization can lead to low self-esteem, feelings of discontinuity, cognitive and social isolation, maladaptive coping mechanisms, symptoms, and dysfunctional behavior when social supports, accurate information, and positive role models are lacking (Hetrick and Martin, 35–41).

FEMINIST VIEWS

Many feminist writers have challenged the main thrust of Mahler's separation-individuation theory as it pertains to women's development. For example, Chodorow (1978) and Gilligan (1982) argue that females have a different individuation process from males because of their primary attachment to a parent of the same rather than the opposite sex. They see mothers and daughters as sharing a greater sense of identification and merger with one another, resulting in a more prolonged closeness and a more diffuse individuation process. Further, female self development when compared to male self development involves more permeable rather than rigid boundaries, an emphasis on relationships rather than autonomy, and a greater capacity for empathy, caring, and intuition.

Members of the Stone Center for Developmental Services and Studies at Wellesley College in Massachusetts echo this point of view and have put forth an important set of ideas, termed self-in-relation theory (Jordan, 1990; Kaplan and Surrey, 1984; Miller, 1977). The Stone Center group, which includes Jean Baker Miller, Judith Jordan, Alexandra Kaplan, Irene Stiver, and Janet Surrey, criticizes the view implicit in Mahler's theory that the healthy person is individuated, autonomous, and separate with clear boundaries and that merger in relationships along with more permeable boundaries is pathological. They regard women's self development as evolving in the context of relatedness, and argue that enhanced connection rather than increased self-object differentiation and separateness is women's major goal. Further, they believe that women grow optimally and change when they experience an interactive process in which mutual engagement, empathy, and empowerment with significant others occur. Nonresponsive relationships and disconnection rather than problems in separation–individuation *per se* result in pathology.

Jessica Benjamin (1988), another prominent theorist, also has critiqued Mahler's theory for emphasizing differentiation and individuation rather than the balance between oneness and separateness, merging and differentiation. In Benjamin's view, true independence involves both self-assertion and mutuality, separateness and sharing, and that the individual's inability to reconcile dependence and independence leads to patterns of domination and submission.

Some writers have utilized these newer theories to suggest a more affirmative view of lesbian development. Traditional conceptions of the early childhood of lesbians saw them as failing to switch their attachment from their mothers to their fathers, remaining fixated on their mothers rather than viewing them as rivals and then identifying with their fathers. Citing the alternative ideas of Chodorow and the self-in-relation theorists, Weille (1993:153–54) speculates that since the little girl normally does not give up her attachment to the mother when she turns to her father but instead maintains this bond, which provides her

with continuity and a core sense of self, it is logical that a normative outcome for women is bisexuality. The daughter maintains
her libidinal connection to the mother while developing a triadic
relational structure. Reiter (1989:138–50) further suggests that
the girl's primary and continuing attachment results in her acquisition of a firm gender identity as a woman, and that women
consequently may have the capacity for greater fluidity in their
sexual interests without its detracting from their sense of female-
ness. This view might help to explain why many lesbians "come
out" later in life, after they have had significant relationships
with men, or else move back and forth between men and women
in their love relationships, thus showing a longstanding bisexual
orientation (Burch, 1993).

Recent research supports the view that lesbian object relations
and self development arise as a variant of positive developmental experiences, in contrast to the traditional belief that they reflect arrested, immature, narcissistic, and undifferentiated object
relations. For example, in Spaulding's study of twenty-four
college-educated lesbians who had positive identities and
achieved high scores on measures of psychological stability, the
women showed "evidence of highly evolved, differentiated and
integrated level of object and reality relatedness" (Spaulding,
1993:17). Further, their views of their parents did not correspond
to common stereotypes, in that they saw both their mothers and
fathers as strong, positive role models who were nurturing, successful, and warm (Spaulding, 1993:19).

The newer perspectives on women's object relations and self
development have major implications for understanding
women's strengths and needs throughout the life cycle and for
redefining behavior that has been viewed as pathological in
more normal terms. They also illuminate the causes of certain
symptoms and difficulties that women experience when they are
deprived of necessary connection or when they experience conflict between a need for affiliation versus a push toward self-
enhancement or more autonomous behavior. Further, these
views of women's needs have significant ramifications for re-
shaping the treatment process into one that is more reciprocal
and relational.

THE BRITISH SCHOOL OF OBJECT RELATIONS

A number of distinctive contributions to understanding personality development came from members of the British School of Object Relations.

Melanie Klein. A children's analyst, Melanie Klein (Segal, 1964) argued that infants possess an inborn awareness of the mother. She emphasized the role in the infant's life of instinctual aggression and fantasy, which determine the nature of perceptions and experiences, although real objects may reinforce or challenge the infant's views. From birth, envy, greed, and destructive fantasies about and impulses toward others make the infant anxious; the infant fears the objects upon whom he or she vents anger. Rage is projected and results in persecutory fears that are heightened during the paranoid/schizoid position in the first six months of life. This stage also is characterized by the use of early defense mechanisms that help the infant to rid him- or herself of this anxiety. In the last half of the first year of life, the infant enters the depressive position in which loving feelings temper the aggressive drive and hate. In order to preserve "good" objects, infants make reparation for their aggressive fantasies and impulses and are capable of experiencing gratitude and guilt. Klein believed that both the paranoid-schizoid and depressive positions shape later personality development and psychopathology and always are active to different degrees.

Fairbairn. Fairbairn (1952), who lived and worked in Scotland, regarded infants as object-seeking rather than pleasure-seeking. He argued that personality develops as a result of interactions with real rather than fantasied objects. Fairbairn believed that the frustration of not feeling loved or lovable, or of feeling that one's love is not welcome and valued, results in aggressive impulses. The inability of external objects to provide these necessary experiences lead the infant to acquire a split ego and to build up a world of internal bad objects, which are themselves split into idealized, rejecting, and exciting parts. The internalization of bad objects and the split in the ego that result become closed systems that influence further personality development and psychopathology. They prevent the individual from progressing from infantile dependence to mature dependence and from establishing loving and satisfying bonds with others.

Winnicott. A pediatrician, Winnicott (1955, 1965), stressed the importance of "good enough mothering" and the provision of a "maternal holding environment" in children's development. He described the child's internalization of personality attributes such as the capacity to be alone as dependent on attuned mothering, as well as the ego defects that result from maternal failures. He also drew attention to the significance of transitional objects as a bridge between children and mothers. According to Winnicott, when good enough mothering is lacking because of either maternal deprivation or too much "impingement," the infant erects a "false" self, which is a facade that comes into being to please others. As the false self rigidifies, the child becomes alienated from his or her true self. Thus, the false self is a defensive organization that both "hides and protects" the true self at the expense of its full expression.

Guntrip. Guntrip (1968, 1971), who was interested in theology, also stressed the importance of early mothering in shaping the personality. He argued that frustrations caused by external objects, primarily the mother, lead the infant or child to turn away from them and that this withdrawal, the schizoid problem, is at the core of all psychopathology. It is characterized by ego-splitting; a withdrawal from interpersonal relationships; attitudes of omnipotence, isolation, and detachment; hopelessness; and a preoccupation with inner reality. The most extreme schizoid mechanisms result in alienation from self and the inability to love or to experience understanding, warmth, and personal concern for others. Deeply hidden in such a person is his or her needy self, which is cut off from the outside world.

KERNBERG'S THEORY OF OBJECT RELATIONS

Otto Kernberg (1975, 1976, 1984), who was influenced by Kleinian theory and the writings of Edith Jacobson and Margaret

Mahler, tried to integrate many Kleinian concepts into American ego psychology and object relations theory. He shares Klein's emphasis on instinctual aggression, unconscious fantasy, and primitive defenses and her view of how the child's inborn dispositions and instincts organize perceptions and internalization of the external world. Kernberg argues that what the child takes in psychically usually differs from the actual objects in the environment, since drives, affects, fantasies, and defenses shape and distort the child's perceptions and experiences. Like the ego psychologists, Kernberg maintains a reliance on structural theory. He traces the development of an individual's *internalized* object relations and internal structure through a series of five sequential stages that are similar to those described by Mahler; however, he tends to minimize the impact of the child's actual parenting experiences. Kernberg relates certain problems in this evolution to the formation of pathological object relations that culminate in borderline and narcissistic disorders. His models for the treatment of these conditions are widely known.

SELF PSYCHOLOGY

Originally identified with classical psychoanalysis and ego psychology, Heinz Kohut (1971, 1974, 1984) gradually evolved a distinctive theoretical model based on his work with narcissistic individuals. Self psychology focuses on the emergence and development of an innate nuclear self, on the role of an empathic caretaking relationship in the evolution of the self, on the role of defects or vulnerability in the self in causing later psychopathology, and on the need for others in the maintenance of self-esteem. Kohut envisioned "a different baby" (Tolpin, 1986) who is more innately intact, creative, organized, self-regulating, and related than the baby portrayed by other theorists; however, the infant does need attuned caretakers or what is termed selfobjects to facilitate and nurture his or her unique nuclear self. The earliest selfobjects are those who perform vital functions for the newborn infant that he or she cannot carry out alone.

Kohut identified three main types of selfobject needs: (1) the need for mirroring that confirms the child's sense of vigor, greatness, and perfection; (2) the need for an idealization of others

whose strength and calmness soothe the child; and (3) the need
for a twin or alter ego who provides the child with a sense of hu-
manness, likeness to, and partnership with others (Elson, 1986).
Rewarding experiences with at least one type of selfobject give
the child a chance to develop a cohesive self. Although early selfobjects are crucial to the development of the infant's self, the
need for others to provide support and sustenance continues all
through life. A strong cohesive self gives the person a sense of
vigor, inner harmony, and self-esteem, but the emergent self may
also reflect deficiencies that result in fragmentation, enfeeble-
ment, lack of zest, and problems in self-esteem regulation that
are so severe as to constitute a self disorder. In Kohut's schema,
not all structural defects in the self result in pathology, since the
child may be able to acquire compensatory structures that
strengthen the self. These structures enable the person to make
up for or repair deficits in one aspect of the self through successful development of its other facets.

STERN'S FOUR SENSES OF THE SELF

A novel account of the developmental process comes from the
work of Daniel Stern (1985), who systematically studied child-
mother interactions. Like Kohut, Stern sees the self, which is
present in a rudimentary form at birth, as the major organizer of
the personality. In contrast to Mahler, he gives evidence that the
infant is born with an innate sense of separateness from others,
and that over time the child's self evolves as a consequence of
complex interpersonal transactions. While Stern identifies stages
in the development of the self as physical and mental maturation
propel the child to face certain adaptive tasks, he does not regard
these phases as time-bound, nor does he believe that the individual grows out of any particular stage. Instead, each one becomes
a distinct form of experience that gets further elaborated over
time as the child and adult deal with later developmental tasks.
For example, the attainment of autonomy is not tied to a particular age but is worked on at various points in the life cycle.

Delineating four phases of self development that he calls "domains of relatedness," Stern views each domain as codetermined

by the growing infant's innate maturational capacities and the nature and degree of caretaker attunement.

The Sense of Emergent Self. From birth onwards, Stern's infant is an active organism that seems able to process important information about the external and interpersonal world. He or she can make distinctions between people by smell and sound, identify familiar objects that have been sucked, and make connections between stimuli based on their intensity. Quickly the infant engages in behavior that confirms his or her own existence as a separate being and build up a stable picture of the physical characteristics of the interpersonal milieu.

The Sense of Core Self. As early as two to three months and continuing until about seven months, the infant forms an organized sense of a core self that is contingent upon satisfying episodes of mutual regulation that build up over time. The infant acquires a clear grasp of both his or her own and the significant other's separate physical presence and also achieves a sense of the mutual influence of others. This view contrasts sharply with that of Mahler, who describes this period as symbiotic. In fact, Stern argues strongly that the infant's ability to merge with the mother is a product of his or her separateness rather than a reflection of a normal symbiotic phase.

The Sense of Subjective Self. Between seven to nine months, the infant moves beyond experiencing itself and others in terms of physical characteristics and discovers inner mental qualities. For example, the child not only reacts positively to the mother's overt comforting or empathic behavior but recognizes her empathic process. Likewise, the child's awareness of his or her own and others' intentions and affects permits an intersubjective relatedness to develop. This period marks the beginning of the child's capacity for true intimacy and sharing of experience.

The child's attainment of a sense of subjective self builds upon but does not supersede or replace the sense of a core self, which continues to expand. Unlike Mahler, who describes the child's differentiation from the mother at this time, Stern draws attention to the child's growing ability to share with the mother. In fact, he criticizes earlier ego psychological views for their overemphasis on separation-individuation and neglect of the beginnings of intersubjective relatedness.

The Sense of Verbal Self. At about fifteen to eighteen months, the child begins to acquire the capacity for language and symbolization. The attainment of this verbal domain of relatedness adds a different dimension to the way the child experiences him- or herself, others, and the world. The child becomes capable of viewing him- or herself objectively, performing empathic acts, engaging in symbolic play, and thinking. Language not only facilitates separation–individuation but also helps to unite two persons in a common use of symbols.

ADULTHOOD REVERBERATIONS

On the one hand adulthood is a time when one can continue to grow through one's identification and loving relations with others. As discussed in Chapter 5, however, the core ego structure has been built by adulthood, although the particular ways in which it evolves and manifests itself are shaped later. Further, even those adults who show optimal functioning may relive separation–individuation themes throughout the life cycle, particularly at life transitional points or during more acute stresses. Nevertheless, the adult who has achieved a relatively stable (psychological) identity and who has an integrated and realistic conception of him- or herself will have the capacity for mature and loving relations with others. Those who do not successfully complete this key developmental task will show serious interpersonal difficulties. While not all interpersonal difficulties reflect developmental arrests, many do. The patterning of adult relationships reflects the developmental successes and failures of the past. Someone who has had less than optimal success or who has had marked developmental difficulties in the area of separation–individuation, with their resultant impact on identity, ego functioning, and the quality of object relations, will be ill-equipped for interpersonal and life transactions. Common difficulties stemming from such developmental failures are detachment from others; clinging dependency on and attempts to merge with others; anxiety regarding rejection and abandonment; fears of, or depression resulting from, independence because it is equated with aloneness and abandonment; inability to empathize with others fully or to see them in realistic ways; abrupt reversals of feelings and attitudes toward others; and lack of self-esteem. Thus some of the difficulties one sees in adult relationships can be traced directly back to particular separation–individuation subphase and other developmental problems.[13]

SUMMARY

This chapter has discussed the complex development of social attachment and object relations. Mahler's theoretical views regarding the separation–individuation process have been presented in detail followed by a critique of her views by feminist writers. Some newer ideas on women's self and object relations development were presented along with alternative formulations from the British School of Object Relations, the work of Otto Kernberg, Kohut's self psychology, and Daniel Stern's research.

NOTES

1. In the United States object relations theory was considered a minor theoretical current within psychoanalysis until recently, although it gained popularity in Europe (particularly England) through the works of Klein, Fairbairn, Winnicott, Guntrip, and others. While there are some points of similarity between these writings and those of the more recent ego psychological-object relations theorists such as Jacobson, Mahler, and Kernberg (who borrow from the British School), these two theoretical lines are relatively independent and often have been viewed by members of both camps as mutually antagonistic. For a summary of the British School of Object Relations see Harry Guntrip, *Psychoanalytic Theory, Therapy and the Self* (New York: Basic Books, 1971; paperback, 1973).
2. Edith Jacobson made the distinction between the real and objective self and object and the self and object representations, which are

unconscious and subjective. See *The Self and the Object World* (New York: International Universities Press, 1964).

3. Piaget's work on cognitive development helps in the understanding of the complex ways in which the organism assimilates and accommodates to the environment. It also provides understanding of the kind of mental structures and processes that underlie ego functioning and the development of object relations. For an excellent summary of Piaget's work see Henry W. Maier, *Three Theories of Child Development* (New York: Harper & Row, 1969).

4. Actually Edith Jacobson, who influenced Mahler's work, originally drew attention to the separation–individuation process and to its role in psychic structuring and the development of internalized object relations. See Jacobson, *The Self and the Object World*.

5. This table represents an integration of ideas put forth by Margaret S. Mahler, Fred Pine, and Anni Bergman, *The Psychological Birth of the Human Infant* (New York: Basic Books, 1975); Jacobson, *The Self and the Object World*; and Otto F. Kernberg, *Object-Relations Theory and Clinical Psychoanalysis* (New York: Jason Aronson, 1976), pp. 55-83.

6. Mahler's early work dealt with autistic and symbiotic psychoses. See Margaret S. Mahler, "On Childhood Psychosis and Schizophrenia: Autistic and Symbiotic Infantile Psychosis," in *The Psychoanalytic Study of the Child* (New York: International Universities Press, 1951): 7:286-305.

7. The works of Spitz and Bowlby are crucial to understanding the nature of the attachment behavior that leads to the emergence and consolidation of this phase. See René Spitz, *The First Year of Life: A Psychoanalytic Study of Normal and Deviant Development of Object Relations* (New York: International Universities Press, 1965), and John Bowlby, "The Nature of the Child's Tie to the Mother," *International Journal of Psychoanalysis*, 39 (1958): 350-73; and *idem*, *Attachment and Loss*, Vol. 1, *Attachment* (New York: Basic Books, 1969).

8. Spitz and Bowlby studied the more dramatic effects of loss, separation, and maternal deprivation on both attachment behavior and ego development. See Bowlby, *Attachment and Loss*, Vol. 1, *Attachment*, and Vol. II, *Separation: Anxiety and Anger* (New York: Basic Books, 1969, 1973), and René Spitz, "Anaclitic Depression: An Inquiry Into the Genesis of Psychiatric Conditions in Childhood," *The Psychoanalytic Study of the Child*, 2 (1946): 313-42.

9. Phyllis Greenacre, a prominent psychoanalyst and theoretician who worked with and observed children, made this observation as quoted in Mahler *et al.*, Psychological Birth, p. 70.

10. A collection of articles on the rapprochement subphase can be

found in Ruth F. Lax, Sheldon Bach, and J. Alexis Burland, *Rapprochement* (New York: Jason Aronson, 1980).

11. This author subscribes to the view that the sex-role stereotypes and biases of the culture affect not only the developmental process *per se* but also the theories about such development and the research that evolves out of particular theoretical systems. For an interesting and provocative discussion that challenges psychoanalytic views of mothering see Nancy Chodorow, *The Reproduction of Mothering* (Berkeley: University of California Press, 1978).

12. It is a debatable issue whether or not this second separation–individuation phase leads to the development of a new ego structure or merely to the reworking of the childhood structure.

13. For an excellent review of Mahler's theory and its implications for adulthood difficulties along with case samples, see Joyce Edward, Nathene Ruskin, and Patsy Turrini, *Separation–Individuation: Theory and Application* (New York: Gardner Press, 1981).

PART III

PRACTICE APPLICATIONS

CHAPTER 7

THE NATURE OF EGO-ORIENTED ASSESSMENT

There is not an integrated, distinctive ego psychological model of assessment. The psychosocial, problem-solving, crisis intervention, and life models, all of which draw heavily on ego psychology, define the nature of assessment somewhat differently.[1] This chapter will discuss the nature of assessment based on ego psychological principles and will explain the focus of assessment using case examples.

THE FOCUS OF ASSESSMENT

Assessment based on ego psychological principles focuses both on the client's current and past functioning and on his or her inner capacities and external circumstances. The practitioner first helps the client to share the problem for which he or she seeks help, to discuss what steps have been taken to help him- or herself, and to identify possible solutions that he or she seeks. The practitioner then tries to assess the problem in the light of the client's total person-in-situation functioning.[2]

QUESTIONS GUIDING ASSESSMENT

The following questions are important guides to the practitioner in the assessment process.

1. To what extent is the client's problem a function of stresses imposed by his or her current life roles or developmental tasks?

2. To what extent is the client's problem a function of situational stress or of a traumatic event?
3. To what extent is the client's problem a function of impairments in his or her ego capacities or of developmental difficulties or dynamics?
4. To what extent is the client's problem a function of the lack of environmental resources or supports or of a lack of fit between his or her inner capacities and external circumstances?
5. What inner capacities and environmental resources does the client have that can be mobilized to improve functioning?

The presence of any one of the etiologies suggested by these questions does not necessarily rule out any or all of the others. It is possible that many problems are a function of the interaction among current life stresses, impairments in ego functioning, developmental arrests, and environmental factors. In many instances, however, the client's problem will stem from one or two of these factors. Some clients who generally function well may become overwhelmed in the face of role and developmental transitions, traumatic events, or stressful environmental conditions. Others may show chronically poor functioning and prove ill-equipped to deal with the stresses of everyday life. Still other clients have little ability to cope effectively with current stresses because of ego deficits, developmental arrests, or a lack of environmental resources.

THE RELATIONSHIP BETWEEN
ASSESSMENT AND INTERVENTION

Ego assessment is not crucial to all forms of help-giving in social work practice. It is not a prerequisite for responding to clients' needs for and entitlements to many types of concrete services. Further, using it as a tool for evaluating whether clients deserve such services violates the values of the social work profession. Ego strength is not synonymous with personal worth or goodness, just as ego weakness or deficits are not to be confused with personal failure or badness.[3]

Ego assessment helps the practitioner determine whether interventive efforts should be directed at (1) nurturing, maintaining, enhancing, or modifying inner capacities; (2) mobilizing, improving, or changing environmental conditions; or (3) improving the fit between inner capacities and external circumstances. Thus the conclusion that a client is overwhelmed by current external stresses but shows good past ego functioning and has many environmental supports points to the need for supportive efforts aimed at reducing the stresses and helping the client to utilize inner and outer resources . In contrast, the conclusion that a client's ego deficits and developmental difficulties are interfering with his or her ability to cope with current life roles suggests the need for efforts aimed at ego-building. The conclusion that a client's maladaptive defenses or characterological patterns are hampering the ability to use his or her capacities points to the need for intervention aimed at modifying such traits; on the other hand, the assessment that a lack of environmental resources is making it impossible for an individual to cope effectively with current role demands suggests the need for intervention aimed at supplying those essential resources. The nature of ego-oriented intervention will be discussed in Chapter 8.

The following five case examples will illustrate the focus of ego assessment.[4] The five guiding questions identified earlier in the chapter will provide a framework for a discussion of the examples. The first two cases, Mr. J and Ms. R, illustrate that the clients' problems are connected not only to difficulties in mastering current life roles and developmental tasks but also to longstanding impairments in ego functioning. Next, the B and F cases show the temporary deterioration of some ego functions resulting from role transition and traumatic crises in individuals whose previous level of ego functioning was good. Finally, the case of Mrs. D illustrates the complex interplay between an acute medical crisis and longstanding characterologic patterns.

THE J CASE

Mr. J, a thirty-year-old Catholic Italian-American, sought help because he felt that his life was "going nowhere." Several months earlier he had returned to college after a ten-year hiatus to complete a business degree.

While he had not done well academically previously, he nevertheless registered for three courses and also accepted a full-time job as a shipping clerk in a manufacturing company in order to support himself. He worked 8:00 A.M. to 4:00 P.M. on the job every day and attended classes in a nearby city three nights a week from 7:00 to 10:00 P.M. He participated actively in class initially but then became withdrawn, hostile, or sarcastic when his comments were ignored by the professor. After a few weeks he had difficulties studying and fell behind. He watched television, smoked marijuana, over-ate, and was easily distracted by friends who wanted to socialize. He felt depressed and worthless. Nevertheless, he fantasized about getting all A's and was surprised and angry when he failed his midterms. At work Mr. J initially invested a great deal, as he liked his boss and the family atmosphere. When he did not receive the recognition he felt he deserved, he began to oversleep and came late on multiple occasions. He became angered when his boss spoke with him about his lateness, feeling that the boss "had it in for him" since Mr. J worked much harder than others who came to work on time. Before his final exams Mr. J had an argument with his boss and quit his job. Not having enough money to support himself, he then dropped out of college.

Mr. J also is concerned about other difficulties in his life. Separated from his wife for fifteen months after a turbulent four-year relationship, Mr. J still clings to her for companionship yet becomes furious with her when she berates him for his difficulties. Mr. J resents the fact that his wife is not taking care of their one-year-old son properly but rarely sees him, nor does he contribute financial support. Mr. J says he has no intention of reconciling with his wife. He dates occasionally, but women seem to give him the brushoff when he becomes possessive early in the relationship. Mr. J responds to their rejection by berating himself, withdrawing into mindless activity, or spending time with his wife.

Mr. J is the oldest son of Italian immigrants. He describes them as self-absorbed, concerned with appearances, unsuccessful financially, and dependent on others. Mr. J was the product of a normal pregnancy and was a healthy baby, although a finicky eater. He does not recall any warmth in his family relationships. He talked and walked early but wet his bed intermittently until he was nine years old. He used to play by himself, feeling lonely and cut off from his parents; he cannot remember that his parents ever played with him. He often daydreamed and play-acted scenes of being loved and admired. He experienced his mother as unreachable and his father as hypercritical, ill-tempered, sarcastic, and ignorant. He resents the attention received by his brothers when they were born and feels that his father favored them over Mr. J. Mr. J attended a small Catholic school, where he liked some of the more kindly nuns and hated others. He earned reasonably good grades, but his father would become verbally and physically abusive if Mr. J did not receive A's. Mr. J then attended a somewhat impersonal and less strict public high school in which he performed erratically, doing well in some courses in which he liked the teachers and barely passing others because of not studying. Mr. J had few friends. He attributes this to his being overweight, a problem that he has had intermittently in his life, as he has always turned to food for comfort. Mr. J attended a local college sporadically, finally dropping out at the beginning of his fourth year to become an actor. While he took acting lessons and appeared in some small parts, Mr. J has not pursued his acting career intensively. He supports himself financially by performing odd jobs requiring a good deal of skill, which comes easily to him. While he views himself as giving in relationships, Mr. J continually feels rejected by both men and women friends. He married his wife after knowing her for three weeks because she was the first woman who seemed sexually attracted to him. Their marriage was problematic from the beginning. Mrs. J worked, and her income often was their main means of financial support. Mr. J describes her as quite demanding, critical, and rejecting. He wanted to leave early in the marriage but was too frightened of being alone. He feels that she "tricked" him into her pregnancy. He fled the relationship, fearing he would become trapped forever. Mr. J sees his parents weekly and still fights with them when they seem not to appreciate him or when they act "stupid." He enjoys his relationship with one younger brother who looks up to him. A recent disappointment was his parents' refusal to help him financially when he wanted to return to school, despite the fact that their economic situation had improved considerably. He feels entitled to their help, whereas their main concern appears to be his getting a job that ensures him a good pension. Mr. J still seeks approval from both his parents and his wife. Mr. J's friendships are superficial. He spends time with unemployed actors whom he feels "put him down" for his going back to school and working at a full-time nontheatrical job.

Discussion. Mr. J is having difficulty in all of his current life roles: student, worker, husband, father, and son. He attains little gratification in these roles and has problems coping with their demands. They generate stress that overwhelms him and leads to maladaptive behavior. Mr. J also is having trouble coping with the age thirty transitional stage of development in which a man seeks to alter or expand his previous life structure. He feels the inner pressure to do so but cannot move toward his goals successfully. Mr. J also has problems with intimacy and generativity.

While wanting close relationships, he is unable to maintain them, is self-absorbed, and does not take an active role in giving to his son or to others.

While it is clear that Mr. J experiences multiple stresses stemming from his current life roles and developmental tasks, his current problems seem related as much to impairments in ego functioning and to developmental difficulties and dynamics as to the current stresses themselves. Mr. J's judgment is problematic. He did not anticipate the stresses of returning to school after such a long absence, working at a full-time job for the first time, and commuting. He overloaded his schedule, did not allow any time for himself, and did not build on any supports to help him study. He did not consider the negative consequences of actions such as coming late to work, not studying, quitting his job, visiting his parents, seeing his wife, and so on. Such difficulties appear to have occurred at other times in Mr. J's life, as evidenced by his sudden marriage, his wife's pregnancy, and his dropping out of high school.

Mr. J's problems in judgment are linked to his impulsivity. He shows difficulties in restraining the urge to discharge his impulses immediately and resorts to food, drugs, and mindless activities to assuage his feelings of anxiety, depression, and loneliness. Again, such difficulties appeared earlier in Mr. J's life. It must be noted, however, that while Mr. J does engage in behavior that undermines him, he is not so impulse-ridden as to threaten his life, his physical well-being, or the lives of others.

Mr. J's common defenses and coping mechanisms are somewhat rigid and maladaptive. He turns his anger at others onto himself, becoming depressed. He rarely takes responsibility for his own role in creating problems (with his wife, employer, parents, friends) and blames others. He often denies important aspects of his own life, as evidenced by his continuing to believe he would get all A's even if he didn't study. He resorts to flight when he is frustrated, as in quitting his job, school, the marriage, and so on. There is some suggestion of a defensive idealization of authority figures such as his employer and wife and then a devaluation of them when they frustrate him. Likewise he seems to hold two contradictory images of himself simultaneously without their influencing one another. He views himself as unworthy on the one hand and quite entitled on the other. While Mr. J's capacity to test reality seems intact, his defenses distort his perceptions (of others' motives, for example), and he does not always act in accord with objective reality. Mr. J also tends to regress under stress and to engage in fantasies when reality is not going well, as evidenced by his preoccupation with obtaining success and approval while he does not do the work necessary to achieve either.

Mr. J's relationships with others reflect his yearning for approval, recognition, and validation rather than a mature give and take or concern for others as individuals. When others do not respond as he wishes, Mr. J feels rejected and frustrated, and turns on the very people he needs. Likewise he lacks a realistically based sense of self-esteem and competence. His sense of himself fluctuates as a function of the responses he gets from others.

While having good intellectual capacities with no obvious impairments in his cognitive and thinking processes, Mr. J cannot fulfill his potential. He cannot sustain his involvement in school or work for their own sake. He cannot move toward his goals in an unambivalent, nonconflicted manner.

While Mr. J is thirty chronologically, he still seems to be "stuck" developmentally in late adolescence and has not consolidated a positive identity, as evidenced by his inability to commit himself vocationally, establish goals, emancipate himself psychologically from his family of origin, achieve some semblance of continuity and sameness within himself, or love and give to others. He searches for someone to become, but his efforts to be different from his family conflict with his need for their love and approval. He is unable to be his own man. This struggle affects all areas of his life, as he seems to create his family in everyone he meets and continues to experience himself as worthless and unlovable as he did with his parents. Mr. J's failure to achieve a stable identity suggests earlier developmental difficulties for which there is evidence in the history. The early frustrations, rejections, and assaults to his self-esteem and the absence of a nurturing and empathic parenting environment that valued Mr. J and supported his independence set the stage for later difficulties. The most important of these are his difficulties with self-esteem regulation, which makes him so dependent on others for validation, and his difficulty coping with his rage when frustrated.

Mr. J has had few supports to bolster his efforts to make something of his life. His parents' value system and life-style do not offer him a model to emulate. Further, they give him negative feedback for pursuing an education, as do his friends and wife. Because he is so dependent on others for approval, this dampens Mr. J's motivation to succeed. The lack of structure provided by the college Mr. J attended and its competitive atmosphere also contributed negatively to his ability to cope, since he lacks internal discipline and a sense of competence. The rivalrous and intense family atmosphere of his job also fueled his conflicts about needing love and recognition. The financial necessity of having to work while in school added to the pressures on him.

Mr. J is motivated to better himself. Despite his academic and work failures he wants to keep trying. He is intelligent, energetic, healthy, and honest. Despite his hypersensitivity to rejection and his frequent bouts of worthlessness he continues to reach out to others and at times feels he can succeed. When he does study he learns easily, and when he works he applies himself and does a good job. While his relationships are turbulent, his wife, parents, and friends remain concerned about him. Despite his problems with internal discipline he is able to function better with structure. He needs approval to keep working, but when he gets it he is able to perform better. He can control his impulses to some extent and can correct distorted perceptions he has of himself and others. He is able to support himself financially in various ways and still is at an age where he has personal and professional options.

In summary it can be seen that Mr. J's problems reflect not only difficulties in mastering current life roles and developmental tasks but also longstanding problems in ego functioning and developmental arrests. These impair his ability to cope effectively with current stresses, particularly in the absence of environmental supports. He does show certain inner and outer resources, however, that can be mobilized in the interventive process.

This tentative assessment suggests that an interventive plan that aims solely at reinforcing Mr. J's motivation to better himself and that mobilizes him to go back to school will not result in Mr. J's ability to maintain his achievements and "get his life together." Such an approach at least must be accompanied by efforts to help Mr. J identify the characteristic behavioral patterns that interfere with his ability to cope effectively, to help mobilize his motivation to work on learning new and more adaptive ways of coping, and to help him restructure his environment in ways that are more nurturing of his ego capacities. Because of his developmental deficits and pervasive and longstanding characterological difficulties, ego-building and ego-modifying procedures will be important. These will be discussed in detail in Chapter 8.

THE R CASE

Ms. R, a twenty-two-year-old Jewish woman, sought help because of increasing anxiety that was affecting her work life. Several months earlier she became acutely anxious anticipating the drive to school on her first day of teaching. She called a neighbor, who also worked at the school, to drive her there. In the ensuing weeks, she continued to be unable to drive by herself but was able to conduct her classes and meet her other responsibilities. She felt fearful at faculty meetings, was worried that other teachers did not like her, and tended to isolate herself at lunchtime or on breaks. Ms. R also is unhappy with other aspects of her life. She lives with her mother, with whom she often is embroiled in conflicts over the latter's expectations that Ms. R do household chores, that she not stay out late, and that she let Mrs. R know where she is at all times. Ms. R has no plans for moving out, as she feels this would not be acceptable to her mother, and besides she feels comfortable at home. Ms. R dates a man whom she sees once a week. While he wants to see Ms. R more often, she feels he is not sensitive to her and wants to date others. At the same time she has trouble mobilizing herself to go out and socialize since she has no one to go with her. She has few friends, not having become close to anyone in college and having lost touch with others from her past. Ms. R is intelligent, but her lack of confidence makes her appear overly tentative and cautious. She fantasizes about traveling but seldom goes anywhere. She likes going to the movies with her boyfriend and double-dating with his friends but often feels left out in conversation. Ms. R easily becomes depressed. At times she feels resentful of her boyfriend, mother, brother, co-workers, and friends but has difficulty expressing her anger. She is plagued by doubts as to whether her anger is justified. Her resentment revolves around the feeling that others never make any effort to be sensitive to her needs. She yearns to be close to others yet always feels distant. Ms. R always showed difficulty starting new undertakings. She cried for months when she began kindergarten, and her mother accompanied her to school until she was nine. She attended camp one summer but came home after a few weeks feeling anxious and upset. She experienced nausea and headaches when starting high school and felt out of place with her peers for some time. As a small child she remembers either being in the company of her mother when the latter would go shopping or do other chores, or being home alone playing by herself. Her father worked long hours. Her mother, a homebody and a dependent woman, was quite close to her family of origin, around which her social life revolved. She is quite traditional in her views as to the role of women, particularly daughters, and feels that Ms. R should not leave home until she marries and should be her assistant in their household. Ms. R remembers little real closeness with her parents, who were in their mid-forties when she was born. Her brother, who is eight years older, was a stranger to her. Ms. R felt quite different from other children when she attended school. She was babyish, was teased a lot, and could not perform as adeptly as the others, although testing done at the time revealed no impairments in her capacities. At home too, Ms. R had difficulties completing tasks quickly and remembers her frustration when her mother grabbed things out of her hands and did not let her finish. She always has yearned for close friends but easily feels rejected or controlled by others. Her father died when she was sixteen, and while she grieved to some extent, she does not miss him. She went to college because it was expected of her and became a teacher because it seemed that she would be able to get a job. She imagines she would like to get married and have children. Ms. R acknowledges that she does not experience her emotions, nor does she feel much enthusiasm or pleasure.

Discussion. Ms. R, at twenty-two, is in a transitional period in which she is entering the adult world and needs to carve out a new life structure. That she is experiencing anxiety in assuming her first real job, which involves moving from the role of student to one of worker, should be no surprise. The degree of anxiety she is experiencing, however, seems disproportionate to the degree of objective stress in her present situation. In fact, her history reveals repeated difficulties at times of increased demands for autonomy and independence. Ms. R's characteristic initial responses to such stress are to become more dependent, childish, fearful, passive, and withdrawn. Thus, this new adulthood transition appears to be stirring up old conflicts and old ways of responding to them. Further, while Ms. R has been able to accommodate to new situations eventually, her characteristic patterns of relating to the world tend to revolve around avoidance, dependency, low self-esteem and confidence, fearfulness, inability to assert herself, and overcontrol of her feelings and impulses. This is evidenced by her difficulties in reaching out and becoming close to others despite her wishes for intimacy, her difficulties in becoming her own person independent of her mother, her anxiety in new situations, the inhibition of her feelings of anger, and her preoccupation with feeling left out and uncared for. At this point in her life, when increased autonomy, emancipation from family, testing of new relationships, and increased capacity for intimacy are important issues, it is likely that Ms. R will be hampered in mastering her adult developmental tasks as a result of previous difficulties.

It can be inferred from the history that Ms. R's parents were emotionally unavailable to her on the one hand but that her mother in particular was hovering on the other. It is likely that Ms. R had early difficulties both in feeling sufficiently close to her mother and in being able to separate and individuate from her without fear and guilt. Ms. R may equate independence and autonomy with being abandoned by her mother. Without a sound internal sense of her mother, any effort toward increased autonomy may stir up her abandonment fears and guilt for leaving her mother. At the same time Ms. R's lack of experience with successful individuation and her early sense of rejection robbed her of a sense of mastery of the world and increased her fearfulness and lack of a sense of competence. Further, Ms. R's tendency to subordinate her wishes and feelings to those of others is evident in her passivity and overt compliance.

At the same time Ms. R has significant areas of autonomous functioning, in contrast to Mr. J. Ms. R, for example, has been able to use her intellectual capacities to advantage, has finished college, is embarking on a career, and is able to teach despite her massive anxiety. She has no difficulties with judgment, reality testing, or impulsivity. In fact, she is overcontrolled. Her defenses are at a higher level and do not distort reality greatly, although they contribute to Ms. R's being out of touch with herself. She rationalizes—"I can't meet men because I have no one to go places with." She uses reaction formation—"I can't move out of my house because I'm comfortable at home." She turns her resentment at others onto herself and becomes depressed. She represses intense feelings of anger, for example, but also uses isolation of affect so that it's hard to know what she really feels.

Ms. R is motivated to become more independent. She is angry at herself for her inability to be more assertive and autonomous. She is aware of some of the patterns that inhibit her ability to get what she wants. Like Mr. J, Ms. R is encountering difficulties in mastering adulthood roles and developmental tasks because of earlier difficulties that have been stimulated by current stresses. In contrast to Mr. J, however, Ms. R has had more successes and has better ego functioning in many areas. Further, she is able to identify, and is motivated to change, many of her dysfunctional patterns.

This tentative assessment suggests two possible though not mutually exclusive directions for intervention. Because Ms. R has had similar difficulties in the past that she has been able to deal with eventually, it should be possible to help her cope with her present situation more effectively by supporting her ability to succeed in this situation and by helping her to explore the fears she has about issues of autonomy and abandonment. Her difficulties, however, also reflect developmental arrests that interfere with Ms. R's functioning in many areas of life and leave her vulnerable to repeated difficulties at later points when separation–individuation issues resurface. Thus, intervention might be directed at helping Ms. R to master these earlier developmental issues in order to strengthen her ego.

THE B CASE

Mrs. B was fifty-three when her mother, a self-sufficient seventy-three-year-old who was visiting from another city, went into heart failure in Mrs. B's presence. The paramedics arrived within minutes of being called. They were able to revive the old woman and transported her to a nearby hospital. For the next week Mrs. B felt as though she was walking in a dream. No one around her seemed real. When she spoke with doctors at the hospital, her voice and theirs seemed far away. She couldn't believe that her mother might die or become bedridden. A highly responsible and well-organized individual who had worked at the same position for eight years, she forgot to call her employer to tell him she would not be at work. When he needed information from her about specific tasks on which she was working, Mrs. B could barely focus on remembering the essential details. While there were many questions she thought of asking the doctor, she was unable to do so. Likewise, while there was a good deal of her mother's business to take care of, Mrs. B was immobilized and felt useless, helpless, and confused. She was fearful of going outside. With the support of solicitous friends and her thirty-year-old son, on whom she became quite dependent during this period, Mrs. B began to cope somewhat better over the next few weeks and returned to work. Her employer was supportive and patient with Mrs. B's difficulty in concentrating. During this time she easily became overwhelmed and tearful. Her mother's condition did not improve markedly, and Mrs. B had trouble thinking about impending decisions that had to be made about where her mother should live and what additional assistance she would need. At the same time she could not consider the possibility that her mother might die or live on severely impaired. She was referred to a hospital social worker for support and help with discharge planning. Soon afterward her mother died, and Mrs. B felt devastated. Mrs. B is an only child and has no living aunts or uncles on her mother's side. When Mrs. B's father died when she was eight, her mother went to work to support them both. Although poor before and after her father died, Mrs. B remembers many good times and a close family life. Mrs. B was a good student, had many friends, and was highly conscientious and responsible. Like her mother, she was cheerful and optimistic, if not a bit of a "goody-goody." Her mother dated other men but did not remarry until Mrs. B herself married at twenty. Mr. and Mrs. B raised one son, who currently is married, works as an accountant, and lives in the suburbs. Mrs. B likes her daughter-in-law, sees her and her son once a month, and talks to her son weekly. She is looking forward to the birth of her first grandchild in several months. She has had a difficult time adjusting to three significant events in her life: her son's departure for the army and Vietnam in 1969, after which she returned to work; her husband's sudden death in 1974; and her mother's retirement to Florida in 1976. Nevertheless, she always has maintained a stiff upper lip and has looked on the brighter side of life. She also feels lucky to have good friends, a devoted son, and a mother who always was there for her emotionally.

Discussion. Mrs. B is a woman whose ego appears to be overwhelmed by the acute stress of her mother's illness. This stress is accompanied by alterations in Mrs. B's autonomous functioning, thought processes, sense of self, synthetic functioning, and sense of competence. She also shows some regression (increased dependency needs and helplessness) and denial (inability to take in the implications of her mother's condition). In sharp contrast to the two cases presented earlier, Mr. J and Ms. R, there is no indication of difficulties related to life role, developmental tasks, or, more important, ego deficits or earlier developmental difficulties. Thus we see an individual who has demonstrated good functioning in and received gratification from her major life roles, past and present, and whose ego functioning has enabled her to lead a life in keeping with her capacities. While she has shown some diminished functioning at points of stress involving separation and loss, Mrs. B nevertheless has regained her equilibrium at these times with the help of her inner coping capacities and external supports, of which her mother has been quite important. The possible death or long-term disability of her mother was very threatening to Mrs. B in the light of their close relationship and the role her mother has played in her life. There is no indication from the history, however, that would suggest that she will not be able to cope with this stress as she has dealt with others in her life, particularly since she still has many external supports on which to draw (sympathetic employer, friends, son, daughter-in-law, and expected grandchild). At the same time the death of her mother, her only parent since she was eight, will require not only a mourning process but one in which Mrs. B will need to come to terms with being an orphan and her own parent. While Mrs. B may be able to undergo a successful mourning process without intervention, her pain may be eased and the length of the acute mourning shortened by a contact that would help her to ventilate, encourage her continued functioning, and decrease her sense of aloneness. This might be important at this time because of the magnitude of her loss and the fact that her mother, who played a prime supportive role in the past, now is the one who is gone.

THE F CASE

Ms. F was twenty-one when she graduated from a small nursing school near her family home in a small town and moved to the city to take a job at a large voluntary hospital. Having lived in a dormitory previously, she was excited at the prospect of living alone in a small rented apartment near the hospital. Aside from one other nurse who also moved to the city, Ms. F knew no one in her new environment. She liked her job but soon became unusually tired and had difficulty concentrating. After work she returned to her apartment exhausted and went to sleep early, not going out. On her days off from work she did her chores but seldom ventured out at night alone, because of crime in the area. She felt more lonely than ever before in her life, although speaking on the telephone to friends and family at home improved her mood. She seemed to be learning the routine at her new job but felt incompetent for the first time in her life. She gave herself pep talks as she knew her family would in order to keep up her spirits. At times she berated herself for not taking hold better. She considered returning home but was determined to succeed, although she comforted herself with the fact that her parents would be supportive whatever her decision. She also considered asking the head nurse for help but thought she would think her babyish. One day her head nurse reprimanded her for a minor error. Ms. F burst out crying and asked a coworker to tell the head nurse that she was ill and had to go home. She then felt ashamed that she had "run away." The next day she returned to work and confided what she was experiencing to the head nurse. The head nurse suggested that Ms. F move into a local nurses' residence during this transition period. While she needed some convincing that such a move was not indicative of her failure to be independent, Ms. F agreed. Almost immediately she felt less desperate. While still frightened about her ability to cope, she felt more able to continue to try. She also sought help from the employee health clinic at the recommendation of the head nurse, and she was referred to a social worker. Prior to her move to the city, Ms. F had lived in the small, close-knit town where she had grown up. She enjoyed good relationships with family and friends, and her teachers were encouraging of her abilities.

She was a good student and was active in school activities. She always wanted to be a nurse, and her family encouraged her. Both parents are of Protestant background and attended church regularly. Her mother worked part time in her father's small business. While somewhat traditional in their values, they try to keep up with the times. Ms. F has two siblings, a brother eight years older, and a sister five years older. Both are married and living in the vicinity, though they went to out-of-town colleges. Her brother is a pharmacist and her sister a homemaker who plans to go back to teaching part time next year. Ms. F wanted to go to an out-of-town nursing school, but economic reversals in the family prevented this. She wants eventually to return to the area in which she grew up to settle, but she hoped to spend some time on her own, as did her siblings. The only experience she had previously in being away from home was during several summers when she attended a music camp in New England. She always adjusted well and remembers those times with pleasure.

Ms. F felt overwhelmed when she moved to the city that she had only visited previously. It, as well as the hospital, seemed enormous, impersonal, and chaotic. Her responsibilities were staggering. She had never seen so many poor, ill, and injured people at one time. Nor was she familiar with the dialect, idioms, and language spoken by many of the patients, who included blacks and Hispanics as well as Caucasians. She felt out of place in her new environment and worried that she would make a serious mistake or not be good enough to keep her position. At the same time she had never failed or given up before and was determined to succeed.

Discussion. Ms. F is having difficulty coping with her role change from student to worker, her developmental transition from late adolescent to young adult, and her geographic move from a small, close-knit environment with many supports to large, impersonal, and unfamiliar surroundings. Like Mrs. B and in contrast to Mr. J and Ms. R, however, there is no evidence that earlier developmental difficulties or ego impairments are contributing to her current difficulties. Rather it appears that Ms. F has shown reasonably good ego functioning and has mastered previous developmental stages, although it is important to note that her capacity to cope with stress had not been tested prior to her recent move. In fact her history reflects an absence of traumatic life events that has fostered Ms. F's personality development. Thus the stresses Ms. F faces currently seem related to the fact that her impetus toward growth and increased autonomy has resulted in her leaving a comfortable niche to enter a new and demanding environment without her usual sources of support. It is necessary to manage awesome work responsibilities, to make new friends, and to maintain a sense of self-esteem in the absence of external feedback and familiar surroundings.

At the same time Ms. F brought very high expectations of herself with her to her new life. The value she places on self-sufficiency and perfect performance suggests an intolerance of her realistic dependency needs and fallibility. She views needing support as babyish and needing to learn or making mistakes as indicative of failure. Her inability to live up to these expectations immediately led to lowered self-esteem and anxiety, which disrupted her functioning and made her feel less competent. Her difficulties in reaching out for help did not allow her to get more support. Ms. F has many inner strengths and external resources to fall back on, however. Even in her new environment she has been able to elicit support from her head nurse, and there are resources (housing, counseling) that can help her mobilize her inner capacities so that she can cope more effectively with her life transitions.

Ms. F might benefit considerably from a period of short-term intervention aimed at helping her to master this important time of her life. It would help to provide her with a support that could enhance her self-esteem, help her to identify activities and resources in her environment, decrease her isolation, and help her to lower her unrealistically high expectations of herself.

THE D CASE

Mrs. D, a divorced fashion consultant, was forty-eight when a malignant tumor of the breast necessitated a radical mastectomy. All of the cancer appeared to be removed, and Mrs. D's initial reactions to the surgery seemed unusually good on the surface. When by herself, however, Mrs. D would burst into tears and become inconsolable. She was irritable with her daughters, did not want other visitors, and did not cooperate with the nurses. When it was suggested that she attend a therapeutic self-help group for mastectomy patients, Mrs. D refused because she did not want to expose her ugliness to others. The doctor's attempts to discuss the need for preventive treatment as well as the devices that would improve her physical appearance were met with a nonchalant, almost blasé attitude. After such discussions Mrs. D despaired or directed her anger at members of the nursing staff, who responded by withdrawing from her. She was referred to the social worker for reasons that were unclear.

All of Mrs. D's life her appearance was a focus of others' attention. As a child she was told she was a beauty. The only memories she has of her mother's interest in her were related to the latter's dressing her and buying her clothes. Otherwise she remembers coming home every day to clean the house, because her mother left it a mess. She was embarrassed to have friends in unless it was clean. She often would find her mother asleep and would try unsuccessfully to get her to wake up. At night her mother would go out and leave Mrs. D. Mrs. D's father left home when she was five. Her mother describes him as a drunk and a womanizer, and he never made efforts to see Mrs. D. Mrs. D was an excellent student all through school and was more like an adult than a child. She was a self-reliant, conscientious, well-disciplined person with high standards for herself and others. She was a cheerleader and very much involved in school activities generally. At times in her life when she feels depressed she becomes very active, and this relieves her. While she was extremely popular with boys, girls shied away from her, which Mrs. D now understands as envy of her looks and popularity. At the time she couldn't understand this, because despite her popularity and beauty she felt alone, unattractive, and self-conscious about her appearance. Her relationships with friends were superficial and characterized by Mrs. D's inability to confide in anyone or to let people get close to her emotionally. She tended to befriend less popular girls who felt chosen to be Mrs. D's friend and who looked up to her. Mrs. D went to college on scholarship. After graduation she became a model, though she hated being looked at and had difficulty competing with other women. Out of financial desperation she married an exceptionally handsome, affluent though irresponsible man whose alcoholism became more apparent after their marriage. Mrs. D stopped modeling at his urging and had two children in quick succession. Mr. D ran away with his secretary after the birth of the second daughter. Despite Mr. D's obvious problems, Mrs. D feels that if she had been more attractive to Mr. D he would not have left her. She raised her daughters with the help of child support, a well-meaning housekeeper, and a good-paying job. She entered the fashion field, worked her way up, and has been employed in a very responsible position for a number of years. Her daughters, ages twenty-one and nineteen, have had their share of difficulties. Both have extremely low self-esteem and are insecure socially. The oldest has been heavily involved in drugs but is doing better recently. The youngest has had psychiatric help because of suicidal impulses but seems to be calmer currently. Mrs. D dates but has refused many offers of marriage. She has not felt that any man has loved her for herself.

Currently Mrs. D is able to take in the implications of her condition at times, but she then feels completely ugly, unworthy, estranged from her body, and guilty for misdeeds that she cannot pinpoint. She feels as if she has no identity, present or future. She feels aware of her age, of her possible death, and of being unable to control life. She becomes panicky and helpless and feels that the carpet has been pulled out from under her. She feels that she has nothing left. Finding this state terribly painful, Mrs. D adopts an arrogant, haughty, angry, and self-reliant attitude in which she does not let anyone get close to her. While ventilating her concerns to the social worker over a time helped to relieve the intensity of Mrs. D's upset and lessened the degree of her uncooperativeness with the staff and her treatment, which was interfering with her physical recovery, Mrs. D's feelings of devastation continued. Even though there was no reason she could not work after her recovery, Mrs. D was unable to mobilize herself to return to her job. She felt that she was not the same person she had been before and did not want to "make others beautiful."

Discussion. The disfiguring surgery that Mrs. D has undergone and the diagnosis of cancer produced a massive crisis for Mrs. D. The assault to her body mobilized severe denial, which has hampered her positive participation in her treatment and rehabilitation. It has been accompanied by efforts to control others, as manifested by her uncooperativeness and success in making others around her feel helpless. Her regression is evidenced by her withdrawal from others. She experiences an inner feeling of badness and ugliness. At the same time her anger is overwhelming her, and she strikes out at others. Her judgment is so impaired that she does not act on her own behalf. She has lost a solid sense of herself and of her future.

Such responses may be present initially in many individuals undergoing similar stresses, who gradually cope more adaptively with these situations. In Mrs. D's case, however, there is little indication that she is coping effectively. The acute stress has triggered a maladaptive response because it has disrupted the mainstays of Mrs. D's adaptation to the world—her physical appearance and her sense of control. Both of these seem critical to her identity and are the major factors in her evaluation of herself. There is evidence in the history that Mrs. D has not had a sound sense of herself as a lovable person able to enjoy close and gratifying relationships with others. While on the one hand she always has felt ugly, her appearance was her main route to obtaining positive feedback from her environment. It is also the factor she focuses on in understanding why bad things have happened to her. Thus it is likely that she experienced the surgery as robbing her of her positive self on the one hand, while reinforcing her bad self on the other. Mrs. D's reactions are suggestive of very early developmental arrests, particularly around the evolution of her attachment to significant others, the evolution of her sense of self, and capacity for self-esteem regulation. The absence of nurturing figures or anyone on whom she could rely or who valued her for herself seems critical. Her self-sufficient adaptation was very important to her psychological survival. This too has been threatened by her illness in that her omnipotence has been challenged.

While Mrs. D has two daughters who might support her emotionally during this time, her relationship with them appears strained and does not reflect much closeness, past or present. While Mrs. D has a good job to return to, in her mind it is tied up to the whole issue of her lost attractiveness and thus is very conflictual for her.

While Mrs. D has shown many strengths in her life, her tenuous sense of self has been devastated by the crisis. Can she learn to value herself differently? Can she see a future if she is not perfect? Can she overcome a sense of being "defective?" Can she transcend her bitterness? These are critical questions.

There is little evidence that she will have the flexibility to adapt positively to the crisis because of her lack of inner resources and outer supports. Work appears to be a possible route to her recovery since it has been a source of esteem, but it will have to become "conflict-free" before it can be used as a support on which to build.

In summary, Mrs. D is a woman whose ego is overwhelmed as a result of current acute stresses but who also shows maladaptive characterologic patterns and developmental difficulties that complicate her reaction to the current crisis. It is doubtful that her emotional rehabilitation can be achieved without extensive help. Her depression and rage, resulting from a massive injury to her sense of self, must be worked through. Because her sense of self was so brittle before the surgery, intervention will need to deal with her profound problem in self-esteem regulation and the ways Mrs. D has characteristically coped all through her life. There is a suicide potential in this case if Mrs. D cannot be helped to deal with her rage and hopelessness and find a reason for living.

DATA COLLECTION

SOURCES OF DATA

The client's self-report is the most direct source of information regarding his or her current and past functioning. Other important sources of data on which to base an assessment are (1) the accounts of relatives and significant others; (2) collateral contacts, e.g., with school, work, or social agency personnel; (3) official records from hospitals, schools, other helping professionals, and so on; (4) the client's behavior within the helping relationship or agency setting; and (5) psychological testing.

Often verbal clients with relatively intact ego functioning are able to give the most accurate and detailed information about themselves, their interactions with others, and their life circumstances. A client's seeming "intactness" can be misleading, however, since people's accounts of themselves and others may reflect selective distortions, misperceptions, contradictions, and omissions. This issue becomes increasingly important the more ego deficits and developmental impairments exist, because chronic maladaptive defenses and problems distort perceptions of the self and others. In clients who show severe ego disorganization, thought processes and capacity for reality testing may be so impaired as to make coherent communication difficult. For all of these reasons it is important to consider obtaining data from more than one source in evaluating the client's functioning.

SHORT-TERM VERSUS EXTENDED INTERVENTION

While assessment should determine whether intervention is short-term or extended, the nature of current social work practice in many settings often reverses this process. Thus, whether short-term or long-term intervention is available determines the nature of the assessment process. The expected duration of interventive efforts, however, should not alter the focus of assessment. It is as critical for a medical social worker in an acute care setting to evaluate whether the client's maladaptive response to illness is embedded in poor ego functioning and developmental difficulties as it is for a psychiatric social work colleague offering extended service to evaluate similar issues in a client presenting with an identity disturbance. Likewise, it is important for both workers to understand the nature and extent of their clients' environmental supports.

The main issue is how to gather sufficient data upon which to make a sophisticated ego assessment in situations where time pressure requires an expedited data collection process. Others have suggested that crisis intervention and short-term approaches require a highly knowledgeable and skillful practitioner who is able (1) to focus actively and selectively on key areas of a client's past and current functioning that are likely to yield the most important data for the purposes of assessment; (2) to make and test tentative hypotheses about the client's level of functioning and reasons for his or her difficulties; (3) to plan intervention based on less detailed and less clear-cut evidence and formulations than might be collected were there less time pressure; and (4) to revise his or her thinking and approach quickly and flexibly in the light of new and contradictory data.[5]

It should be noted, however, that while there is more leisure to refine and readjust one's assessment as new information is accumulated in extended intervention, the importance of having a working assessment early in the contact is crucial. This helps to avoid vagueness in the formulation of goals and in the selection of appropriate foci.

SUMMARY

This chapter has proposed five questions that the practitioner can use as a guide in the assessment process. These questions concern the degree to which the client's problem stems from stresses in his or her current life roles and developmental stages, from situational stress or a traumatic event, from ego impairments or developmental difficulties or dynamics, or from a lack of environmental resources or fit between inner capacities and outer circumstances. They also focus on the internal and external resources that may be mobilized to improve the client's coping. The chapter also has discussed the importance of multiple sources of data in making an assessment, the relationship between assessment and intervention, and the commonalities between assessment in short-term and extended or long-term intervention.

NOTES

1. For discussion of the assessment process in the psychosocial, problem-solving, and crisis intervention models, see Robert W. Roberts and Robert H. Nee, eds., *Theories of Social Casework* (Chicago: University of Chicago Press, 1970). For a discussion of the life model see Carel B. Germain and Alex Gitterman, *The Life Model of Social Work Practice* (New York: Columbia University Press, 1980).
2. The practitioner has a responsibility to use professional knowledge and expertise to evaluate the client's view of his or her problem and his or her request. Otherwise, as pointed out by Carol Meyer, there is no professional practice. See Carol H. Meyer, "Issues in Clinical Social Work: In Search of a Consensus," in Phyllis Caroff, ed., *Treatment Formulations and Clinical Social Work* (Silver Spring, Md.: National Association of Social Workers, 1982), pp. 19–26.
3. Meyer has underscored the idea that assessment of possible pathology is not an effort to assign fault or responsibility or "to blame the victim." This is an important issue. See *ibid.*, p. 22.
4. In the interests of space, the case examples have been abbreviated. The data presented have been edited to highlight the main points for discussion. It should be kept in mind that the conclusions drawn are tentative, working hypotheses about cases. More detailed information would be needed to confirm or disconfirm these.
5. See, for example, Naomi Golan, *Treatment in Crisis Situations* (New York: Free Press, 1978), and Lydia Rapoport, "Crisis Intervention as a Mode of Brief Treatment," in Roberts and Nee, *Theories of Social Casework*, pp. 265–312.

CHAPTER 8

THE NATURE OF EGO-ORIENTED INTERVENTION

E go psychological concepts guide many different interventive models. While ego-oriented practice is generally associated with casework, it also informs group and family intervention. This chapter will discuss the goals, techniques, and modalities of intervention that are consistent with an ego psychological perspective.

EGO-SUPPORTIVE VERSUS EGO-MODIFYING APPROACHES

Generally ego-oriented approaches can be grouped according to whether their goals are ego-supportive or ego-modifying.[1] Ego-supportive intervention aims at restoring, maintaining, or enhancing the individual's adaptive functioning as well as strengthening or building ego where there are deficits or impairments. In contrast, ego-modifying intervention aims at changing basic personality patterns or structures. In addition to this dual classification, further distinctions can be made according to whether intervention is psychological (direct) or environmental or social (indirect). Ego-supportive intervention tends to rely on both psychological and environmental work, whereas ego-modifying intervention tends to be more psychological.[2] Ego-supportive intervention may be short- or long-term, while ego-modifying intervention tends to be long-term.

Distinctions between ego-supportive and ego-modifying approaches however, are not clear-cut in practice. First, it is possible that efforts to improve adaptive functioning result in qualitative modifications of personality, thus blurring the distinction between the goals of ego support and ego modification. For example, helping an individual to overcome his or her anxiety sufficiently to return to college, perform well, and graduate may not only enhance feelings of competence but also alter his or her basic self-concept so that he or she no longer views him- or herself as a failure. Likewise, an ego-supportive approach with clients who manifest ego deficits may foster developmental mastery that results in a creation of a new personality structure. Second, in reality ego-supportive and ego-modifying approaches are not always easy to differentiate, because practitioners do not use a pure model but often move back and forth between or blend the two approaches in a given case. Third, there are some clients with severe ego deficits and maladaptive patterns who require a modifying approach concurrent with supportive structuring of their external lives through the use of hospitalization, halfway houses, sheltered workshops, or residential schools. Finally, while ego-modifying approaches generally are equated with long-term intervention, ego modification may result from crisis or short-term intervention, as well as from the impact of life events themselves.

Despite the blurring between ego-supportive and ego-modifying approaches, important differences have been identified. The accompanying table summarizes these distinctions.

DIFFERENCES BETWEEN EGO-SUPPORTIVE AND EGO-MODIFYING APPROACHES

Criteria	Ego-supportive	Ego-modifying
Focus of intervention	Current behavior and conscious thoughts and feelings; some selected focus on past	Past and present; conscious, preconscious, and unconscious
Nature of change	Ego mastery; increased understanding; learning and positive reinforcement; emotionally cor-	Insight and conflict resolution

**DIFFERENCES BETWEEN EGO-SUPPORTIVE
AND EGO-MODIFYING APPROACHES** *continued*

Criteria	Ego-supportive	Ego-modifying
	rective experiences, neutralization of conflict; better person-environment fit	
Use of relationship	Experience of the real relationship; positive transference; corrective relationship; worker's relationship with others in client's environment	Understanding of positive and negative transference
Psychological testing	Directive, sustaining, educative, and structured; some reflection	Nondirective, reflective, interpretive
Work with social environment	Environmental modification and restructuring; provision and mobilization of resources; improving conditions	Not emphasized but may be used
Appropriate client populations	Those encountering life transitions, acute or situational crises, or stress; those with ego deficits; those with maladaptive patterns and low anxiety tolerance and impulse control	Those with good ego strength who have maladaptive patterns interfering with optimal functioning; in some cases those with severe maladaptive patterns, defenses, and ego deficits
Duration of intervention	Short-term or long-term	Generally long-term

THE FOCUS OF INTERVENTION

Ego-supportive intervention focuses on the client's current behavior and on his or her conscious thought processes and feelings, although some selected exploration of the past may occur. Generally, however, it is more here-and-now-oriented than is ego-modifying intervention, which focuses additionally on the client's childhood past as well as on his or her preconscious and unconscious conflicts. A here-and-now and reality-oriented focus identifies current stresses on the client; restores, maintains, and enhances the client's conflict-free areas of functioning, adaptive defenses, coping strategies, and problem-solving capacities; and mobilizes environmental supports and resources. It may identify the client's past maladaptive patterns, but it does so in order to enable the client to develop better ways of dealing with inner needs and outer reality within his or her existing personality. In cases where a client's autonomous ego functioning has been disrupted by conflict, ego-supportive intervention identifies the conflict and attempts to diminish its impact on the client's current behavior. In many cases a here-and-now focus is used to strengthen and build ego that may have been impaired as a result of past developmental failures or to help enhance the ego through the mastery of current life crises and transitional stages.

THE NATURE OF CHANGE

In contrast to ego-modifying intervention, which stresses the role of insight into unconscious conflicts and their impact on behavior as fundamental to personality change, ego-supportive approaches aim for changes in an individual's adaptive functioning. Change results from a variety of additional and complementary factors, including (1) the exercise of autonomous ego functioning in the service of mastering new developmental, life transitional, crisis, or other stressful situations; (2) greater understanding of the impact of one's behavior on others; (3) learning and positive reinforcement of new behavior, skills, attitudes, problem-solving capacities, and coping strategies; (4) the utilization of conflict-free areas of ego functioning to neutralize conflict-laden areas; (5) the use of relationships and experiences to correct for previous difficulties and deprivations; and (6) the use of the environment to provide more opportunities and conditions for the use of one's capacities.[3]

THE USE OF RELATIONSHIP

Ego-supportive intervention emphasizes the more realistic rather than transferential aspects of the helping relationship. It relies on the client's ability to perceive and use the relationship with the worker in a nondistorted and benign way rather than as an arena in which he or she plays out the unconscious conflicts from the past. Consequently the worker in an ego-supportive approach encourages the client's accurate perception of the worker as a helping agent rather than as a transference figure. The worker provides a human and genuine experience in the helping relationship. In many instances, however, the worker uses the positive transference and becomes a benign authority or parental figure who fosters the client's phase-appropriate needs and development. In some instances the worker becomes a "corrective" figure to the client. A client may develop intense reactions to the worker of an unrealistic kind even in an ego-supportive approach. Such reactions do need to be worked with, but the aim, in most cases, is to restore the positive relationship rather than to trace the negative reactions back to their original sources in the client's past.[4]

Another important aspect of the use of relationship in an ego-supportive approach is the worker's willingness to use him- or herself outside of the client-worker relationship to function in a variety of roles on behalf of the client. It may be important for the worker to be an advocate or systems negotiator for the client, to meet with members of his or her family, and so on. Because of the significance of the client-worker relationship in the interventive process, it will be discussed more fully in Chapter 9.

PSYCHOLOGICAL TECHNIQUES

Among the psychological techniques used in ego-supportive intervention are those that are more sustaining, directive, educative, and structured, in contrast to those that are more nondirective, reflective, confronting, and interpretive. Hollis (1972:72–88), dissatisfied with the dichotomy between supportive and modifying types of intervention, developed a classification of techniques based on dynamic considerations that she felt offered a more fluid and flexible way of describing intervention. She differentiated six main groups of psychological techniques:

1. Sustaining techniques consisting of sympathetic listening and receptiveness, conveying an attitude of acceptance of the client's worth and uniqueness, and providing reassurance and encouragement.

2. Direct influence consisting of suggestion and advice to the client.
3. Exploration, description, and ventilation, consisting of eliciting the client's subjective and objective feelings and experiences and helping the client to express his or her feelings.
4. Person-situation reflection, consisting of focusing on the client's current situation and relationships. The client is helped in developing (a) better understanding of others or of any other objective situation external to him or her; (b) insight into the nature of his or her behavior and its effects on others; (c) awareness of why he or she behaves in certain ways in specific situations; and (d) his or her evaluation of his or her inner feelings, self-concept, attitudes, values, and so on. Person-situation reflection may involve rational discussion or thinking through of the pros and cons of taking certain actions.
5. Pattern-dynamic reflection, consisting of helping the client to identify and consider his or her pattern of behavior including defenses and their impact. The goal is to help the client to develop greater dynamic understanding of the nature of and reasons for his or her behavior. This may involve the worker's pointing out (confronting) maladaptive, contradictory, but often ego syntonic[5] behavior as well as interpretations of the underlying reasons for it.
6. Developmental reflection, consisting of helping the client to think about the past and the way it is affecting his or her current behavior. As with pattern-dynamic reflection, the goal is to help the client gain greater insight into the dynamics of his or her maladaptive behavior that may stem from irrational feelings and fears, from past conflictual situations, or from developmental arrests.

The first three groups of techniques (sustainment, direct influence, and ventilation) help the client to feel less alone and overwhelmed; diminish anxiety, guilt, depression, anger, and other unpleasant emotions; make problems more manageable; move the client toward appropriate or necessary action that he or she may not be able to take on his or her own; and instill hope, motivation, self-confidence, and self-acceptance. Along with person-situation reflection, these techniques are used extensively in ego-supportive intervention. Pattern-dynamic and developmental reflection arouse anxiety, insofar as they help to make the client aware of his or her maladaptive or irrational behavior, thoughts and feelings. They must be utilized with caution with clients who cannot tolerate anxiety. These techniques are used extensively in ego-modifying approaches.

Important techniques that are not described fully by the Hollis classification but are useful in ego-supportive intervention are:

7. Educative techniques, consisting of providing the client with information essential to functioning in various roles or in negotiating external systems; helping to reflect on the effects of his or her behavior on others; and helping to gain understanding of others' needs and motivations. Educative techniques also involve modeling, role-playing and rehearsal, anticipatory planning, and the promotion of new behavior within the client-worker relationship.

8. Structuring techniques, consisting of partializing problems, focusing intervention on key areas, using time limits flexibly, assigning homework tasks, and planning activities. Many of these techniques have arisen out of crisis-oriented, planned short-term, or task-centered intervention.[6]

WORK WITH THE SOCIAL ENVIRONMENT

Environmental intervention has not been well conceptualized in the social work literature.[7] It is critical, however, to interventive efforts within an ego psychological perspective. For example, it may be important to mobilize resources and opportunities that will enable the individual to use his or her inner capacities. It may be necessary to restructure the environment so that it nurtures or fits better with individual needs and capacities. Environmental work also may be essential to modifying maladaptive patterns within an individual. For example, it may be utilized where the family system is perpetuating, reinforcing, or aggravating a family member's difficulties.

Work with the environment within an ego psychological perspective generally has two main foci:

One can think in terms of treatment through the environment and treatment of the environment. The former makes use of resources and opportunities that exist or are potentially available for the benefit of the client in his total situation. The latter deals with modifications that are needed in order to lessen pressures on or increase opportunities or gratifications that exist [Hollis, 1972: 81–82].

Numerous efforts to classify such intervention have been attempted. For example, Hollis (1972: 82–83) grouped environmental work according to (1) type of resource employed, e.g. social agency, host setting, or an expressive relationship to the client; (2) the type of communication utilized, e.g. sustainment, direct influence, ventilation, or person-situation reflection; and (3) type of role assumed, e.g. provider of a resource, locater of a resource, or mediator.

It can be seen that the view of the social environment most consistent with ego psychological theory sees it as a backdrop or context that impinges on the individual and that can be mobilized, manipulated, restructured, modified, and so on in order to improve the individual's functioning. While there may be limitations to this view,[8] it is a useful conceptualization in many instances.

It can be said however, that, ego psychology did not generate a systematic framework that guides environmental intervention. Further, the skills essential to environmental intervention often were viewed as similar to those needed for psychological intervention. In this connection several authors (Grinnell, Kyte, and Bostwick, 1981) have discussed the various complex roles that have been identified with environmental intervention: activist, lobbyist, bargainer, advocate, mediator, aggressive intervener, broker, ombudsman, enabler, and conferee. Using a problem-solving paradigm, they outline the specific skills involved in what they consider to be the three main roles: broker, mediator, and advocate.

APPROPRIATE CLIENT POPULATIONS

Ego-supportive approaches generally are recommended for two types of clients: (1) those whose characteristic ego functioning is disrupted by current stress and (2) those who show severe and chronic ego deficits. Ego-modifying approaches usually are recommended for (1) those clients with reasonably good ego strength who show maladaptive patterns that interfere with the optimal use of their capacities and (2) selected clients with severe and chronic maladaptive patterns who can tolerate or be helped to tolerate the anxiety associated with ego-modifying procedures. For this second group, interventive efforts often may include the use of hospitalization or other types of environmental structuring.

DURATION OF INTERVENTION

Ego-supportive approaches may be crisis-oriented, short-term, or long-term. This is related to the fact that the individual may benefit from ego support in both acute and chronically stressful life circumstances and from long-term support of efforts aimed at improving selected areas of ego functioning. In contrast, ego-modifying efforts generally are long-term because of the difficulties involved in altering entrenched personality patterns or characteristics.

THE NATURE OF EGO-SUPPORTIVE INTERVENTION

The goals of restoring, maintaining, and enhancing client functioning overlap and often coexist or are used sequentially in the same case. Likewise the means to achieving these goals relies on the same armamentarium of techniques. Despite their overlap and similarities it is useful to consider the somewhat different thrust of each of these goals, because it helps in considering the needs clients bring to the interventive process.

RESTORING CLIENT FUNCTIONING

Ego-restorative efforts help the individual to regain his or her previous level of functioning and thus to return to his or her previous equilibrium. Such efforts are important particularly with clients undergoing stress or crises that disrupt or overwhelm their usual ego functioning temporarily. Often such individuals show reasonably good ego functioning in their precrisis state.

While they eventually may resume their previous level of functioning without intervention, this is not always the case. Some individuals worsen and never achieve their precrisis adaptation. In other instances intervention may help the client function more appropriately and optimally, may diminish anxiety and other unpleasant emotions, and may curtail the duration of the crisis state. Ego-restorative efforts also are important with clients who demonstrate marginal or poor functioning in normal conditions and who undergo a sudden disorganization or deterioration in their functioning. This is exemplified by some schizophrenic clients in the community who develop rapid-onset acute psychotic episodes or who begin to show signs of worsening. In such cases intervention that returns the client to his or her usual level of functioning may prevent hospitalization, self-destructive behavior, further disruptions of social functioning, and the erosion of self-esteem and social supports.

MAINTAINING CLIENT FUNCTIONING

Ego-maintaining efforts enable the individual to continue an optimal level of functioning within the constraints and resources of his or her particular capacities and life situation and thus to maintain equilibrium. Such efforts are important particularly with clients who show chronic difficulties in dealing with the stress of everyday life or with those whose social functioning is threatened by stressful circumstances. Often such individuals' functioning will worsen, or they will suffer greatly without intervention.

ENHANCING CLIENT FUNCTIONING

Ego-enhancing efforts enable the individual to achieve more optimal functioning in selected areas and thus to reach a new equilibrium based on a higher level of functioning. The use of ego-enhancing intervention does not imply that the client necessarily has ego deficits but rather that an improvement or expansion of his or her capacities may be beneficial. For example, such intervention may be used to help individuals master developmental, role, and life transitions in which they must learn new coping skills.

Often the terms "ego-strengthening" and "ego-building" are used to refer to efforts to enhance the ego functioning of clients whose ego deficits hamper their ability to cope effectively. For example, a client who manifests impulsivity when becoming anxious may benefit from experiences in which he or she has the opportunity to practice or test new ways of handling anxiety. Similarly, a client with poor reality testing may be helped to learn how to correct distortions by getting feedback from others. A client who is bombarded by strong emotions that disrupt his or her ability to concentrate may improve functioning through the strengthening of intellectual defenses. Ego-building may entail helping an individual to relive, experience, and master earlier developmental stages and thereby acquire the capacities associated with them for the first time. For example, a client who never obtained object constancy or the ability to make sound judgments may be helped to develop these critical capacities.

It is important to note that the goals of restoring, maintaining, and enhancing client functioning are global. Such goals must be individualized and specified more precisely in a given case. Thus in an ego-supportive approach (and in an ego-modifying approach) the practitioner should indicate whether he or she is directing his or her efforts at enhancing parenting skills, restoring self-esteem, strengthening impulse control, maintaining ability to cope with work stress, or something else. An important aspect of specifying goals involves delineating the criteria for achieving them. Thus it is necessary to consider what would constitute an improvement in parenting skills, impulse control, or whatever. Without such specification of goals and the criteria for achieving them, interventive efforts remain unfocused. Both client and practitioner lack the means for evaluating progress, and research on effectiveness will be hampered.

The following case examples illustrate the nature of ego-supportive intervention. The first two examples (Mrs. G and Mr. K) show individuals who at least initially need to be restored to their previous level of functioning. The cases of Mrs. C and Ms. D illustrate the importance of ego-maintaining efforts. Finally, the last two cases (Ms. F and Ms. M) show efforts to enhance the clients' usual ego functioning.

THE G CASE

Mrs. G, age forty-two, a bookkeeper for fifteen years, is a self-reliant, tightly controlled, somewhat rigid individual who is quite intelligent, hardworking, and perfectionistic. She was referred to the social worker for help in dealing with her daughter's increasing rebelliousness at home and at school. Mrs. G is increasingly critical of her daughter, J, and seems unable to allow her phase-appropriate independence. One month ago Mrs. G left a job she had worked at for eight years, where she was respected highly for her competence. Her new responsibilities are radically different from anything she has done before. She is acutely anxious, feels incompetent, and has difficulty asking for supervisory help. She works long hours in order to teach herself the new system and comes home exhausted, frustrated, and demoralized. She is more irritable and strict with J, and fighting between the two has escalated. The social worker, upon evaluating Mrs. G, concluded that her job change had upset Mrs. G's usual equilibrium, which was based largely on being in control, competent, and respected. Her efforts to restore her sense of well-being have been frustrated, and in order to make herself feel better she has resorted to more controlling behavior at home. This has created additional difficulties with her daughter, however. While the worker thought that Mrs. G would benefit from help in dealing with her daughter's changing needs, it seemed important first to help restore Mrs. G's usual equilibrium. The worker encouraged Mrs. G to express her concerns and feelings about the difficulties she encountered at work and at home and accepted and sympathized with her frustration, loss of security, and loss of self-esteem. The worker helped Mrs. G to identify the stresses stemming from her new and different responsibilities. She helped her to recognize that she was being too hard on, and expecting too much of, herself and that it would take time to learn her new responsibilities. She also helped her to separate her feelings of being a failure and incompetent from the actual reality. The worker validated Mrs. G's ability to learn a new system by reminding her of her previous experiences in mastering difficult and complex tasks. She helped Mrs. G to see that her usual self-reliant form of coping was self-defeating in this situation and made suggestions about better ways of dealing with her work situation. The worker also helped Mrs. G reflect on the relationship between her feeling out of control on her job and her increased efforts to control her daughter at home in order to help herself feel better. After approximately a month Mrs. G began to regain her sense of mastery and competence at work. She became less critical of her daughter, whose behavior improved somewhat. It was then ᵖossible to help Mrs. G begin to explore her relationship with her daughter, whose adolescence and challenging behavior were threatening Mrs. G's need to feel respected and in control.

Discussion. In this example the worker directed her efforts to restoring Mrs. G's self-esteem and ability to cope effectively on the job before she undertook the goal of enhancing Mrs. G's ability to deal with her adolescent daughter's changing needs. The worker focused on the client's here-and-now experiences and on her conscious thoughts and feelings. She used herself to provide a sympathetic, accepting, and permissive relationship in which Mrs. G could ventilate her concerns, lower her high expectations of herself, identify new ways of coping with stress, and identify some of her dysfunctional responses at work and at home. The worker primarily utilized the techniques of sustainment, direct influence, and ventilation, along with some person-situation reflection. Important to the improvement in Mrs. G was the sense of mastery and reinforcement she experienced in being more able to cope with work. This in turn led to diminished pressures at home. The reduction of her anxiety freed Mrs. G, enabling her to look more closely at her relationship difficulties with her daughter. To some extent the relationship with the worker also provided a source of positive feedback and self-esteem for Mrs. G. This first phase of the intervention was short-term, lasting about six weeks.

THE K CASE

Mr. K is a thirty-six-year-old college professor who is recognized as an excellent teacher. Over the past five years he has become more successful professionally and has published numerous articles. He lives with a male friend in a homosexual relationship that has lasted for six years. They get along very well and have a small circle of intimate male and female friends. Both dislike the gay bar scene and tend toward more intellectual pursuits. Mr. K looked forward to being promoted with tenure in his position and felt reasonably content until six months ago, when his parents visited from another city. On the last night of their visit they found fault with the dinner he prepared. Usually quiet and submissive with his family, Mr. K commented on how upset it made him when his parents criticized him. The parents left suddenly in a burst of anger, and Mr. K did not hear from them for weeks until he received a letter from his father. The letter expressed the sentiment that while Mr. K was doing well professionally, he was a "queer" and would never be a success in Mr. and Mrs. K's eyes. Since this episode, Mr. K has been depressed and unable to write. Work feels like drudgery, and he pushes himself to meet his commitments, which he still does very well. He has been more dependent on his lover and friends for moral support. Mr. K knows he is upset because of his parents' visit and his father's letter but he has been unable to pull himself out of his depression. Fearful that his writing block would interfere with his chances for promotion, Mr. K sought help at a gay counseling center. After evaluating Mr. K, the worker concluded that his level of functioning was excellent prior to the incident that triggered old conflicts regarding Mr. K's relationship with his father. Mr. K has never been able to please his father and has struggled in his life to develop and maintain a sense of self-esteem despite feelings of rejection and anger. At some level Mr. K hoped that his professional success would change his father's attitude. The visit thwarted this hope and stirred up Mr. K's rage and underlying doubts about himself. He turned his anger at his father against himself, experienced a lowering of his self-esteem, and his writing, a most valued accomplishment, became associated with this conflict. Instead of experiencing his anger at his father, he punished himself.

The worker helped Mr. K to experience his justifiable anger at his father's attitude and behavior and to get in touch with his disappointment in him. He helped Mr. K to consider his father's limitations rather than blame himself. The worker also helped Mr. K to see that he was punishing himself as well as accepting his father's lifelong negative view of him by his inability to write and pursue his successful career. The worker helped Mr. K to connect his current response to those at other times in his life when he also felt angry at and disappointed with his father. The worker supported all that Mr. K had accomplished in his life without his family's help and helped him to separate his father's rejection of him from the reactions of people close to Mr. K who valued him highly. After about ten weeks Mr. K began to feel better and begin writing again, although it took some time for him to put this episode in perspective. He also began to feel that he had come to terms with his father's limitations and with the likelihood that Mr. K would never be able to win his father's approval and love.

Discussion. In this example, as in the previous one, the worker directed his efforts at restoring Mr. K to his usual level of functioning prior to the visit from his parents. This involved helping Mr. K to overcome his depression resulting from his introjected rage toward his father, to regain his self-esteem, and to return his writing pursuits to the autonomous sphere. As in the G case, the worker supplied a sympathetic and accepting relationship and actively validated the appropriateness of Mr. K's anger at his father and his realistic perception of his father's difficulties. The worker focused on the client's present situation as well as on some aspects or his past relationship with his father. He utilized the techniques of sustainment and ventilation as well as person-in-situation and person-dynamic reflection. To some extent the worker also functioned as a benign parental figure who helped to correct for the rejection and disapproval of Mr. K's father. Again the duration of this phase of the work was short-term. In this example, however, Mr. K appears to have gained more from the intervention than a restoration of his functioning, since he feels he has resolved more fully his longstanding feelings of anger at and disappointment with his father.

THE C CASE

Mrs. C is a thirty-two-year-old Hispanic mother of four children, ages ten, seven, four, and eighteen months, who lives with her husband in a crowded apartment in a deteriorated neighborhood of the city. Until recently Mr. C was employed as a waiter and worked from 4:00 P.M. until midnight six days a week. He earned only a little more than the family would receive if they were collecting welfare but was very proud of his independence. A few months ago two serious problems confronted the C's. Their oldest son, R, age ten, was diagnosed as having kidney disease necessitating hemodialysis every other day for four hours a day. Shortly thereafter Mr. C was mugged on his way home from work and sustained a broken hip as a result of being pushed down the subway stairs. The family was forced to go on welfare, and Mr. C is quite depressed. He is able to help watch his three small children when Mrs. C takes R to the hospital for dialysis. The children are energetic and mischievous, however, and Mr. C, because of his immobility, cannot restrain them. Thus it is necessary to keep them confined in one room when Mrs. C is away. They are irritable and very demanding when Mrs. C returns home. She also is quite upset about R, whose prognosis is poor. She cannot speak to her husband about her feelings, because he is convinced that R will be all right. In addition to accompanying R to the hospital, Mrs. C spends most of her time with him, as he is quite needy. She feels torn between his demands and those of her husband and the other children, and has no time for herself. She gets little sleep and is nervous and taut. Mrs. C was referred to the social worker on the hemodialysis unit by the head nurse, who saw Mrs. C crying silently while holding R's hand. Mrs. C spoke emotionally to the worker about her hopelessness and helplessness. The worker listened, accepted Mrs. C's feelings, and began to explore all the facets of her situation. She offered to meet with her regularly for a while to see if they could help find ways of reducing the burden on Mrs. C. Over the next few weeks the worker helped Mrs. C ventilate about her day-to-day worries and her despair about R. She also arranged with the welfare department to have a home care aide come to the C's apartment for a half-day three times a week to help Mr. C and the children. The worker also helped Mrs. C to see that while it was important that she help R, it was not good for her to treat him like a baby. She helped her to recognize that despite his illness and poor long-term prognosis he might live a long time and needed her help in being as independent as possible. The worker assisted Mrs. C in setting priorities related to her appropriate involvement with R. The worker also visited the home to see Mr. C and was able to persuade him to put in an application for vocational training, which he could begin more quickly than a job. Ultimately such training would provide him with a better salary and a more secure position. Mrs. C still had to deal with the same stresses as before, yet she began to feel better, and her functioning improved. She felt less alone, less hopeless, and more able to begin to plan with her husband how they could work together to improve their lives. Mr. C, feeling more hopeful, was able to provide more emotional support to Mrs. C.

Discussion. In this example the worker helped Mrs. C to maintain her ability to cope with the multiple stresses inherent in her life situation, which were making Mrs. C increasingly desperate. The worker provided Mrs. C with a relationship in which she could share her burden and thus decrease her aloneness. Perhaps more important, she helped to reduce the actual stress on Mrs. C by obtaining essential concrete services for her. She also provided an important resource for Mr. C and helped to link him to it. The worker focused exclusively on Mrs. C's current situation and on her conscious thoughts and feelings. Among the techniques the worker utilized were those involving intervention in the social environment as well as sustainment, direct influence, and ventilation. Within a short time Mrs. C became less desperate and more able to cope with her life situation.

THE D CASE

Ms. D, age twenty-two, lived in a furnished room in a building that housed formerly hospitalized mental patients. The social worker met with her in her first aftercare visit after being discharged from a city hospital where she had been for two weeks. Ms. D had been hospitalized six times in the past two years since her father's death. Each time she was discharged to a furnished room as her mother refused to let her come home. She would attend aftercare a few times and then stop, because she did not like seeing someone new every time. She also would discontinue her medication, precipitating greater disorganization and eventual rehospitalization. Before her father's death Ms. D's parents fought about what to do with her. Mr. D prevailed upon Mrs. D to permit their daughter to remain home, where she "would be safe and would not hurt anyone." She enjoyed rug-weaving and was quite skilled at it. After the father's death Mrs. D refused to let Ms. D live at home. Ms. D has been receiving financial assistance from the city. When the social worker met with her she seemed subdued. She was given medication by injection, which appeared to suppress her more bizarre symptoms but also left her feeling apathetic. She spent her time wandering around the city because she couldn't stand being by herself in her room. She had not seen her mother for more than a month and had lost contact with the one friend she had. The worker, reviewing the recent history, felt that Ms. D might respond to a more structured and actively supportive approach. The worker arranged to see Ms. D weekly initially and helped her apply to a sheltered workshop program that she could attend daily. It offered socialization, a systematic evaluation of work skills, and on-the-job training in a range of positions at various levels of skill. The worker also consulted with the psychiatrist administering Ms. D's medication to see if something could be done to help counteract the negative drug effect she experienced. He agreed to lower the dose somewhat on a trial basis as well as to add another medication that might help reduce side effects. Since the enrollment in the sheltered workshop would take several weeks and the worker was concerned about Ms. D's use of her time, she arranged for her to attend a Day Hospital program nearby that would at least provide some structure during the day. Ms. D responded to the worker's interest in her and to her enthusiasm. She formed a dependent relationship on the worker quickly but was able to use it to decrease her isolation and foster her motivation to try the things suggested by the worker. The Day Hospital was quite effective, as Ms. D found a niche for herself and made a new friend. While she was fearful of trying the sheltered workshop when she was accepted, she began the program with the worker's encouragement. The demands of the program were stressful, but the staff were trained in helping patients deal with the stresses. The staff kept in contact with the worker, who also discussed Ms. D's everyday concerns with her. While the worker tried to establish a connection with Ms. D's mother in order to improve their relationship, this was unsuccessful. The worker continued to see Ms. D weekly and served as a benign figure who encouraged Ms. D, was a sounding board, and gave advice on practical matters. She helped Ms. D to evaluate the world around her and her interactions with others more realistically. While she did not make significant progress in the sheltered workshop, as her ability to tolerate work and interpersonal demands was low, she nevertheless was able to maintain herself outside of the hospital, to make friends, and to obtain some pleasure in what she was doing.

Discussion. In this example the worker helped Ms. D to maintain her marginal level of functioning, thus preventing a downward slide leading to repeated psychiatric rehospitalizations. The worker engaged in numerous activities with others on behalf of the client and helped to link her to important resources. In addition, the worker provided Ms. D with a relationship in which she could share her everyday activities and stresses and learn new, more adaptive ways of coping. The worker intervened in the current life space of the client. She utilized sustainment, ventilation, direct influence, education, and structuring techniques, as well as environmental intervention. While some of the work was accomplished quickly, the worker continued with Ms. D over a longer period of time, as she needed the ongoing supportive contact to maintain her gains.

THE F CASE

Ms. F is a twenty-six-year-old black high school graduate with two years of college who works as a secretary at a social service agency in a large city. She has been married for seven years to a man with whom she fights constantly and differs about almost everything. They met during the Vietnam War before Mr. F went overseas. Ms. F became pregnant, and they married. When Mr. F returned home, the couple seemed ill-suited to one another. Mr. F earns a good salary but gambles and drinks excessively. The couple have had frequent financial difficulties. Mr. F shows little interest in their seven-year-old daughter, S, or in Ms. F, spending most of his time with his friends. More recently S is expressing resentment at her father and feels rejected by him. The teacher has reported that she is preoccupied at school. Ms. F wants to leave Mr. F but fears raising her daughter on her own. She began working a year ago in order to make herself financially independent of her husband. Recently she has considered going back to college at night in order to better herself. She does not know if she can handle a full-time job, attend college, and be a mother, however. Ms. F's mother, to whom she confides, has advised Ms. F to make the best of her marriage, as she is lucky to have a husband who earns a living, doesn't beat her, and leaves her alone sexually. Feeling desperate, Ms. F shared her problems with her employer, who suggested it might be helpful for Ms. F to talk her difficulties over with someone at the agency and arranged for Ms. F to be seen by a social worker there. The social worker Ms. F saw was, like herself, a reasonably youthful black woman, came from a similar background, and showed a special sensitivity to Ms. F's struggle. She validated the legitimacy of Ms. F's strivings for herself. She helped to diminish Ms. F's guilt over disloyalty for wanting to be different from her mother. She also helped Ms. F reflect on the contradiction between her self-image as dependent and weak in contrast to her strength, particularly her ability to be independent and competent in the past. The worker also accepted Ms. F's assessment of her marital situation and its negative effects on her and her daughter. She helped her to express her fears about being on her own, to think through how she could manage realistically, and to plan what she needed to do in order to make the changes that she desired. The worker helped Ms. F to set priorities so that she would not overload herself with too many new stresses simultaneously. She was an ongoing source of encouragement to Ms. F. With this help, Ms. F was able to separate from her husband and find a new apartment. This enhanced her sense of competence and mastery and her feeling that she was doing the right thing as a mother, since her daughter appeared to feel better and her school work greatly improved. Within a year Ms. F enrolled in college part time at night while her mother babysat, and she was able to do extremely well.

Discussion. In this example the worker helped Ms. F to make positive changes in significant areas in her life that enhanced her overall functioning. She was helped to leave an unsuccessful and disturbing marriage, to manage on her own, to return to college in order to prepare herself for a new career, and to continue to care for her daughter sensitively. The worker supported Ms. F's ego capacities, validated her right to a better life, helped her to share her fears about being on her own and to plan her future action, reduced her sense of guilt and disloyalty, and reinforced a new self-concept. The process occurred over a year and involved the techniques of sustainment, ventilation, direct influence, and person-in-situation reflection. The worker focused on Ms. F's current situation, thoughts, and feelings as well as on her past struggles and experiences. She also functioned as a role model with whom Ms. F identified, which seemed to strengthen Ms. F's ability to make changes in her own life. The positive reinforcement that Ms. F received in undertaking new behavior also was important in maintaining her ability to function.

THE M CASE

Ms. M is a single thirty-year-old unemployed commercial artist who receives unemployment insurance. She has no close friends and spends every weekend visiting her parents. She would like to work in order to earn more money but is reluctant to seek full-time employment because of the demands it will make on her.

Usually Ms. M likes to read, to take long walks by herself, and to go to the movies, but recently she has been feeling desperate about her life and gets little pleasure from her solitary activities. Several months ago she became acutely psychotic and was hospitalized briefly. She recovered quickly, was discharged from the hospital, and began seeing a social worker at an outpatient clinic.

Among Ms. M's major difficulties are her extreme suspiciousness and her tendency to merge with others in close relationships. On her last job she began to feel that her female employer wanted to have a sexual relationship with her merely because she was friendly and supportive. Ms. M became fearful and withdrew from her to the point of being unable to work. Similarly in efforts to make friends with men or women Ms. M is overly sensitive to every nuance of their interaction with her or to their nonverbal expressions. She reads malevolent or sexual motivation into their behavior. At times she thinks others can read her mind and often attributes her own thoughts to others. While she tells herself that she is imagining these things, she is never fully convinced and expends a great deal of energy trying to contain her anxiety. She rarely asks people directly for reassurance, nor does she question them about what they mean when they say things she does not fully understand.

Ms. M has learned to deal with these stressful interactions by avoidance, although this results in excessive loneliness as well as in interference with work. The social worker experienced the struggle between Ms. M's observing ego and her irrational perceptions and fears within their own beginning relationship itself. When asked how she experienced her meeting with the worker, Ms. M responded that she felt the worker was sympathetic but wondered if she was tape-recording her. When asked what gave her that idea, Ms. M pointed to a dictating machine that was on the worker's desk. The worker let Ms. M check to see if the dictating machine was running, and Ms. M seemed satisfied that it was not. Then she replied that she guessed it was a ridiculous idea but it just seemed to her for a moment that the worker might be recording the session. The worker commented that it was good that Ms. M could ask her about the tape recording so that she could clear up her confusion. Ms. M acknowledged that she lived in this kind of confusion most of the time and that this was a problem to her. They agreed that this was something they could work on together.

The worker met with Ms. M weekly, and they used the sessions to identify what Ms. M was feeling, to help her sort out her feelings from the worker's, to help her expand her understanding of the possible motivations of the worker that did not relate to Ms. M specifically, to help her find ways of recognizing when her perceptions might be distorted, and to find ways of correcting them before becoming overwhelmed by anxiety. Simultaneously the worker helped Ms. M think through the ways she could pursue both work and interpersonal relationships gradually, not exposing herself to too much stress at once. They decided that free-lancing was a good option for Ms. M, since it permitted her to work by herself. The worker also suggested that Ms. M attend a weekly discussion group at a local church. The group had a specific topic of interest each night and was followed by a coffee hour where people could socialize. Because of its structured nature, it seemed a less threatening way for Ms. M to begin to involve herself in activities and meet others. Ms. M and the worker discussed what happened at these meetings in order to help Ms. M to find new ways of coping with stressful situations she encountered and to reinforce her for her good handling of situations that arose. After a year Ms. M felt much less fearful, seemed more related to the world around her and to herself, and was able to venture out to a somewhat greater extent. She was still fearful of one-to-one relationships but felt ready to begin working on this. She was doing well in her free-lance work and felt some enhanced self-esteem.

Discussion. In this example the worker engaged in ego-building efforts with Ms. M, whose severe ego deficits were hampering her ability to use her capacities. The worker used the client-worker relationship as a testing ground in which Ms. M could identify the difficulties she had in perceiving and communicating with others and could improve these important skills. The worker used Ms. M's observing ego in this process and tapped her motivation to improve herself. The worker helped Ms. M to understand her needs and capacities and to structure her external life to meet these. The worker also provided a forum in which Ms. M could discuss her current problems of everyday life and learn new ways of approaching these better. Part of this process was improving Ms. M's sensitivity to the motivations and needs of others. This work took a year and involved the techniques of sustainment, ventilation, direct influence, education, structuring, and person-in-situation reflection.

THE NATURE OF EGO-MODIFYING INTERVENTION

The goal of modifying defenses and maladaptive patterns is indicated for those individuals whose characteristic traits, mechanisms for dealing with anxiety and stress, and modes of interacting with others are hampering the full use of their capacities, are interfering with their functioning or well-being, or are endangering themselves or others. At the same time such individuals must be able to tolerate or must be protected against the potentially hazardous upsurge in anxiety associated with ego-modifying procedures. Individuals whose rigid, maladaptive defenses nevertheless protect them from disorganization may become more disorganized if their defenses are challenged. This may require emergency supportive measures ranging from reassurance in extra sessions or on the telephone to hospitalization or medication. Likewise, individuals with severe impairments in impulse control or judgment, for example, may become more impulsive and destructive to themselves or others if their defenses are weakened; individuals whose grandiosity protects them from low self-esteem, hopelessness, and potentially suicidal behavior may become acutely depressed if their grandiosity is threatened. This leads to a paradox. Many individuals with serious impairments of ego functioning who may benefit from ego-modifying intervention cannot tolerate it without the help of external structuring of their lives such as hospitalization, residential treatment, and so on. One sees this with many clients who are antisocial, impulse-ridden, or self-destructive, or who regress to psychosis easily.

The following case example illustrates the nature of an ego-modifying approach.

THE D CASE

Mr. D is a thirty-five-year-old single administrative assistant to the managing editor of a magazine. Mr. D considers himself a writer, and is working on a novel he hopes will be a commercial and literary success. He has given numerous chapters to literary agents, all of whom indicate that while he has some talent, the writing needs extensive revision. Mr. D disregards this advice and tells himself that his judgment is superior to that of the agents. Mr. D has never published before, as he considers his articles too good to be commercially successful. He has had difficulties maintaining jobs because of his arrogant and disdainful attitudes. He considers clerical work of any kind beneath him yet has repeatedly sought positions assisting successful men in the publishing field. Considering them his intellectual peers, Mr. D resents being treated like an employee. While he regards those who criticize his work as inferior or jealous of his talent, at times Mr. D becomes morose, hopeless, and bitter and stops writing. Mr. D has a wide circle of acquaintances but no close friends, as he gets tired and bored easily. His involvements with women reflect his yearning to be admired and special and his inability to tolerate those who differ with him, who have outside interests, or who do not give him the respect he feels he deserves. Mr. D has become more depressed recently. He is angry that he has not had financial success or recognition and that he has to struggle when so many others with mediocre talent make it. His usual fantasies about achieving wealth, power, and success are no longer satisfying him. At times he feels desperate and recently has been unable to write. At a low ebb he sought help. Mr. D is the elder of two sons of first-generation American parents who are financially affluent and who have had high expectations of their children. His father is a self-made man from a poor background who became a prominent attorney. His mother was an overindulged child of parents who wanted her to have everything. Mr. D feels bitter that his father was unavailable to him when he was growing up. He harbors great resentment against his younger brother, who was his father's favorite and who has achieved more personal and professional success than Mr. D. Mr. D's mother lavished attention and material possessions on Mr. D but was emotionally cold toward him. Mr. D was used to getting his own way, was disciplined rarely, and was able to control and manipulate his mother. He also recalls feeling lonely and isolated. He kept a diary in order to soothe himself, and that started his interest in writing. Mr. D has not felt close to anyone in his life. While initially charming, he becomes quite competitive with others and is rather insensitive to their needs. The social worker who met with Mr. D concluded that his difficulties are related to a lifelong defensive pattern involving grandiosity as a protection against profound feelings of lack of worth. He also shows feelings of entitlement, devaluation of others, difficulties in taking responsibility for his own behavior, and low frustration tolerance. He prefers fantasies of stardom to the work of obtaining success and becomes deflated when reality does not conform to his wishes and needs. His sense of himself is therefore quite disturbed and unrealistic, as are his relationships with others. Yet his maladaptive defenses (denial, splitting, projection, idealization, devaluation, and omnipotent control) protect his unrealistic perceptions of himself and others while at the same time keeping him from achieving the success that he craves. Mr. D's difficulties appear to have developed as a response to a childhood in which he did not derive a realistic sense of being valued and cared for while at the same time he was treated like a prince. He never developed an integrated identity, although his grandiosity gives him the appearance of someone whose identity is based on a sense of superiority. In later life he perpetuated the expectation that he be treated as special while at the same time never developing his own sense of worth.[9] The worker felt that these basic patterns needed to be altered in order for Mr. D to be able to attain some gratifications in his life. Further, Mr. D did appear to have talent that could be channeled into successful endeavors and ego strengths in important areas that would permit an ego-modifying approach to be attempted.

The worker and Mr. D met twice weekly, and the worker attempted to help Mr. D identify those patterns that were self-defeating and to engage him in trying to modify these. This attempt was met by Mr. D's increasing defensiveness and anger at the worker, which threatened their work together. While Mr. D sought help because he wanted to feel better and achieve more, he really did not think it was his behavior that was creating the problem. Efforts to help Mr. D reflect on how he was causing his own difficulties threatened his self-image as a superior person, stimulated anxiety and underlying feelings of unworthiness, and produced resistance.

The worker shifted his approach to one in which he empathized with Mr. D's view of himself and others. He also helped Mr. D share his thinking about his book and encouraged him to continue his writing efforts. As Mr. D became more comfortable with the worker he was able to share some of the feelings of worthlessness that he had. They explored the origins of these feelings in Mr. D's past relationships with his family. The worker then helped Mr. D to identify the characteristic patterns and defenses that he developed and still exhibited in order to cope with his early feelings of rejection, helplessness, inadequacy, unlovability, and anger. They were able to reflect on how Mr. D continued to see himself (as all-good and all-powerful) and others (as all bad and weak) in order to protect himself from psychological injuries similar to those of his past. He was able to see how his constant need for reinforcement of the self-image he had constructed drove others away and left him feeling bad and weak when he was frustrated. At many points Mr. D exhibited all of the feelings toward the worker that he did toward others in his life: disdain, contempt, possessiveness, boredom, and demandingness. He accused the worker of being envious and jealous of him, would threaten to quit, or would withdraw. He was helped to understand the origins of these feelings in his early relationships and to see the worker more realistically as someone who had a sincere respect for and desire to help him. Mr. D was able to tolerate his rage at the worker without terminating their contact as the worker himself seemed able to tolerate Mr. D's emotional displays without withdrawing from him emotionally. After a year, Mr. D relinquished his tenacious hold on his characteristic patterns. This was accompanied by acute anxiety and depression, as Mr. D felt that to be realistic about himself was to be worthless. He could barely work and didn't write at all for a number of months. He continued with the worker, however, and promised that he would do nothing to hurt himself physically. With the support of the worker for Mr. D's actual capacities as well as with continued reflections on and interpretations of Mr. D's reactions in the light of his early childhood experiences, Mr. D emerged from his depression after six months. He seemed more realistic in his perceptions of himself and others and took more responsibility for his actions. Together he and the worker began to identify areas in which he could begin to alter his behavior, and their work continued for another year. During this time his functioning with friends at work and in his pursuit of his writing career improved considerably.

Discussion. In this example the worker attempted to modify entrenched maladaptive defenses and patterns. His initial efforts to utilize person-in-situation reflection techniques were met with increased resistance that threatened the tenuous helping alliance between client and worker. The use of sustaining and ventilating techniques lessened the resistance and enabled the alliance to be formed more solidly. This ushered in more insight-oriented techniques such as person-dynamic, person-developmental, and person-situation reflection. This approach aroused anxiety, resistance, and transference storms that threatened the ongoing work but also were reflected upon and interpreted in terms of their dynamics and developmental origins. At the same time the worker maintained an empathic, accepting, and respectful stance that was very different from the client's experience of significant people in his life. This helped to correct for his earlier experiences. As the client's defenses lessened, he underwent a severe depressive reaction that was difficult to tolerate but was able to work this through with support and increased understanding of its developmental and dynamic components. As Mr. D emerged he became more able to work on learning new, more adaptive behavior.

GROUP AND FAMILY MODALITIES

Although group and family modalities generally draw on theoretical systems other than ego psychology and follow interventive principles different from those governing individual intervention, there are linkages between ego psychological concepts and group and family intervention. Unfortunately, proponents of individual, group, or family modalities tend to advocate their particular approach to helping individuals rather than identifying the types of situations or client problems for which one approach or the other is most suited. Even when there is an attempt to establish criteria for the use of one modality over another, the bias of the author asserts itself.[10] In the absence of research as to the efficacy of one modality as against another with specific target problems or client populations, the decision of which modality to employ depends more on the knowledge, skills, and biases of the practitioner making the assessment and on the agency's pattern of service delivery than on the client's need, level of functioning, or specific problem.

It is beyond the scope of this chapter to discuss fully the ramifications of ego psychology for group and family intervention. Rather, it will suggest a few of the important linkages.

EGO-ORIENTED GROUP INTERVENTION

Groups are a potent force in offering clients acceptance, reassurance, and encouragement; promoting problem-solving; enhancing and developing ego capacities; teaching skills and developing a sense of competence; providing information; promoting mastery; shaping or changing attitudes and behavior; and mobilizing people for collective action. Moreover, groups can be used to help individuals collaborate with helping agencies and personnel and to overcome their resistance to or discomfort with being a client.[11]

Ego-oriented groups have been used successfully in work with clients who:

1. Face similar life transitions such as retirement, widowhood, geographic relocation, leaving home, or hospital discharge
2. Are going through similar developmental phases, such as adolescence or middle age
3. Occupy similar social or occupational roles or statuses or share common concerns such as women, gays, executives, managers, or supervisors
4. Face similar life crises such as death, surgery, or psychiatric hospitalization
5. Need help in developing specific skills such as socialization or problem-solving
6. Need help in enhancing or building ego functioning such as impulse control, reality testing or self-esteem
7. Show similar types of maladaptive patterns

EGO-ORIENTED FAMILY INTERVENTION

While the family has its own life cycle[12] that is different from that of its individual members and can be characterized by unique internal processes (communication, roles, structure, and so on), it nevertheless is a potent force in personality development, is a crucial resource for the individual, reinforces adaptive or mal-adaptive patterns, and reacts to the problems encountered by individual members. Thus, intervention with the family does not always have to be thought of as systemic in nature. One can intervene to improve parent-child relationships or parenting skills,[13] to enlist the family's positive participation in the treatment of a relative,[14] to resolve marital conflict,[15] or to help individual family members cope with the impact of illness or disability of a member.[16]

The following two case examples illustrate the uses of family intervention within an ego-oriented framework. The first (the W's) shows the use of couple work to resolve the difficulties a remarried couple have in coming together successfully. The second (the E family) illustrates the importance of work with family members when one of the offspring has a severe emotional disturbance.

THE W CASE

Mrs. W is a fifty-year-old divorced mother of three children, ages twenty-seven, twenty-four, and twenty-one, who married a widower, Mr. W, two months ago. They live in the house that Mr. W resided in with his former wife. Living with Mr. and Mrs. W are his eleven-year-old daughter, J, and a housekeeper who looked after J when her mother died a year and a half ago. Mrs. W's oldest child, a son, is married, and her two daughters are on their own. Prior to her remarriage Mrs. W sold the house she had lived in for twenty years. This event stirred up many feelings associated with the loss and failure of her first marriage eight years ago. It also upset her two daughters in particular. It was as if the selling of the house finally concretized the breakup of the family. While Mrs. W looked forward to her new marriage, she felt a sense of disloyalty to her children for having sold their home and for undertaking the responsibilities of a new family, particularly another daughter. In the first two months of her new marriage, Mrs. W felt left out and a stranger in her own home. Mr. W and J seemed allied with each other and the housekeeper, and Mrs. W experienced herself as their enemy. She had definite ideas about how to raise J, whom she felt was excessively spoiled. While Mr. W seemed to agree with her, he was passive in his support of Mrs. W and in setting limits on the housekeeper, who undermined Mrs. W's disciplining of J. Prior to the marriage J seemed quite positive toward Mrs. W and seemed quite needy of her. Now J was sullen and resentful toward Mrs. W, clung to her father, and was manipulative with the housekeeper. Mr. W was quite upset that Mrs. W was so unhappy, yet he felt torn between his daughter and her.

The social worker from whom the W's sought help felt that Mr. and Mrs. W each were reacting to the impact of the remarriage in different and non-complementary ways. Mrs. W felt disloyal to her children and a sense of loss at having concretely dissolved her first marriage with the sale of the house. She also felt the loss of the house itself, which symbolized an important part of her identity and past. It became all the more important for her to find a new home and family, and she threw herself into assuming her new responsibilities quickly without giving herself, Mr. W, and J time to adjust. At the same time, because of her guilt toward her daughters she was more remote emotionally from J, who experienced her as cold and punitive. Further, Mrs. W had particular difficulties in asserting herself with the housekeeper, who reminded her of her domineering mother, with whom she felt forced to comply. Mr. W, who felt extremely needy of and dependent on Mrs. W, also felt disloyal to J for marrying Mrs. W so soon after her mother's death. He was fearful that Mrs. W would leave him and J as his wife had. He also had not mourned the death of his first wife completely. Rather than allying with Mrs. W, who needed his support, he withdrew from Mrs. W in order to protect himself. He also clung to J and was reluctant to be firm with the housekeeper, whom he had relied on previously and might need again. The worker educated the W's about the usual problems encountered by remarried couples and helped them to identify the issues that were affecting them particularly. She helped them to share their feelings with each other and assisted them in dealing with the past losses, feelings of disloyalty, and guilt with which they were both struggling. She then helped them to identify the dysfunctional ways in which they were dealing with each other, with J, and with the housekeeper and made suggestions that might improve the situation. The worker also helped the couple to identify the tasks they had to deal with as a family and to talk about how they could better work together on these. As Mr. W became less depressed and fearful, he stopped withdrawing and was able to be more of a support to Mrs. W. She began to feel more secure and became less frantic in her efforts to take over the household. As her sense of self returned and her disloyalty and guilt feelings subsided, Mrs. W was able to reach out more to J and to be more firm and sensitive in dealing with her. Mr. and Mrs. W began to spend more time together and drew closer.

Discussion. In this example the worker helped Mr. and Mrs. W to cope more effectively with their new marriage. She used her understanding of their individual personalities and unique reactions to the stresses posed by their marriage in order to help the couple to come together. The work was short-term and involved the techniques of sustainment, ventilation, direct influence, education, and person-in-situation reflection.

THE E CASE

Ms. E is a twenty-nine-year-old grade school teacher who lives near her parents. Recently she began to show increased agitation, inability to sleep, feelings of being estranged from her body and the world, increased suspiciousness, and mounting antagonism toward her parents. Mr. and Mrs. E were called by the principal of Ms. E's school, who was concerned about her functioning on the job. Mr. and Mrs. E became panicky and contacted a social worker they had seen previously for advice on how to deal with the situation. Ms. E had been hospitalized for acute psychotic episodes on three occasions in the past when she was twenty-five and twenty-seven. The episodes were preceded by rejections. Previously she experienced delusions and hallucinations; escalated in her fights with her parents, whom she experienced as intrusive and suffocating; ran away from home; and became so lacking in impulse control and judgment that she had to be hospitalized for her own safety. In their panic Mr. and Mrs. E tend to become volatile with and controlling of Ms. E, which appears to escalate her panic and disorganization. They have opposed psychiatric treatment in the past and have taken Ms. E out of the hospital against the advice of the staff. After the third hospitalization, however, the parents agreed to see a social worker for help in dealing with Ms. E while she was referred to a private psychiatrist. Gradually Mr. and Mrs. E were helped to express their anger and disappointment that Ms. E has turned out as she has and to share their fears about her future and their own. The worker also helped the E's to recognize how they were allowing their concern about E to interfere with their freedom and pleasure. She encouraged them to spend more time having fun. They became more tolerant of Ms. E's idiosyncrasies and set more realistic limits on her demands of them without treating her as either an invalid or totally well. They have been able to support Ms. E's independence to a greater extent and have spent more time together. The worker also helped the E's to share their misgivings about psychiatric treatment and educated them as to the importance of treatment and their positive involvement with Ms. E as well. Two months ago Ms. E's psychiatrist went on a month's vacation, and she has refused to see him since. Mr. and Mrs. E,. who stopped seeing the social worker some months earlier, did not encourage Ms. E to return. When the parents contacted the social worker, they indicated that they wanted to make Ms. E return home so that they could watch her and to ask her principal to insist that she take a week off from work. The worker helped the E's to express their anger and disappointment that Ms. E had become ill again. She pointed out that on previous occasions their efforts to help Ms. E had been interpreted by her as their intruding and she had escalated in her rebellion against them. The worker helped them to anticipate that their taking over might again have the result that Ms. E would experience them as undermining her, causing a worsening of her condition. The worker also indicated she felt that Ms. E was feeling rejected by and enraged at her psychiatrist. As in previous situations where she felt rejected, this might be stimulating the exacerbation of her symptoms. She suggested that it was important to encourage Ms. E to recontact her psychiatrist and offered to call Ms. E, whom she knew, to arrange an appointment for a talk. In her discussion with Ms. E the worker indicated that Ms. E's parents had called to express their concern about how Ms. E was feeling, wanted to help her, but didn't know the best way. She indicated that she knew that Ms. E was having a hard time and that it might be beneficial for her to discuss her feelings with someone. Ms. E agreed to see the worker. Ms. E acknowledged feeling on the verge of being out of control. The worker helped her to recognize that in the past her episodes followed feelings of rejection and that it was possible that she was feeling rejected by her psychiatrist because he went on vacation. The worker emphasized the progress Ms. E had made over the year and that it would be a shame to let her anger at her doctor interfere with her efforts to be independent. She indicated that she felt they could all work together to avoid Ms. E's having to be rehospitalized. Ms. E refused to call her doctor herself but agreed to let the social worker make an appointment for her to see Dr. H. Ms. E kept the appointment and Dr. H was able to help her express her anger at him for rejecting her by going away. Ms. E was able to reestablish her sense of positive connection with Dr. H. He also gave her some medication to help reduce her level of anxiety. Meanwhile the worker helped the parents to maintain an available but restrained presence in the situation. Within a week Ms. E, while still somewhat shaky, was in much better control, and the crisis subsided.

Discussion. In this example the worker intervened with all members of the family to prevent the escalation of a crisis that would lead to Ms. E's rehospitalization. Her previous work with the family had established their ability to use support to lessen their own distress caused by Ms. E's condition and to enhance their ability to deal with her constructively. This appeared to help Ms. E and her parents to get along better and to support Ms. E's efforts to be independent. The parents, however, were unable to carry on as well without the active help of the worker. In a crisis their anxiety called forth their familiar pattern of responding, with the exception that they called for the worker. She enabled them to restrain their natural impulse to take over by allowing them to ventilate their anger and disappointment, helping them to reflect on the past and present implications of their usual course of action, explaining what Ms. E was experiencing, and giving them firm guidance. This quelled their panic and enabled them to collaborate in the helping process. Meanwhile the worker, a less threatening figure to Ms. E, appealed to her observing ego, her desire to be independent, and her wish to avoid hospitalization to enable her to make the connection with her psychiatrist that she needed. There is hope that this experience will reinforce the parent's ability to be more effective in their dealings with similar situations, should they occur, as well as decrease the degree of their apprehensiveness about Ms. E's condition. It may also serve as an important message to Ms. E and the family that hospitalization can be avoided.

SUMMARY

This chapter has discussed and illustrated the differences between ego-supportive and ego-modifying approaches with respect to their focus, the nature of change, the use of relationship, the types of techniques employed, the nature of work with the social environment, the nature of appropriate client populations, and the duration of intervention. Some of the similarities and differences among restoring, maintaining, and enhancing ego functioning were pointed out and illustrated. The importance of ego-oriented group and family intervention in addition to individual intervention was discussed.

NOTES

1. For a discussion of efforts to classify social work practice after the impact of ego psychology on casework, see Florence Hollis, *Casework: A Psychosocial Therapy,* 2d Ed. (New York: Random House, 1972), pp. 57-71.
2. Insofar as ego-modifying intervention attempts to alter personality patterns, it is logical that psychological techniques are emphasized. Such an emphasis should not discount the fact that even individuals with maladaptive patterns live in an environmental context that shapes their behavior and supplies or withholds needed resources.
3. A discussion and illustration of some of these factors can be found in Hollis, *Casework.*
4. For a discussion of the nature of the client-worker relationship, see Annette Garrett, "The Worker-Client Relationship," *American Journal of Orthopsychiatry,* 19, No. 2 (1949). Reprinted in Howard J. Parad, ed., *Ego Psychology and Dynamic Casework* (New York: Family Service Association of America, 1958), pp. 53–72; Florence Hollis, *Casework,* pp. 228–46; and Helen Harris Perlman, *Social Casework: A Problem-Solving Process* (Chicago: University of Chicago Press, 1957).
5. Ego syntonic refers to characteristics or behavior that an individual feels to be an acceptable part of him- or herself and does not associate with causing difficulties or suffering. In contrast, ego dystonic or ego alien characteristics or behavior are those that an individual finds disagreeable or problematic and wants to change.
6. A discussion of some of these techniques can be found in Naomi Golan, *Treatment in Crisis Situations* (New York: Free Press, 1978), pp. 104–105.
7. This issue has been discussed by many authors. For example, see Richard M. Grinnell, Nancy S. Kyte, and Gerald J. Bostwick, "Environmental Modification," in Anthony J. Maluccio, ed., *Promoting Competence in Clients: A New/Old Approach to Social Work Practice* (New York: Free Press, 1981).
8. An ecological perspective or life model of social work practice attempts to reconceptualize the role of the social environment and it defines problems and intervention in more reciprocal and transactional terms. See Carel B. Germain, ed., *Social Work Practice: People and Environments* (New York: Columbia University Press, 1979), and Carel B. Germain and Alex Gitterman, *The Life Model of Social Work Practice* (New York: Columbia University Press, 1980).
9. This is a greatly oversimplified assessment and statement about the etiology of Mr. D's problems. The reader may conclude that a nar-

cissistic personality is being described. A full discussion of this disorder is beyond the scope of this chapter.

10. An example of this bias can be found in Rubin Blanck, "The Case for Individual Treatment," *Social Casework,* 46 (February 1965): 70–74, in which criteria are given for selecting one modality over another on the basis of theoretical points while no empirical evidence is given.

11. There is a plethora of literature on the use of groups to enhance ego functioning. Two interesting articles are Ruth R. Middleman, "The Pursuit of Competence through Involvement in Structured Groups," and Judith A. B. Lee, "Promoting Competence in Children and Youth" in Maluccio, ed., *Promoting Competence,* pp. 236–63.

12. Interesting articles on the family life cycle and its implications for work with families can be found in Elizabeth A. Carter and Monica McGoldrick, eds., *The Family Life Cycle: A Framework for Family Therapy* (New York: Gardner Press, 1980). For a perspective on ego-oriented casework with families, see Howard J. Parad, "Brief Ego-oriented Casework with Families in Crisis," in Parad and Miller, eds., *Ego-oriented Casework,* pp. 145–64; and Eda G. Goldstein, "Promoting Competence in Families of Psychiatric Patients," in Maluccio, ed., *Promoting Competence,* pp. 317–42.

13. For example, see Herbert S. Strean, "Casework with Ego Fragmented Parents," *Social Casework,* 49 (April 1968): 222–27.

14. For example, see Eda G. Goldstein, "Mothers of Psychiatric Patients Revisited," in Germain, ed., *Social Work Practice: People and Environments,* pp. 150–73.

15. For example, see Dorothy Fahs Beck, "Marital Conflict: Its Course and Treatment as Seen by Caseworkers," *Social Casework,* 47 (September 1966): 575–82.

16. For example, see Eda G. Goldstein, "Promoting Competence in Families of Psychiatric Patients," in Maluccio, ed., *Promoting Competence,* pp. 317–42.

CHAPTER 9

THE NATURE OF THE CLIENT–WORKER RELATIONSHIP

The relationship between the client and the worker is the medium through which help is given and received. Different social work practice models attach different levels of importance to the client–worker relationship as a force for client change or improvement. The relationship is a pivotal element in intervention based on ego psychological concepts. Applications of ego psychology to social work practice through the years clarified important characteristics of the helping relationship; led to a greater appreciation of the complex factors influencing it; enlarged upon its uses; added to our understanding of important issues in it; and expanded the strategies for managing the relationship. This chapter will discuss the characteristics, the factors affecting, the uses, and the management of the client–worker relationship in ego-oriented intervention.

CHARACTERISTICS OF THE CLIENT–WORKER RELATIONSHIP

The client-worker relationship is similar in some ways to other types of relationships but also has singular qualities. The client–worker relationship is a helping relationship. It has a purpose. It embodies professional values and attitudes, and it elicits characteristic responses. These will be discussed below.

THE CENTRALITY OF CLIENT NEED IN DETERMINING PURPOSE

The client–worker relationship exists for a purpose. It focuses on the client's need. Many authors[1] have tried to capture the essence of the helping relationship:

> . . . it is a condition in which two persons with some common interest between them, long-term or temporary, interact with feeling. . . . Whether this interaction creates a sense of union or antagonism, the two persons are for the time "connected" or "related" to each other. . . . In everyday life the formation of a relationship may be an end in itself. . . . But a professional relationship is formed for a purpose recognized by both participants and it ends when that purpose has been achieved or is judged to be unachievable. The mutual concern is the resolution or modification of the problem the client is encountering. . . . Whatever personal rewards or frustrations may accrue to the professional helper from such relationships are irrelevant to the management of them, for the need of the client is his central focus. Thus . . . the relationship develops out of the professional business the caseworker and client have to work on together [Perlman, 1957:65–69].

THE WORKER'S DISCIPLINED USE OF SELF

The worker is not a blank screen upon which the client projects fantasies, wishes, and fears, nor is the worker always neutral in providing interventions.[2] In ego-oriented intervention the worker generally permits his or her personal qualities to enter the client–worker relationship in a disciplined way based on his or her determination of the client's need and therapeutic goals. The worker is neither a mechanical robot who refrains from involvement with the client, nor an aloof, walled-off figure who views the client from an emotionally removed position. The worker shows human concern for clients but controls the nature of involvement with the client in keeping with his or her assessment, goals, and professional values and ethics. The worker whose personal feelings intrude upon the relationship in ways that are irrelevant to the work being done is allowing his or her own needs to take precedence over the client's needs. There is a fine line, however, between expressing feelings and involvement for one's own sake and doing so for the client's benefit. The crucial issues are whether the worker is disciplined (consciously purposeful) in using him- or herself in the relationship and bases his or her actions on an assessment of the client.

IMPORTANT VALUES AND ATTITUDES

The worker should convey certain key values and attitudes in the relationship with the client irrespective of the worker's or client's personal characteristics or difficulties. These include acceptance of the client's worth, a nonjudgmental attitude toward the client, appreciation of individuality and uniqueness, respect for the right to self-determination, and adherence to therapeutic rights to confidentiality.

REALISTIC AND UNREALISTIC COMPONENTS
OF THE RELATIONSHIP

The client–worker relationship can be characterized by two main types of responses: (1) realistic and appropriate reactions to the personalities involved, behavior displayed, and professional business transacted, which occur in what may be termed the real relationship and the working alliance,[3] and (2) unrealistic and inappropriate responses that stem from the client's and worker's past relationships with, and unconscious conflicts regarding, significant others, or as a result of developmental deficits in the area of object relations, which are characteristic of transference and countertransference. Ego-oriented intervention places more emphasis on the former group of responses than did psychoanalytically oriented casework, but the latter group is also important. The ways of dealing with these reactions in ego-oriented intervention will be discussed in more detail later in the chapter.

The Real Relationship and the Working Alliance. Both client and worker react to their respective "real" personalities as they manifest themselves in their relationship. At the same time both client and worker must decide whether they can work together on helping the client. While their realistic feelings about each other as people may influence their perceptions of their mutual capacity to work on problems successfully, such influence is not always predictable. It is possible for a client not to like actual aspects of the worker's personality and behavior—e.g. his or her appearance, sarcasm, mannerisms, or office decor—and yet to respect the worker's expertise because of professional credentials or reputation, to believe the worker has the capacity to be helpful, and to be willing to cooperate with the plan they arrive at for working together. Conversely, the client may feel the worker is sincere in desiring to help but he or she may lack confidence in the worker's abilities. The worker may dislike the client's demandingness and arrogance but be able to empathize with his or her feelings, feel qualified to help the client, and be able to create the conditions essential to their working together, as will be discussed in detail later in this chapter.

The development and maintenance of the willingness and ability to work jointly on the problems for which the client seeks help is called the working alliance, as distinct from the real relationship. Without a working alliance the work cannot proceed. The working alliance requires that the client's rational and observing ego remain in contact with the worker as a reasonable helping person and that he or she continue to cooperate in achieving the goals they have identified. In large part, it is the working alliance that enables the client to continue to struggle with his or her problems even as he or she experiences intense unrealistic feelings about and perceptions of the worker or other forms of resistance as part of the interventive process.

In principle the working alliance should be based on the client's realistic perceptions of the worker's ability to help, but sometimes in practice what appears to be a working alliance really reflects the client's unrealistic, highly idealized, or magical expectations that an authority figure will "cure" his or her problems. Consequently when the worker does not live up to the client's expectations, the worker loses his or her magic in the eyes of the client, who may terminate the relationship. In other cases the working alliance is fragile because of the client's mistrust or lack of a sound observing ego, for example. As intense reactions to the worker develop, they become so extreme that the client loses the ability to see the worker realistically. While such reactions can be managed, as will be discussed later in the chapter, the best approach is to recognize the potential for such problems in or disturbances of the working alliance early in the contact so that they can be anticipated and prevented to some extent.

Transference and Countertransference. Unrealistic reactions that occur in the client–worker relationship generally are thought to be of two types: transference and countertransference. According to Greenson (1967), transference is the experience of feelings, drives, attitudes, fantasies, and defenses toward a person in the present that do not befit that person but are a repetition of reactions originating in regard to significant persons of early childhood, unconsciously displaced onto figures in the present (Greenson, 1967:171). While both worker and client can experience such unrealistic reactions, the term "transference" applies to the client's reactions, while the term "countertransference" refers to the worker's reactions. Transference and countertransference reactions may be positive, that is, based on loving, caring, affectionate, or related feelings, or negative, that is, based on angry, aggressive, destructive, or related feelings.

In psychoanalysis, transference reactions are viewed as essential to the therapeutic process in that their interpretation is believed to result in conflict resolution and personality change. Psychoanalysis therefore encourages transference reactions and a "transference neurosis" (the creation of one's core conflicts with past figures in the therapeutic relationship). It uses such procedures as free association; lying on a couch; frequent sessions; a focus on dreams, fantasies, wishes, fears, and childhood memories; therapist neutrality and anonymity; and a dimly lit room, among others. These foster regression and stimulate the client's transference distortions.

Transference reactions are dealt with differently in ego-oriented intervention, which does not rely on insight or conflict resolution alone as the major change mechanisms. In ego-supportive approaches the interventive process generally is structured to minimize, regulate, or selectively stimulate and use transference reactions. Face-to-face contact, a here-and-now reality-oriented focus, more rational and focused discussion, less frequent sessions, and more therapeutic activity, among other procedures, reinforce the client's rational thought processes and realistically based relationship to the worker. A positive transference in which the worker is viewed as a benign parental figure may be fostered in order to facilitate the process of identification, to affirm a sense of worth, to encourage adaptive attitudes and behavior, or to provide an emotionally corrective experience. Intense positive or negative reactions are viewed as regressive, nonproductive, and potentially harmful to the ongoing intervention or to the client's well-being. Such reactions, if they occur, need to be identified and diffused.[4] In ego-modifying approaches transference reactions are encouraged to some extent by the use of nondirective and reflective techniques and by greater attention to the client's inner life and to selected aspects of his or her childhood. Their intensity is regulated carefully by the measures discussed above and those illustrated later in this chapter, and there is an effort to avoid the development of a full regression to a transference neurosis. Transference reactions are interpreted selectively, however, in order to help the client understand his or her maladaptive defenses and patterns and their origins in past relationships.

Transference reactions sometimes disrupt the working alliance. The client becomes convinced that his or her distorted perception of and intense feelings toward the worker are "real." Clients who show impaired object relations stemming from early developmental arrests generally will need more help in maintaining a working alliance than will clients who have reached the Oedipal stage of development and who have developed object constancy. The former group of clients are easily frustrated by the worker's responses, and this produces stormy reactions. Sometimes the client lacks sufficient observing ego to maintain the working alliance and sufficient impulse control to sustain the frustration without disrupting the relationship or hurting themselves. Other such clients, because of the force of their needs, succeed in getting the worker to play the role they seek, irrespective of whether this is growth-enhancing.

Countertransference reactions, to the degree that they represent the worker's unrealistic and inappropriate reactions to the client as a result of his or her own unconscious conflicts or developmental arrests need to be understood, controlled, or resolved in all therapeutic endeavors. The term "countertransference" has come to have a broader meaning, however. It refers not only to the worker's unrealistic, unconsciously motivated reactions but also to all the reality-based reactions he or she has to the client's behavior.[5] The broadening of the meaning of countertransference has an important implication, namely, that the worker's often uncomfortable or potentially hindering reactions may be induced by the client rather than produced by the worker's conflicts. Thus a client who relates to others and to the worker in a clinging, demanding, and intrusive way may evoke in the worker a strong wish to withdraw that seems difficult to overcome. While the worker must control and refrain from acting upon personal feelings in this instance, his or her understanding of such a reaction is important to assessing and working with the client. It may be that the client is provoking the worker to abandon him or her, as the client was abandoned in the past; or the client may be attempting to control the worker as he or she did others. The use of the worker's own reactions as a diagnostic clue in this way may help the worker to respond more appropriately to the client and enable the client to gain increased understanding of his or her own needs. Clearly, however, the worker must be reasonably sure that he or she is not reacting to the client out of his or her own difficulties before attributing certain feelings to the client's behavior.[6] Likewise the worker must consider whether the client's responses represent transference or are appropriate reactions to the worker's behavior, as will be discussed later.

FACTORS INFLUENCING THE CLIENT–WORKER RELATIONSHIP

There are numerous factors in the client, the worker, and the practice setting that shape the client–worker relationship. The worker must understand the particular interplay of these factors with each client so that he or she can maximize the client's ability to engage in the helping process.

FACTORS IN THE CLIENT

Among the factors in the client that affect participation in the helping relationship are (l) motivation and expectations; (2) values, experiences, and sociocultural background; (3) ego functioning; and (4) current life situation.

Motivation and Expectations. Client motivation is a complex subject.

> Two conditions must hold for the sustainment of responsible willingness to work at problem-solving: discomfort and hope. . . . Thus a person must feel more uncomfortable than comfortable with his problem in order to want to do something about it and this malaise will serve to push him. Accompanying this push from within (or some push without that results in discomfort) must be some promise of a greater ease or satisfaction and this promise pulls the person to bend his effort to some goal. . . . [D]iscomfort without hope spells resignation, apathy, fixation. . . . Hopefulness without discomfort . . . is the mark of the immature, wishful person, he who depends on others or on circumstances to work for his interest [Perlman, 1979:186–87].

Thus, client motivation is fueled by the "push of discomfort" and "the pull of hope." Sustained motivation in some instances, however, also requires that the client be willing to invest time, energy, and often financial resources on a process that stirs up painful emotions and arouses anxiety. Such feelings may diminish motivation or increase resistance. Further, the client, while seeking to feel better, may not identify the aspects of his or her behavior that are maladaptive. Hence he or she may not feel the impetus to work on particular problems. The client also may experience relief from the acute distress that prompted the effort to seek help, and lose the motivation to work on other difficulties that leave him or her vulnerable to repeated episodes of distress or with problematic characteristics that affect functioning. Thus motivation is a dynamic concept; it has to be understood in terms of changing needs, feelings, and circumstances. The worker's task is to enhance and sustain client motivation to work on the problems they have both identified.

An important related factor is the nature of the client's expectations of the worker and of the interventive process as well as his or her goals. Many client dissatisfactions with the helping process stem from discrepancies between their expectations and goals and what actually occurs.[7] Thus the client who seeks advice from an expert may experience distress when asked to reflect on his or her behavior and to consider the pros and cons of various solutions he or she has identified. The client who seeks short-term and tangible assistance may be frustrated by exploration of his or her feelings. Therefore it is crucial for the worker to establish goals with the client that are consistent with the client's needs and expectations and for the worker to explain the specific nature of the interventive process and its rationale to the client.

Values, Experiences, and Sociocultural Background. The client's values, life experiences, and sociocultural background are important factors affecting the client–worker relationship. The worker must consider whether the client views the act of seeking help and of sharing his or her private concerns with a stranger as antagonistic to or a violation of established mores and values; whether it stigmatizes the client in his or her reference group; or whether it requires an adaptation to new and difficult practices. Further, the worker must understand the degree to which the client has had unpleasant or destructive experiences with other helping persons or institutions and whether he or she has felt controlled by, alienated from, or discriminated against by individuals or organizations that the worker and his or her agency represent.[8] Such understanding will enable the worker to intervene in ways that help the client to participate in the helping process.

Ego Functioning. The nature of the client's ego functioning itself affects the client–worker relationship. The worker must be alert to the client who lacks trust, easily feels controlled, cannot differentiate his or her thoughts and feelings from those of others, cannot distinguish fantasy from reality, harbors distorted perceptions of others and the world, or cannot contain intense and potentially destructive impulses. In some instances the degree of the client's disorganization, regression, or impulsivity may make it impossible temporarily for the client and worker to communicate meaningfully and safely. The worker's ability to assess accurately those aspects of the client's impaired ego functioning and the conditions that stimulate it will permit the worker to design his or her interventions appropriately. The task is to maximize the client's ability to engage in the helping process.

Current Life Situation. Many factors in the client's current life situation may impinge upon the client–worker relationship. Financial and time pressures and constraints, medical problems and disabilities, and other responsibilities affect the client's ability to engage in the helping process. The degree to which the worker and agency can flexibly respond to the issues will play an important role in enabling clients to participate in the helping process.

FACTORS ON THE WORKER'S SIDE

From the foregoing discussion it follows that the worker's understanding of and responses to the client are crucial in enabling the client to develop a working alliance. Among the more important attributes of the worker are his or her ability to (1) assess and relate to the impact of the client's motivation, expectations, goals, values, life experiences, sociocultural background, life situation, and ego functioning on the helping process; (2) show empathy, positive regard, genuineness, commitment, openness, and flexibility when interacting with the client;[9] (3) be skillful in making the goals and nature of the interventive process explicit and engage the client as a collaborator in the helping process; (4) adapt interventions and practices flexibly to the client's expectations where appropriate; (5) mobilize the client's motivation and capacity and foster the client's understanding of the rationale for the interventive process; (6) remain focused on achieving the goals arrived at jointly or reformulate these with the client; and (7) recognize quickly any signs of threat to the working alliance and intervene to lessen these. Clearly these characteristics reflect not only the worker's knowledge and skill but also his or her personality and ability to be useful and resourceful when working with clients.

FACTORS IN THE AGENCY OR PRACTICE SETTING

The agency or practice setting from which the client seeks help affects the client–worker relationship through its function, through the flexibility of its practical arrangements and policies, and through the respect it accords the client as a consumer of service.

The agency's function dictates its ability to help certain clients. If the agency cannot meet the client's request for help, it must not force its particular services or way of delivering services on clients whose needs, goals, or expectations are at variance with the agency's mandate. Timely and appropriate referrals are important factors in the client's ability to get help. Likewise the agency's flexibility with respect to waiting lists, fees, easy access, scheduling, and other practical arrangements is a key element in enabling clients to use services

The attitude the agency conveys to the client about his or her status is another major factor that affects the client–worker relationship. Clients often experience vulnerability, neediness, dependency, shame, failure, and fear when they seek help. This is so irrespective of their need for or entitlement to service or of whether the auspices of the service are public or private. Unfortunately it too often is the case that the attitudes, conditions, and procedures of the agency or practice setting intensify the client's uncomfortable reactions. Cramped, poorly lit, and dirty waiting rooms; rude and insensitive personnel; bureaucratic procedures; lack of sharing of important information; unavailability or lack of access to professional staff; and blaming or demeaning attitudes are but a few of the factors that convey a lack of respect for the client as a worthwhile human being and as a consumer of service. Attitude and practices that convey that the client is unable to think for him- or herself, to act rationally, to understand his or her own or other's problems or conditions, and is an object to be manipulated, controlled, or changed are inimical to the client's ability to be a collaborator in the helping process.[10]

THE USES OF THE CLIENT–WORKER RELATIONSHIP

In ego-oriented intervention the client–worker relationship can be used in a variety of ways to help the client. The major uses of the relationship are discussed below.

ASSESSING THE CLIENT

The client's reaction to the worker and his or her behavior within the client–worker relationship are important sources of data that contribute to assessment. While the client reacts to the worker's behavior in the relationship, he or she also brings characteristic ways of perceiving and relating to others. The worker must be cautious, however, in concluding too quickly that the client's responses in the relationship reflect his or her characteristic behavior or difficulties. He or she must ascertain whether the client's reactions are being provoked or elicited by the worker's interventions, behavior, or attitudes. Thus the client's anger may be a justifiable response to the worker's insensitivity. The fact that the worker may have provoked the client's response does not in itself imply that the client's reaction is not diagnostic. It also is possible, however, that the client's quick anger at others for not understanding as well as he or she would like is a problem in functioning. Thus it is important for the worker also to determine whether reactions that surface within the client–worker relationship reflect the client's typical responses to others in his or her life. This issue is complicated further by the fact that some clients seem different in the client–worker relationship from the way they describe themselves or the way they actually are in other areas of their lives. Sometimes these seeming contradictions reflect important data. For example, a client may describe others as always controlling him or her, whereas in the client–worker relationship the worker feels controlled by the client. This would lead the worker to wonder whether the client is controlling in other relationships, thus eliciting power struggles in which he or she feels controlled. Clearly there can be many pitfalls to this type of approach if the worker is not skillful in its use.

SUSTAINING HOPE AND MOTIVATION

The worker provides the client with an experience in which he or she is valued and viewed in a nonjudgmental way. The worker helps the client to express his or her thoughts, feelings, needs, and worries. The worker's acceptance and empathy help the client to feel less alone and to validate needs and wishes for him- or herself. The worker's identification of the client's strengths and capacities and possible solutions to or ways to approach finding the solutions to difficulties offers the client hope and encouragement.

ENHANCING AUTONOMY, PROBLEM-SOLVING, AND ADAPTIVE BEHAVIOR

The worker helps the client to find solutions by exercising his or her own problem-solving and decision-making abilities. He or she encourages and facilitates the client's taking of positive actions on his or her own behalf. The worker may explore the reasons for and origins of the problems in order to help the client gain more understanding of him- or herself and more control over his or her life. The worker may impart information, advice, or direction essential to the client's successful management of his or her life. This must be undertaken with caution so as to minimize both unnecessary dependency and the possibility of imposing one's views or biases on the client. The worker helps the client find ways of acquiring the information and resources he or she needs. The worker also helps the client to understand better the needs, motivation, and behavior of him- or herself and others and to learn new ways of thinking, feeling, perceiving, and behaving. The worker reinforces the client's efforts to act more adaptively.

PROVIDING A ROLE MODEL AND CORRECTIVE EXPERIENCE

In an emotionally charged positive relationship it is not unusual to take on (identify with) and take in (internalize), selectively and unconsciously, the attitudes, interests, values, and behavior of the loved or admired person. This process sometimes occurs in the client–worker relationship as a byproduct of it. At other times the worker may foster this process. Such role modeling can be helpful in strengthening the client when the attitudes or behavior he or she adopts is consistent with his or her own needs, talents, capacities, and well-being. It also can be helpful in enabling individuals to acquire characteristics that improve their functioning. The important issue this process raises is how to avoid manipulating the client or imposing one's own values on the client consciously or unwittingly. There is no simple answer to this. The worker has a responsibility to help the client find his or her own solutions and develop values, attitudes, and behavior that enhance the client's functioning and sense of self.

Because of its positive characteristics the client–worker relationship may provide the client with a new kind of relationship that enhances his or her feelings of being cared for, lifts his or her self esteem, and allows him or her to view him- or herself and others differently. To this extent the relationship has a corrective aspect. The worker, however, may purposely use the relationship with the client in ways that attempt to correct for earlier deprivation, bad experiences, or developmental arrests and to foster the growth process. The worker who uses the relationship as a primary means of helping the client in this way is attempting to provide an emotionally corrective experience.[11]

PROMOTING PERSONALITY CHANGE

The worker may help the client gain an understanding of and modify his or her maladaptive patterns, defenses, and conflicts and make connections between the client's current difficulties and past childhood experiences. This involves more systematic attention to the client's transference reactions and patterns of resistance within the client–worker relationship. It also requires more attention to exploring the origins of such reactions on the client's part and to how such behavior manifests itself in areas of the client's current functioning.

MOBILIZING RESOURCES

The worker may help the client locate appropriate resources and may help link the client to these resources.

MODIFYING THE ENVIRONMENT

The worker may help the client to restructure or change selected aspects of his or her environment so that they are more conducive to meeting his or her needs. Also, the worker may intervene directly in the environment, e.g. with the client's family in order to modify those characteristics that are obstructing the client's successful adaptation.

MEDIATING, EDUCATING, COLLABORATING, AND ADVOCATING

The worker may intervene with others on behalf of the client. He or she may mediate conflicts between the client and others or provide others with important information that helps in their understanding of and dealing with the client. The worker also may collaborate with other professionals, friends, family members, or significant individuals in the client's life in order to help the client. Finally the worker may actively represent the client's interests and needs to others with the goal of influencing them to take positive action on behalf of the client.

MANAGING THE CLIENT–WORKER RELATIONSHIP

In addition to possessing assessment and general interventive skills, the worker must be skillful in attuning his or her relationship with the client to the client's needs at different phases of the interventive process and in dealing with specific aspects of the client–worker relationship during the course of intervention. Thus the worker must be able to engage the client, to use the relationship as a positive force in promoting the client's growth, to recognize and deal with transference reactions, and to terminate the client–worker relationship successfully. While a full exploration of these issues is beyond the scope of this chapter, what follows is a discussion of some of the important considerations.

ENGAGING THE CLIENT

Developing a working alliance involves helping the client to engage with the worker in identifying the problems to be worked on and the means for working on them. The term "contracting" means the process whereby the worker makes explicit to the client the goals, nature, and shared responsibilities of the interventive process.[12]

What is important is not the mechanical or legalistic establishment of a contract between worker and client but rather the process whereby the worker enlists the client's ego in the helping process. This process must occur at the beginning of intervention, but it often must continue over a period of time or be renegotiated at points during the course of intervention.

At the time clients seek help, however, their egos may be overwhelmed by their problems or life situations. Before the client can formulate goals he or she must be helped to decrease his or her level of stress and increase his or her ability to work on his or her difficulties. Thus sustaining techniques that diminish anxiety, strengthen appropriate defenses, partialize problems, validate strengths, and encourage hope are critical. Some clients may lack understanding of, confidence in, or ease with the helping process. It is important to explain the helping process and its rationale to the client, to elicit his or her concerns about it, and to identify those aspects of the process that might be altered where appropriate in order to help the client feel more comfortable. Some clients may have sought help at the urging of others and may lack motivation; they may have concerns that are at variance with the worker's. It is important for the worker to reach out actively and sensitively to such clients, to help identify common areas of concern, and to build upon whatever motivation does exist. With clients whose sociocultural background or lifestyle differs markedly from the worker's, the worker must build a bridge between him- or herself and the client.

The following four brief case examples illustrate some common issues that arise in the engagement process.

Mr. P is a forty-eight-year-old construction worker who has been drinking heavily for the past two years. When sober, Mr. P is stubborn and ill-tempered. He spends little time with his children or with Mrs. P, who has repeatedly threatened to leave him. This time Mrs. P insisted that Mr. P seek help for his drinking problem. When Mr. P spoke with the social worker, he said he wanted help to stop drinking but soon admitted that his main concern was keeping his wife from leaving him. He enjoyed alcohol and saw nothing wrong in the way he managed himself. He felt he was a good breadwinner, did not cheat on his wife, and was bringing his kids up right. While he acknowledged that his drinking had worsened two years earlier when he became depressed after not receiving a promotion, he could not understand how seeing the worker would help matters. He only wanted to change his wife's mind about leaving. The worker helped Mr. P to identify what he felt he could do to influence her and explained how talking things over might help accomplish his goal. Mr. P somewhat reluctantly agreed to see the worker for six weeks in order to get support in accomplishing his goals. During these sessions the worker focused on helping Mr. P to improve his home situation and to find ways of controlling his drinking. At the same time he helped Mr. P to express his frustrations regarding his job and his hopelessness about the future. The worker sympathized with Mr. P's anxiety about getting older and his feelings of failure at having little to give his children. He also acknowledged his hurt sense of pride that his wife had to work. The worker supported Mr. P's efforts as a breadwinner and as a concerned parent. He also tried to mobilize Mr. P's hope that he could do more to help himself were he to take more control of his life and his concern about how his drinking was affecting his health and his relationship with his children. After six weeks Mr. P felt the situation at home was better and felt enormous relief as well as a sense of mastery at having been able to accomplish something. Nevertheless, he agreed to continue seeing the worker for help with getting his work and family life back on the right track.

Ms. G, a thirty-four-year-old woman, sought help in extricating herself from a relationship with a man with whom she had been having an affair and who borrowed money from her and gambled heavily. Recently she learned accidentally that he was seeing another woman. Ms. G wanted to ask him to move out but was fearful that he would physically hurt her and refuse to leave. Ms. G, however, seemed to have a pattern of involving herself in relationships with men who exploited and mistreated her. The worker agreed to help Ms. G in the current situation, but she also indicated that Ms. G was likely to continue to get herself into similar difficulty unless she could understand her need to involve herself in self-destructive relationships with men. The worker indicated that she felt Ms. G needed to work on this over a long-term period and that this would help her greatly. Ms. G was dubious about this and was most concerned about her current situation. She agreed, however, to see the worker, who helped Ms. G to develop a plan for leaving her boyfriend and explored the difficulties Ms. G had in implementing it. As Ms. G shared her fears about being on her own, her feelings of self-blame for the relationship, and her lack of positive expectations of men, the worker supported Ms. G's ability to take action on her behalf. At the same time the worker helped her to make connections between her current concerns and her lifelong patterns of relating to men. She instilled hope that Ms. G could have different kinds of relationships. It never had occurred to Ms. G that she may have needed to get herself into some of the bad situations of her life. She used the worker's support to help her leave the boyfriend successfully after a few months but also agreed to continue seeing the worker to help her prevent recurrent difficulties.

Mr. Y is a twenty-five-year-old Chinese engineering student who requested help for anxiety and depression related to his impending graduation from engineering school and his resultant difficulty in deciding whether or not to return to his country. After several sessions the young and inexperienced worker assigned to the case began feeling very frustrated by Mr. Y. He had difficulty providing her with information about himself and sharing his thoughts and feelings. He seemed to keep her at a distance, always acting extremely polite and formal with her. The more she questioned Mr. Y and tried to develop a friendly relationship with him, the more Mr. Y clammed up and withdrew. With the help of her supervisor, the worker caught on to the fact that she had neglected to consider the impact of Mr. Y's cultural background on his attitude and behavior in the interventive process. She assumed that because Mr. Y had voluntarily sought help that he had no conflicts about this. She failed to realize that he might feel extremely ashamed and disloyal. She also had failed to consider that Mr. Y might value privacy, formality, and self-sufficiency, that he might have difficulty taking help or sharing feelings and difficulty with her particular manner. She recognized that her entire approach to Mr. Y was making it more difficult for him to participate in working with her and that it would be necessary for her to restrain her natural friendliness, to permit Mr. Y more distance, and to go at his pace rather than her own. As the worker acknowledged directly to Mr. Y her awareness of not having appreciated fully what he was feeling, showed more respect for his way of interacting with her, and helped him verbalize his concerns about taking help, talking to a stranger, and sharing his feelings, Mr. Y began to relax more. They were able to find a way of working together.

Ms. F is a twenty-two-year-old unemployed aspiring actress living with her parents. Since returning home after graduating from college, Ms. F has been "vegetating," becoming more and more depressed. She looks for work sporadically without enthusiasm and has not enrolled in acting classes or socialized. Her parents are unaware that Ms. F is a lesbian and that she had an intense involvement with a female classmate for one and a half years prior to her graduation. They decided it would be best if both returned to their home states to pursue their careers after graduation. They correspond but miss each other terribly. Ms. F feels more alone because she cannot share anything of her personal life with her parents, whom she feels will condemn her, a fear that has a reality basis. Ms. F also feels burdened in that she cannot engage in relationships with other gay individuals freely, fearing that her parents will find out about her sexual preference. With increasing desperation she sought help from a local suburban mental health clinic and was assigned a middle-aged married woman who was quite friendly and supportive. After a few sessions she shared the fact that she was gay and her fear that the worker would disapprove. The worker, in an attempt to be supportive and reassuring, commented that she was not there to judge Ms. F and that besides it was likely that Ms. F was going through a phase as many young women did. She further added that Ms. F was attractive, intelligent, and talented, and that together they could help her live a normal life. Ms. F sensed the worker's sincere efforts to help her but felt devastated by the worker's response. She felt completely misunderstood by the worker but did not press the issue further at the time. The worker suggested that the first thing it was important for Ms. F to do was to mobilize herself to start acting classes and to find part-time work. Ms. F said that she felt trapped at home, missed her friend, and didn't know where to turn. When Ms. F spoke of her love for her former classmate and said how much she missed her, the worker sympathized but indicated that it was natural for someone like Ms. F, who had such intense dependency needs, to confuse these with sexual love. Ms. F was able to tell the worker at this point that she felt misunderstood by her and felt it would be better for her to speak with someone who could understand her predicament. The worker interpreted Ms. F's wish to see someone else as indicative of her fear of becoming dependent on the worker. Soon after this Ms. F stopped attending sessions but sought help from a gay counseling center advertised in a newspaper. She made an immediate connection with a social worker there. Ms. F found a part-time job in order to pay for the sessions.

In the first two cases, both Mr. P's and Ms. G's initial motivations were to alleviate their current situations (Mr. P's wife's threat of leaving him and Ms. G's desire to extricate herself from her relationship with a boyfriend). In each case the worker felt that these current situations were symptomatic of longstanding difficulties that needed to be addressed. The therapeutic issue was how to engage both clients. In both cases the workers met the clients where they were. They engaged them in working on the immediate goals Mr. P and Ms. G identified. In the P case it was necessary additionally for the worker to identify how he could help Mr. P to achieve his limited goal. At the same time the workers in both instances helped these clients to develop motivation to work on their longstanding difficulties. This was achieved by helping to meet the clients' identified needs while also exploring their underlying feelings, supporting their strengths, instilling hope, and making connections between current and longstanding difficulties.

In the latter two cases (Mr. Y and Ms. F) the workers' initial efforts to engage their clients were misguided. With Mr. Y the worker intervened without individualizing the client in terms of his sociocultural background and the impact this had on the interventive process. Fortunately the worker, with the help of supervision, recognized her mistake and was able to adjust her style and interventions to be more in tune with where Mr. Y was. With Ms. F, however, the worker's inability to understand, accept, and relate sensitively to Ms. F's sexual orientation, to the significance of her separation from her lover, to what it meant to be gay in her family, and to her sense of aloneness made it impossible for her to engage the client. Fortunately Ms. F had the strength to leave the worker and was able to locate and use a more appropriate therapeutic resource.

USING THE RELATIONSHIP POSITIVELY

The worker's ability to provide and manage a specific kind of relationship with the client in order to foster the client's functioning is an important skill. It is often difficult to do this while at the same time controlling one's emotional involvement, keeping a reality focus, minimizing irrational or regressive reactions, and maintaining the client's autonomy. The following case illustrates this complex process.

Ms. M is a twenty-six-year-old graduate student who sought help because of her inability to complete her doctoral dissertation. Her problems seemed related partly to the fact that she had difficulty spending many hours by herself, since this made her feel alone and cut off from others. She also equated the completion of her dissertation with her emotional emancipation from her parents, who disapproved of and never showed an interest in her academic pursuits.

Ms. M formed a positive working relationship with the worker, who validated Ms. M's academic strivings and abilities and who actively encouraged Ms. M to finish her work. Ms. M felt reassured by the worker's confidence in her. The worker encouraged Ms. M's identification with her by selectively sharing with Ms. M some of her own academic and professional struggles. Ms. M viewed the worker as a woman who had made it and who could help Ms. M to do likewise.

In their meetings together the worker helped Ms. M to talk about her ideas, to outline the tasks that she needed to undertake, to help her set priorities, to plan a course of action, and to talk about the work Ms. M was doing each day. She asked to read material that Ms. M prepared and discussed it with her. The worker thus not only mobilized Ms. M's ego capacities but also provided a relationship that, unlike Ms. M's relationship with her parents, reflected the worker's interest in and approval of Ms. M. This helped to decrease Ms. M's sense of isolation and guilt. Ms. M viewed the worker as a special kind of friend and mentor who had idealized qualities. When she left each session she jokingly would comment on how it was time for her to pack the worker up and put the worker in her bookbag so that she could carry her around. The worker regulated the intensity of the relationship by her reality focus, by weekly sessions, and by reinforcing what Ms. M was doing independently to finish her work.

At several points in their contact, however, Ms. M began to view the worker as similar to her parents and became depressed and hopeless. She accused the worker of feeling that she was not working hard enough or fast enough and of thinking that it was useless for her to try to finish her dissertation. The worker, after reviewing whether Ms. M was correct in her perceptions, concluded that she had not responded sufficiently sensitively to Ms. M, who assumed that she, like Ms. M's parents, was not truly interested in her. She communicated this to Ms. M and also reassured her of her continued interest and concern. While Ms. M always denied being angry at the worker, her mood would shift as a result of the worker's intervention and she would again become involved in the task of completing her work. Ms. M was able to meet her deadline. No attempt was made to alter Ms. M's basic personality. Following the termination of their contact Ms. M corresponded with the worker, who always remained "a good mother" in the client's eyes.

RECOGNIZING AND DEALING WITH TRANSFERENCE REACTIONS

While transference reactions may be minimized or kept at a positive level in many therapeutic encounters, at times intense reactions threaten the working alliance and need to be recognized and lessened in order for the work to continue. In other situations transference reactions are encouraged and used to help the client gain understanding of his or her maladaptive patterns. The following four case examples illustrate the importance of dealing effectively with such reactions.

Ms. D, a twenty-five-year-old mother of three small children, ages seven, four, and two, was suspected of neglecting them and was referred to a city agency for help. The social worker assigned to the case began to see Ms. D weekly in order to enhance her parenting skills. While somewhat suspicious of the worker and her motives initially, fearing she might take her children from her, Ms. D became emotionally extremely attached to and dependent on the worker, who was sensitive, accepting, warm, and available and who treated her as no one else in her life had treated her.

With the worker's help Ms. D began to pay more attention to her children and seemed more sensitive to their needs. Ms. D became excessively demanding of attention from the worker, however, whom she felt was like a real mother to her. Her own mother left the home when Ms. D was a baby, and her grandmother cared for her. Ms. D also became frustrated, however, when the worker would not fulfill some of her requests, such as going shopping with her, coming for lunch, and showing physical affection toward her. She felt extremely jealous of the attention the worker gave to other clients.

When the worker went on a two-week vacation, Ms. D refused to see the worker upon her return. Despite the worker's repeated attempts to reestablish the reason for their work together and to reach out to and reassure Ms. D of her interest and concern, and despite the risk Ms. D was taking with respect to the agency's expectations, she nevertheless remained adamant in her refusal to see the worker. At the agency's insistence she did agree to see someone else.

Ms. L is a thirty-three-year-old formerly hospitalized mental patient who was referred to the worker for help in maintaining herself in the community. She lives alone, is lonely and isolated, and tends to withdraw from others. Among her difficulties in relationships is a marked tendency to see women as hateful and controlling of her. Such women remind her of her deceased mother, on whom she was quite dependent but toward whom she felt enraged. In relationships with others Ms. L often not only becomes convinced of a friend's malevolent intention toward her but also begins to feel that her mother has invaded the friend's body and through her is continuing to communicate with Ms. L. The worker took an active role in helping Ms. L to find activities in which she could socialize in a nonthreatening way and in helping her to take an interest in improving her appearance and manner of approaching people. While Ms. L spoke of her anxieties about the motives of others in her meetings with the worker, the worker did not focus on improving Ms. L's perceptions of others. Nor did she explore the degree to which Ms. L was distorting the worker's motives toward her. After two months Ms. L stopped attending sessions, and the worker learned that Ms. L had been rehospitalized. Apparently Ms. L had become increasingly suspicious and had talked to others about how the worker had teamed up with her mother. Upon her discharge she refused to return to the worker.

Mr. J is a thirty-year-old unemployed actor who wanted help in "getting his act together." He could not make a commitment to work, had failed in his efforts to return to school, had failed in his marriage, and had unsatisfying relationships with friends and family, who he felt did not care about him and who demeaned him. In Mr. J's early meetings with the social worker he seemed motivated, attended sessions promptly, talked freely, and began making efforts to take care of everyday matters he had let go. Soon he began to call frequently between sessions when he felt out of control, anxious, or depressed. The worker spoke with him and would offer him support at these times. One day the worker was ten minutes late for a session. While Mr. J did not seem upset at the time, he began missing appointments and was withdrawn and noncommunicative when he appeared after the worker would call him and make another appointment. He talked about quitting and finally acknowledged feeling rejected and demeaned by the worker's having been late to the session several weeks earlier. He felt he was no longer important to her, was angry at what he felt was her cavalier attitude toward him, and accused her of exploiting him for charging a fee for just listening to him. The worker was able to empathize with Mr. J's feelings but also took the opportunity to point out that his reactions were part of a pattern involving the escalation of his demands on others in order to see if people cared and his concomitant feelings of rejection when they inevitably disappointed him. She helped him to reflect on the degree to which he set these situations up. Mr. J was able to acknowledge the accuracy of what the worker pointed out, to correct his perceptions of the worker's motives toward him, and to refrain from impulsively terminating the contact, as he had done with others in his life.

Mr. M is a thirty-four-year-old accountant who sought help because of repeated difficulties retaining employment. Typically he obtained good positions, felt valued by his male employers, and became dependent on them for their approval. Then he became depressed at not getting the recognition he felt he deserved and felt exploited. He would become angry at the way he was being treated and would engineer being fired. This pattern seemed related to Mr. M's relationship with his father, who was erratic in his emotional availability and critical in his attitude toward Mr. M, who never knew where he stood. This left him with strong yearnings to be close to and valued by men in authority, who represented his father. At the same time his exaggerated need for approval always left him feeling unsatisfied, as his expectations could not be fulfilled. His original anger at his father would then be displaced onto his employers, who really did like and value him but who disappointed him. His employers would become perplexed by Mr. M's change in attitude toward them, experience him as demanding and angry, and feel compelled to fire him as he created an unpleasant work environment.

The goal of the intervention was to help Mr. M understand and alter this pattern. The worker maintained an emotionally empathic but somewhat neutral stance with Mr. M in which he helped him to focus on understanding his relationship with his father and how he might be carrying it over into his adult relationships. As the worker continued to help him explore and reflect upon his reactions, Mr. M became depressed and felt worthless. He then became enraged at the worker for what appeared to be his cold and critical attitude. The worker used this experience to highlight to Mr. M the degree to which he wanted support from his father and was angry at not receiving it.

The worker helped Mr. M to see that in the absence of overt positive feedback he experienced the worker in a way similar to the way he experienced his father, when in fact the worker was quite different and felt a good deal of concern for and interest in Mr. M. The worker suggested that it was possible that Mr. M was misperceiving his employers in the same way. Mr. M was able to correct his distortion of the worker's attitude toward him. The same issue cropped up numerous times and was handled the same way. Finally the emotional impact of this pattern was extremely helpful in getting Mr. M to understand the nature of his relationships with other men.

In the first case Ms. D's initial suspiciousness masked her enormous neediness stemming from her past deprivations. The worker underestimated what a giving relationship would evoke in Ms. D and overestimated her ability to regulate the client's intense needs and feelings within the relationship. Further, when faced with Ms. D's escalating demands the worker was unable to restore a reality focus and diffuse the intensity of the client's reactions to her. Thus the relationship stirred up the client's longings while it also frustrated her. The client became very sensitive to any signs that the worker was going to abandon her (as did her mother), and the worker's vacation symbolized this abandonment and betrayal.

Similarly, in the second case the worker could have anticipated that Ms. L would develop suspicious feelings toward her as their relationship progressed, since this was characteristic of her response to women. This response was all the more likely to occur because of the active, somewhat directive role the worker took, which would stimulate Ms. L's perception of the worker as being like her mother. Had the worker anticipated these reactions and helped the client to improve her ability to perceive others' motivations toward her, the worker might have avoided becoming an "enemy."

In the third and fourth cases (Mr. J and Mr. M) the workers were able to help the clients identify and lessen their transference distortions in the client–worker relationship. In the case of Mr. J his responses within the relationship threatened his ongoing participation. The worker, however, was able to tap Mr. J's observing ego in order to help him perceive the worker and himself more realistically and to inhibit his pattern of terminating relationships. With Mr. M the worker utilized Mr. M's reactions to the worker to help him gain understanding of his needs and characteristic patterns of dealing with others.

TERMINATING THE CLIENT–WORKER RELATIONSHIP

The ending of any emotionally charged relationship evokes powerful emotions. Among these are feelings of loss, with related experiences of anger and guilt; feelings of narcissistic injury and related experiences of worthlessness and anxiety; and feelings of success and mastery. Because current losses reawaken past losses, the mastery of current separations can result in the mastery of previous ones. Because current feelings of narcissistic injury stimulate old injuries, the healing of current wounds may heal old wounds. Because experiences of success and mastery accrue to the ego's overall sense of competence, the ability to move forward in the present can lead to an enhanced sense of self-esteem and competence.[13]

There are many factors that affect the outcome of the termination process, such as the reasons for the termination, the time given to the process, the way it is dealt with, and the client's satisfaction with the help received. The nature and phases of the process also vary. The most important goals of the termination process are to prepare the client to (1) leave the relationship in a way that helps him or her maintain the gains that have been made, (2) master the separation and its unique meanings, and (3) be equipped to locate and use further therapy if indicated. Thus, terminating the client–worker relationship involves more than ending it after it has achieved, failed to achieve, or can no longer go on attempting to achieve its purpose. The process of termination itself is ego-building.

The following example illustrates the importance of handling this important phase of the interventive process.

Ms. P was thirty-seven when she accepted a new position in another city that necessitated her leaving the social worker she had seen weekly for four years, who she felt had helped her considerably. While Ms. P knew the change would be a good one since it offered the promise of more professional growth and advancement, better financial rewards, and greater recognition, the prospect of the rupture in her ties with the worker was experienced as an enormous loss.

While in reality Ms. P would lose an ongoing source of support as a result of leaving the social worker, her fears were extreme. She felt that she would be totally alone. She also felt unexplainable guilt for leaving the worker behind while she bettered herself. She found it difficult to imagine that the worker would still exist and care about her if Ms. P was no longer seeing her. Ms. P knew many people in her new environment and had positive feelings about her approaching move, but her sadness and depression absorbed her energy.

Significant in Ms. P's history was that she had struggled to achieve her autonomy from a suffocating yet nonsupportive family. The struggle was evident all through her development, and Ms. P's success professionally and personally involved acts of self-assertion in the face of her family's discouraging attitude toward her academic pursuits, anger at her leaving home, ridicule of her life-style, and refusal to help her financially. Despite her success the family remained critical of and unresponsive to her. She felt estranged from her family because of her independence and difference from them.

A major issue in her sessions with the social worker had been helping Ms. P to feel good about her success without experiencing terrible feelings of abandonment, depression, and guilt. It seemed likely that Ms. P's current anxiety and depression represented her fear that her lifelong fear would come true—that she would choose greater individuation but as a result lose her sense of belonging to a family as symbolized by the worker. With this came feelings of guilt about her own individuation. Further, because she had never been able to internalize "a good mother" who loved her and thus had difficulties maintaining a good sense of self, it was difficult for her to trust that the positive relationship with the worker would remain a part of her. The thought of leaving the worker resulted in a loss of her sense of herself.

In this termination process the worker was able to help Ms. P identify her lifelong pattern of experiencing loss in the process of individuation and recognize that she was reliving these feelings associated with her past. Many of these painful feelings were revisited in the termination process, and the worker empathized with them. The worker helped Ms. P to see that she was in a very different situation now from before, that she needed to trust more in the relationships she had established, and that her individuation, which Ms. P equated with aggression, would not destroy the worker or the worker's positive feelings toward Ms. P. The worker underlined the fact that the key issue in Ms. P's struggle was being evoked now, and that her ability to master it was important to her well-being.

This process was difficult for the worker too. She wanted to foster Ms. P's autonomy while remaining available to her as a support. The worker indicated she would be glad to correspond with Ms. P and to learn of her successes and that Ms. P did not have to terminate "cold turkey."

During the year following Ms. P's departure, she adapted to her new position quite easily and made many new friends. Nevertheless she experienced an enormous sense of loss resulting from the change in her important relationship with the worker, and her sense of herself was shaky. She was able to restrain her tendency to see the worker as rejecting her or to withdraw as she had done in the past with other relationships. She wrote to the worker and called her occasionally, and this reassured her that the quality of the relationship had not changed with the passage of time. Ms. P not only began to feel more secure about the relationship but also felt a sense of mastery over her problems with separation. This was the first time she felt that her growth and pleasure did not have to be at the expense of a relationship with an important person. This experience was corrective for Ms. P and allowed for a reworking of a major difficulty in her life. Thus it was only in completing termination that Ms. P overcame a core problem affecting her well-being and relations with others.

In this example the anticipated separation from the worker stirred up Ms. P's lifelong difficulties around separation–individuation, even though it was she who decided to terminate the client–worker relationship. The worker's ability to help Ms. P experience her feelings, to help her understand the nature of the worker's response, to validate and support her ability to handle the situation, and to remain available as someone on whom Ms. P could concretely rely while she moved forward were important factors in Ms. P's gradual ability to master not only the termination but the longstanding separation–individuation issues that it stirred up.

SUMMARY

This chapter has discussed many of the important characteristics of the client–worker relationship: its purpose, the values guiding it, and the nature of responses within it. It also has discussed the attributes of the client, the worker, and the practice setting that influence the relationship and the uses of the relationship. The chapter concluded with case examples illustrating the management of important features of the client–worker relationship. Among these are the engagement and termination process, the use of the positive relationship, and recognizing and dealing with transference.

NOTES

1. For example, see Annette Garrett, "The Worker Client Relationship," In Howard J. Parad, ed., *Ego Psychology and Dynamic Casework* (New York: Family Service Association of America, 1958), pp. 53–72; Gordon Hamilton, *Theory and Practice of Social Casework*, 2nd Ed., Rev. (New York and London: Columbia University Press, 1951), Chapter 2; Florence Hollis, *Casework: A Psychosocial Therapy*, 2nd Ed. (New York: Random House, 1972), Chapter 13; Helen Harris Perlman, *Social Casework: A Problem-Solving Process* (Chicago: University of Chicago Press, 1957), Chapters 6 and 12; *idem*, *Relationship* (Chicago: University of Chicago Press, 1979); and Virginia Robinson, *A Changing Psychology in Social Casework* (Chapel Hill: University of North Carolina Press, 1930).
2. The therapist as a blank screen is a model adopted from psychoanalytic theory and practice. It followed from the premise that change in the client resulted from his or her ability to gain insight into unconscious conflicts as a result of their being enacted within the client–worker relationship. Consequently the worker was supposed to refrain from allowing his or her personality to intrude upon the helping process at all in order to minimize the client's realistic perceptions of him or her and to foster the client's irrational distortions. Also, the term "therapeutic neutrality" is used in psychoanalysis to describe the stance of the analyst. His or her interventions must not side with any of the three structures of the mind (id, ego, or superego). Supportive techniques violate this neutrality, whereas reflective techniques do not.
3. These distinctions were made originally in the psychotherapy literature. See, for example, Ralph R. Greenson, *The Technique and Practice of Psychoanalysis*, Vol. 1 (New York: International Universities Press, 1967), and Lewis Wolberg, *Techniques of Psychotherapy*, 2 Vols. (New York: Grune & Stratton, 1969).
4. Two important writers who discuss how to deal with transference in this manner are Franz Alexander and Thomas M. French. See *Psychoanalytic Therapy* (New York: Ronald Press, 1946).
5. See, for example, Otto F. Kernberg, *Borderline Conditions and Pathological Narcissism* (New York: Jason Aronson, 1975), Chapter 2.
6. This is a complex issue. How can one know if one's reactions are unconsciously motivated if one cannot know the unconscious? One hopes that the practitioner has reasonably good self-awareness, including knowledge of his or her blind spots and trouble spots. What is important here is the awareness that clients do induce strong feelings in workers.

7. For a study of the importance of shared expectations and goals in the interventive process, see John Mayer and Noel Timms, *The Client Speaks: Working Class Impressions of Casework* (New York: Atherton Press, 1970). See also Anthony N . Maluccio and Wilma D. Marlow, "The Case for the Contract," *Social Work*, 19 (January 1974): 28–36.

8. For an interesting book that contains numerous articles dealing with the topic, see James A. Goodman, *Dynamics of Racism in Social Work Practice* (Washington, D.C.: National Association of Social Workers, 1973).

9. For studies of therapist characteristics associated with therapeutic effectiveness, see C. R. Rogers, "The Necessary and Sufficient Conditions of Therapeutic Personality Change," *Journal of Consulting Psychology*, 21 (1957): 95–103; C. B. Truax and R. R. Carkhuff, *Toward Effective Counseling and Psychotherapy: Training and Practice* (Chicago: Aldine, 1967); and R. R. Carkhuff and B. G. Berenson, *Beyond Counseling and Psychotherapy* (New York: Holt, Rinehart & Winston, 1967).

10. The worker's own self-awareness is an important component of skillfulness, and the constraints on his or her self-knowledge will disturb effectiveness.

11. Lucille Austin was among the first social workers to stress this aspect of the casework relationship. The idea originated in the work of Alexander and French, *Psychoanalytic Therapy*.

12. See Allen Pincus and Anne Minahan, *Social Work Practice: Model and Method* (Itasca, Ill.: F. E. Peacock, 1973), Chapter 9.

13. For a discussion of the termination process, see Evelyn F. Fox, Marian A. Nelson, and William M. Bolman, "The Termination Process: A Neglected Dimension," *Social Work*, 14 (October 1969): 53–63.

EGO-ORIENTED INTERVENTION WITH DIVERSE AND OPPRESSED POPULATIONS

W hile ego psychology provided social work with a biopsychosocial theoretical foundation for direct practice, its critics have tended to equate it with a narrow psychodynamic, psychotherapeutic, and pathology-oriented framework. At its best, however, ego-oriented practice reflects a person–environmental focus, a respect for individual differences, and a focus on mobilizing strengths. As society generally has shown greater appreciation of ethnicity, race, and culture and the impact of sexism, racism, homophobia, discrimination, and victimization on human functioning, ego psychology has expanded to include new knowledge regarding these phenomena. Consequently, ego-oriented practitioners are showing more individualized understanding of the needs and concerns of clients who belong to diverse and oppressed populations and are utilizing more affirmative and empowering interventions in their practice. In light of these developments, this chapter will discuss the main principles and selected foci of intervention with women, people of color, and gays and lesbians.

GENERAL PRINCIPLES

While more recent perspectives on work with women, people of color, and gays and lesbians reflect their own distinctive foci, they embody similar guidelines. The following ten common principles have been put forth.

APPRECIATING THE IMPACT OF THE SOCIOPOLITICAL CONTEXT

The practitioner must be able to view clients who belong to diverse and oppressed populations in terms of the effects of the sociopolitical context instead of their personal development only.[1] This requires an appreciation of the impact of sexism, racism, homophobia, discrimination, stigma, victimization, lack of resources, and rigid role requirements on personality functioning and in causing stress and dysfunction. Such an emphasis has led some individuals to discount all theories that place importance on the development of individual capacities and their role in adaptation or maladaptation and to advocate an exclusive focus on changing society rather than on helping individuals improve their functioning through direct practice. In contrast to those who hold this extreme view, the ego-oriented practitioner, who possesses an awareness of the contributions of the sociopolitical context to human functioning, recognizes that personal problems often reflect broader social realities. He or she refrains from relying on a pathology model to explain the difficulties of oppressed groups and from mechanically applying diagnostic labels and theories based on personal weakness or biased observations and attitudes.

The ego-oriented practitioner does not discard all theory or all attempts to understand the personality of the client but uses concepts selectively and on an individualized basis when they fit the facts of a particular case. Moreover, he or she helps the client to understand him- or herself in relationship to sociopolitical forces and cultural values as well as his or her unique personal and family history. For example, in working with a depressed Puerto Rican mother who is self-sacrificing in her behavior toward all the members of her extended family and who maintains dependent and submissive relationships with exploitative men, a practitioner would be making a serious error in quickly labeling her "a masochistic personality" and focusing on her pathology. Instead, the worker should explore the client's needs as she sees them and help her to reflect on the ways in which she has had to adapt to her own culture's and family's expectations of her and to the lack of available options, role models, and encouragement for her to act with greater self-interest and independence. Similarly, in working with a young African-American male substance abuser who has grown up in poverty, it is important to go beyond a narrow focus on his character traits and possible ego deficits and to consider the role that drugs may play in helping him cope with his underlying rage and depression and his experience of being a second-class citizen who is closed out of the mainstream of life. Likewise, in trying to help a Puerto Rican mother who has recently moved to the mainland United States in order to secure a better economic future, leaving her two small children behind with their grandmother, it would be crucial to recognize her efforts to provide for her family rather than assume that she is ambivalent about caring for her children or that she has abandoned them.

EXERCISING SELF-AWARENESS

While the worker's exercise of self-awareness is an important component of all practice efforts, it takes on a special significance in work with those who show very different values, attitudes, backgrounds, life experiences, and personal styles. Nevertheless, there is a fallacy to the commonly articulated view that helping professionals who are like their clients in terms of gender, cultural background, or sexual orientation, for example, will be free from negative attitudes, and thus more effective in the helping process than those who are unlike their clients. There are many instances in which the use of workers who share characteristics with their clients may be therapeutically indicated, enabling the clients to feel more easily understood and accepted and providing them with positive role models. Sameness of worker and client, however, is not always a panacea and may lead to mutual blind spots.[2] For example, while it may be difficult for some male therapists to understand a woman client's fear that self-assertion and autonomy may result in abandonment, female practitioners who have been raised with conventional values may have problems helping a female client who feels trapped in her marriage to choose less traditional options. Likewise, while a white middle-class therapist may unwittingly reflect stereotyped and prejudiced attitudes in his or her work with a poor African-American single mother who is dependent on others, a female worker from the same background who has struggled to be financially successful and independent may expect her client to behave as she did and fail to empathize with her unique plight. Similarly, while some non-gay male workers may have difficulty accepting a gay client's interest in other men, it may be equally difficult for a closeted lesbian practitioner who herself suffers from internalized homophobia to help a lesbian client who is demeaning of other lesbians and reluctant to disclose her sexual orientation out of shame and fear. The ability to be empathic and respectful of clients, whether one is similar to or different from them, requires the practitioner to scrutinize his or her own values, attitudes, experiences, and theoretical biases, since these shape all aspects of the interventive process.

BALANCING A FOCUS ON GROUP MEMBERSHIP AND INDIVIDUALIZATION

It is important for the practitioner to be sensitive to the common problems, life experiences, values, characteristics, and strengths that clients have by virtue of their group membership. For example, those who have recently immigrated to this country often lack skills for negotiating their new environment, necessary resources, and support systems. Further they may be experiencing loss of relationships, income, status, familiar surroundings, and language; disorientation; disillusionment; and feelings of powerlessness (Hirayama and Cetingok, 1988: 41–47). Collier (1982: 57–77) has noted eight common difficulties that women clients present: powerlessness; limited behavioral and emotional options; anger; inadequate communication skills; inability to nurture themselves; problems balancing independence and dependence; lack of trust in self-direction; and adherence to old rules and expectations. Gutierrez (1990: 149–54) and Pinder-hughes (1983: 331–38) emphasize the lack of a sense of personal power that is characteristic of many people of color who become clients. Further, the practitioner must recognize their frequent and understandable distrust of authority, social institutions, and helping professionals, as well as their culturally specific patterns of giving and receiving help (Solomon, 1983: 873–74). Fear of mental health professionals is also widespread among gay and lesbian individuals, who may suffer from internalized homo-phobia or anticipate being judged negatively, labeled inappro-priately, and otherwise mistreated by homophobic practitioners who may attempt to "cure" their "deviance" rather than relate to their human concerns.[3] On the positive side, different popula-tions have developed certain strengths that have helped them to cope adaptively. For example, strong kinship and religious ties and spiritual leanings are crucial to the functioning of African-Americans, Latinos, and Asians.

While sensitivity to the commonalities that stem from the clients' group membership is crucial to accurate assessment and all aspects of the interventive process, the principle of individu-alization always must be a central concern of the practitioner. Since members of diverse and oppressed populations do not al-ways share the same experiences or show the same degree of group identification, the practitioner needs to avoid over-gener-alizing and stereotyping.

ENHANCING CLIENT STRENGTHS

Many proponents of gender- and culture-sensitive interventive approaches have accused clinicians of focusing narrowly on deficits, conflicts, problems, and other types of pathology instead of identifying, mobilizing, and enhancing clients' strengths. While in principle the support of adaptive functioning is central to all ego-oriented intervention, it sometimes has received less attention than attempts to modify pathology. A focus on enhanc-ing clients' positive capacities is consistent with an emphasis on the impact on social functioning of oppressive social and envi-ronmental attitudes and conditions or a dearth of necessary re-sources.[4] Such an approach also takes on particular significance in work with clients who feel stigmatized or oppressed and who show low self-esteem, low-self confidence, feelings of powerlessness, and hopelessness about alternative courses of action. Emphasizing areas of dysfunction or pathology may be experienced by these clients as blaming, thereby contributing to their negative self-regard. Instead, it is vital for the practitioner to convey respect for the ways in which the client has attempted to cope with difficult life circumstances and to search out, validate, and enhance the positive features of the client's functioning. Crucial as a strengths perspective is, however, it does not obviate the need for the worker to assess the obstacles to more adaptive functioning that may stem from the client's inadequately developed or impaired coping mechanisms. There is a role for remedial interventions in many instances. A main concern for the practitioner is how to achieve the proper balance between maximizing strengths and modifying dysfunctional behavior and attitudes.

BUILDING SELF-CONFIDENCE, SELF-ESTEEM, AND PERSONAL POWER

Since powerlessness is so pervasive among clients who belong to diverse and oppressed populations, empowerment is the most important goal of intervention with them.[5] It involves helping clients to increase the sense of personal control over their lives, to feel good about themselves, and to believe that they can have an impact on others and the world around them. Gutierrez (1990: 150–52) describes four general aspects of the empowerment process: increasing self-efficacy, developing group consciousness, reducing self-blame, and assuming personal responsibility for change. Among the empowering practices she suggests are: employing a more collaborative and egalitarian model in the therapeutic relationship; accepting the client's definition of the problem; utilizing role-playing in which clients practice assertiveness, taking control, helping, and leadership; actively involving clients in the process of change; identifying and building on existing strengths; engaging in a power analysis of the client's situation; teaching specific skills; linking clients to resources and support systems; and advocacy.

EQUALIZING POWER IN THE THERAPEUTIC RELATIONSHIP

In order to empower clients effectively, it may be necessary to reconceptualize the worker–client relationship. Critics of the traditional model of the therapeutic interaction, which reflects a hierarchical arrangement between helper and client, have stressed its embodiment of society's inequitable power arrangements. They argue that it runs the risk of reinforcing dependence on authority. Believing that it is important for clients to experience a helping relationship that is based on collaboration, trust, and the sharing of power, they have strongly urged the adoption of a more egalitarian model of the therapeutic relationship.[6] Solomon (1983: 878) cautions, however, that there are exceptions to this principle and notes that the value placed on authority by some Third World groups might make clients with certain backgrounds uncomfortable and distrustful of a more egalitarian helping relationship. For example, Japanese and other Asian-Pacific cultures accept authority when they are learning and do not feel demeaned by being in a subordinate position.

Finding ways of equalizing power between worker and client does not mean that the helper should withhold his or her expertise from the client. It does necessitate that the practitioner strive to find ways of engaging the client in a collaborative problem-solving effort in which the client is accorded respect and dignity. Some writers (Gutierrez, 1990: 151; Valentich, 1986: 572) have suggested that it is necessary to demonstrate this equality in concrete ways such as using first rather than last names, creating a more informal atmosphere, engaging in self-disclosure, and being more genuine in communicating with the client. Since clients differ, however, in their expectations of the treatment relationship, fears of exploitation, values with respect to authority, level of comfort with informality, and need for clear boundaries, a flexible rather than doctrinaire approach to structuring the client–worker relationship is indicated.

EDUCATING ABOUT OPTIONS AND MAXIMIZING CHOICE

Individuals who feel trapped and powerless may lack knowledge of available options, be unaccustomed to and uncomfortable with making decisions, and be fearful of and reluctant to take risks that seem to threaten their security. Often such individuals have not had access to role models to lead the way with respect to different ways of thinking, feeling, and acting. The client's self-determination may be enhanced rather than undermined by the worker's taking an active role in educating him or her about options, providing a vision for change, and encouraging constructive actions consistent with his or her needs and abilities. Advocating for the client's right to realize his or her potential is different from imposing one's own values and opinions on the client indiscriminately and suggesting solutions that may be too frightening, guilt-producing, or alienating given the client's cultural background. For example, in working with a depressed Puerto Rican woman who is slavishly devoted to and dominated by her elderly parents and strongly attached to her siblings and other relatives, efforts to help her identify and implement ways of developing her own life must be undertaken with an appreciation of her need to remain loyal to her family.

LINKING CLIENTS TO NEEDED RESOURCES

When clients lack needed resources, their personal power is diminished. Thus a crucial aspect of the interventive process linking clients to services, entitlements, and other forms of material assistance. Effectively connecting clients to environmental resources requires that the worker not only help them in locating appropriate help but also assist them in understanding the application procedures and eligibility requirements and in developing coping skills for dealing with bureaucratic systems. Further, it may be necessary for the worker to facilitate the application process, accompany clients, and advocate on their behalf.

CONNECTING CLIENTS TO MUTUAL AID
GROUPS AND PEER SUPPORTS

Consciousness-raising, educational self-help, and other types of support groups often are important in empowering individuals who belong to diverse and oppressed populations (Gutierrez,

1990: 150; Valentich, 1986: 574–75). Such experiences help clients to decrease their isolation, strengthen their group identification, clarify issues of common concern, increase feelings of acceptance and self-esteem, develop their problem-solving skills, learn new ways of negotiating interpersonal relationships, gain support from others, and acquire experience in collective action.

ENCOURAGING COLLECTIVE AND POLITICAL ACTION

In addition to creating the conditions that promote personal change, both individual and group intervention can empower clients to advocate for themselves more effectively and to contribute to collective efforts for change in the community and larger society. Not only do such activities help clients to feel that they can make a difference, but they are also necessary to achieving freedom from oppression and equal access to social resources. That there truly is strength in numbers can be seen from the successful struggle for equality and social justice on the part of women, people of color, and gays and lesbians that we have witnessed in the last decades.

SELECTED ISSUES IN WORK WITH WOMEN

While some feminist practitioners might object to a formal assessment, viewing it as part of a pathology model, others emphasize that there is a need for a thorough understanding of the presenting problem that encompasses gender-specific factors, avoids inappropriate diagnostic labels, and focuses on present concerns. Further, the practitioner may utilize the client's history to facilitate his or her understanding of the social context and any oppression to which the client has been exposed. Besides the questions (discussed in Chapter 7) that generally guide an ego-oriented assessment as a starting point, additional important considerations can assist the practitioner in arriving at a gender-sensitive understanding of a female client. It is important to appreciate the role that gender is playing in the presenting problem, for example, in the client's experience of financial inequity, sexual harassment, discrimination, or low status in the workplace; inadequate income, child care, housing, medical care, or other resources in her parenting role; isolation and lack of family and peer supports; limited gender roles; traumatic events such as death of a spouse, parent, or child or personal or family illness; health problems; and sexual abuse, rape, or domestic violence.

In evaluating a woman's ego capacities, personality traits, and unique strengths, it is important to explore the components of her self-concept; to identify the roles, activities, and relationships that help her sustain and regulate her self-esteem; to understand how she has been socialized in terms of her view of herself as a woman; to evaluate her feelings of competence and personal power; and to consider what options are available for her and how she thinks significant others would view and treat her were she different. Characteristics such as passivity, lack of assertiveness, difficulty expressing anger, self-sacrifice and self-abnegation, and even self-destructiveness need to be understood as adaptive solutions to oppressive social conditions or traditional social roles, rather than as innate or pathological. Other traits, such as self-sufficiency and aggressiveness, that might erroneously be considered pathological in women must be appreciated in light of their appropriateness or their role in aiding psychological survival.

Further, in assessing women who seem to show certain diagnostic syndromes such as eating disorders, depression, substance abuse, avoidant behavior, and anxiety states, it is necessary to understand the socialization patterns, interpersonal relationships, absence of positive outlets and supports, and environmental conditions that may be contributing to these symptomatic manifestations.[7]

Women have special treatment needs that stem from their personality development and socialization, life cycle events and roles, economic status, health needs, and vulnerability to certain kinds of trauma.

Personality Development and Socialization. Several emphases in the traditional socialization of women have had major ramifications for their later personality functioning: the emphasis on caring for others at the expense of gratifying one's own needs; the value placed on passivity and dependence on others rather than on active and autonomous behavior; the importance of defining oneself in terms of one's relationships with husband and children; the ambivalence about entering and succeeding in the work arena; and the prohibition against enjoying sex. Intervention must offer women alternatives to traditional roles and ways of viewing themselves and assist them in expanding their repertoire of behavior and in actualizing themselves.

Life Cycle Events and Roles. In the usual view, a woman's life cycle is composed of events such as menarche, pregnancy, mothering, menopause, and widowhood that have special significance psychologically and that require certain external supports. The expansion of alternatives for women has led to greater variation in their predictable life course. For example, the needs of single mothers and of unmarried, childless, lesbian, separated, divorced, and remarried women have come into focus to a greater extent than was true previously.[8] The widening of options for women, while liberating, also creates stress. Women today struggle with blending family and work, conflicting choices, the absence or inadequacy of necessary resources and support systems, new ways of negotiating their relationships with men, and the anxiety associated with moving into unfamiliar territory in the absence of maternal or other role models.

Economic Status. As a group, women are more economically disadvantaged than men and they constitute the vast majority of those who are considered poor in this country (Simon, 1988:6–17). They make up the bulk of those on welfare rolls and carry the brunt of parenting in female-headed households; when they work they tend to receive lower salaries, have positions of lesser status, and have fewer opportunities for advancement than do men. Women of color have the additional burden of being doubly oppressed.

Health Issues. Women experience numerous health-related issues that warrant special attention throughout their lives. The staggering amount of teenage pregnancy[9] and the large numbers of women who give birth when they are addicted to alcohol or drugs or who are carriers of the HIV virus underscore the need for preventive counseling around managing sexuality, the effects of substance abuse, birth control, abortion, and prenatal care. Likewise, there is a need for preparation for menarche, childbirth, and menopause as well as education and supportive intervention around postpartum reactions, breast cancer, breast augmentation and reduction and other forms of plastic surgery, estrogen replacement therapy, osteoporosis, and hip replacement surgery.

An important women's health issue that has major psychological, physical, and treatment implications involves their concern with weight loss and body image. Eating disorders in women are of epidemic proportions and chronic dieting is commonplace even among those who are not overweight by objective standards. Feminists have argued that women's obsession with food and thinness is a direct result of a society that places a primary value on women as sexual objects and that equates thinness as attractiveness (Orbach, 1978). They encourage women to reject this emphasis but most women have difficulty doing so, having been taught to think otherwise and encountering the message that "thin is beautiful" on a regular basis.

One cannot leave the topic of women's health issues without noting the high incidence of depression in the female population. Some have suggested that the statistics reflect women's willingness to express their feelings and their tendency to come for help, rather than women's greater biological, psychological, or sociological vulnerability. After reviewing the evidence, however, Weissman (1981:160–95) argues that the extensive amount of depression in women is real. Research on the causes of depression in women has produced suggestive findings but there is no clear evidence that it results from biological rather than psychosocial factors.

Vulnerability to Trauma. Women are vulnerable to rape and spouse abuse and frequently need help in dealing with the immediate and ongoing impact of traumatic assaults and episodic and chronic violence. Further, the staggering amount of childhood sexual abuse of females leaves severe emotional scarring along with more subtle residues in adult survivors, all of which warrant special interventive efforts (Courtois, 1988). This important topic will be discussed in more detail in Chapter 11.

Rape is a devastating experience psychologically even if the woman is not harmed physically. It has both short- and long-term effects and may result in post-traumatic stress reactions long after the actual event has occurred. Despite the increasing prevalence of sexual assault, most rapes are not reported to the police because of the victim's shame, fear, uncertainty about others' reactions, and lack of confidence in the police or criminal justice system.[10] Women's reluctance to reveal the fact that they have been raped out of concern for the repercussions of such disclosure has resulted in large part from society's suspicion of, negative attitudes toward, and poor treatment of rape victims. This is particularly true in cases of acquaintance and marital rape, which people often view as less serious than stranger rape (Abarbanel and Richman, 1990:102–107; Bowker, 1983:347–52).

Usually there are stages in a survivor's reactions to rape, although these differ in nature from person to person. The initial stage of shock, numbness, terror, and disbelief tends to be followed by denial. This gives way to more acute symptoms such as shame, anxiety, fear of being alone or fear for one's personal safety, self-blame, guilt, emotional lability, intrusive thoughts and nightmares, feelings of powerlessness, depression, rage, low self-esteem, sleep disturbances, somatic distress, social withdrawal, and sexual problems. After these responses lessen, reorganization or resolution of the event occurs in the final stage. It is not unusual, however, for survivors to have continuing reactions for a long time and recurrent symptoms episodically after the event (Abarbanel and Richman, 1990:102–107; Lee and Rosenthal, 1983:593–601). When untreated, many survivors may later show post-traumatic stress disorders. In addition to the crippling symptoms that are associated with rape, a woman may undergo a change in her view of the world. Rape and other types of violent assault violate a woman's basic sense of security and invulnerability and often leave survivors questioning their judgment and ability to take care of themselves.

The greater availability of rape hot lines and crisis centers and the effort of law enforcement officers and the press to change their attitudes toward and treatment of the victims of rape have helped countless numbers of women to reach out for help. Most writers agree that the first steps in the treatment of rape survivors who are in crisis should be to assess where they are in the process of coping with the rape as well as their strengths and support systems; help them to discuss what happened to them and to express their feelings; provide validation for and education about their reactions; elicit their concerns; partialize and problem-solve about immediate courses of action such as reporting to the police, creating a sense of safety, and sharing with others; mobilize their strengths; and involve their support systems.

In the early ventilation stage of intervention, the worker should help the client to discuss the details of the rape experience in manageable doses; it also may be necessary for her to go over these experiences repeatedly both initially and at various points in the treatment. As the treatment continues, the worker helps the client to deal with the losses and other reactions she may be experiencing and to find ways of going on with her life in the face of what has occurred. Sometimes the rape experience evokes other events and situations in a woman's life, or it may trigger and serve to reinforce her negative view of herself and the world around her. The worker assesses the degree to which the present crisis can be resolved without more extensive ongoing treatment of underlying issues. Finally the worker prepares the client for ongoing reactions and how to cope with them and evaluates her ability to function on her own.

Wife battering, like rape, is widespread in our society[11] and its victims likewise tend to be viewed negatively for provoking, enjoying, or withstanding the abuse "masochistically," rather than setting limits on the spouse's violent behavior or leaving the relationship. While there are women who cannot leave their abusive partners for deep-seated psychological reasons that cause them to hold onto a destructive relationship, this fact has obscured other more important factors in their inability to remove themselves from the abusive situation. These involve fear of being murdered; fear of their children's being harmed; lack of knowledge about alternatives; lack of economic resources; psychological and economic dependency; low self-esteem; and religious and cultural beliefs. Moreover, many wife batterers are not merely impulsive but actively engaged in manipulating and terrorizing their wives, convincing them that they are worthless, incompetent, and deserving of mistreatment (Brekke, 1990: 161–78). Because of this, victims of battering often blame themselves and feel humiliated, isolated, powerless, and resigned to their plight. Moreover, they have been taught to distrust those who might otherwise help them and are secretive about and denying of their abuse.

Intervention with women who are the victims of domestic violence requires information about alternative living arrangements and economic resources as well as supportive treatment. Fortunately, the availability and visibility of hot lines and shelters, and media attention to the prevalence of spouse abuse, are important in enabling women to seek help. The unprecedented publicity about the battering of Nicole Simpson and the subsequent charges against her husband, O. J. Simpson, for her murder led to a significant increase in the use of hot lines and shelters. These dramatic and tragic events seemed to mobilize women to take action on their own behalf. It is important to note, however, that even when women who are battered seek help, they are ambivalent and fearful about leaving their partners.

In the interventive process, the victim of battering must feel that she is safe in disclosing the extent of her abuse, and that she will not be judged or asked to take actions for which she is not fully ready. The worker must make an assessment of the urgency of the woman's plight and of her ability to leave the abusive relationship. Educating a woman about the nature and prevalence of battering, available resources and alternatives, and her legal rights is indicated. When the client is ready, problem-solving with her and arriving at a safety plan that addresses not only where she can go when she leaves home but how she can make the move without endangering herself or her children are crucial. Before engaging in this strategy, however, considerable work may be necessary that is aimed at empowering the client. The worker must help the client to express her feelings, understand the positive aspects of life with the batterer, explore her fears and misgivings about leaving, deal with her losses, correct distortions and point out the realities of her situation, and support her strengths. In some instances, it may be necessary to explore the woman's self-concept and the longstanding attitudes and patterns that have contributed to her dependence on destructive relationships.

SELECTED ISSUES IN WORK WITH PEOPLE OF COLOR

An ego-oriented assessment should encompass additional important foci so that the practitioner can achieve a more culturally sensitive understanding of people of color. In working with African-Americans, Caribbean-Americans, Latinos, Asian-Americans, and Native Americans it is important for the practitioner to explore the contributions of race, ethnicity, immigration, acculturation, minority status, poverty, and oppression to the presenting problem. Clients may be experiencing stress related to cultural conflict; difficulties coping with loss, unfamiliar surroundings, new demands and customs, a different language, lack of resources, and the absence of support systems; outright discrimination in housing, employment, and acceptance by the community; the effects of negative stereotyping; the daily assaults of living with the threat of sudden violence and even death, the pervasiveness of drugs, substandard housing, devastated neighborhoods, and lack of basic necessities; and feelings of isolation, alienation, and powerlessness. Crucial to the assessment of whether ethnicity and race are playing a role in the presenting problem is the degree of group identification a particular client has with those who share his or her cultural background.[12] Further, because clients may not feel free to share their view that racism or discrimination is contributing to their problems, particularly with a white American worker, the practitioner must be sensitive and alert to the messages being conveyed and willing to ask questions in ways that give clients permission to disclose their concerns (Robinson, 1989:323–29).

In evaluating certain symptoms and seemingly dysfunctional behavior, the worker should have knowledge regarding the ways in which different groups cope with stress. Ryan (1985: 337–38) points out, for example, that for Chinese-Americans, the cultural emphasis on self-control, middle-position virtue, adherence to the mean, and inhibition of strong feelings takes a toll and that many Chinese tend to somatize rather than express their emotions and problems. In fact, complaining of anxiety or depression would be considered a failing. Thus, it is not unusual for such individuals to present with physical distress and disorders rather than with concerns about difficulties with school, work relationships, or their emotional states and psychological problems. Further, because of certain factors in their family background and values, Chinese-Americans may be prone to depression. Moreover, suicide is considered to be an honorable way of saving face and solving problems. Along with these general considerations, it is important for the practitioner to bear in mind that there is diversity within special populations and to refrain from viewing all members of certain cultural groups as similar in all respects.

In evaluating ego capacities, personality traits, and unique strengths, the worker must recognize the characteristics that a particular culture considers desirable as well as the strengths that have developed as adaptive solutions to oppressive social conditions or to promote survival. In this regard, Darielle Jones (1979:112–18) points to the importance of gender role flexibility, strong kinship bonds, high achievement strivings, strong work orientation, and firm religious leanings in African-Americans. She further identifies four common distortions that clinicians have tended to make in diagnosing individuals who come from this cultural background, including a tendency to see them as having poor impulse control, inappropriate rage, concrete thinking, and dependent and helpless character traits. Jones argues that these characteristics are likely to result from the cumulative effects of racism, limited opportunities, adaptation to sparse resources, the need for day-to-day survival mechanisms, environmental assaults, and an accumulated sense of social injustice. Similarly, Solomon (1983:872–73) discusses the different values that many Puerto Ricans hold in comparison to middle-class whites that might lead some practitioners to label their characteristic stance as maladaptive. She notes Puerto Ricans show present rather than future time orientation; a preference for collateral decision-making by consensus over individualistic decision-making; a tendency toward "being," in the sense of enjoying spontaneity and expressiveness, rather than "doing";

and a belief that human nature has a large component of evil rather than being neutral or having a mix of good and evil. Ghali (1982:98–102) emphasizes the importance of understanding frequent practices and attitudes among Puerto Ricans, including common-law marriage; men's sexual freedom and feeling of superiority to women; women's submission, obedience to men, and self-sacrificing commitment to mothering; and the institution of "companion parents," in which children are given over to the care of close relatives in order to help them have a better future.

An important issue in the assessment of people of color is their patterns of taking help and their expectations and behavior in the interventive process. The tendency to use natural support networks such as family, friends, schools, and spiritual leaders for assistance in times of need is characteristic of Latinos and Asians in particular. Ryan (1985:338–40) notes that Chinese-Americans characteristically seek help from family and friends but may be forced to turn to strangers when necessary support systems are lacking or when problems become so extreme that usual means of assistance are not effective. Thus they tend to use professional services reluctantly, if at all, and may appear to be guarded in sharing their concerns. Their discomfort may be intensified by their common belief that expressing feelings and worries is a sign of weakness and that problems are physical rather than psychological in nature. Consequently, they may appear to be denying, resistant, and suspicious. On the positive side, their respect for authority may allow positive connections to be made to helping professionals and agency settings, and a worker's willingness to be active in structuring concretely helpful, nonintrusive, and respectful contacts may enable the process to move forward.

Many people of color have special treatment needs that stem from their adaptation to immigration and acculturation, their vulnerability to poverty and other stressful life circumstances, and their exposure to personal and institutional forms of racism and oppression.

Immigration and Acculturation. Both the steady flow of immigrants and numerous episodic waves of immigration have resulted in large numbers of Asian-Americans, Latinos, and Caribbean-Americans seeking a new life in this country. Culturally sensitive interventive approaches must recognize and address their various stages of adjustment in attempting to acculturate to American society,[13] the range of troubling reactions that they experience, their frequent lack of adequate coping skills, and the absence of necessary resources and support systems. The change in values, mores, and expectations as well as the loss of relationships, status, familiarity, and other mainstays of self-esteem regulation are disorienting and often debilitating even among those who adapt successfully. Further, emigres who adjust well always have to contend with their own biculturalism and the ongoing strains that this imposes, for example, on parenting, on the ability to achieve a sense of belonging in a society in which one looks and speaks differently from others and may have lower status, and on native values.

Poverty. The fact that people of color are disproportionately represented among the economically disadvantaged in this country has significant implications for intervention. Many individuals present with concrete material and reality-based needs as well as a host of difficulties coping with limited resources and the problems that are ravaging poor and minority communities. While teen pregnancy, violence, substance abuse, child maltreatment, AIDS, and mental illness affect all classes of society and poor communities show certain strengths in coping with stress and traumatic events, members of minorities who also lack economic resources are highly vulnerable to these and other pervasive social ills. The treatment of some of these problems will be considered in Chapter 11.

Racism and Oppression. Personal and institutional racism and oppression affect the daily lives of many people of color in very concrete and more subtle ways that need to be addressed in terms of both broader societal change and direct practice. Discrimination in housing, employment, and service delivery; lack of access to economic opportunities and resources; unfair treatment by police and the court system; and the constant awareness of being viewed negatively by others has insidious effects on

self-esteem and successful coping. The client's use of professional services and the worker–client relationship itself are not
free from the effects of racism, on the part of both the client and
the worker. The practitioner's awareness of his or her own negative stereotypical attitudes, his or her ability to create a safe, respectful, and accepting environment in which clients can
verbalize and explore their concerns, and his or her ability to
help empower and advocate for clients are crucial elements of effective intervention.

SELECTED ISSUES IN WORK WITH GAYS AND LESBIANS

Homosexuality is not a psychiatric illness nor does its presence
in men and women mean that they are suffering from a disease
that needs to be cured or that they are showing psychological
maladjustment or some type of personality pathology. Some of
the presenting concerns of gay men and women do relate specifically to their sexual orientation, for example, how to deal with
their emerging feelings of attraction to same-sex individuals or
whether or not to disclose their homosexuality to family, friends,
or co-workers. Most gays and lesbians, however, usually seek
professional help for a range of reasons that have little to do with
their sexual orientation *per se* or are related to it only indirectly.[14]
Like their so-called "straight" counterparts, they seek help in
dealing with the problems of living, career issues, relationship
problems, life crises, depression, anxiety, physical illness, unemployment, parenting concerns, and the like. In order for practitioners to be sensitive to the particular needs and concerns of gay
and lesbian clients, however, they must appreciate that the
client's membership in a stigmatized and oppressed group has
shaped his or her identity and may be playing a role in the presenting problem. For example, a woman's relationship problems
with her female partner may stem from her reluctance to include
her partner in family gatherings or to socialize with her publicly.
This may result from her own negative attitudes toward her sexual orientation and her fear of being viewed as a lesbian by others. Likewise, a gay man's difficulty in pursuing his career

actively and assertively may stem from his low self-esteem and the fear that if he calls attention to himself he will be exposed as gay. Similarly, a lesbian's depression and alcoholism may be caused by her attempts to deny her own wish and need to be with women; this may lead her to try unsuccessfully to have relationships with men, leaving her with tormenting doubts about her ability to love.

Whether or not the presenting problem itself is related to the client's sexual orientation, the worker who intervenes with gay clients must be well-acquainted with the special features of gay and lesbian life, develop expertise in working with this population, and acquire knowledge of community resources. While it is necessary to recognize that there is no one type of gay individual or gay relationship and that there are major differences between gay men and lesbians, it also is important to understand the common attitudes, developmental issues, relationship patterns, and concerns of many members of the gay community.

The indiscriminate use of diagnostic labels that characterized the assessment of homosexual men and women in the past led to an antidiagnostic stance on the part of many gays.[15] The fact that homosexuality is not a disease does not mean that gay men and women are free of emotional disorders. Like everyone else, they may show the full range of problems encountered by helping professionals. The use of clinical diagnoses can be integrated with an affirmative perspective on gays and lesbians. The practitioner must bear in mind, however, that certain syndromes may be intensified, if not caused, by the stigmatizing and oppressive conditions to which gay men and women were exposed during their development and which they may continue to experience in their adult lives. For example, in a society that has viewed homosexuality so negatively, coming out to oneself, while liberating for many individuals, may have dramatic and unsettling consequences and lead to an acute outbreak of symptoms or to more ongoing dysfunction. Likewise, the psychological consequences of having to hide an essential part of oneself from family, friends, and associates are great and often contribute to identity conflicts, problems with intimacy and sexuality, substance abuse, depression, and other disorders.

Gay men and lesbians often have special treatment needs that are related to the effects of stigma and oppression, identity formation and the process of coming out, violence against gays, and relationships issues. While the AIDS epidemic has had an enormous impact on the gay community, the disease is now more widespread within the society and will be discussed separately in Chapter 11.

The Effects of Stigma and Oppression. While progress is gradually being made in altering society's negative attitudes toward and treatment of gays, oppressive policies and practices are manifested concretely in discrimination in housing, employment, insurance, inheritance and other forms of legal protection, child custody, foster care, adoption proceedings, medical care, and the like. Although they are undergoing some modification, stereotypical and inflammatory portrayals of gays in the media abound. Violence against gays and lesbians has increased to a startling degree, even as gay men and women are achieving more equitable treatment. Society's fear and oppression of gays engenders internalized homophobia in gays and lesbians themselves; this takes the form of negative attitudes toward themselves identical to those held by others.

Practitioners must be sensitive to the presence of internalized homophobia in their gay clients, refrain from inadvertently reinforcing it through their own biases and stereotypes, and help to empower their clients.[16] For example, when a male client expresses ambivalence about pursuing his interest in men, the worker needs to consider whether he is demonstrating characteristic features of the early stage of coming to terms with a stigmatizing identity and help him to explore and validate his feelings, rather than quickly interpret his ambivalence as a sign that the client should pursue "straight" life. Likewise, in working with a lesbian who is fearful of disclosing her sexual identity to her family despite the fact that she is living with a female partner, the worker must help her consider the negative consequences of her continuing to hide rather than collude with her staying in the closet.

Another frequent problem that arises as a result of the stigma attached to homosexuality is the relative isolation of many gays and lesbians. Because of their fear of exposure, their own internalized homophobia, and their lack of knowledge about or reluctance to use gay support networks, many gay and lesbian individuals lack connections to the larger gay community. This may be particularly acute for those who are older and who have lived a more closeted existence, perhaps in a very long-term relationship that ended in the death of one of the partners. It also may be very stressful for younger individuals who live with disapproving parents or relatives or for those who have had a recent breakup or loss of a relationship. The practitioner must provide clients with information about available resources, explore their reluctance to reach out to the gay community, and encourage them to develop support systems.

Identity Formation and the Process of Coming Out. A crucial aspect of the interventive process is helping gays and lesbians to cope with their own identity formation, or what is known as the coming out process, which was discussed in Chapter 5. While the adolescent and young adult periods are extremely important for gay identity formation (Hetrick and Martin, 1988:25–43), this process often occurs much later, particularly for women, and may extend for many years. The practitioner who is sensitive and affirmative in his or her work with gay clients needs to understand the psychological, behavioral, and attitudinal features of each of the stages of coming out and gear his or her interventions accordingly.[17] Lack of familiarity with these common characteristics and sequences will cause the practitioner to misinterpret the client's reactions and to miss opportunities to help the client move forward in the process of identity formation.

Relationship Issues. Gay and lesbian couples often seek help in dealing with relationship issues and a number of common problems and concerns have been identified. For example, Roth (1985:273–86) argues that the most significant factors influencing lesbian couples is the fact that both partners are socialized as women, that they are not a socially sanctioned unit, and that their full commitment to one another requires the acceptance of a stigmatized identity. She describes the five major issues presented by lesbian couples in therapy as being related to distance regulation and boundary maintenance; sexual expression; unequal access to resources; stage differences in coming out and the management of identity; and problems in ending the relationship. Likewise, George and Behrendt (1988:77–88) identity four stresses that cause conflict in gay males: stereotypical male roles; stereotypical sexual roles; homophobia and the coming out process; and sexual dysfunction. Colgan (1988:101–23) identifies the two patterns of over-separation and over-attachment, one or anther of which occurs in many gay male couples and creates problems in intimacy. As more gays and lesbians are entering relationships in which there are children, or are having or adopting children as couples, there is a need for help around parenting and related concerns (Baptiste, 1987:223–239).

SUMMARY

This chapter has discussed ten common themes that characterize work with women, people of color, and gays and lesbians: appreciating the impact of the sociopolitical context; exercising self-awareness; balancing a focus on group membership and individualization; enhancing client strengths; building self-confidence, self-esteem, and personal power; equalizing power in the therapeutic relationship; educating about options and maximizing choice; linking clients to needed resources; connecting clients to mutual aid groups and peer supports; and encouraging collective and political action. The chapter then described some of the distinctive foci that arise in work with these populations.

NOTES

1. This view is expressed in Nan Van Den Bergh and Lynn B. Cooper, "Feminist Social Work," in Ann Minahan, Ed.-in-Chief, *Encyclopedia of Social Work*, 18th Ed. (Silver Spring: National Association of Social Workers, Vol. 1., 1987), pp. 610–18 and Barbara Bryant Solomon, "Value Issues in Working with Minority Clients," in Aaron Rosenblatt and Diana Waldfogel, eds., *Handbook of Clinical Social Work* (San Francisco: Jossey-Bass, 1983), pp. 866–87.
2. For a discussion of this issue, see Robert D. Schwartz, "When the Therapist is Gay: Personal and Clinical Reflections," *Journal of Gay and Lesbian Psychotherapy*, 1 (1) (1989): 41–53.

3. For interesting discussions of these attitudes on the part of practitioners and clients, see Teresa A. DeCrescenzo, "Homophobia: A Study of Attitudes of Mental Health Professionals Toward Homosexuality," in R. Schoenberg and R. Goldberg with D. Shore, eds., *With Compassion Toward Some: Homosexuality and Social Work in America* (New York: Harrington Park Press, 1984), pp. 115–36; Alan K. Malyon, "Psychotherapeutic Implications of Internalized Homophobia in Gay Men," in John C. Gonsiorek, ed., *Homosexuality Psychotherapy: A Practitioner's Handbook of Affirmative Models* (New York: Haworth Press, 1982), pp. 59–70; and April Martin, "Some Issues in the Treatment of Gay and Lesbian Patients," *Psychotherapy: Theory, Research, and Practice,* 19 (Fall 1982): 341–48.

4. For an interesting discussion of this view, see for example, Ann Weick, Charles Rapp, W. Patrick Sullivan, and Walter Kisthardt, "A Strengths Perspective for Social Work Practice," *Social Work,* 34 (July 1989): 350–54.

5. For excellent discussions of empowerment, see Lorraine Gutierrez, "Working with Women of Color: An Empowerment Perspective," *Social Work,* 35 (March 1990): 149–54; Hisashi Hirayama and Muammer Cetingok, "Empowerment: A Social Work Approach for Asian Immigrants," *Social Casework: The Journal of Contemporary Social Work,* 69 (January 1988): 41–47; and Elaine B. Pinderhughes, "Empowerment for Our Clients and for Ourselves," *Social Casework: The Journal of Contemporary Social Work,* 64 (June 1983): 331–38.

6. For a discussion of this view, see Gutierrez, "Working with Women of Color: An Empowerment Perspective," p. 151; Solomon, "Value Issues in Working with Minority Clients," pp. 866–87, and Mary Valentich, "Feminism and Social Work Practice," in Francis J. Turner, ed., *Social Work Treatment,* 3d Ed. (New York: Free Press, 1986), pp. 572–74.

7. For interesting articles that reconceptualize selected pathological syndromes in women, see for example, Marlene Boskind-Lodahl, "Cinderella's Stepsisters: A Feminist Perspective on Anorexia Nervosa and Bulimia," in Elizabeth Howell and Marjorie Bayes, eds., *Women and Mental Health* (New York: Basic Books, 1981), pp. 248–62; Barbara G. Collins, "Reconstructing Codependency Using Self-in-Relation Theory," *Social Work,* 38 (July 1993): 470–76; Harriet E. Lerner, "The Hysterical Personality: A 'Woman's Disease,'" in Howell and Bayes, *Women and Mental Health,* pp. 196–206; Alexandra Symonds, "Phobias After Marriage: Women's Declaration of Dependence," in Howell and Bayes, *Women and Mental Health,* pp. 228–239.

8. A comprehensive collection of articles that deal with the treatment implications of these life events and roles can be found in Howell and Bayes, *Women and Mental Health.*

9. For a review of research on teenage pregnancy, see Catherine S. Chilman, "Teenage Pregnancy: A Research Review," in Howell and Bayes, *Women and Mental Health*, pp. 325–339.

10. For a summary of studies reporting the likely incidence of sexual assault and women's reporting patterns, see Gail Abarbanel and Gloria Richman, "The Rape Victim," in Howard J. Parad and Libbie G. Parad, eds., *Crisis Intervention Book 2: The Practitioner's Sourcebook for Brief Therapy* (Milwaukee, Wis.: Family Service America, 1990), pp. 93–118.

11. For a discussion of the prevalence of spouse abuse, see John Brekke, "Crisis Intervention with Victims and Perpetrators of Spouse Abuse," in Parad and Parad, *Crisis Intervention Book 2: The Practitioner's Sourcebook for Brief Therapy*, pp. 161–78 .

12. For a discussion of this issue, see Jeanne B. Robinson, "Clinical Treatment of Black Families: Issues and Strategies," *Social Work*, 34 (July 1989): 323–29 .

13. For a discussion of the stages of adjustment to immigration and the factors that affect the acculturation process, see Hirayama and Cetingok, "Empowerment: A Social Work Approach for Asian Immigrants," pp. 41–47.

14. Because of the accessibility of gay organizations and support groups, which often are staffed by volunteers in large cities, and the distrust of more establishment mental health professionals, many gay and lesbian individuals seek help outside the usual network of mental health services.

15. For a discussion of this issue see John C. Gonsiorek, "The Use of Diagnostic Concepts in Working with Gay and Lesbian Populations," in Gonsiorek, *Homosexuality and Psychotherapy: A Practitioner's Handbook of Affirmative Models*, pp. 9–20.

16. For a discussion of some of the ways in which societal attitudes, worker bias, and internalized homophobia enter the treatment relationship, see Alan K. Malyon, "Psychotherapeutic Implications of Internalized Homophobia in Gay Men," in Gonsiorek, *Homosexuality and Psychotherapy: A Practitioner's Handbook of Affirmative Models*, pp. 59–70, and April Martin, "Some Issues in the Treatment of Gay and Lesbian Patients," pp. 341–48.

17. For some excellent discussion of the coming out process, see Eli Coleman, "Developmental Stages of the Coming Out Process," in Gonsiorek, *Homosexuality and Psychotherapy: A Practitioner's Hand-*

book of Affirmative Models, pp. 31–44; Kristine L. Falco, *Psychotherapy with Lesbian Clients: Theory into Practice* (New York: Brunner/Mazel, 1991); Emery S. Hetrick and Damien A. Martin, "Ego-Dystonic Homosexuality: A Developmental View," in Emery S. Hetrick and Terry S. Stein, eds., *Innovations in Psychotherapy with Homosexuals* (Washington, D.C.: American Psychiatric Press, 1984), pp. 2–21; Richard A. Isay, *Being Homosexual: Gay Men and their Development* (New York: Farrar, Strauss, and Giroux, 1989); Lou Ann Lewis, "The Coming-Out Process for Lesbians: Integrating a Stable Identity," *Social Work,* 29 (September-October 1984): 464–69.

CHAPTER 11

EGO-ORIENTED INTERVENTION WITH SPECIAL POPULATIONS

The interventive principles that have been discussed so far provide the worker with general guidelines for ego-oriented practice with a broad range of clients. The effective treatment of many types of problems for which people seek help in today's world, however, requires that practitioners have specialized knowledge and expertise. Intervention must address the particular needs of special populations. This chapter will explore the use of ego-oriented intervention and its integration with other types of services in working with selected problems that are prevalent and disabling and that necessitate creative interventions and programs for their amelioration. It will discuss work with individuals who abuse alcohol and drugs, who are schizophrenic and chronically mentally ill, who have AIDS, and who are adult survivors of sexual abuse. What follows is not meant to be a comprehensive discussion of intervention with these conditions but is intended to offer a perspective on how to integrate ego psychological theory and principles into one's treatment.

WORKING WITH SUBSTANCE ABUSERS

According to the DSM-IV™ (American Psychiatric Association, 1994: 112), substance abuse is defined as "a maladaptive pattern of substance use leading to clinically significant impairment or distress, as manifested by one (or more) of the following, occurring within a 12-month period": failure in fulfilling major social role obligations at work, school, or in the household; engaging in physically hazardous activities; substance-related legal problems; and continued substance use despite its contribution to personal and interpersonal problems. Substance abuse may be with or without physiological dependence. Since the move away from a moralistic view of substance abuse, which sees it as reflecting personal weakness, lack of willpower, and a failure to resist sin and evil, different models for understanding and treating addiction have been put forth and there is considerable debate over the best approach.

PERSPECTIVES ON SUBSTANCE ABUSE

Those who use a mental health model in working with addiction tend to regard substance abuse as an attempt at self-medication or as an expression of and way of dealing with underlying personality difficulties. Consequently, psychodynamically oriented practitioners often have chosen not to address a client's use of alcohol or drugs directly, believing that it would diminish and abate if the client's ego were strengthened, inner conflicts resolved, or longstanding personality problems modified. Those with special expertise in working with substance abusers generally have regarded this approach as seriously flawed and have characterized mental health professionals as lacking in concrete knowledge regarding the manifestations and effects of chemical dependence. Moreover, they have accused them of having "blinders on" with respect to their clients' substance abuse, either failing to recognize or "denying" its presence, thereby colluding with or "enabling" their clients' addictive behavior (Fewell and Bissell, 1978:6–13; Levinson and Straussner, 1978: 14–20; Mulinski, 1989:333–39).

Alternatively, specialists in the chemical dependency field focus on treating the addiction itself. They argue that substance abuse is a disease[2] and that many individuals have a biological predisposition to addiction that can easily be triggered by any substance use. According to this view, the potential for addiction always is present and cannot be "cured." Symptoms such as depression and anxiety and problems in ego functioning are viewed as caused by rather than as causing chemical dependence. In the recovery model that flows from this view, self-help groups such as Alcoholics Anonymous or Narcotics Anonymous and more structured treatment programs require that the afflicted person accept the presence and chronicity of his or her disease and engage in lifelong, total abstinence. They usually advocate confrontation of dysfunctional behavior that is thought to protect the client's addiction and that interferes with sobriety. Individuals are helped to engage in new ways of thinking, feeling, and behaving that support abstinence and alternative ways of dealing with addiction. Followers of the disease or recovery model tend to negate the importance of making a thorough psychosocial assessment of the individual and rarely attend to underlying ego weakness or emotional disorder that may require treatment in its own right. Consequently, mental health practitioners have criticized this approach, as well as the learning model described below, for ignoring the whole person.

In the learning model, alcohol and substance abuse are seen as resulting from maladaptive habits or patterns that can be modified through education, conditioning, and the acquisition of new behaviors. It emphasizes helping individuals gain control over their substance abuse either through abstinence or controlled use of alcohol or drugs. A current controversy in the field of chemical dependency is whether controlled substance abuse is possible or whether it leads to continuing and escalating abuse (Levy, 1992:251–56).

Yet another perspective on the causes of substance abuse focuses on the impact of social conditions such as poverty, unemployment, and oppression.[4] It advocates interventions that focus on ameliorating the environmental stresses that push people to drink or to abuse drugs, and on helping those who abuse substances to find better ways of coping with external forces. Some have suggested that this view contributes to substance abusers' shirking responsibility for their behavior, since they are encouraged to externalize their problems.

INTEGRATIVE APPROACHES

Increasingly, there is recognition that the causes of chemical dependence are varied and complex and that substance abusers are not uniform in their treatment needs. A multifaceted rather than singular approach to understanding and treating substance abuse seems desirable (Brower, Blow, and Beresford, 1989:147–57; Evans and Sullivan, 1990:13–39). There are significant barriers to the implementation of such a model in practice, however, since settings and staff tend to be organized around a particular approach to the treatment of chemical dependency. One way of integrating diverse views has been through the use of the concept of "dual diagnosis," which refers to the fact that an individual may present with both the syndrome of substance abuse and a personality or mental disorder. While in some instances one disorder may be primary and the other secondary, this distinction is not always useful since both disorders reinforce one another.

Proponents of the dual diagnosis perspective argue that those who present with multiple disorders have special treatment needs that require a blending of techniques that address both the substance abuse and the concurrent personality or mental disturbances (Orlin and Davis, 1993:50–68). For example, while supporters of the recovery model have tended to refrain from recommending psychoactive drugs such as antidepressants and antipsychotic medications or psychotherapy in treating substance abusers, dual diagnosis proponents argue that the use of such medications may be an important adjunct in the treatment of individuals who present with substance abuse and a major depression or schizophrenia. Likewise, they are more likely to concede that psychotherapy with those substance abusers who have personality disorders and severe ego weakness may be crucial in helping them to attain and sustain their sobriety. Such treatment, however, always must keep the substance abuse at the center of the treatment and set abstinence as a goal (Millman, 1986: 103–109).

Another way of integrating diverse models with the treatment of substance abuse is through the use of a biopsychosocial perspective to guide the practitioner in his or her assessment and interventive focus. The practitioner recognizes that individuals become chemically dependent for various reasons and that treatment, while always focusing on the substance abuse *per se*, must draw on a range of interventions based on an individualized assessment of the client.

THE NATURE OF ASSESSMENT

While some substance abusers seek help with their addiction, many receive help for other kinds of problems and may conceal or minimize their substance abuse. It is important that practitioners in a range of agency facilities and in private practice be familiar with the signs and symptoms of different types of substance use, the common ways in which an individual's life is affected by alcohol and drugs, and who is at risk for developing chemical dependence. Each major group of substances—for example, alcohol and other central nervous system depressants, central nervous system stimulants, narcotics or opiates, psychedelics or hallucinogens, and designer drugs—has its own unique physical effects (Straussner, 1993:3–32), and there is an identifiable progression in the addiction cycle for many individuals. Persons with a family history of substance abuse seem to be more at risk than those without such a background; age, gender, and cultural background are also important factors. While male substance abusers far outnumber female substance abusers and the major views about the causes and treatment of substance abuse are based on studies of men, there is increasing information about the particular patterns of substance abuse in women and their special treatment needs (Pape, 1993:251–69). Stereotypical notions about what constitutes serious substance abuse need to be examined, since an individual's use of alcohol or drugs may not seem to be problematic but his or her pattern of use may be such that he or she is likely to be at an early stage of a full-blown addiction.

Evaluating the Nature and Severity of Substance Abuse. Because of the prevalence of substance abuse and the fact that it often is concealed or denied, practitioners should routinely ask about alcohol and drug use, particularly when there are signs that an individual is unpredictable or volatile and is having problems in his or her daily life and social roles that are not readily explainable. Straussner (1993:15–18) outlines a series of questions that can be used to assess the nature and severity of substance abuse and advises that the practitioner also assess the effects of the abuse on the client's life.

A Biopsychosocial Framework. While it is important to assess the nature and severity of a client's substance abuse and its impact, it is essential not to lose sight of the whole person. Assessment must encompass the individual's biological endowment, family and cultural background, life stage, developmental achievements, ego functioning and coping capacities, characteristic defenses, interpersonal relationships, medical and psychiatric history, current environmental stressors, supports and resources, level of motivation, and strengths. Most of us take for granted certain capacities that substance abusers often lack, such as a stable sense of identity; good judgment; impulse control; self-soothing mechanisms when feeling anxious, frustrated, or depressed; the ability to recognize and verbalize feelings; object constancy when alone or separated from significant others; and the capacity for empathy with others' motivations and feelings. Deficits in these and other areas impair thee ability of substance abusers to function in the world without alcohol or drugs and to cope effectively in many areas of their lives. In many instances, substance abusers have a concurrent personality or mental disorder that may require a special evaluation.

Assessment also should focus on the family of the substance abuser. Families may show interlocking pathology that contributes to and sustains a member's substance abuse, or family members may experience shame, guilt, low self-esteem, frustration, fatigue, helplessness, and hopelessness (McIntyre, 1993: 171–95; Zelvin, 1993:196–213). Children of substance abusers suffer are at risk to show later problems (Markowitz, 1993:214–32).

CLINICAL INTERVENTIONS

Based on an individualized assessment of the client, the practitioner can draw on a range of interventions in a flexible manner rather than follow a doctrinaire approach to treatment.

Individual Treatment. There is a role for individual treatment even in the beginning stages of work with substance abusers. A crucial focus of the first phase of treatment is to motivate clients to stop their substance abuse and to help them develop better ways of dealing with their pressing needs and impulses so that sobriety can be attained and maintained. In later stages of treatment, when sobriety is more secure, many clients come to realize that they do not know how to deal with life without alcohol and drugs and that their problems are still pressing despite their abstinence; ego-supportive and ego-modifying work can be undertaken at these times.

The establishment of a therapeutic holding environment is always important in the beginning of treatment, but achieving this is not an easy task with substance abusers. The treatment structure should be individualized rather than mechanistic. Some clients can benefit from strict rules to help them maintain control of their behavior, while others may need more access to the therapist or other staff and a more flexible approach. Treatment should aim at helping clients to achieve a stable sobriety, to restore, develop, or strengthen their adaptive coping mechanisms, to modify dysfunctional defenses and patterns of behavior, to build new social networks and supports, and to connect to necessary community resources. Such an approach initially focuses on here-and-now issues and should be attuned to the client's ability to tolerate exploration of his or her feelings. While it may not be advisable to pursue this approach early in the treatment, helping substance abusers to get in touch with what is disturbing to them, to track the relationship between their feelings and their use of substances, and to get validation for their needs can have soothing and ego-strengthening effects.

Whether or not total abstinence should be an immediate goal is a controversial question. The answer is clearer when substance abuse is out of control and is having obvious and immediate destructive consequences for the individual or others. In these instances, steps must be taken to enable the client to become free of alcohol or drugs. While this may be possible on an out-patient basis in some instances, an in-patient phase of the treatment will be necessary in many cases. When the substance abuse is erratic though severe and the client shows more denial of the problem and resistance to addressing it, the worker's timing in placing expectations for sobriety on the client is important to the success of the treatment. The worker may need to wait until the therapeutic alliance is stronger and he or she has more leverage, or until the client fails in his or her repeated attempts to control the substance abuse, before making abstinence a clear condition of treatment. Waiting does not imply that the therapist is being inactive or is ignoring the client's substance abuse. It is advisable (1) to let the client know that abstinence is a goal; (2) to keep the negative consequences of substance abuse in the forefront of the treatment; (3) to identify the defenses that protect the abuse; (4) to identify the underlying problems that give rise to the abuse; (5) to acknowledge and explore the gratification obtained from the abuse; (6) to explore fears of and resistance to abstinence; and (7) to problem-solve with the client about ways to control the abuse. The worker must be vigilant about his or her own fears of raising these issues with the client and must not succumb to the erroneous belief that eventually the client will gain control of his or her substance abuse as a matter of course. Eventually it may be necessary to pressure the client to take decisive action, but it may take a long time before this tactic can be effective.

Because of the substance abuser's frequent use of denial and other maladaptive defenses and coping mechanisms, many authors have stressed the use of confrontation in the treatment process (Chernus, 1985:67–75; Fewell and Bissell, 1978:6–13). While this may be indicated at times, too much confrontation early in treatment may rigidify defenses, escalate acting out, and increase resistance, since clients may feel attacked or threatened. The practitioner does need to address self-defeating behavior, but it is generally preferable to do so in ways that show an understanding of what the client is experiencing and the factors that are contributing to his or her compulsive behavior. This can be accomplished through empathically relating to the client's urgent needs and feeling states, exploring their origins in the client's early life, and pointing out negative consequences of behavior that may have been learned in order to survive early neglect, abuse, or other kinds of trauma. For example, the therapist might say that the client's need to get immediate relief from his or her emotional pain through the use of a chemical was understandable, particularly since no one ever responded to his or her feelings early in life or offered needed protection, but that it is important for the client to find other ways of dealing with discomfort.[3]

While the setting of limits and the use of behavioral contracts may be helpful with some clients, substance abusers are vulnerable to slips, repeated crises, and failure in keeping the terms of the contract.[4] There should be sufficient flexibility in the treatment structure to help them through these difficulties and prevent their being discharged or terminated. Further, the limit-setting strategy should be put aside at times with some clients. Workers also may find that being "real," selectively meeting some of the client's needs at times, and refraining from interpreting the client's efforts to get his or her needs met as "manipulations" are important. This does not mean that one always gratifies the client's requests, since this may enable self-defeating behavior, stimulate regressive behavior, or eventually lead to worker burnout, frustration, or withdrawal.

There is general consensus that practitioners who work with substance abusers are especially vulnerable to countertransference reactions that can obstruct their work because of the impact of the client's urgent needs, aggressive behavior, acting out, and primitive defenses (O'Neill, 1993:127–46). Sometimes they even "induce" particular responses in those around them in order to rid themselves of uncomfortable feelings. There is a risk, however, in assuming that this is always the case. Workers themselves need to be vigilant in understanding their own attitudes toward substance abusers and in their use of themselves. They must refrain from retaliating in anger to provocative and attacking behavior, or from giving too much to the point of exhaustion. In order to provide a therapeutic holding environment in in-patient settings and other more structured treatment programs, staff must understand the treatment philosophy that guides their work and have ample opportunity for open communication and help in recognizing and managing their intense reactions to clients.

Twelve-Step Programs and Other Self-Help Groups. A substance abuser's regular participation in a twelve-step program such as Alcoholics Anonymous or Narcotics Anonymous generally is a crucial ingredient in maintaining sobriety,[5] although there are other self-help groups that can be utilized as well. In dealing with the client's initial resistance to entering such programs, the practitioner can indicate that he or she is unable to really be helpful to the client unless certain supports are in place, that the client's efforts to control his or her substance abuse are not working, that the chemical dependence is too great a burden for the client to attempt to handle alone, and that the client has nothing to lose by taking the worker's advice on a trial basis. If this strategy fails, the worker can suggest that the client try it his or her own way for a specified period of time but accept the worker's advice if he or she is unable to attain sobriety.

The clinician who works with clients attending twelve-step programs must be knowledgeable about and comfortable with them and able to help the client integrate the generally compatible but sometimes conflicting foci of the two approaches. For example, in the early stages of sobriety, clients may interpret the twelve-step program as telling them not to dwell on feelings, and they may question the worker's effort to explore emotionally laden issues. The worker needs to know when it is helpful to minimize or suppress such exploration of feelings and when it is necessary to help clients to get in touch with, verbalize, and get validation for their feelings.

In-Patient Treatment. Some substance abusers are admitted to psychiatric hospitals following overdoses, psychotic episodes, or other types of destructive behavior. For many addicts, a phase of in-patient treatment in a detoxification facility or another type of in-patient or residential drug treatment program may be essential to beginning recovery (Chernus, 1985:6–13).

The Role of Psychotropic Drugs. While abstinence itself can relieve many symptoms of depression and anxiety, for example, there are some positive indications for the use of medication by those who display a depressive disorder, panic states, or disorganized thinking concurrent with substance abuse. A rule of thumb is to give antidepressants for an affective disorder or for panic states and small doses of major tranquilizers for pathology that is close to the psychotic range of symptoms. Psychotropic drugs always should be used cautiously as some are addictive, many have serious side effects, and others can be lethal if taken in large quantities or with other substances. Further, noncompliance with and abuse of medication are common since substance abusers tend to use drugs in their acting out of intense feelings.

The Use of Groups. Support, activity, and task-oriented groups can be used effectively with many substance abusers. They provide opportunities for the development of specific skills and the enhancement of ego functioning, interpersonal relationships, and social functioning. Many structured settings utilize encounter groups that are very confrontational in their approach to substance abusers, but the automatic use of this type of intervention is problematic, especially with dually diagnosed individuals.

Work With Families. While it might be advisable, if not necessary, for partners of substance abusers or other family members to obtain treatment of their own, they may feel too threatened to seek treatment or attend a twelve-step program initially. The worker should approach family members with acceptance, empathy, and respect, educate them about substance abuse and the important role a family can play in the recovery of a substance abuser, and help to connect them with social supports and treatment.

Mobilizing Community Resources. The practitioner who works with substance abusers needs to be knowledgeable about community resources that can be used to support clients' recovery. Early and prolonged substance abuse may have resulted in their inability to pursue work, education, or committed relationships, or their vocational and personal lives may have been drastically affected by their substance abuse. They may need job training, education, vocational counseling, housing, financial, medical, and legal assistance, or new avenues for socialization and leisure activities.

WORKING WITH THE SCHIZOPHRENIC CHRONICALLY MENTALLY ILL

Since the discovery of Thorazine, the first major psychotropic medication that was effective in alleviating some of the more flagrant symptomatology of schizophrenia, and the beginning of the deinstitutionalization movement in the late 1950s, the care of the chronically mentally ill shifted substantially from large state mental hospitals to communities (Zuckerwise, 1990:228–29). The services necessary to deal with the needs of this massive population have lacked financial support and have been slow to develop. In large urban centers particularly, the situation has deteriorated as psychiatric admissions to local treatment facilities have been restricted, services have shrunk, and increasing numbers of chronically mentally ill individuals have joined the ranks of the homeless. While the chronically mentally ill population is composed of individuals with different types of disorders, a substantial number suffer from schizophrenia. Not all schizophrenic individuals have the same degree of disability and many are able to achieve some degree of independence and stability. Nevertheless, they characteristically show disorganized and bizarre thinking and behavior and serious impairments in their daily living skills, their ability to care for themselves, and their occupational and other social roles (American Psychiatric Association, 1994:142–53).

PERSPECTIVES ON SCHIZOPHRENIA

Three basic models for understanding and treating schizophrenia have been put forth: the biological model, the developmental or psychodynamic model, and the family systems model.[6] The most prevalent view today is that schizophrenia is a biological disorder requiring psychotropic drugs for its treatment either alone or in combination with other types of intervention. Various hypotheses about the role of genes, hormones, biochemical imbalances, brain size, and neurotransmitters in causing schizophrenia have been studied (Taylor, 1987:115–21). Research has yielded some important associations, but no clear and indisputable biological factor or group of factors has been identified as yet. Psychodynamically oriented theorists have tended to view schizophrenia as being caused by serious deficiencies that occur during the developmental process, believing that it, like other milder emotional problems and disorders, can be treated successfully by intensive psychotherapy. There have been many speculations about the link between specific developmental failures and schizophrenia but rigorous studies connecting early experiences to schizophrenia have lagged or been largely disappointing. Further, as Parloff (1979:296–306) notes, studies of the treatment of schizophrenia, while sparse, have tended to favor drug treatment alone or in combination with other psychosocial interventions.

While scientific evidence supporting the psychodynamic model of causality for schizophrenia is lacking, individuals with this disorder show severe disturbances in their ego functioning, whatever the causes may be. Their ability to cope with both internal and external stimuli and environmental demands is impaired. In addition to presenting with hallucinations and delusions, they generally are prone to a breakdown of their ego boundaries and a failure of reality testing and become confused in their ability to distinguish between themselves and others, the internal and external world, and fantasy and reality. Their sense of themselves may be chaotic or bizarre and their thinking processes may become disorganized and illogical. Impulse control, judgment, perception, memory, concentration, comprehension, the ability to organize and synthesize may be affected.[7] Even when schizophrenic individuals show less flagrant symptoms and interference with ego functioning, they often lack basic problem-solving capacities, skills in daily living, and ability to cope with stress.

A third view of the causes of schizophrenia comes from the work of numerous family systems theorists who view dysfunc-

tional family processes and interlocking family pathology as crucial determinants of the disorder. They have advocated treating
the whole family rather than the identified schizophrenic individual only. Like the individual psychodynamic approach, the
family systems perspective has yielded rich views of the linkages
between family life and schizophrenia but no conclusive findings have been forthcoming. The treatment of families in which
there is a schizophrenic member has not been studied extensively and there are many unanswered questions about its
efficacy. A different perspective on families of schizophrenic individuals and their treatment needs has emerged from studies of
the family burden in caring for a mentally ill member and on the
role of the family in helping the schizophrenic individual to remain in the community. For example, it has been observed that
there are family characteristics associated with both higher
and lower rates of reinstitutionalization (Vaughn and Leff,
1976:157–65) and that families need help in dealing with the impact of mental illness and in performing a supportive role.

A BIOPSYCHOSOCIAL APPROACH

While there seems to be a growing belief that biological factors
may contribute to schizophrenia, there also is general agreement
on the following points: schizophrenic individuals are whole
persons who vary in their ego capacities, family supports, and
environmental resources; psychological deficits and impairments
are associated with this disorder; psychotropic drugs, either
alone, or in combination with psychotherapy, are not sufficient to
help schizophrenic individuals remain in the community or
function more independently; families are severely stressed in
dealing with schizophrenic members, lack understanding of the
disorder and specific skills for dealing with it in a positive way;
and structured settings in the community, social resources, and
supports are essential in social rehabilitation and in preventing
reinstitutionalization. Consequently, there is growing consensus
that the treatment of the schizophrenic chronically mentally ill
requires an individualized assessment and a broad range of interventive roles and treatment methods.

The Role of Psychotropic Medications. Major tranquilizers or antipsychotic drugs seem to help many, though by no means all schizophrenic individuals to become less symptomatic and more organized in their thinking, behavior, and general ego functioning, but they do not necessarily enable clients to function more autonomously and to cope with interpersonal relationships, work, and other social roles more effectively. Noncompliance with medication is a serious problem in causing repeated psychotic episodes. Further, many schizophrenic individuals are at risk of developing more acute flare-ups of psychotic symptoms whether or not they take medication regularly. The use of psychotropic drugs is not without its problems since they tend to have side effects, some of which are quite severe and irreversible. Individuals have the right to be informed of the benefits and risks associated with medications and to refuse treatment under certain conditions. Yet some schizophrenic persons may not be able to take in this information and make an informed decision. Family members who may be involved with the client often lack understanding of or themselves have negative attitudes toward the use of medication. Nonmedical practitioners, who generally are on the front lines in working with the chronically mentally ill, must understand the rationale for the use of psychotropic drugs, have knowledge of their side effects, and be sensitive to the psychological, sociocultural, ethical, and legal issues involved in their use (Matorin and De Chillo, 1984:579–89).

The Use of Structured Settings. The provision of an external structure seems to be helpful, if not essential, in enabling schizophrenic chronically mentally ill individuals to remain in the community. Supervised independent apartment arrangements, halfway houses or residences, group homes, day hospitals, and sheltered workshops for vocational training offer protection and support. They serve to stabilize and bolster the ego functioning of schizophrenic individuals.

Case Management Case management has become an increasingly important component of the social rehabilitation process since it addresses many schizophrenic individuals' lack of organizing and problem-solving skills and their tendency to feel overwhelmed and isolated. The case manager generally functions as a kind of auxiliary ego for the schizophrenic individual, overseeing and coordinating the client's treatment, living arrangements, and functioning in the community. Harris and Bergman (1987:296–302) have suggested that the process of case management may be internalized by the client, enhancing his or her overall coping capacities, and that the case manager is well-suited to intervene clinically. This will in large part depend, however, on the training, experience, and skill of the case manager. The case management function, in its more narrow sense, promotes the stabilization of the client in the community and enables him or her to make use of the services that will sustain and enhance his or her coping capacities. Part of the case manager's role is also to assess the client's ongoing needs, monitor his or her condition, plan with the client, locate resources, advocate on behalf of the client, and intervene in crisis situations.

Individual Treatment. An important aspect of working with schizophrenic individuals in the community involves efforts to sustain, strengthen, and enhance their coping capacities. Ego supportive and ego-building interventions are indicated in the context of an ongoing helping relationship between the worker and client. The worker must identify the client's strengths and build on these. Basic types of intervention are useful, such as offering sustainment; helping clients to partialize; enabling them to exercise and enhance their problem-solving and decision-making capacities by discussing alternative courses of action, evaluating consequences, and planning strategies for accomplishing goals; enabling them to find better ways of dealing with anxiety and social isolation; providing opportunities for anticipating and rehearsing ways of coping with new or stressful situations or interactions with others; strengthening their ability to test reality by discussing and stretching their perceptions and understanding of others' motivations, increasing their ability to verify interpretations of events, and correcting distortions. The client–worker relationship itself, which may take a long time to establish, may become an important source of role-modeling and internalization.[8]

Working with Families. While the stress caused by mental illness on families and the importance of providing them with support and education has long been appreciated, an emphasis on the treatment of family pathology has received greater attention in mental health circles since the burgeoning of the family therapy field. Because of increasing interest in and research on family burden and the role of families in enabling schizophrenic clients to remain in the community, a psychoeducational approach to intervention with such families was developed in the early 1980s and has been utilized extensively ever since (Anderson, Hogarty, and Reiss, 1980:490–505; Iodice and Wodarski, 1987:122–28; Simon *et al.*, 1991:323–34). It combines elements of support, education, and counseling and attempts to engage families in a collaborative relationship with the treatment team, focusing on provision of information regarding schizophrenia and teaching of more effective management skills and ways to decrease dysfunctional patterns of relating. While more intensive treatment of family pathology might be recommended in some instances, it would rarely he the first or major approach utilized.[9]

The Use of Groups. Structured task, guided support, self-help, and advocacy groups are useful in working with schizophrenic individuals and their families. They provide opportunities for the development of specific skills; the enhancement of ego functioning, interpersonal relationships, and social functioning; the communication of knowledge and information about mental illness and treatment resources; ventilation, peer support, and the sharing of ideas about the management of difficult situations that arise; socialization; and the development of incentive and strategies for collective action.

Social Resources and Supports. Schizophrenic chronically mentally ill individuals often do not have families willing to help them and require financial assistance, housing, job training, education, vocational counseling, medical and legal assistance, opportunities for socialization; shelters, partial hospitalization programs, mobile units that seek out needy clients in the community, and emergency psychiatric services are also needed for those who are homeless or in the midst of crises (Zuckerwise,

1990:227–50). Further, there are increasing numbers of schizo-phrenic individuals who also abuse substances or have AIDS, and so have special and complex treatment needs.

Effective discharge planning when clients are hospitalized and comprehensive after- and out-patient care must help link schizophrenic individuals to necessary resources in the commu-nity. Shortened hospital stays and insufficient services in the face of enormous demand makes this task a daunting one.

WORKING WITH PERSONS WITH AIDS

Acquired immune deficiency syndrome (AIDS) has posed a medical crisis of staggering proportions throughout the world since the early 1980s. It has been estimated that at the end of 1994, more than ten million cases of AIDS will have been diag-nosed in the world, with more than 500,000 of these being in the United States. Further, over two million Americans will have been infected and 400,000 will have died (Grinspoon, 1994:1–4). AIDS is contracted mainly through unprotected sexual relations, the sharing of intravenous needles, and *in utero* from mother to fetus. It is transmitted through exchange of blood, semen, vagi-nal fluid, and possibly other bodily fluids. While certain protec-tive measures can be taken by the general population and by health workers, fear of contagion has been known to cause near panic reactions (Grinspoon, 1994:1–4). Because there is no known cure for AIDS at the present time, it is viewed as a "killer" dis-ease and its very mention creates overwhelming anxiety. While its initial victims in the United States were largely gay men and intravenous drug abusers, increasing numbers of cases are now being found in heterosexual men, women who engage in sex with infected partners, and newborn children of infected moth-ers. Further, as Dane (1989: 305) notes, poverty and minority sta-tus are becoming associated with the epidemic as AIDS becomes concentrated among poor, black, and Hispanic intravenous drug users and their sexual partners and children. Across the world, AIDS has affected non-gay individuals to an even greater degree and has wiped out small communities. Despite the spread of AIDS to more varied populations, the social stigma attached to the victims of AIDS in this country has been severe. Gay men, in particular, who are seen as both at risk and responsible for the spread of the disease, are subjected to civil rights violations, social ostracism, bigotry, and even violence.

NATURE OF THE ILLNESS

AIDS is spread by the HIV retrovirus, which undermines the immune system causing the infected individual to be subject to a host of opportunistic diseases that destroy vital organs if not treated. When a person contracts the virus, he or she may become ill briefly with flu-like symptoms but generally a long period (an average of eight to ten years) elapses before he or she develops serious symptoms and is said to have full-blown AIDS. Consequently many individuals do not know that they are infected and thus can spread the disease unwittingly; others who are aware they have the virus (through testing) must live with this knowledge for years without having active or severe symptoms. Once the illness becomes more apparent, its course varies from individual to individual. It is not unusual for persons with AIDS to have repeated bouts with illness and hospitalization alternating with periods of more normal functioning. Over time they get progressively weaker and may deteriorate physically and mentally. On average, persons with AIDS die within eighteen months of the onset of symptoms, but many live for years, particularly as more drugs that treat the opportunistic infections are developed. These medications often are quite costly and have serious side effects themselves.[10]

PSYCHOSOCIAL IMPACT ON INDIVIDUALS AND FAMILIES

In addition to having to face that they have an increasingly debilitating illness that affects all areas of functioning and that inevitably leads to death, persons with AIDS must deal with the stigma of the disease. The stigma surrounding AIDS affects not only the victim's feelings about him- or herself and the disease but may also result in a more immediate and greater loss of social supports than would otherwise necessarily follow from his or her health status alone. Persons with AIDS may lose their jobs, means of supporting themselves financially, medical benefits, housing, friends, and family connections.

Since persons with AIDS may need material help from family members from whom they are estranged or with whom they have conflictual relationships, they may be thrust into tense and difficult family situations. Others may have no one to whom they can turn, their families having been destroyed by AIDS and few resources remaining.

Even before they know whether or not they have been infected with AIDS, individuals who believe they are at risk face certain dilemmas. The main one is whether or not to be tested for the presence of the HIV virus. This decision has complex ramifications. Knowing that he or she is infected may make an individual better able to take care of his or her health, to obtain drugs that may prolong life, and to protect others. On the negative side, many persons do not want to live with the knowledge that they are likely to develop an incurable disease sometime in the future, or they fear that their rights may be violated by breaches of confidentiality regarding their health status.

There are different stages in an individual's attempts to cope with the AIDS diagnosis, since persons with AIDS can live a long time with the disease in an inactive or active form. In the initial stage, the AIDS diagnosis constitutes a crisis that produces an immediate upheaval and mobilizes defensive or highly charged reactions. Individuals may experience shock, denial, anger, shame and humiliation, fear, guilt, and loss. Having internalized society's negative attitudes, they may feel that AIDS is a punishment for their behavior. They may become terrified at the prospect of having such a debilitating and fatal illness and become severely depressed or suicidal before they become more acutely ill. The issue of whether or not to disclose one's health status to friends and family usually is a central concern, as are the ongoing issues of whether and how to disclose one's diagnosis to potential sexual partners, how to manage one's sexual behavior, and how to deal with drug-taking behavior and pregnancy.

Life does not stop with the AIDS diagnosis. After the initial crisis subsides the person goes on living, uncertain about when severe symptoms and death will strike. Various issues arise, particularly with respect to intimate and family relationships, planning for the future, arranging health care, and the like. A certain type of adaptive denial may occur when individuals who remain symptom-free for a long time are able to "forget" that they are infected, even though they are protecting others and taking good care of themselves. Some may even begin to feel that they have escaped. In other cases denial or self-destructiveness may be severe, causing an individual to continue to behave recklessly.

When symptoms and bouts of illness become more frequent and severe, the person with AIDS has to deal more actively with assaults on his or her body image and self-esteem, increasing deterioration, curtailment of financial resources and life-style, hospitalization and side effects of medication, dependence on others, anticipatory grief, death and dying, and planning for survivors.

Lovers, parents, siblings, and children have a host of reactions when they learn that a significant other or family member has AIDS.[11] Like the person with AIDS, they may experience shock, denial, anger, shame and humiliation, fear, guilt, and loss. Partners of those infected with HIV are themselves thrust immediately into crisis. They must deal with their own reactions to the diagnosis and its stigma and to the loss of security about the future. They too will need to make decisions about disclosure and determining their own health status. In later stages, they often become involved in the care of the person with AIDS and will experience the burdens of the often roller-coaster like and progressively debilitating course of the illness and the death of their loved one. During this process, role reversals in couple relationships may occur. Even positive relationships are taxed heavily and those that have had a history of conflict may not survive the added stress. In some instances, partners will not be able to overcome their own feelings of fear, anger, blame, or guilt. This state of affairs often worsens if the caretaker has been infected or is responsible for the transmission of AIDS to his or her partner. Even when this is not the case, partners are in a difficult situation because of the anticipated loss or guilt about their own good health. In the gay community, which has banded together during the epidemic, friends and former lovers often play a vital role in caretaking; those who survive may witness the death of many friends and have to cope with multiple and chronic losses. As one gay man put it, "I don't keep an address book because I can't bear to cross out any more names."

Some families who learn that a child, sibling, parent, or spouse has AIDS and at the same time that he is gay must cope with a double stigma. They fear disclosing to others that someone in the family is ill. Maintaining secrecy distorts communication and increases social isolation at a time when families need support. While some families become more cohesive and help one another, others have trouble accepting and coping with the illness.

In many African-American, Caribbean-American, and Hispanic families, AIDS has struck multiple times and few are left who are not infected. Grief becomes chronic. Children with or without AIDS are born to mothers and fathers who become ill and die during the infancy of those who survive. Their care often is thrust upon grandmothers or aunts, or they are given over to foster care or institutional settings (Dane and Miller, 1992).

ISSUES FACING PRACTITIONERS
WHO WORK WITH PERSONS WITH AIDS

Those who are on the front lines in working with persons with AIDS and their caregivers often show a strong commitment to the work and feel that it is deeply rewarding and growth enhancing. At the same time, they are subjected to the same stigma as are those who have the disease and struggle with stresses that arise because of the work. Others may think they are crazy for working with this population, or that they have AIDS or are members of a risk group themselves; they may shun them or be uninterested in their work. Dunkel and Hatfield (1986:114–17) identify eight countertransference issues reported by health care providers, including social workers, who work with persons with AIDS: (1) fear of the unknown, (2) fear of contagion, (3) fear of dying and of death, (4) denial of helplessness, (5) fear of homosexuality, (6) over-identification, (7) anger, and (8) the need for professional omnipotence. In dealing with their reactions, workers may become over-involved in their work to the point of exhaustion, develop self-protective attitudes of detachment, show severe anxiety and depression, and become burned out. With their special empathy for AIDS victims, those who have experienced many personal losses or who are at risk themselves may become overwhelmed. They require agency personnel and social supports to help them sustain their commitment and effectiveness.

ASSESSMENT

In working with persons with AIDS a biopsychosocial assessment must include an understanding of (1) the stages, symptoms, and impairments caused by AIDS; (2) the effects of the illness on the person's ability to function in his or her major social roles and to manage daily living and survival needs; (3) the degree of recognition of the illness and the meaning of AIDS to the individual; (4) the coping mechanisms and defenses that the person is using to deal with the illness; (5) the impact of AIDS on the person's self-esteem and personal identity; (6) the individual's prior experiences with medical and psychiatric illness and death; (7) his or her past and current ego functioning and strengths; and (8) the availability of friends, family, and social supports. As the AIDS population becomes increasingly varied, the practitioner must focus on the special needs and concerns of gay and bisexual men, women, children, intravenous drug users, people of color, and those from diverse cultural backgrounds.

PRACTICE ROLES

The practitioner who works with persons with AIDS must have a thorough knowledge of the nature of the illness and of community resources as well as clinical skills. Caputo (1985:361–65) stresses the importance of role flexibility in working with this population. At various times the worker must be (1) an educator who provides important information about the illness and available services; (2) an advocate who helps to represent the client's needs to others and who helps him or her obtain necessary services; (3) a mediator who helps resolve conflicts and disputes that develop between the client and other persons and organizations; (4) a social broker who helps the client to use the system;

and (5) an enabler or counselor who enhances the client's strengths and coping skills.

CLINICAL FOCI

Intervention with persons with AIDS will have different foci depending on the stage of the illness. While helping clients cope with loss is crucial all through the illness, individuals who are dealing with the crisis of a recent diagnosis will present with different needs from those who have been living with AIDS for a long period of time or those who are steadily deteriorating and facing death. Moreover, there are special issues that surface in working with gay or bisexual men, intravenous drug users, women, and so on. Lopez and Getzel (1984:387–94) comment on seven important foci in working with gay men that include providing material and supportive services; linking clients to close family and friends; maximizing clients' choices about the type of care available to them; preventing and challenging service delivery discrimination or neglect; preparing clients for life-threatening events and possible death; supporting clients through periods of emotional upheaval and in coming to term with their past life and the prospect of death; and providing some degree of concern to counter social and existential loneliness. To this list should be added helping persons with AIDS to deal with issues of disclosure, manage their sexuality, deal with relationship problems and issues, cope with their families, and make legal and other arrangements for their survivors. While it is beyond the scope of this discussion to address the ethical and legal issues around euthanasia and suicide, it is not uncommon for persons with AIDS to express suicidal wishes and to make plans for carrying them out. Health care workers will need to address this issue in their work and determine whether such thoughts and behavior are part of a depression that warrants a psychiatric evaluation and treatment or whether it reflects a client's adaptive efforts to take control of his or her own life and death.

WORKING WITH CAREGIVERS

Caregivers are extremely important to persons with AIDS and generally carry considerable burdens. In instances in which the caregivers lack necessary information about AIDS, education is important. Practitioners need to be sensitive in reaching out to caregivers and in assisting them to get the supports they need to sustain them. They will need help in doing their own grief work and in caring for themselves as well as the person with AIDS. Support and mutual aid groups are being used extensively in helping AIDS victims and their families and caregivers. In some situations, however, caregivers may be highly judgmental and nonsupportive in their attitudes and behavior toward the person who is ill, particularly when there is a history of underlying and longstanding interpersonal conflict. The use of couple and family therapy may be an important adjunct in helping family members confront and resolve old issues and to become more able to play a positive role in the caregiving process.

WORKING WITH ADULT SURVIVORS OF SEXUAL ABUSE

Chapter 5 discussed the severe trauma that children experience when they are sexually abused in childhood and the impact of these experiences on all aspects of a child's or an adolescent's sense of self and personality functioning. It also noted that sexual abuse leads to characteristic defenses, personality traits, and symptoms in later life. There has been growing interest in the treatment of adult survivors of sexual abuse, who are thought by many to have a distinct type of disturbance and special treatment needs. While there is reason to believe that there is a sizeable percentage of male as well as female survivors, the following discussion will focus on women who have been sexually abused.

PRESENTING PROBLEMS AND CHARACTERISTICS

Increasing numbers of women are coming for help specifically to deal with their past experiences of incest and other forms of sexual abuse. Some have always been conscious of those experiences but others struggle with flashbacks, intrusive thoughts and feelings, or disturbing dreams that make them anxious and upset. Sometimes these reactions are stimulated by seeing films, for example, in which there are scenes of sexual abuse or by life situations that trigger memories or a reexperiencing of the abuse. More commonly, women who are aware of having been sexually abused seek help for other problems and do not readily disclose their abuse history. Still others seek help for a variety of problems but have little if any conscious memory of having been abused. While women in the first category identify themselves as survivors, those in the second group often conceal their abuse out of shame and guilt or reveal it later in the treatment or when asked about it directly. In a third group the presence of sexual abuse may go unrecognized unless the practitioner is alert to the clues that it has occurred (Faria and Belohlavek, 1984:465–71). Some of the more common symptoms that adult survivors display are severe apprehension and anxiety attacks; sleep disturbances, nightmares, flashbacks, or intrusive thoughts; fears, phobias, and chronic depression; suicidal thinking and behavior; low self-esteem and negative views of themselves; physical problems and complaints such as headaches, stomach ailments, skin disorders, backaches, and other pain; hypervigilance, distrust of others, and interpersonal disturbances; compulsive, impulsive, and addictive behavior; problems in social functioning or sexual functioning; and a tendency toward revictimization (Courtois, 1988:104–115).

DIAGNOSTIC AND OTHER CONTROVERSIES

Because of the presence of severe trauma in the histories of abuse victims, the resultant changes in their personality, and the repetitive nature of their characteristics in adulthood, Herman (1992:115–29) argues that the term "complex post-traumatic stress disorder" be used in diagnosing the particular problems of such women. She feels that the survivor's symptoms mimic a personality disorder but have very different origins. In fact, Herman decries the diagnostic mislabeling and mistreatment of those who have been sexually abused that she believes occurs in the mental health field. She notes that a large percentage of women who are diagnosed with borderline personality disorder, multiple personality disorder, and somatization disorder have a history of sexual abuse.

In contrast to those who seek to highlight the trauma of sexual abuse, some individuals have protested the amount of attention given to this subject. They argue that traumatic memories are false and that they are stimulated by the therapeutic process. Media attention has been given to this controversy when allegations of sexual misconduct are made against so-called innocent victims. Unfortunately, this runs the risk of intimidating true survivors and the helping professionals who work with them, thus making the recovery process more difficult.

ASSESSMENT

It is important for the practitioner to recognize and understand some of the common defenses used by those who have a history of sexual abuse as well as some of the main dynamic issues that adult survivors reflect. Perhaps the most important defense that victims of sexual abuse utilize is dissociation, in which they totally repress memories of disturbing events and/or the painful and overwhelming affects associated with them. While the use of dissociation may result in a survivor's not even remembering that she has been abused, it also may lead to recall of the event without the affects. As Blake-White and Kline (1985:397) note, women who have been sexually abused do not feel the stronger emotions of terror, despair, abandonment, betrayal, pain, and total aloneness that they experienced as children.

As part of the dissociation process, survivors often distrust their own memories. Sometimes this is accompanied by idealization of the abuser and a tendency to protect the memory of his or her "good" aspects through the use of splitting. The survivor finds it emotionally preferable to blame herself for being "bad," even though this causes low self-esteem, guilt, and shame. These feelings may be particularly intense when the abuser played a kind and nurturing role in the child's life.

While helping adult survivors to recover their lost memories and painful affects so that they can recover from their trauma is usually advocated, this work must be based on an individual-ized assessment of the client's ego functioning and ability to tol-erate exploration of her overwhelming earlier experiences. An assessment of the support systems that a client has in her life also is important, as the recovery work can become quite intense and anxiety-producing, sometimes necessitating emergency in-tervention.

CLINICAL INTERVENTIONS

Work with adult survivors is easier when the client can recall painful events and has sufficient self-esteem, ego strength, and social supports to endure exploration of the original traumatic experiences.

Correct Timing of Interventions. When clients are reluctant to dis-close or discuss their abuse or when they cannot recall it the worker must proceed with caution. While it is important for the practitioner to be alert to the possibility that sexual abuse has oc-curred and to be comfortable with exploring the client's early ex-periences, the timing of this must be well thought out. All too often, inexperienced and zealous workers push for details of the abuse situation or attempt to recover traumatic memories before the client feels safe or has experienced some lessening of her de-fenses and feelings of fear, badness, shame, and guilt. These must be dealt with sensitively and empathically before more in-tensive exploration can occur.

Creating a Holding Environment. Acceptance, consistency, empa-thy, genuineness, safety, and validation are important ingredi-ents of a therapeutic holding environment in the beginning stages of working with survivors. It is difficult for many sur-vivors of abuse to trust others, including those from whom they seek help. They have been exploited and not protected by the most significant people in their lives. People have had hidden agendas and have violated their boundaries. They may expect others upon whom they depend to act similarly and may even unwittingly act in ways that lead to their revictimization. This tendency may show itself in the therapeutic relationship, and the worker must be alert to its manifestations and refrain from being drawn into a destructive recreation of the original abuse situation. Likewise, as the client begins to feel closer to the worker, she may begin to feel more frightened and try to distance herself or flee. The worker will need to understand the client's fear and help her to stay connected to the treatment.

Working Through Past Trauma. When the client has a greater feeling of safety and self-esteem and diminished feelings of fear, shame, and guilt, the memory work and the process of recovery can begin. This may take a long time and the client may undergo periods of resistance or show intense and overwhelming affects. The worker will need to be available and sustaining in order to help the client to contain her feeling states. Sometimes crises will occur during this process as the client reexperiences her pain. Anger usually accompanies retrieval of memories of the abuse experience and the client undergoes a mourning process for her lost childhood. This work can be very difficult for the practitioner as well as the client. Ultimately the treatment helps the client to connect the effects of her past experiences to her current life and to learn to reshape relationships and reconnect to others in new ways.

FAMILY INTERVENTION

Sometimes during the treatment process the adult survivor wants to disclose that she was sexually abused to family members or she wishes to confront the perpetrator. It is important that the worker help the client to anticipate the likely consequences of taking these steps and to help her prepare for the reactions she may get. In selected cases in which revelations are contemplated or have been made, it can be useful to offer to meet with the client and members of her family. This may help the client to feel supported and also may enable the family to assimilate the information without having to attack the client or defend themselves against knowledge of the abuse in other dysfunctional ways.

In other instances, adult survivors may finally be able to disclose the fact that they were sexually abused to their spouses or children. In addition to helping the client prepare for this sharing, it may be important for the worker to help the client's significant others to understand the significance of the abuse and to offer ways they can be of assistance to the client in her recovery.

GROUP INTERVENTION

The use of self-help and support groups is a valuable modality in work with adult survivors of sexual abuse, particularly as an adjunct to individual treatment. However, not every client is ready to participate in a group experience at the outset. While groups can be effective in enabling clients to feel less alone, to get validation for their feelings, to share experiences with others who can empathize with them, to enhance self-esteem and lessen feelings of stigma, shame, and guilt, and to obtain help in other aspects of the recovery process, they can make certain clients feel more vulnerable and exposed. Consequently, the recommendation that the client attend a group should be based on the worker's assessment of where the client is and should be discussed with her.

SUMMARY AND CONCLUSION

This chapter has discussed important issues in the treatment of four major problem populations: substance abusers, the schizophrenic mentally ill, persons with AIDS, and adult survivors of sexual abuse. It has shown how ego-oriented intervention can be used as part of a holistic and multifaceted approach. While the chapter has emphasized direct practice, the problems of substance abuse, mental illness, AIDS, and sexual abuse are public issues as well as private troubles. Their amelioration requires changes in social policy and service delivery as well as intervention at the level of individuals, families, and groups.

NOTES

1. For excellent discussions of the different models of chemical dependency and their treatment implications, see Kirk J. Brower, Frederic C. Blow, and Thomas Beresford, "Treatment Implications of Chemical Dependence Models: An Integrative Approach," *Journal of Substance Abuse Treatment*, 6 (1989):147–57, and Katie Evans and J. Michael Sullivan, *Dual Diagnosis: Counseling the Mentally Ill Substance Abuser* (New York: Guilford Press, 1990), pp. 13–37.

2. For a discussion of issues in the treatment of alcoholism in certain groups that are vulnerable to social stress, see Sandra C. Anderson and Donna C. Henderson, "Working with Lesbian Alcoholics," *Social Work*, 30 (November-December 1985):518–25; Beverly Creigs, "Treatment Issues for Black Alcoholic Clients," *Social Casework: The Journal of Contemporary Social Work*, 70 (June 1989):370–74; and Joanne E. Turnbull, "Treatment Issues for Alcoholic Women," *Social Casework: The Journal of Contemporary Social Work*, 70 (June 1989): 364–69.

3. The rationale for this approach is discussed in more detail in Eda G. Goldstein, "The Borderline Substance Abuser," in Shulamith Lala Ashenberg Straussner, ed., *Clinical Work with Substance-Abusing Clients* (New York: Guilford Press, 1993), pp. 270–90.

4. For an interesting article that deals with the effects of contracting with clients in methadone treatment, see Stephen Magura, Cathy Casriel, Douglas S. Goldsmith, and Douglas S. Lipton, "Contracting with Clients in Methadone Treatment," *Social Casework: The Journal of Contemporary Social Work*, 68 (October 1987):485–93.

5. For a discussion of twelve-step programs, see Betsy Robin Spiegel, "12-Step Programs as a Treatment Modality," in Straussner, ed., *Clinical Work with Substance-Abusing Clients*, pp. 153–70.

6. For a discussion of the models, see Eda G. Goldstein, "Mental Health and Illness," *Encyclopedia of Social Work*, 18th Ed., Vol. 2 (Silver Spring, Md: National Association of Social Workers, 1986), pp. 105–08.

7. An excellent discussion of these characteristics can be found in Esther S. Marcus, "Ego Breakdown in Schizophrenia: Some Implications for Casework Treatment," *American Journal of Orthopsychiatry*, 31 (April 1961): pp. 368–87. Reprinted in Francis J. Turner, ed., *Differential Diagnosis and Treatment in Social Work*, 2d Ed., (New York: Free Press, 1976), pp. 322–40.

8. For interesting articles on this subject, see Ethel J. Panter, "Ego-building Procedures that Foster Social Functioning," *Social Case-*

work, 47 (March 1966): 139–45, and Judith A. Nelsen, "Treatment Issues in Schizophrenia," *Social Casework,* 56 (March 1975): 145–51.

9. For discussions of how to engage families of schizophrenic patients, see Eda G. Goldstein, "Promoting Competence in Families of Psychiatric Patients," in Anthony N. Maluccio, ed., *Promoting Competence in Clients: A New/Old Approach to Social Work Practice* (New York: Free Press), pp. 317–42, and Joseph Walsh, "Engaging the Family of the Schizophrenic Client," *Social Casework: The Journal of Contemporary Social Work,* 70 (Feb 1989): 106–13.

10. For a detailed discussion of the nature of the illness, see Grinspoon, Lester, ed., "AIDS and Mental Health—Part I," *The Harvard Mental Health Letter,* 10 (January 1994):1–4.

11. For a discussion of these reactions see Barbara O. Dane and Samuel O. Miller, *AIDS: Intervening with Hidden Grievers* (Westport, Ct.: Auburn House, 1992).

CHAPTER 12

THE DIAGNOSIS AND TREATMENT OF THE BORDERLINE CLIENT

The borderline diagnosis is applied frequently to individuals who show certain entrenched, rigid, maladaptive patterns and characteristics that impair their functioning or cause subjective distress.

Borderline individuals show severe personal and relationship problems and often present with substance abuse, eating disorders, self-destructive behavior, and even violence. Characteristically they are crisis-prone, nonreflective, and live in the immediacy of their experience. Some may have extreme difficulty knowing what they feel and verbalizing their feelings. Others are quite articulate and insightful but their self-understanding does not enable them to manage their impulsive or destructive behavior. Generally they are angry, volatile, and highly contradictory in their feelings and behavior. Their identity is fluid and diffuse and their self-esteem fluctuates dramatically. They may alternate between extreme feelings of grandiosity and entitlement on the one hand and feelings of worthlessness on the other. They yearn for and fear closeness so that they fluctuate between merging with and distancing from others and their relationships are turbulent. They do not tolerate stress well and often are flooded with anxiety and panic. The main thing that is stable about them is their instability.

Borderline individuals are difficult to engage and maintain in treatment but they often become extremely dependent on therapy for a sense of connection and well-being. Even when successful, the treatment process is characterized by missed appointments; threats to leave and premature terminations; alcohol, drug, and food abuse; self-mutilation; nonpayment of fees; noncompliance with agency or therapeutic requirements; suicidal rumination and gestures; insistent requests for personal information, additional time, or extra-therapeutic contact; and behavior that requires hospitalization.

This chapter will discuss the concept of borderline conditions and will describe criteria for their diagnosis from both clinical and developmental perspectives. It will discuss different theories of the etiology and treatment of such conditions. It then will explore important issues in clinical work with borderline clients.

Borderline conditions have been selected for discussion because (1) they are common among the clients seen by social workers in a variety of settings; (2) work with such clients is difficult and exemplifies important applications of ego-oriented intervention; (3) there still is a great deal of confusion about the diagnostic criteria and most effective treatment for these conditions; (4) ego psychology has made important contributions to understanding the ego pathology of borderline conditions; and (5) it is important for social workers to understand what is meant by this diagnostic category.

THE CONCEPT OF BORDERLINE CONDITIONS

The concept of borderline conditions stems from clinicians' experiences with individuals who do not fit traditional diagnostic criteria for neuroses and psychoses and whose clinical course differs from the usual characteristics and responses during the treatment process. While there are references to borderline patients earlier than 1938, the term began to appear more frequently at that time among psychoanalytic authors. Despite the growing interest of clinicians in borderline conditions, it was not until 1980 that the American Psychiatric Association included the category of borderline personality disorder in its *Diagnostic and Statistical Manual of Mental Disorders: Third Edition* (1980) (DSM III) and later editions (Spitzer, Williams, and Skodol, 1980:1050–54).

The main questions with respect to borderline conditions historically were (1) whether they represented a severe but nonpsychotic form of personality disorder or a variety of schizophrenia; (2) their distinguishing features; (3) their causes; and (4) their treatment implications. While a full review of the historical development of the term "borderline" is beyond the scope of this chapter, some of the major benchmarks and issues will be discussed briefly.[1]

BORDERLINE PERSONALITY OR BORDERLINE SCHIZOPHRENIA

Two usages of the term borderline are present in the literature. One stems from the interest of psychoanalytically oriented clinicians in identifying a group of patients who looked neurotic but were too disturbed to undergo psychoanalysis. A second emanates from the efforts of clinicians who worked with hospitalized patients to identify those who, despite their healthier appearance, nevertheless shared characteristics with core schizophrenic individuals. Adolf Stern (1938), for example, who is credited with initially popularizing the term "borderline," belongs to the former group. He identified ten characteristics of office patients that were associated with their getting worse, resisting change, or not cooperating with psychoanalysis. Among these were narcissism, psychic bleeding, inordinate hypersensitivity, psychic and body rigidity, negative therapeutic reaction, constitutional feelings of inferiority, masochism, organic insecurity, projective mechanisms, and difficulties in reality testing. Likewise, Schmideberg's (1947) concept of the borderline was that it was a form of personality disorder "stable in its instability." She felt that borderline individuals (1) were unable to tolerate routine and regularity; (2) tended to break many rules of social convention; (3) were often late for appointments; (4) were unable to free associate during their sessions; (5) were poorly motivated for treatment; (6) failed to develop meaningful insight; (7) led chaotic lives in which something dreadful was always happening; (8) would engage in petty criminal acts; (9) could not easily establish emotional contact.

In contrast to Stern and Schmideberg, among others, Zilboorg (1941) described a group of ambulatory schizophrenic patients. Hoch and Polatin (1949) identified the pseudoneurotic schizophrenic category, and Federn (1947) described latent schizophrenia. These categories refer to patients who seem to function better than the usual schizophrenic patient but nevertheless possess the basic characteristics of schizophrenia.

Thus historically it was not clear if the term "borderline" referred to a distinct diagnostic entity that had its own unique characteristics, development, prognosis, and treatment implications, if it was a less severe form of schizophrenia, or if it was a wastebasket category encompassing patients that did not fit traditional diagnostic criteria.

RESEARCH ON DISTINGUISHING FEATURES

Even among authors who agreed in their usage of the term "borderline," there was disagreement about its main characteristics (Perry and Klerman, 1978:141–50).

Grinker and his colleagues (1968), for example, were among the first clinicians to undertake a research study of the characteristics of a large group of borderline individuals. They identified four common characteristics: (1) anger as the main or only affect; (2) defect in affectional (interpersonal) relations; (3) absence of consistent self-identity; and (4) depression. They further described four subtypes: *Type I*, the Psychotic Border, is manifested by inappropriate, nonadaptive behavior; deficient self-identity and sense of reality; negative behavior and anger; and depression. *Type II*, the Core Borderline Syndrome, is manifested by vacillating involvement with others, anger acted out, depression, and inconsistent self-identity. *Type III*, the Adaptive, Affectless, Defended, "As If" Persons, show appropriate, adaptive behavior, complementary relationships, little affect or spontaneity, and defenses of withdrawal and intellectualization. *Type IV*, The Border with the Neuroses, is manifested by anaclitic depression, anxiety, and a resemblance to neurotic narcissistic character.

Likewise, Gunderson and Singer (1975), in their extensive review of the literature on borderline clients, identified six characteristics that they consider common to most descriptions of such individuals: (1) the presence of intense affect, usually depressed or hostile; (2) a history of impulsive behavior; (3) a certain social adaptiveness; (4) brief psychotic experiences; (5) loose thinking in unstructured situations; and (6) relationships that vacillate between transient superficiality and intense dependency. It should be noted, however, that neither Grinker's nor Gunderson and Singer's studies attempted to link the identifiable characteristics of borderline individuals to developmental concepts.

CAUSAL EXPLANATIONS

Explanations as to why borderline conditions develop have emphasized either constitutional and hereditary factors or developmental ones. Helene Deutsch (1942) was among the first to emphasize the pathology of internalized object relations in her discussion of "as if" personalities, another term used to describe borderline individuals. Knight's (1953) seminal efforts to define the borderline client systematically reflected an attempt to apply ego psychological understanding. He called attention to the nature of ego weakness in borderline clients and focused particularly on their defects in secondary process thinking and realistic planning, and on their defenses against primitive impulses. Until recently, however, these views were not systematized, nor was it clear how developmental difficulties were linked to the manifest pathology observed in borderline patients.

A major perspective in the early study of borderline disorders saw them as linked genetically to schizophrenia but this view did not predominate. More recently, biologically oriented researchers have argued that so-called borderline individuals suffer from an underlying mood disorder. While a large percentage of those who are diagnosed as borderline do have a concurrent depressive disorder and others complain of depression, they seem to differ substantially from those who have the usual types of depression (Kroll, 1988).

TREATMENT CONSIDERATIONS

The main controversy regarding the psychodynamic treatment of borderline individuals was whether they required supportive psychotherapy or classical psychoanalytic psychotherapy with special modifications (parameters). Stern and Knight, for example, both argued for a supportive, ego- and reality-oriented approach that maximized the patient's ego strengths and did not foster regression. They viewed these patients as unable to tolerate the demands of a more modifying type of approach without getting worse. Their views influenced prevailing ideas about the optimal treatment of borderline individuals for many years, until recently.[2] Other writers, such as Eissler (1953), however, advocated more traditional psychoanalytically oriented approaches that contained modifications (parameters) of technique to handle the special problems of the borderline patient. Eissler argued that a supportive approach would not modify the basic pathology of internalized object relations and defenses that the borderline patient presented.

While some clinicians believed that patients at the psychotic border required hospitalization in order for intensive psychotherapy to be effective, others felt it was regressive and should be avoided. There were similar differences of opinion about whether short-term or long-term intervention was indicated and whether borderline patients should receive drugs along with or instead of psychotherapy. The lack of research on treatment outcome fostered continued debate on these points.

CLINICAL OR DEVELOPMENTAL DIAGNOSIS

The use of clinical diagnoses in categorizing emotional problems traditionally has been associated with a medical model (Spitzer, Williams, and Skodol, 1980). Certain human difficulties are seen as mental disorders that can be identified and grouped by their common symptoms or characteristics. Such clusters are thought to have similar causes, prognoses, and implications for treatment (Lazare, 1973:345–51; Mechanic, 1980:1–28).

Many psychodynamically oriented clinicians favor the use of developmental diagnoses. They seek to establish how problems arise in the course of an individual's efforts to adapt to the environment (Lazare, 1973:345–51; Mechanic, 1980:1–28). Psychopathology is viewed on a continuum with normal development.

The use of clinical diagnoses has been challenged for the following reasons: (1) Its conception of causality does not encompass the cultural, environmental, or interpersonal context. Consequently social workers, for example, have attempted to develop classifications systems that address person-in-situation problems that clients present (Finestone, 1960:139–54). (2) Diagnostic pigeonholing or labeling rather than individualized understanding is encouraged. It is argued that such labeling leads to abuses in client care. (3) The use of diagnostic categories is unreliable, that is, clinicians differ markedly with respect to the criteria they use to make their judgments. Thus the same client may be diagnosed differently by various clinicians. (4) Sociocultural bias affects the diagnostic process. What is viewed as psychopathology may represent class, sex-role, cultural, or life-style difference. Further, such biases lead to the use of premature, unnecessary, or incorrect treatment approaches. (5) Diagnosis is a means of social control in which those who are viewed as deviant or undesirable can be labeled as sick, punished, or deprived of their rights (Mechanic, 1980). Many of these issues also apply to the use of developmental diagnoses.

Hollis (1972) and Shevrin (1972), among others, have defended the use of clinical diagnosis, although they agree that the above criticisms are valid in some instances. Shevrin points out, however, that the potential value of clinical diagnoses and the ideal process by which they are achieved ought not be confused with their abuse by untrained, unskilled, unethical, or misguided individuals. While there are dangers in the use of clinical and developmental diagnoses, they shed light on certain types of difficulties that clients present. Further, while they do not constitute the main diagnostic models that social workers utilize, they offer social workers an important framework that enhances their diagnostic understanding.

DSM IV CRITERIA

The conception of the clinical diagnosis of borderline conditions was reflected in the DSM-III. The most recent edition of the American Psychiatric Association's official classification system, the DSM-IV (1994), defines borderline personality disorder by overt signs and symptoms that are believed to cluster together irrespective of underlying developmental pathology.

According to the DSM-IV, borderline conditions represent one of many types of personality disorder, along with paranoid, schizoid, schizotypal, histrionic, narcissistic, antisocial, dependent, compulsive, passive-aggressive, and atypical personalities. It is possible, however, to have one of these disorders along with borderline personality disorder.

According to the DSM-IV, borderline individuals show at least five of the following characteristics: (1) desperate attempts to avoid real or imagined abandonment; (2) unstable and intense interpersonal relationships; (3) identity disturbance; (4) impulsiveness; (5) recurrent suicidal threats, gestures, or behavior, or self-mutilating behavior; (6) unstable, intense, and transient feeling states; (7) chronic feelings of emptiness; (8) inappropriate, intense anger or difficulty controlling anger; and (9) temporary stress-related paranoid or dissociative states (American Psychiatric Association, 1994:280–81).

DEVELOPMENTAL CHARACTERISTICS

From a contemporary psychodynamic perspective, ego psychological, object relations, and self psychological theories emphasize the developmental pathology that is associated with borderline conditions. A main controversy that cuts across these frameworks is whether borderline personality disorder reflects a rigid and faulty defensive structure that arises to ward off anxiety and structural conflict (Kernberg, 1975, 1984; Masterson, 1972), or whether it reflects deficits, gaps, missing, or underdeveloped elements in the personality (Adler, 1985; Adler and Buie, 1979; Blanck and Blanck, 1974, 1979; Kohut, 1971, 1977).

Drawing on both the conflict and deficit models, the following discussion reflects thirteen major characteristics that are important in diagnosing borderline disorders from a developmental perspective (Goldstein, 1990).

Identity Disturbances. Most individuals are able to convey a coherent, stable, and three-dimensional view of themselves and of significant others in their lives. With acquaintances, friends, and loved ones there is a secure sense of their basic predictability and sameness over time. People grow and change and may act differently in differing circumstances, but they show a continuity with their past or usual behavior. They rarely demonstrate radical shifts within hours, days, or weeks without an unusual reason. Such individuals experience themselves and others as having this sameness over time. They do not experience abrupt reversals of feelings and attitudes in themselves or in others. Such individuals also have a sense of their multifaceted feelings and characteristics. They are "human" with imperfections, and they regard others similarly. Sometimes they are aware of what may be troubling contradictions in themselves, but they attempt to resolve rather than to deny these.

In contrast, the borderline client presents him- or herself and others in puzzling, contradictory, vague, or stereotyped ways. One may obtain a great deal of information about a person but not be able to add it all up or make sense of it. It may be difficult to get any meaningful information about the client or about others in his or her life, even though the client does not withhold such information. Rather, his or her descriptions lack depth. One may obtain contradictory data that cannot be reconciled or the impression that there are either saints or villains in the client's life. The client may express uncertainty about his or her identity and may show difficulty in acknowledging certain characteristics, thoughts, and feelings.

Borderline individuals present themselves differently even in similar circumstances. Each way they appear is genuine but represents only one facet of the client. When appearing one way, moreover, the client may deny that he or she has ever been different. Thus a client may seem ingratiating and dependent one week, haughty and aloof another week, and charming and affable on yet a third occasion despite the worker's constancy of attitude and response. The client's perception of others in his or her life is that they are changing constantly. The client does not recognize that others remain the same and that it is he or she who changes.

Splitting and Other Primitive Defenses. In mature individuals ambivalence is recognized and tolerated. One can become angry at a spouse whom one loves without the anger destroying the relationship. One can accept being angry without feeling that one is no longer worthwhile. In other individuals feelings that are taboo become repressed so that they are not consciously experienced. Rather than experience anger at her husband, a wife may utilize (unconsciously) reaction formation and become more solicitous toward him.

In contrast, the borderline client utilizes the splitting defense and cannot tolerate or even recognize the coexistence of two conscious, contradictory feeling states such as love and hate. He or she tends to experience and perceive him- or herself and others as all good or all bad. Often these perceptions and experiences shift so that someone who is viewed as all good suddenly, when perceived as frustrating, becomes all bad. Conversely someone who is seen as all bad may become all good if he or she is perceived as gratifying. What is important, however, is that these feelings do not influence one another. Thus one denies the existence of good traits in someone who is perceived as bad even if one hour earlier that individual was seen as good. For example, a loved one who is sensitive to one's needs ninety-nine times out of a hundred still may be perceived as unloving if, on the hundredth occasion, he or she is insensitive.

Often certain characteristics of the individual or of others become associated with goodness and badness and also are split. Thus one can view assertiveness as bad and compliance as good. One may refuse to acknowledge evidence of one's own assertive behavior or impulses. These become split off from one's self-concept. Other defenses related to splitting, such as denial, projective identification, idealization, devaluation, and omnipotent control, also serve to maintain splitting (see Chapter 4).

The Capacity for Reality Testing. Most individuals are able to differentiate self from non-self or inner from outer stimuli, and can evaluate their behavior, thoughts, and feelings in terms of ordinary social norms. Psychotic individuals lack this capacity. Borderline clients may show certain psychotic-like symptoms. At times they may regress to a psychotic level of functioning. Thus it is sometimes difficult to differentiate between a borderline individual and a schizophrenic individual. Borderline clients, however, do have the capacity to test reality despite their psychotic-like symptoms. Thus, a borderline individual may appear to have bizarre beliefs about his or her special capacities or about others' motivations, for example. Upon exploration and confrontation of these ideas however, the client is able to correct or modify the distortions or beliefs and to become more realistic. Likewise a borderline client may experience difficulties in his or her sense of reality as evidenced by feelings of depersonalization. He or she may experience him- or herself as looking at his or her actions from outside of his or her body, while all the time recognizing that this is a strange experience and that his or her body really is intact. While some borderline clients may become acutely psychotic at times of stress, these episodes are transient, lasting a few hours, days, or in some instances weeks. They often respond to structuring of their lives or to brief hospitalization and do not require medication or more extensive treatment.

Problems in Impulse Control. Borderline individuals generally are impulsive in one or more areas of their lives. Their impulsiveness may be chronic and seemingly without environmental triggers or episodic in response to internal or external events, such as blows to self-esteem, loss, or the threat of abandonment.

Problems in Anxiety Tolerance. Many borderline individuals are anxious most of the time or have recurrent, disabling bouts of diffuse anxiety. They may experience dread when they awake in the morning or even in the middle of the night. Increases in stress are disorganizing or overwhelming. They also may experience panic reactions intermittently in response to life events, especially separations.

Problems in Affect Regulation. Borderline individuals often escalate rapidly in their feelings so that, for example, irritation becomes rage; sadness becomes despair; loneliness becomes aloneness; and disappointment becomes hopelessness. They become overwhelmed by too-intense positive or negative feelings. Seemingly happy at one moment, they plunge into a painful depression the next. They often show intense and inappropriate anger, temper tantrums, or affect storms. When these displays are coupled with impulsiveness, borderlines can become frightening, physically violent, or self-destructive.

Negative Affects. Often complaining of chronic depression, many borderlines show persistent feelings of anger, resentment, dissatisfaction, and envy. Sometimes they experience inner emptiness and feel bereft of positive or meaningful connections to others.

Problems in Self-soothing. Borderline individuals lack the capacity for self-soothing. They are at the mercy of any upsurge of uncomfortable feelings and have "no money in the bank" to draw upon in moments of stress. They become overwhelmed by feelings of panic, rage, and aloneness. Even minor separations such as leaving a therapy session can generate panic that prompts them to engage in desperate efforts to make contact. Some immerse themselves in constant activity or engage in addictive or other types of self-destructive behavior in order to escape from their feelings.

Abandonment Fears. Borderline individuals commonly show fears of abandonment. Some attempt to merge with others in efforts to deny or ward off their aloneness and to reassure themselves that they will never be abandoned. They seek constant proximity to or contact with those upon whom they are dependent and want to know their exact whereabouts or minute details of their activities. At the same time, most borderline individuals have a need-fear dilemma that makes them ward off or withdraw from the positive experiences with others for which they long. They often show an oscillating cycle of clinging and distancing behavior. When they are not feeling intense loneliness, many borderline individuals manage their abandonment fears by regulating interpersonal closeness and engage in many superficial relationships, avoiding intimacy.

Problems in Self-Esteem Regulation. Individuals with a sound sense of their self-worth are able to seek attention, affirmation, and praise without being driven to do so. They can survive being hurt by criticism, rejection, disapproval, insults, failures, or setbacks without feeling devastated, and they are able to have empathy for others. Borderline individuals often are highly vulnerable in their self-regard. Some show either highly grandiose or devalued conceptions of their abilities and talents and tend to feel either very entitled to special treatment or unworthy of help, or they fluctuate between these extremes.

Superego Difficulties. While some borderline individuals show an absence of guilt and empathy in their dealings with others and are capable of ruthless and exploitative acts, many experiencing remorse, self-contempt, and self-recriminations after they mistreat others. Nevertheless they find themselves unable to stop the very behavior that they hate.

Intense and Unstable Interpersonal Relationships. Intimacy is a problem since the borderline tends to merge with others or regulates closeness so that it is not threatening. Moodiness, possessiveness, insecurity, and highly charged interactions are common. Fights, accusations, and sudden breakups frequently occur and are usually related to feelings of being rejected or abandoned. Feelings of victimization are frequent. Separations are difficult, however, and cause anxiety and severe depression. They may lead to desperate and often seemingly manipulative and attention-getting behavior such as suicidal threats and attempts or other types of acting out.

Problems in Self-Cohesion. Some borderline individuals are vulnerable to psychotic decompensation under stress. They have a profound lack of self-cohesion that leaves them susceptible to transient periods of fragmentation that can be quite disturbing. When in equilibrium, borderline individuals can maintain their self-cohesiveness by regulating the degree of intimacy in their relationships and thus avoid the loss of ego boundaries involved in closeness.

THE CAUSES OF BORDERLINE CONDITIONS

The writings of Kernberg (1975), Mahler (1971), Masterson (1972, 1976) and Masterson and Rinsley (1975), Blanck and Blanck (1974, 1979), Adler (1985) and Adler and Buie (1979), and Kohut (1971, 1977) reflect contemporary psychodynamic perspectives on the developmental origins of borderline disorders.

A conflict model theorist, Kernberg attributes the development of the borderline structure to the child's inability to integrate good and bad self- and object representations in the third stage of the development of normal internalized object relations, which occurs from approximately the fourth month of life to the end of the first year. This stage is ushered in by the child's differentiation of self-representations from object representations. Within his or her self- and object images, however, good and bad self- and object representations remain separated. For example, while the mother is seen as distinct from the self, she is viewed as all good when she gratifies the child. Conversely, she is seen as all bad when she frustrates the child. Splitting, a defense, arises to protect the child from the loss of the good object and good self. When, because of excess aggression, the child's fear of destruction of the good self- and object representations is great, splitting continues along with other primitive defenses.

Although the child is able to differentiate him- or herself from others, a capacity that permits the development of reality testing and firm ego boundaries, his or her identity does not coalesce. He or she does not go on to the fourth stage of development, in which good and bad self- and object images become integrated into a whole and three-dimensional conception of self and others. The child remains fixated, his or her identity remains diffuse, and primitive defenses dominate perceptions. The id, ego, and superego do not consolidate into a mature intrapsychic (neurotic) structure. The capacity to neutralize aggressive instinct is deficient, and other ego functions such as the control of drives are impaired. The persistence of these structural deficits results in characteristic difficulties in perceiving and relating to others. Kernberg is equivocal as to whether constitutional factors or early frustration predispose children to the excess aggression that is central in this development.

Mahler's view of the sequential development of the borderline's difficulties in early childhood is similar to Kernberg's. She locates the timing somewhat later, however, during the rapprochement subphase of the separation–individuation process. In contrast to Kernberg, Mahler emphasizes the importance of the primary caretaker's (mother's) emotional unavailability and lack of attunement to the child's unique characteristics and phase-appropriate needs for separation–individuation in the genesis of borderline conditions.

During the rapprochement subphase the mother must support the child's efforts to be more autonomous from her while simultaneously remaining available to him or her. She must be a reliable figure on whom the child can count and with whom he or she can check out new achievements. The failure to master the rapprochement crisis impairs the child's ability to achieve object constancy (a secure inner representation of the mother). He or she does not consolidate the sense of self, nor does he or she develop a realistic view of others. Ego functioning becomes impaired.

In Masterson and Rinsley's conflict model, maternal unavailability during the rapprochement subphase is seen as being responsible for borderline disorders. Some children experience maternal withdrawal or punishment for their independent moves and rewards for dependency. In order to maintain the connection with the rewarding object and to avoid the withdrawal associated with autonomy, the child erects defenses against the depression, rage, fear, guilt, passivity, and emptiness that are associated with his or her independent strivings. The mother's alternating good (rewarding) and bad (withdrawing) attitudes toward the child's dependent and autonomous behavior, respectively, are internalized and kept split. Later life events that are associated with greater independence may reactivate the abandonment depression and its defensive constellation.

Gertrude and Rubin Blanck, who also draw on Mahler's research and writings, see borderline pathology as resulting from a developmental arrest during the separation–individuation process. They take a broader view of the origins of borderline conditions, however. They argue that there is a range of pathology within the neurotic and psychotic borders and that in some instances there is a crossing over into the neurotic border. Thus there is more than one type of borderline pathology, and the exact nature of the difficulties depends on how the ego has negotiated what they refer to as the fulcrum of development and how the processes of differentiation and integration are handled in each of the subphases of the separation–individuation process. Where particular subphase difficulties occur will determine the specific manifestations of borderline pathology.

Alternatively, Kohut, the initiator of self psychology, believed that true borderlines display a core deficit in the formation of the self. Unlike narcissistic personalities, however, they cover this basic deficit with a rigid defensive structure, for example, a schizoid or paranoid personality. Other borderlines, who on the surface may appear more similar to narcissistic personalities, show greater underlying narcissistic vulnerability. Severe and protracted failures in parental empathy with the selfobject needs of the child are the cause of borderline pathology. The necessary transmuting internalizations that transform archaic narcissistic needs for idealization, mirroring, and twinship do not occur. The self is arrested in its development, becomes enfeebled, and lacks cohesion.

Brandchaft and Stolorow (1984a and b) applied Kohut's self psychological principles to the problem of borderline pathology. As opposed to Kernberg's view of borderline disorders as representing a fixed, pathological defensive organization that resides within the person alone, they argue that what appears as borderline structure is iatrogenically created, that is, it is induced by unattuned and antitherapeutic treatment techniques. They reinterpret behavior that has been labeled by others as defenses, such as splitting and projective identification, as reflecting developmental arrests and resulting from selfobject failures. Thus the more flagrant and seemingly intractable behavior of so-called borderline individuals is stimulated by the failure of the environment (including the therapist) to meet their selfobject needs.

Adler and Buie (1979) describe the borderline's primary deficit as an inability to evoke a positive mental representation of a sustaining, holding, or soothing caretaker because he or she did not have good-enough mothering as a child. They do not regard the splitting defense as central in borderline disorders since they think borderlines have not internalized enough experiences with good objects to make splitting of good and bad objects possible. Borderline individuals also have a need–fear dilemma. They yearn for closeness but maintain distance out of fear of abandonment. When separated from those upon whom they depend, however, they become overwhelmed by a sense of aloneness and panic and rage reactions develop.

The views discussed so far have not encompassed the role of trauma or of family systems in the genesis of borderline disorders.[3] There has been increasing attention paid recently to the staggering amount of incest and other forms of sexual abuse in the histories of female borderlines (Herman and Van der Kolk, 1987; Kroll, 1988; Wheeler and Walton, 1987). Other families of borderlines show a history of physical abuse, psychiatric illness, divorce, parental death, and alcoholism. These findings raise the question of whether childhood trauma is pivotal in causing borderline disorders, which reflect a type of post-traumatic stress reaction. Presumably, traumatic experiences might result in the predominance of the defenses and symptoms that are associated with borderline conditions.

There are other aspects of family life that may be important in the development of borderline disorders. In this connection, an important contribution comes from the work of Shapiro and his colleagues (1975, 1977), who link ongoing family characteristics to the emergence of borderline pathology in adolescent and young adult offspring. They observe that both parents of borderline offspring show similar defenses as do the offspring themselves. They view such parental traits as stable structures that generate pathological developments in the offspring's early separation–individuation phase. They believe that these structures are reactivated in the parents during the adolescent's second separation–individuation phase, exerting pressure on the vulnerable adolescent and creating a family regression. The parents are seen as disavowing or idealizing many of their own characteristics, which remain unintegrated in their own personalities. These are projected onto their offspring. In turn the offspring internalizes the parental projections and conforms to the image that has been projected onto him or her. The offspring's acceptance of a particular identity such as the "good" or "bad" one interferes with identity integration. With demands for increased autonomy in adolescence, the underlying ego pathology emerges. The adolescent cannot separate from the family and cannot consolidate his or her identity because of family pressure, internalized difficulties, and impaired ego functioning. The families that were studied all appeared highly overinvolved or enmeshed, and primitive defenses dominated their family transactions. Others who have studied so-called borderline families found that many followed these patterns but others did not, showing more rejecting and neglectful characteristics.[4]

TREATMENT MODELS

Those clinicians who tend to follow the conflict model attempt to modify the rigid or faulty defensive structure of borderline individuals, usually through the use of insight-oriented, confrontative, and interpretive techniques, sometimes in conjunction with strict limit-setting and external structuring of the client's life. In contrast, those clinicians who favor the deficit model believe that treatment must build the internal structure that does not exist as well as strengthen and consolidate what is there.

Kernberg, for example, advocates an approach that attempts to modify the borderline's internal, pathological defensive structure and thus promote identity integration. He argues that while a supportive approach may lead to some improvement in the client's behavior, it only perpetuates his or her maladaptive defenses and identity diffusion. The individual remains vulnerable to impoverished functioning and requires the interminable presence of a therapist to promote adaptive behavior.

Kernberg's treatment approach to the borderline patient attempts to prevent undue regression by focusing on the reality of the patient's current life and relationships, by face-to-face contact, and by less frequent sessions (in comparison to psychoanalysis). He recommends (1) interpreting the latent and manifest negative transference that distorts the therapeutic relationship; (2) confronting and interpreting the primitive defenses that threaten the working alliance along with examining the patient's similar reactions to others in his or her life; (3) setting limits on the expression of destructive impulses and the patient's unrealistic demands on the therapist; (4) structuring the patient's life to control acting out, and (5) confronting and interpreting the defensive operations that impair the patient's here-and-now functioning and that reduce reality testing. Kernberg assumes that this treatment strategy will strengthen the patient's ego and lead to structural change.

Masterson, in contrast, advocates a special type of psychotherapy that aims to (1) help the patient deal with his or her current acute abandonment depression; (2) help the patient resolve his or her underlying abandonment depression; (3) correct and repair the ego deficits associated with the developmental arrest stemming from the patient's early separation–individuation phase; and (4) foster the mastery of separation–individuation tasks. Masterson recommends both supportive and reconstructive therapy. His supportive approach shares certain elements with Kernberg's modifying approach (the confrontation of defenses and the blocking of acting out).

The Blancks recommended an ego-building approach for the more disturbed borderlines that also aims to (1) correct and repair ego deficits stemming from particular separation–individuation subphase difficulties and (2) foster mastery of separation–individuation tasks. Because they emphasize the range of borderline difficulties, they advocate a therapeutic strategy that is geared specifically to the patient's subphase needs. While –confrontation and interpretation may be indicated with the higher-level borderline patient, it would be discouraged in the treatment of lower-level borderline patients. The Blancks rely heavily on the therapist's use of him- or herself as a real object with the patient in order to help provide an experience in which the patient's separation–individuation difficulties can be reexperienced and mastered.[5] They recommend (1) providing diagnostically specific "measured gratifications"; (2) supporting the client's highest level of functioning; (3) aiding verbalization and affect differentiation; (4) correcting distortions; and (5) engaging in a variety of ego-building techniques. They alert therapists to the fact that client behavior that looks like resistance may actually be in the service of separation–individuation.

Self psychological treatment requires the therapist's empathic immersion in a client's subjective experience, with the goal of helping him or her to develop a greater degree of self-cohesion. Interpretation and other technical interventions focus on helping clients to understand their selfobject needs—for example, for affirmation, admiration, and soothing—and the failures in attunement of parents and significant others in childhood. The empathic climate and experience of the therapy as much as its contents strengthen the client's self. There are differences of opinion even among self psychologists about whether therapists should restrict their interventions to empathic understanding or whether it is necessary or desirable to meet some of the client's selfobject needs. Kohut acknowledged that empathy in itself had a corrective emotional effect on clients and was an important aspect of therapeutic cure.

According to Adler and Buie, the borderline's need–fear dilemma must be addressed and worked through early in treatment through the provision of a good-enough holding environment and empathic interpretations so that the client will establish and maintain a positive relationship with the therapist. Since Adler and Buie argue that it is the absence of positive introjects rather than splitting that leads to the borderline client's overwhelming sense of aloneness and unmodulated rage, they seek to foster new internalizations rather than to confront and interpret pathological defenses. The therapist may selectively gratify the client's needs for contact and soothing, for example, in the treatment. Brief telephone calls, extra appointments, and the use of transitional objects such as vacation addresses and postcards may be necessary to help clients contain their feelings and impulses and maintain their positive connection to the therapist during periods of separation, however seemingly brief. It may be necessary at times for the therapist to set limits or to take a strong position on the dangerous or destructive behavior in which clients engage. In some instances, the devastating impact of longer separations—over summer vacations, for example—may actually cause the client to require hospitalization. Eventually, the client internalizes the therapist as a sustaining and soothing introject. This permits clients to overcome the terrible, chronic states of aloneness, panic, rage, and emptiness that occur when they are separated from those upon whom they depend for sustenance, as well as their fears of abandonment, which keep them from developing close attachments. The therapy also attempts to help clients replace pathological defenses and destructive patterns that they have used to cope with their turbulent inner experiences with more adaptive behavior.

Consistent with their view that borderline conditions reflect both individual and family pathology, Shapiro and his colleagues (1977) recommend intensive individual psychotherapy similar to Kernberg's approach with the identified borderline patient, concurrent with marital (parental) and family (including the borderline patient) therapy. They also advocate the use of two therapists (one for the identified patient and one for the patient's parents), who come together for family sessions.[6]

CLINICAL INTERVENTIONS

It is most useful to think of borderline pathology as reflecting a range of developmental difficulties that necessitate highly individualized and attuned therapeutic interventions. A worker who is wedded to one approach runs the risk of serious misattunement. While the worker's understanding of the borderline client's unique characteristics is crucial to most helping efforts, the therapeutic task varies from case to case. The client's presenting problem, expectations, and motivation; the agency's mandate; the worker's skill; and the availability of treatment resources all influence the determination of goals. While much can be learned and utilized from the treatment approaches to the borderline client suggested in the foregoing discussion, individualization is essential in establishing social work practice goals with this client population.

With some borderline clients the goal may be to help them over a particular crisis. With others the goal may include helping them to recognize the longstanding and entrenched nature of their personality difficulties in order to motivate them to work on these problems. With some clients the goal may be to help promote more adaptive behavior in selected areas of functioning, such as work or parent-child relationships. With others it may be to help build and strengthen some aspects of their ego functioning such as the capacity for impulse control. With some clients one may undertake more ambitious efforts to alter their borderline personality and to foster personality integration. With others ego-building efforts may be aimed at mastery of separation–individuation issues. While individual treatment generally is recommended for borderline clients, group (Horowitz, 1977) and family (Shapiro et al., 1977) intervention may be useful. Similarly, although long-term treatment is advocated for the modification of the borderline personality itself or for ongoing supportive efforts, short-term approaches (Wolberg, 1982) can be used successfully, particularly in dealing with more circumscribed difficulties. A detailed discussion of interventive techniques and modalities is beyond the scope of this chapter but the following comments highlight some important facets of the treatment process.

DEVELOPING AND MAINTAINING THE WORKING ALLIANCE

It is difficult to maintain a secure working alliance with borderline clients irrespective of whether one engages in a supportive or modifying approach with them. Their primitive defenses, proclivity to develop negative or highly charged transference reactions, capacity for regression, and impulsivity are activated readily during the interventive process. Borderline clients frequently drop out of treatment suddenly, prematurely, and dramatically. Their impulsivity or regressive behavior often results in self-destructive acts, excessive demands for and intrusions on the worker's time, or habitual crises that themselves command the immediate focus of interventive efforts.

A supportive approach does not stimulate as much anxiety or activate the client's maladaptive responses as much as does a modifying approach, but it does not eliminate these reactions. The client's tendency to shift suddenly in his or her feelings toward others in his or her life and to break off relationships with those who were formerly needed and idealized will occur in the client-worker relationship. Even the most sensitive and supportive worker will inevitably frustrate or disappoint the client by having to cancel a session due to illness, for example. Likewise a client's tendency to abuse drugs or alcohol when depressed may result in self-destructive behavior at times when he or she feels rejected by the worker. Further, the client's tendency to lose him- or herself in or merge with those upon whom he or she becomes dependent may be stimulated by the relationship with the worker, whom he or she comes to need.

Thus even if the goal of interventive efforts is to promote more adaptive behavior rather than to modify the client's internal defenses, structure, or personality patterns, the worker must be able to anticipate, recognize, and deal with those characteristics of the client that are likely to lead to disruption of the working alliance.

Establishing a Therapeutic Holding Environment. The establishment of a therapeutic environment that helps borderline individuals to feel safe and to contain their impulses is essential. While stability, consistency, clarity about expectations, and firmness are important in achieving these goals, the treatment framework should be individualized rather than mechanistic. While strict rules may be indicated for some clients, many who have severe deficits may require more flexibility and accessibility than is often recommended in the treatment of borderlines. The question of how best to help borderline individuals to contain their characteristic anxiety, impulsiveness, and self-destructiveness is an important one. Worker availability, real object experiences, empathic understanding and responsiveness, the use of transitional objects, selected confrontation, the use of limits and external structure are different ways of providing essential holding. Others have recommended that the client write down thoughts and feelings during periods of separation or use fantasy and visualization experiences involving the worker.

When limits and structure are needed, it is important for the worker to engage borderline clients collaboratively in a problem-solving effort about what will enable them to contain their impulses and self-destructive behavior. All too often, workers set limits unilaterally or as a result of anger or frustration. Likewise, while some clients will experience even the most gentle confrontation of their self-defeating patterns as an attack, the worker can try to communicate concern in nonassaultive and respectful ways.

Dealing with Primitive Defenses and the Negative Transference. The worker can help the client to gain more control of, correct, or alter the nature of his or her dysfunctional reaction during the interventive process by appealing to the client's observing ego. The first step in this process involves anticipating with the client some of the likely responses he or she may have in the course of interventive efforts and establishing guidelines as to how these might be handled should they occur. For example, a client may have a history of multiple therapeutic contacts characterized by initial idealization followed by disillusionment and termination of the treatment. This pattern also may be evident in the client's relationships with friends. The client tells the new worker that she (the worker) is the most sensitive and skillful person he has ever known and that he is sure she will be able to help him. It is important that the worker not be flattered or comforted by what she may feel to be the client's accurate perception of her talents. She needs to understand the likelihood that the client's comments reflect his beginning idealization of the worker and the recreation of his usual pattern. The worker must recognize the inevitability of her falling from her pedestal in the client's eyes, with the probable consequence that the client will leave treatment as he has done previously unless the worker is able to help the client gain control of this pattern, at least temporarily. The worker would be well advised to share her concern with the client by suggesting to him that should he begin to feel disappointed in or angry with her it is important that he express these feelings directly to the worker rather than act on them. The worker may explain to a client who tends to experience all authority figures as controlling that he may begin to feel this way toward the worker, and that it is important for their work together that these feelings be discussed openly.

The aim of anticipating the client's reactions with the worker is not to prevent their occurrence but to set the stage for helping the client to use his or her observing ego to block the potentially disruptive effects of those reactions. It is the beginning of an overall strategy. The second step in this strategy is for the worker to be alert to various signs that, despite the client's seeming cooperativeness, he or she may be feeling, thinking, and behaving in ways that are "split off" from the interventive process and may threaten it. The defense of splitting has the effect of keeping important information about the client from surfacing directly in what the client shares with the worker. For example, a client gives no hint of anger in what appears to be an agreeable session, but at the end of it announces that he no longer wishes to see the worker because he is feeling much better and doesn't need her any more. The worker asks if the client is angry that she was unable to see him the preceding week because of illness. The client acknowledges that he is angry. When asked why he didn't bring this up himself, however, he responds that he lost his anger upon seeing the worker but wants to leave treatment anyway. The worker then responds that she feels the client is fearful of expressing his anger at the worker and would rather leave than talk about his feelings. In this example, the worker did not recognize the client's use of splitting until it threatened the continuance of intervention. The worker who understands the likelihood that the client cannot express anger directly despite its being consciously experienced will be alert to and able to elicit the client's split-off reactions. That will enable him or her to block their disruptive consequences. In order to do this successfully, the worker must be attuned to what feelings, thoughts, and behavior are not communicated as well as those that are verbalized.

A third step in the process of using the client's observing ego to help him or her maintain the working alliance is to help the client recognize the true nature of defensive and transference reactions as they emerge in the client–worker relationship and their connection to similar experiences he or she has had with others in the past and present. In order to do this the worker needs to (1) help the client clarify how he or she is perceiving and reacting to the worker; (2) help the client reflect on his or her contradictory perceptions of, sudden shifts in attitudes or feelings toward, or distortions of the worker; (3) help the client connect his or her perceptions of or reactions to the worker to those he or she has had with others; and (4) help the client reflect on the possible reasons for his or her reactions or distortions. If the worker has anticipated with the client the possibility of developing certain reactions in the course of the intervention, the worker can remind the client of their earlier discussion in an effort to help him or her recognize that indeed he or she is reexperiencing the usual pattern as predicted.

For example, a client who in previous session has repeatedly praised the worker's sensitivity and skill becomes disparaging and verbally assaultive after the worker accepts a telephone call briefly during their meeting time. The worker asks the client to consider how it is possible for the client to change his view of the worker so totally after one incident. The client indicates that this is because the worker has changed. The worker suggests that it is the client and not the worker who has changed. She indicates that the client, feeling rejected by her, now wants to reject her as all bad as he has done with others in his life whom he perceived as hurting him when they did not respond to his needs as he wished. Another client who has shared many intense feelings with the worker begins to offer very little in response to the worker's questions. Whatever the worker says is regarded as wrong or stupid, so that the worker feels she must be very careful what she says to the client and feels controlled. The worker then asks the client if he perceives the struggle going on between them. She reflects on the client's contradictory behavior of opening up and then shutting off and his trusting the worker one moment and treating her like an enemy the next. The worker suggests that the client may fear that he will be vulnerable to the worker's power and control if he confides in her and that he may be protecting himself by controlling what he shares with the worker. She adds that this seems to happen to the client in other close relationships and may stem from his feelings of having been exploited and dominated by his parents.

Because defenses and entrenched patterns of relating or reacting are experienced as intrinsic and essential to their very being, borderline clients, like those with other types of personality disorder, may view the worker's efforts to point out and interpret their feelings, thoughts, and behavior as criticisms or assaults. Thus it is very important that the worker convey his or her comments in a respectful and sensitive way and refrain from being judgmental, punitive, sarcastic, mocking, or in other ways hostile to the client. The worker's attitude is important to the client's ability to hear and take in what the worker has to say. Further the worker's confidence that he or she is not guilty of the client's accusations will enable him or her to aid the client in perceiving the worker more realistically.

Controlling Regression and Impulsive or Destructive Behavior. There are many ways the worker can try to regulate the nature of the client's regression during the interventive process. Among these are (1) focusing on the client's here-and-now functioning; (2) structuring the sessions; (3) minimizing the transferential nature of the relationship by being more real and seeing the client at well-spaced intervals (once a week); (4) establishing clear expectations regarding the length of sessions, the nature of payment, and the worker's availability by telephone or for extra sessions, and so on; and (5) helping to clarify the client's perceptions of and reactions to the worker and correcting distortions that occur, as discussed above. Sometimes the use of more than one worker at least temporarily may dilute the intensity of regressive transference reactions. The use of group treatment instead of or in addition to individual treatment may also be helpful in this regard.

When there is more than one helping person, however, there must be close coordination and collaboration among helping efforts. Otherwise the nature of the client's splitting defense and identity problems is likely to create serious difficulties. It is not uncommon for two workers to see the client differently, because the client presents him- or herself differently to each of them. Each may be unaware of certain aspects of the client's self-presentation or behavior. In becoming aware of these differences, each worker may feel that his or her view of the client is the more accurate. This may lead to disagreements among the workers, to their being played one against the other by the client (not necessarily consciously), or to unresolvable collaborative problems. This scenario is not infrequent when the borderline patient is treated within a hospital or residential setting, where there are multiple staff members involved in the patient's care. It also occurs in outpatient practice, however, among all those involved with the patient (helpers, friends, family, and so on).

There also are ways to help clients control their potentially impulsive or destructive behavior by building structure into their lives outside of their meetings with the worker. The feasibility and success of these will vary from case to case. The use of day treatment or recreational centers, halfway houses or residences, vocational programs or employment itself, and rehabilitative groups like Alcoholics Anonymous can provide external structure to clients who lack internal structure. Other helpful strategies involve (1) discussing with the client ways of building certain routines or accomplishing certain tasks in daily life so that he or she is not overwhelmed by hours of unstructured time and activity; (2) helping the client find more appropriate ways of dealing with unpleasant emotions or anxiety-provoking stimuli and situations; and (3) helping the client find ways of reducing the stresses that stimulate increased impulsivity or destructive behavior.

USING THE SELF

The traditional view that workers should remain neutral and frustrating needs to be reexamined when working with borderlines. Since these individuals have such profound developmental arrests, this stance may reexpose them to the neglect they experienced early in life. Workers may need to be more real, selectively share personal information, and provide validation and affirmation (Goldstein, 1994). This does not mean that one always gratifies the client's needs and requests. The very uncharted nature of this territory makes for uncertainty and error. We lack criteria for when one does what to whom. While there are dangers in being "manipulated" or "drawn in" by clients, or in acting out one's own need to be nurturing or rescuing to the detriment of clients, there also are dangers inherent in withholding from and frustrating clients and reexposing them to deprivation and rejection.

EGO-BUILDING

Treatment must attempt to help borderline clients to restore, develop, or strengthen their adaptive coping mechanisms. A variety of ego-building techniques can be used in this process based on a careful assessment of the client's ego functioning. It is important to partialize and focus, particularly when treatment is short-term in nature (Rowland, 1975).

USING PSYCHOTROPIC MEDICATION

While the common view is that psychotropic drugs do not help borderlines and are generally contraindicated because they tend to be abused, there are some positive indications for the use of medication with clients who show depression, panic states, or disorganized thinking. A common practice is to give antidepressants when there is evidence of a concurrent affective disorder or panic states and to prescribe small doses of major tranquilizers for pathology that is close to the psychotic range of symptoms. Psychotropic drugs always should be used cautiously with borderlines since noncompliance with drug regimens as well as abuse are common.

PSYCHIATRIC HOSPITALIZATION

Many borderlines are admitted to psychiatric hospitals following suicide attempts, psychotic episodes, or self-destructive behavior. Hospital treatment is usually short-term and focuses on resolving the immediate crisis that led to hospitalization, although some settings do provide long-term treatment. When treatment is short-term, a multifaceted, active treatment approach with partialized goals is necessary. Family must be involved in the treatment from the beginning not only as part of the problem but as part of the solution. Since borderline clients typically are admitted to hospitals at times of crisis, when they are extremely agitated, impulsive, or disorganized, the short-term model emphasizes the control function of the setting. It tries to limit disruptive behavior by maintaining a firm, highly structured, unified, and predictable atmosphere in which clients must meet all rules and expectations. In order to provide "optimal holding," it is equally important for staff to relate empathically rather than distance themselves from clients' panic and aloneness (Adler, 1975). Discharge planning is paramount, often requiring creativity, advocacy, systems negotiation skills, and persistence. Clients and families need to be involved in this process and much of the groundwork can be laid by family members. Linkages to community resources or out-client settings generally should be made prior to the client's leaving the hospital so that there is ample time to discuss the client's reactions.

WORKING WITH COUPLES AND FAMILIES

There are many instances in which therapeutic success with borderline individuals necessitates work with the family system. An approach that is sensitive to the family's needs and defenses and that respects their need for information and their rights as consumers will lessen their more extreme reactions and lead to a therapeutic alliance (Anderson, Hogarty, and Reiss, 1980; Goldstein, 1983b). The family of the borderline client requires a therapeutic holding environment that helps them to contain their anxiety and to become true collaborators in the treatment process. Avoiding power struggles, being accessible, providing information, and involving family members in decision-making facilitates their engagement. While many families may require treatment of their own, they may be threatened by such efforts and without necessary support will resist and act out, often undermining the primary client's recovery.

GROUP INTERVENTION

Arguing that unstructured groups mobilize regression and stimulate volatility and defensiveness in borderline individuals, most clinicians have cautioned against the use of intensive group therapy with this population. Supportive, structured, and task-oriented groups, however, can be used effectively with many borderlines to develop skills and promote ego functioning and interpersonal relationships.

SUMMARY

This chapter has reviewed the important issues in the diagnosis and treatment of borderline conditions historically. It considered current conceptions of the diagnosis and treatment of borderline conditions as a form of personality disorder or as a type of structural organization or developmental arrest and the various diagnostic criteria associated with each approach. Discussing the implications of these conceptions for social work practice, it focused on the worker's ability to recognize the borderline client, to maintain the working alliance, and to establish individualized interventive goals.

NOTES

1. Excellent historical reviews can be found in Eda G. Goldstein, *Borderline Disorders: Clinical Models and Techniques* (New York: Guilford Press, 1990), pp. 14–29; Otto F. Kernberg, *Borderline Conditions and Pathological Narcissism* (New York: Jason Aronson, 1975); Michael H. Stone, *The Borderline Syndromes* (New York: McGraw-Hill, 1980); and Arlene Robbins Wolberg, *Psychoanalytic Psychotherapy of the Borderline Patient* (New York: Grune & Stratton, 1982).
2. These views were adopted in the social work literature. See Irving Kaufman, "Therapeutic Considerations of the Borderline Personality Structure," in Howard J. Parad, ed. *Ego Psychology and Dynamic Case Work* (New York: Family Service Association of America, 1958), pp. 99–111; Richard Stuart, "Supportive Casework with Borderline Patients," *Social Work*, 9 (January 1964):38–44; and Jerome Weinberger, "Basic Concepts in Diagnosis and Treatment of Borderline States," in Parad, *Ego Psychology and Dynamic Casework*, pp. 111–16. For an article that applies more recent views, see Anne O. Freed, "The Borderline Personality," *Social Casework: The Journal of Contemporary Social Work*, 61 (November 1980):548–58.
3. For a discussion of this issue see Eda G. Goldstein, *Borderline Disorders*.
4. For studies of the families of borderline patients see, for example, Roy R. Grinker and Beatrice Werble, eds., *The Borderline Patient* (New York: Jason Aronson, 1977); John Gunderson, John Kerr, and Diane Woods Englund, "The Families of Borderline Patients: A Comparative Study," *Archives of General Psychiatry*, 37 (January 1980):27–33; and Froma Walsh, "Family Study 1976: 14 New Borderline Cases," in Grinker and Werble, eds., *Borderline Patient*, pp. 158–77.
5. For an illustration of this approach see Joyce Edward, Nathene Ruskin, and Patsy Turrini, *Separation–Individuation: Theory and Application* (New York: Gardner Press, 1981).

6. Kernberg cautions against this approach. He suggests that in cases where family treatment accompanies individual treatment of borderline patients the family should be seen by a separate therapist, and the patient's therapist should never participate in family meetings. See Otto F. Kernberg, "Psychoanalytic Psychotherapy with Borderline Adolescents," in Sherman Feinstein and Peter L. Giovacchini, eds., *Adolescent Psychiatry*, Vol. 7 (Chicago: The University of Chicago Press, 1979), pp. 294–321.

BIBLIOGRAPHY

Abarbanel, Gail, and Gloria Richman. "The Rape Victim." In Howard J. Parad and Libbie G. Parad, eds., *Crisis Intervention Book 2: The Practitioner's Sourcebook for Brief Therapy.* Milwaukee, Wis.: Family Service America, 1990. Pp. 93–118.

Abelin, Ernest L. "The Role of the Father in the Separation-Individuation Process." In J. B. McDevitt and C. F. Settlage, eds., *Separation Individuation: Essays in Honor of Margaret S. Mahler.* New York: International Universities Press, 1971. Pp. 229–52.

Abell, Neil, and James R. McDonnell. "Preparing for Practice: Motivations, Expectations, and Aspirations of the M.S.W. Class of 1990." *Journal of Social Work Education,* 26 (Winter 1990):57–64.

Adler, Alfred. *The Practice and Theory of Individual Psychotherapy.* New York: Humanities Press, 1951.

Adler, Gerald. "Hospital Management of Borderline Patients and Its Relation to Psychotherapy." In Peter Hartacollis, ed., *Borderline Personality Disorders.* New York: International Universities Press, 1977. Pp. 307–24.

Adler, Gerald. *Borderline Psychopathology and its Treatment.* New York: Jason Aronson, 1985.

———, and Daniel H. Buie. "Aloneness and Borderline Pathology: The Possible Relevance of Child Development Issues." *International Journal of Psychoanalysis,* 60 (1979):83–96.

Ainsworth, M. D. S. "The Development of Mother-Infant Attachment." In B. Caldwell and H. Ricciuti, eds., *Review of Child Development Research.* Vol. 3. Chicago: University of Chicago Press, 1973. Pp. 1–94.

———, and S. Bell. "Some Contemporary Patterns of Mother-Infant Interaction in the Feeding Situation." In A. Ambrose, ed., *Stimulation and Early Infancy.* London: Academic Press, 1969. Pp. 133–70.

Alexander, Franz. *Fundamentals of Psychoanalysis.* New York: W. W. Norton, 1963.

———, and Thomas M. French. *Psychoanalytic Therapy.* New York: Ronald Press, 1946.

Allport, Gordon W. *Pattern and Growth in Personality.* New York: Holt, Rinehart, & Winston, 1961.

Ambrose, J. A. "The Concept of a Critical Period in the Development of Social Responsiveness." In B. M. Foss, ed., *Determinants of Infant Behavior*. Vol. 2. New York: John Wiley & Sons, 1963. Pp. 201–25.

American Psychiatric Association. *Diagnostic and Statistical Manual of Mental Disorders: Third Edition*. Washington, D.C.: American Psychiatric Association, 1980.

———. *Diagnostic Criteria from DSM-IV,*™ Washington, D.C.: American Psychiatric Association, 1994.

Anderson, Carol; Garard E. Hogarty; and Douglas J. Reiss. "Family Treatment of Adult Schizophrenic Patients: A Psychoeducational Approach." *Schizophrenia Bulletin*, 6 (3) (1980):490–505.

Anderson, Sandra C., and Donna C. Henderson. "Working with Lesbian Alcoholics." *Social Work*, 30 (November–December 1985): 518–25.

Arieti, Silvano. *Interpretation of Schizophrenia*. New York: Basic Books, 1974.

Austin, Lucille N. "Trends in Differential Treatment in Social Casework." *Social Casework*, 29 (June 1948):203–11.

———. "Qualifications of Social Caseworkers for Psychotherapy." *Journal of Orthopsychiatry*, 26 (January 1956):47–57.

Babcock, Charlotte G. "Inner Stress in Illness and Disability." In Howard J. Parad and Roger Miller, eds., *Ego-Oriented Casework*. New York: Family Service Association of America, 1963. Pp. 45–64.

Bandler, Bernard. "The Concept of Ego-Supportive Therapy." In Howard J. Barad and Roger Miller, eds., *Ego-Oriented Casework*. New York: Family Service Association of America, 1963. Pp. 27–44.

Bandler, Louise. "Some Casework Aspects of Ego Growth Through Sublimation." In Howard J. Parad and Roger Miller, eds., *Ego-Oriented Casework*. New York: Family Service Association of America, 1963. Pp. 89–107.

Baptiste, Jr., David A. "Psychotherapy with Gay/Lesbian Couples and Their Children in 'Stepfamilies': A Challenge for Marriage and Family Therapists." *Journal of Homosexuality*, 14 (1/2 1987):223–39.

Barnett, Rosalind C. "The Anxiety of the Unknown—Choice, Risk, Responsibility: Therapeutic Issues for Today's Adult Women." In Grace Baruch and Jeanne Brooks-Gunn, eds., *Women in Midlife*. New York: Plenum Press, 1984. Pp. 341–57.

Bartlett, Harriet. *The Common Base of Social Work Practice*. New York: National Association of Social Workers, 1970.

Bauer, Steven; Eda G. Goldstein; Kay Haran; and Barbara Flye. "Differential Diagnosis and Adolescence: The Use of the Hospital Milieu." *Hospital and Community Psychiatry*, 31 (March 1980):187–91.

Beck, Aaron T.; A. John Rush; Brian F. Shaw; and Gary Emery. *Cognitive Theory of Depression*. New York: Guilford Press, 1979.

Beck, Aaron T.; Arthur Freeman; and Associates. *Cognitive Therapy of Personality Disorders.* New York: Guilford Press, 1990.

Beck, Dorothy Fahs. "Marital Conflict: Its Course and Treatment as Seen by Caseworkers." *Social Casework,* 47 (September 1966):575–82.

Belcher, John R., and Paul H. Ephross. "Toward an Effective Practice Model for the Homeless Mentally Ill." *Social Casework: The Journal of Contemporary Social Work,* 70 (September 1989):421–27.

Bellak, Leopold; Marvin Hurvich; and Helen Gediman, eds. *Ego Functions in Schizophrenics, Neurotics, and Normals.* New York: John Wiley & Sons, 1973.

Benedek, Therese. "Parenthood During the Life Cycle." In James Anthony and Therese Benedek, eds., *Parenthood—Its Psychology and Psychopathology.* Boston: Little, Brown, 1970. Pp. 185–208.

Benjamin, Jessica. *The Bonds of Love: Psychoanalysis, Feminism, and the Problem of Domination.* New York: Pantheon, 1988.

Beres, David. "Ego Deviation and the Concept of Schizophrenia." In *Psychoanalytic Study of the Child.* Vol. XI. New York: International Universities Press, 1956. Pp. 164–233.

Berger, Raymond M. "Research on Older Gay Men: What We Know, What We Need to Know." In N. J. Woodman, ed., *Gay and Lesbian Lifestyles: A Guide for Counseling and Education.* New York: Irvington Publishers, 1992. Pp. 217–32.

———, and James J. Kelly. "Working with Homosexuals of the Older Population." *Social Casework: The Journal of Contemporary Social Work,* 67 (April 1986):203–10.

Berlin, Sharon, and Diane Kravetz. "Women as Victims: A Feminist Social Work Perspective." *Social Work,* 26 (June 1981):447–49.

Beverly, Creigs. "Treatment Issues for Black Alcoholic Clients." *Social Casework: The Journal of Contemporary Social Work,* 70 (June 1989): 370–74.

Bibring, Grete. "Psychiatric Principles in Casework." In Cora Kasius, ed., *Principles and Techniques in Social Casework: Selected Articles 1940–1950.* New York: Family Service Association of America, 1950. Pp. 370–79.

Biringen, Zeynep. "Attachment Theory and Research: Application to Clinical Practice." *American Journal of Orthopsychiatry,* 64 (July 1994):404–20.

Birns, Beverly. "The Mother-Infant Tie: Fifty Years of Theory, Science, and Science Fiction." *Works in Progress.* 21. Wellesley, Mass.: The Stone Center for Developmental Services and Studies, 1985. Pp. 1–19.

Blake-White, Jill, and Christine Madeline Kline. "Treating the Dissociative Process in Adult Victims of Childhood Incest." *Social Casework: The Journal of Contemporary Social Work,* 66 (September 1985):394–402.

Blanck, Gertrude, and Rubin Blanck. *Ego Psychology in Theory and Practice.* New York: Columbia University Press, 1974.

———. *Ego Psychology II: Psychoanalytic Developmental Psychology.* New York: Columbia University Press, 1979.

Blanck, Rubin. "The Case for Individual Treatment." *Social Casework,* 46 (February 1965):70–74.

Bloom, Martin. "Empirically Based Clinical Research." In Aaron Rosenblatt and Diana Waldfogel, eds., *Handbook of Clinical Social Work.* San Francisco: Jossey-Bass, 1983. Pp. 560–82.

Blos, Peter. "The Second Individuation Process of Adolescence." In Aaron Esman, ed., *The Psychology of Adolescence: Essential Readings.* New York: International Universities Press, 1975. Pp. 156–77.

Blum, Harold P., ed. *Female Psychology.* New York: International Universities Press, 1977.

Blythe, Betty J., and Scott Briar. "Developing Empirically Based Models of Practice." *Social Work,* 30 (November-December 1985):483–88.

Borzenzweig, H. "Social Work and Psychoanalytic Theory." *Social Work,* 16 (1971):7–16.

Boskind-Lodahl, Marlene. "Cinderella's Stepsisters: A Feminist Perspective on Anorexia Nervosa and Bulemia." In Elizabeth Howell and Marjorie Bayes, eds., *Women and Mental Health.* New York: Basic Books, 1981. Pp. 248–62.

Bowker, Lee H. "Marital Rape: A Distinct Syndrome." *Social Casework: The Journal of Contemporary Social Work,* 64 (June 1983):347–52.

Bowlby, John. "The Nature of the Child's Tie to the Mother." *International Journal of Psychoanalysis,* 39 (1958):350–73.

———. *Attachment and Loss.* Vol. I: *Attachment.* New York: Basic Books, 1969.

———. *Attachment and Loss.* Vol. II: *Separation: Anxiety and Anger.* New York: Basic Books, 1973.

———. "Developmental Psychiatry Comes of age. *American Journal of Psychiatry,* 145 (January 1988):1–10.

Boyd-Franklin, Nancy. *Black Families in Therapy: A Multisystems Approach.* New York: Guilford Press, 1989.

Brandchaft, Bernard, and Robert D. Stolorow. "The Borderline Concept: Pathological Character or Iatrogenic Myth." In Joseph Lichtenberg, Melvin Bornstein, and Donald Silver, eds., *Empathy II.* Hillsdale, N.J.: Analytic Press, 1984a. Pp. 333–58.

———. "A Current Perspective on Difficult Patients." In Paul E. Stepansky and Arnold Goldberg, eds., *Kohut's Legacy: Contributions to Self Psychology.* Hillsdale, N.J.: Analytic Press, 1984b. Pp. 117–34.

Brekke, John. "Crisis Intervention with Victims and Perpetrators of Spouse Abuse." In Howard J. Parad and Libbie G. Parad, eds., *Crisis*

Intervention Book 2: The Practitioner's Sourcebook for Brief Therapy. Milwaukee, Wis.: Family Service America, 1990. Pp. 161–78.

Brennan, Eileen M., and Ann Weick. "Theories of Adult Development: Creating a Context for Practice." *Social Work,* 62 (January 1981):13–19.

Brenner, Charles. *An Elementary Textbook of Psychoanalysis.* New York: International Universities Press, 1955.

Briar, Scott, and Henry Miller. *Problems and Issues in Social Casework.* New York: Columbia University Press, 1971.

Bricker-Jenkins, Mary; Nancy R. Hooyman; and Naomi Gottlieb, eds. *Feminist Social Work Practice in Clinical Settings.* (Sage Sourcebook for the Human Services Series, vol. 19). Newbury Park, Calif.: Sage Publications, 1991.

Brodsky, Annette M., and Jean Holroyd. "Report of the Task Force on Sex Bias and Stereotyping in Psychotherapeutic Practice." In Elizabeth Howell and Marjorie Bayes, eds., *Women and Mental Health.* New York: Basic Books, 1981. Pp. 98–112.

Brooks-Gunn, Jeanne, and Barbara Kirsh. "Life Events and the Boundaries of Midlife for Women. In Grace Baruch and Jeanne Brooke-Gunn, eds., *Women in Midlife.* New York: Plenum Press, 1984. Pp. 11–30.

Broverman, Inge K.; Donald M. Broverman; Frank E. Clarkson; Paul S. Rosenkrantz; and Susan R. Vogel. "Sex-Role Stereotypes and Clinical Judgments of Mental Health." In Elizabeth Howell and Marjorie Bayes, eds., *Women and Mental Health.* New York: Basic Books, 1981. Pp. 86–97.

Brower, Kirk J.; Frederic C. Blow; and Thomas Beresford. "Treatment Implications of Chemical Dependence Models: An Integrative Approach." *Journal of Substance Abuse Treatment,* 6 (1989):147–57.

Burch, Beverly. "Heterosexuality, Bisexuality, and Lesbianism: Rethinking Psychoanalytic Views of Women's Sexual Object Choice." *Psychoanalytic Review,* 80 (Spring 1993):83–98.

Butler, Robert N. "The Life Review: An Interpretation of Reminiscence in the Aged." *Psychiatry,* 26 (January 1963):65–76.

Caputo, Larry. "Dual Diagnosis: AIDS and Addiction." *Social Work,* 30 (July–August 1985):361–65.

Carkhuff, R. R., and B. G. Berenson. *Beyond Counseling and Psychotherapy.* New York: Holt, Rinehart & Winston, 1967.

Carter, Elizabeth A., and Monica McGoldrick, eds. The Family Life Cycle: A Framework for Family Therapy. New York: Gardner Press, 1980.

Cass, Vivienne C. "Homosexual Identity Formation: A Theoretical Model." *Journal of Homosexuality,* 3 (Spring 1979):219–35.

Cath, Stanley. "Fathering from Infancy to Old Age: A Selective Overview of Recent Psychoanalytic Contributions." *The Psychoanalytic Review,* 73 (Winter 1986):469–79.

Chernus, Linda A. "Clinical Issues in Alcoholism Treatment." *Social Casework,* 66 (February 1985):67–75.

Chestang, Leon W. 1972. "Character Development in a Hostile Environment." In Martin Bloom, ed., *Life Span Development: Bases for Preventive and Interventive Helping.* New York: Macmillan, 1980. Pp. 40–50.

————. "Competencies and Knowledge in Clinical Social Work." In Patricia L. Ewalt, ed., *Toward a Definition of Clinical Social Work.* Washington, D.C.: National Association of Social Workers, 1987. Pp. 1–112.

Chilman, Catherine S. "Teenage Pregnancy: A Research Review." In Elizabeth Howell and Marjorie Bayes, eds., *Women and Mental Health.* New York: Basic Books, 1981. Pp. 325–39.

Chodorow, Nancy. *The Reproduction of Mothering.* Berkeley: University of California Press, 1978.

Cockerill, Eleanor E.; Lewis J. Lehrman; Patricia Sacks; and Isabel Stamm. *A Conceptual Framework of Social Casework.* Pittsburgh: University of Pittsburgh Press, 1953.

Coehlo, George V.; David A. Hamburg; and John E. Adams., eds. *Coping and Adaptation.* New York: Basic Books, 1974.

Colarusso, Calvin, and Robert A. Nemiroff. *Adult Development.* New York: Plenum Press, 1981.

Coleman, Eli. "Developmental Stages of the Coming Out Process." In John C. Gonsiorek, ed., *Homosexuality and Psychotherapy: A Practitioner's Handbook of Affirmative Models.* New York: Haworth Press, 1982. Pp. 31–44.

Colgan, Philip. "Treatment of Identity and Intimacy Issues in Gay Males." In Eli Coleman, ed., *Integrated Identity: Gay Men and Lesbians.* New York: Harrington Park Press, 1988. Pp. 101–23.

Collier, Helen V. *Counseling Women—A Guide for Therapists.* New York: Free Press, 1982.

Collins, Barbara G. "Defining Feminist Social Work." *Social Work,* 31 (May-June 1986):214–20.

————. "Reconstructing Codependency Using Self-in-Relation Theory." *Social Work,* 38 (July 1993):470–76.

Comas-Diaz, Lillian, and Marilyn Minrath. "Psychotherapy with Ethnic Minority and Borderline Clients." *Psychotherapy,* 22 (Summer 1985):418–26.

Courtois, Christine A. *Healing the Incest Wound: Adult Survivors in Therapy.* New York: W. W. Norton, 1988.

Dane, Barbara Oberhofer. "New Beginnings for AIDS Patients." *Social*

Casework: The Journal of Contemporary Social Work, 70 (May 1989): 305–09.

———, and Samuel O. Miller. *AIDS: Intervening with Hidden Grievers.* Westport, Conn.: Auburn House, 1992.

Davies, Jody Messler, and Mary Gail Frawley. *Treating the Adult Survivor of Childhood Sexual Abuse: A Psychoanalytic Perspective.* New York: Basic Books, 1994.

DeCrescenzo, Teresa A. "Homophobia: A Study of Attitudes of Mental Health Professionals Toward Homosexuality." In R. Schoenberg and R. Goldberg with D. Shore, eds., *With Compassion Toward Some: Homosexuality and Social Work in America.* New York: Harrington Park Press, 1984. Pp. 115–36.

de la Cancela, Victor. "A Critical Analysis of Puerto Rican Machismo: Implications for Clinical Practice." *Psychotherapy,* 23 (Summer 1986):291–96.

Deutsch, Helene. "Psychology of Women in Relation to the Function of Reproduction." *International Journal of Psycho-Analysis,* 6 (June 1925): 405–18.

———. "The Significance of Masochism in the Mental Life of Women." *International Journal of Psycho-Analysis,* 11 (November 1930):48–60.

———. "Some Forms of Emotional Disturbance and Their Relationship to Schizophrenia." *Psychoanalytic Quarterly,* 11(1942):301–21.

Devore, Wynetta. "Ethnic Reality: the Life Model and Work with Black Families." *Social Casework: The Journal of Contemporary Social Work,* 64 (November 1983):525–31.

Dinnerstein, Dorothy. *The Mermaid and the Minotaur.* New York: Harper Colophon, 1977.

Dunkel, Joan, and Shellie Hatfield. "Countertransference Issues in Working with Persons with AIDS." *Social Work,* 31 (March-April 1986):114–17.

Edward, Joyce; Nathene Ruskin; and Patsy Turrini. *Separation-Individuation: Theory and Application.* New York: Gardner Press, 1981.

Eissler, Kurt R. "The Effects of the Structure of the Ego on Psychoanalytic Technique." *Journal of the American Psychoanalytic Association,* 1 (1953):104–43.

Elson, Miriam. "Parenthood and the Transformation of Narcissism." In Rebecca S. Cohen, Bertram J. Cohler, and Sidney H. Weissman, eds., *Parenthood: A Psychodynamic Perspective.* New York: Guilford Press, 1984. Pp. 297–314.

———. *Self Psychology in Clinical Social Work.* New York: W. W. Norton, 1986.

Erikson, Erik. Childhood and Society. New York: W. W. Norton, 1950.

———. "Identity and the Life Cycle." *Psychological Issues,* 1, No. 1 (1959):50–100.

————. "The Inner and Outer Space; Reflections on Womanhood."
   Daedalus, 93 (1964):582–606.

————. *Identity: Youth and Crisis*. New York: Norton, 1968.

————. "Once More the Inner Space." In Juliette Strauss, ed., *Women in
   Analysis*. New York: Dell, 1974. Pp. 333–64.

Escalona, Sibylle K. *The Roots of Individuality: Normal patterns of Development in Infancy*. Chicago: Aldine, 1968.

Espin, Olivia M. "Psychological Impact of Migration on Latinas." *Psychology of Women Quarterly*, II (December 1987):489–503.

Evans, Katie, and J. Michael Sullivan. *Dual Diagnosis: Counseling the
   Mentally Ill Substance Abuser*. New York: Guilford Press, 1990.

Ewalt, Patricia. *Toward a Definition of Clinical Social Work*. Washington,
   D.C.: National Association of Social Workers, 1980.

Fairbairn, W. Ronald D. *Psychoanalytic Studies of the Personality*. London:
   Routledge & Kegan Paul, 1952.

Falco, Kristine L. *Psychotherapy with Lesbian Clients: Theory into Practice*.
   New York: Brunner/Mazel, 1991.

Farber, Laura. "Casework Treatment of Ambulatory Schizophrenics."
   Social Casework. 39 (January 1958):9–17. Reprinted in Francis J.
   Turner, ed. *Differential Diagnosis and Treatment in Social Work*. 2d Ed.
   New York: Free Press, 1976. Pp. 341–51.

Faria, Geraldine, and Nancy Belohlavek. "Treating Female Adult Survivors of Childhood Incest." *Social Casework: The Journal of Contemporary Social Work*, 65 (October 1984):465–71.

Federn, Paul. "Principles of Psychotherapy in Latent Schizophrenia."
   American Journal of Psychotherapy, 1 (1947):129–39.

————. *Ego Psychology and the Psychoses*. New York: Basic Books, 1952.

Fewell, Christine Huff, and LeClair Bissell. "The Alcoholic Denial Syndrome: An Alcohol-Focused Approach." *Social Casework*, 59 (January 1978):6–13.

Field, Martha Heineman. "Social Casework Practice During the Psychiatric Deluge." *Social Service Review*, 54 (December 1980):483–507.

Finestone, Samuel. "Issues Involved in Developing Diagnostic Classifications for Casework." *Casework Papers 1960*. New York: Family Service Association of America, 1960. Pp. 139–54.

Finkelhor, David. *Childhood Sexual Abuse*. New York: Free Press, 1984.

Fischer, Joel. *The Effectiveness of Social Casework*. Springfield, Ill.: Charles
   C. Thomas, 1976.

————, and Walter Hudson. "Measurement of Client Problems for Improved Practice." In Aaron Rosenblatt and Diana Waldfogel, eds.,
   Handbook of Clinical Social Work. San Francisco: Jossey-Bass, 1983. Pp.
   673–93.

Foote, Nelson N., and Leonard S. Cottrell. *Identity and Interpersonal
   Competence*. Chicago: University of Chicago Press, 1965.

Fox, Evelyn F.; Marian A. Nelson; and William M. Bolman. "The Termination Process: A Neglected Dimension." *Social Work,* 14 (October 1969):53–63.

Frank, Margaret G. "Clinical Social Work: Past, Present, and Future Challenges and Dilemmas." In Patricia L. Ewalt, ed., *Toward a Definition of Clinical Social Work.* Washington, D.C.: National Association of Social Workers, 1980. Pp. 13–81.

Freed, Anne O. "The Borderline Personality." *Social Casework: The Journal of Contemporary Social Work,* 61 (November 1980):548–58.

Freud, Anna. *The Ego and the Mechanisms of Defense.* New York: International Universities Press, 1936.

———. *Normality and Pathology in Childhood.* New York: International Universities Press, 1965.

Freud, Sigmund. *The Standard Edition of the Complete Psychological Works of Sigmund Freud.* 24 vols. Edited by James Strachey. London: Hogarth Press, 1953–66.

———. 1900. *The Interpretation of Dreams.* In *The Standard Edition.* Vols. 4 and 5. London: Hogarth Press, 1955.

———. 1905. *Three Essays on the Theory of Sexuality.* In *The Standard Edition.* Vol. 7. London: Hogarth Press, 1953.

———. 1923. *The Ego and the Id.* In *The Standard Edition.* Vol. 19. London: Hogarth Press, 1961.

———. 1926. *Inhibitions, Symptoms, and Anxiety.* In *The Standard Edition.* Vol. 20. London: Hogarth Press, 1959.

———. 1933. "Anxiety and the Instinctual Life." Lecture XXXII. *New Introductory Lectures in Psychoanalysis.* In *The Standard Edition.* Vol. 23. London: Hogarth Press, 1964.

———. 1933. "Femininity." Lecture XXXIII. *New Introductory Lectures in Psychoanalysis.* In *The Standard Edition.* Vol. 23. London: Hogarth Press, 1964.

———. 1940. "An Outline of Psychoanalysis." In *The Standard Edition.* Vol. 23. London: Hogarth Press, 1964.

Friedan, Betty. *The Feminine Mystique.* New York: Dell, 1963.

Friedman, Richard C. *Male Homosexuality: A Contemporary Psychoanalytic Perspective.* New Haven, Conn.: Yale University Press, 1988.

Friedman, Robert M. "The Psychoanalytic Model of Male Homosexuality: A Historical and Theoretical Critique." *Psychoanalytic Review,* 73 (Winter 1986):483–519.

Fromm, Erich. *Escape from Freedom.* New York: Farrar & Rinehart, 1941.

Garrett, Annette. "The Worker-Client Relationship." In Howard J. Parad, ed., *Ego Psychology and Dynamic Casework.* New York: Family Service Association of America, 1958a. Pp. 53–72.

———. "Modern Casework: The Contribution of Ego Psychology." In

Howard J. Parad, ed., *Ego Psychology and Dynamic Casework*. New York: Family Service Association of America, 1958b. Pp. 38–52.

George, Kenneth D., and Andrew E. Behrendt. "Therapy for Male Couples Experiencing Relationship Problems and Sexual Problems." In Eli Coleman, ed., *Integrated Identity: Gay Men and Lesbians*. New York: Harrington Park Press, 1988. Pp. 77–88.

Germain, Carel B. "Casework and Science: An Historical Encounter." In Robert W. Roberts and Robert H. Nee, eds., *Theories of Social Casework*. Chicago: University of Chicago Press, 1970. Pp. 3–32.

———. "An Ecological Perspective on Social Work Practice and Health Care." *Social Work in Health Care*, 3 (Fall 1977):67–76.

———. *Social Work Practice: People and Environments*. New York: Columbia University Press, 1979.

———. "The Physical Environment in Social Work Practice." In Anthony N. Maluccio, ed., *Promoting Competence in Clients: A New/Old Approach to Social Work Practice*. New York: Free Press, 1981. Pp. 103–24.

———. "Letter to the Editor." *Social Casework: The Journal of Contemporary Social Work*, 64 (January 1983):61–62.

———, and Alex Gitterman. *The Life Model of Social Work Practice*. New York: Columbia University Press, 1980.

Ghali, Sonja Badillo. "Understanding Puerto Rican Traditions." *Social Work*, 27 (January 1982):99–103.

Gilligan, Carol. *In a Different Voice: Psychological Theory and Women's Development*. Cambridge, Mass.: Harvard University Press, 1982.

Gladwin, Thomas. "Social Competence and Clinical Practice." *Psychiatry*, 30 (February 1967):30–38.

Golan, Naomi. *Treatment in Crisis Situations*. New York: Free Press, 1978.

Goldstein, Eda G. "Social Casework and the Dying Person," *Social Casework*, 54 (December 1973). Reprinted in Francis J. Turner, *Differential Diagnosis and Treatment in Social Work*. 2d Ed. New York: Free Press, 1976. Pp. 156–66.

———. "Mothers of Psychiatric Patients Revisited." In Carel B. Germain, ed., *Social Work Practice: People and Environments*. New York: Columbia University Press, 1979. Pp. 150–73.

———. "The Knowledge Base of Clinical Social Work." *Social Work*, 25 (May 1980):173–78.

———. "Promoting Competence in Families of Psychiatric Patients." In Anthony N. Maluccio, ed., *Promoting Competence in Clients: A New/Old Approach to Social Work Practice*. New York: Free Press, 1981. Pp. 317–42.

———. "Issues in Developing Systematic Research and Theory." In Diana Waldfogel and Aaron Rosenblatt, eds., *Handbook of Clinical Social Work*. San Francisco: Jossey-Bass, 1983a. Pp. 5–25.

———. "Clinical and Ecological Approaches to the Borderline Client." *Social Casework: The Journal of Contemporary Social Work,* 64 (June 1983b):353–62.

———. "Mental Health and Illness." *Encyclopedia of Social Work.* 18th Ed. Vol. 2. Silver Spring, Md.: National Association of Social Workers, 1986. Pp. 102–11.

———. *Borderline Disorders: Clinical Models and Techniques.* New York: Guilford Press, 1990.

———. "Borderline Personality Disorder." In Francis J. Turner, ed., *Mental Health and the Elderly: A Social Work Perspective.* New York: Free Press, 1992a. Pp. 220–48.

———. Narcissistic Personality Disorder." In Francis J. Turner, ed., *Mental Health and the Elderly: A Social Work Perspective.* New York: Free Press, 1992b. Pp. 249–70.

——— "The Borderline Substance Abuser." In Shulamith Lala Ashenberg Straussner, ed., *Clinical Work with Substance-Abusing Clients.* New York: Guilford Press, 1993. Pp. 270–90.

Gonsiorek, John C., ed. *Homosexuality and Psychotherapy: A Practitioner's Handbook of Affirmative Models.* New York: Haworth Press, 1982a.

Gonsiorek, John C. "The Use of Diagnostic Concepts in Working with Gay and Lesbian Populations." In John C. Gonsiorek, ed., *Homosexuality and Psychotherapy: A Practitioner's Handbook of Affirmative Models.* New York: Haworth Press, 1982b. Pp. 9–20.

Goodman, James A. *Dynamics of Racism in Social Work Practice.* Washington, D.C.: National Association of Social Workers, 1973.

Gordon, William E. "Basic Constructs for an Integrative and Generative Conception of Social Work." In Gordon Hearn, ed., *The General Systems Approach: Contributions Toward an Holistic Conception of Social Work Practice.* New York: Council on Social Work Education, 1969. Pp. 5–11.

———, and Margaret Schutz. "A Natural Basis for Social Work Specialization." *Social Work,* 22 (September 1977):422–27.

Gould, Roger L. *Transformations: Growth and Change in Adult Life.* New York: Simon & Schuster, 1978.

Greenberg, Jay R., and Stephen A. Mitchell. *Object Relations in Psychoanalytic Theory.* Cambridge, Mass.: Harvard University Press, 1983.

Greenson, Ralph. *The Technique and Practice of Psychoanalysis.* Vol. 1. New York: International Universities Press, 1967.

Greenspan, Miriam. *A New Approach to Women in Therapy.* New York: McGraw-Hill, 1983.

Grinker, Roy R., and John D. Spiegel. *Men Under Stress.* Philadelphia: Blakiston, 1945.

Grinker, Roy R., and Beatrice Werble, eds. *The Borderline Patient.* New York: Jason Aronson, 1977.

Grinker Roy R.; Beatrice Werble; and Robert Drye. *The Borderline Syndrome.* New York: Basic Books, 1968.

Grinnell, Richard M.; Nancy S. Kyte; and Gerald J. Bostwick. "Environmental Modification." In Anthony N. Maluccio, ed., *Promoting Competence in Clients: A New/Old Approach to Social Work Practice.* New York: Free Press, 1981. Pp. 152–84.

Gunderson, John; John Kerr; and Diane Woods Englund. "The Families of Borderlines: A Comparative Study." *Archives of General Psychiatry,* 37 (January 1980):27–33.

Gunderson, John, and Margaret T. Singer. "Defining Borderline Patients: An Overview." *American Journal of Psychiatry,* 132 (January 1975):1–10.

Guntrip, Harry. *Schizoid Phenomena, Object-Relations, and Self.* New York: International Universities Press, 1968.

———. *Psychoanalytic Theory, Therapy and the Self.* New York: Basic Books, 1971.

Gutierrez, Lorraine M. "Working with Women of Color: An Empowerment Perspective." *Social Work,* 35 (March 1990):149–54.

Hamilton, Gordon. *Theory and Practice of Social Casework.* New York: Columbia University Press, 1940.

———. *Theory and Practice of Social Casework.* 2d ed. New York: Columbia University Press, 1951.

———. "A Theory of Personality: Freud's Contribution to Social Work." In Howard J. Parad, ed., *Ego Psychology and Dynamic Casework.* New York: Family Service Association of America, 1958. Pp. 11–37.

Harris, Maxine, and Helen C. Bergman. "Case Management with the Chronically Mentally Ill: A Clinical Perspective." *American Journal of Orthopsychiatry,* 5 (October 1987):296–302.

Hartmann, Heinz. *Ego Psychology and the Problem of Adaptation.* New York: International Universities Press, 1939.

———, and Ernst Kris. "The Genetic Approach in Psychoanalysis." *Psychoanalytic Study of the Child,* 1 (1945):11–29.

———, and Rudolph M. Lowenstein. "Comments on the Formation of Psychic Structures." *Psychoanalytic Study of the Child,* 2 (1946):11–38.

Hendrick, I. "Instinct and the Ego During Infancy." *Psychoanalytic Quarterly,* 11 (1942):33–58.

———. "Work and the Pleasure Principle." *Psychoanalytic Quarterly,* 12 (1943):311–29.

Herman, Judith Lewis. *Trauma and Recovery.* New York: Basic Books, 1992.

———, and Bessel Van der Kolk. "Traumatic Antecedents of Borderline Personality Disorder." In Bessel A. Van der Kolk, ed., *Psychological*

Trauma. Washington, D.C.: American Psychiatric Press, 1987. Pp. 111–26.

Hetrick, Emery S., and Damien A. Martin. "Developmental Issues and Their Resolution for Gay and Lesbian Adolescents." In Eli Coleman, ed., *Integrated Identity: Gay Men and Lesbians.* New York: Harrington Park Press, 1988. Pp. 25–43.

———. "Ego-Dystonic Homosexuality: A Developmental View." In Emery S. Hetrick and Terry S. Stein, eds., *Innovations in Psychotherapy with Homosexuals.* Washington, D.C.: American Psychiatric Press, 1984. Pp. 2–21.

Hill, Reuben. "Generic Features of Families Under Stress." *Social Casework,* 39 (February-March 1958):139–50.

Hirayama, Hisashi, and Muammer Cetingok. "Empowerment: A Social Work Approach for Asian Immigrants." *Social Casework: The Journal of Contemporary Social Work,* 69 (January 1988):41–47.

Hoch, Paul, and Philip Polatin. "Pseudoneurotic Forms of Schizophrenia." *Psychoanalytic Quarterly,* 23 (April 1949):248–76.

Hollis, Florence. "Techniques of Casework." *Journal of Social Casework,* 30 (June 1949):235–44.

———. "Contemporary Issues for Caseworkers." In Howard J. Parad and Henry Miller, eds., *Ego-Oriented Casework.* New York: Family Service Association of America, 1963. Pp. 7–26.

———. *Casework: A Psychosocial Therapy.* New York: Random House, 1964.

———. *Casework: A Psychosocial Therapy.* 2d Ed. New York, Random House, 1972.

Horner, Althea J. *Object Relations and the Developing Ego in Therapy.* New York: Jason Aronson, 1979.

Horney, Karen. *The Neurotic Personality of Our Time.* New York: W. W. Norton, 1937.

———. *New Ways in Psychoanalysis.* New York: W. W. Norton, 1939.

———. *Our Inner Conflicts.* New York: W. W. Norton, 1945.

Horowitz, Leonard. "Group Psychotherapy of the Borderline Patient." In Peter Hartacollis, ed., *Borderline Personality Disorders.* New York: International Universities Press, 1977. Pp. 399–422.

Howell, Elizabeth. "Women: From Freud to the Present." In Elizabeth Howell and Marjorie Bayes, eds., *Women and Mental Health.* New York: Basic Books, 1981. Pp. 3–25.

———, and Marjorie Bayes, eds. *Women and Mental Health.* New York: Basic Books, 1981.

Ichikawa, Alice. "Observations of College Students in Acute Distress." In Howard J. Parad, ed., *Crisis Intervention: Selected Readings.* New York: Family Service Association of America, 1965. Pp. 167–73.

Inkeles, Alex. "Social Structure and the Socialization of Competence." *Harvard Educational Review,* 36 (February 1966):30–43.

Iodice, Jody D., and John S. Wodarski. "Aftercare Treatment for Schizo-phrenics Living at Home." *Social Work,* 32 (March-April 1987): 122–28.

Isay, Richard A. *Being Homosexual: Gay Men and their Development.* New York: Farrar, Strauss, and Giroux, 1989.

Jackel, Merl M. "Clients with Character Disorders." *Social Casework,* 44 (June 1963):315–22. Reprinted in Francis J. Turner, ed., *Differential Diagnosis and Treatment in Social Work.* 2d Ed. New York: Free Press, 1976. Pp. 196–206.

Jacklin, Carol Nagy. "Female and Male: Issues of Gender." *American Psychologist,* 44 (February 1989):231–36.

Jacobson, Edith. *The Self and the Object World.* New York: International Universities Press, 1964.

———. *Depression.* New York: International Universities Press, 1971.

Janis, Irving. *Psychological Stress.* New York: John Wiley & Sons, 1958.

Johnson, Geneva B. "American Families: Changes and Challenges." *Families in Society,* 72 (October 1991):502–07.

Jones, Darielle L. "African-American Clients: Clinical Practice Issues." *Social Work,* 24 (March 1979):112–18.

Jordan, Janet V. "Relational Development Through Empathy; Thera-peutic Applications." The Stone Center for Developmental Services and Studies, *Works in Progress.* 40. Wellesley, Mass.: 1990. Pp. 11–4.

Kammerman, Sheila; Ralph Dolgoff; George Getzel; and Judith Nelsen. "Knowledge for Practice: Social Science in Social Work." In Alfred J. Kahn, ed., *Shaping the New Social Work.* New York: Columbia Uni-versity Press, 1973. Pp. 97–148.

Kaplan, Alexandra, and Janet L. Surrey. "The Relational Self in Women: Developmental Theory and Public Policy." In Lenore Walker, ed., *Women and Mental Health Policy.* Beverly Hills, Calif.: Sage Publica-tions, 1984. Pp. 79–94.

Kaplan, David. "A Concept of Acute Situational Disorders." *Social Work,* 7 (April 1962):15–23.

Kaufman, Irving. "Therapeutic Considerations of the Borderline Per-sonality Structure." In Howard J. Parad, ed., *Ego Psychology and Dy-namic Casework.* New York: Family Service Association of America, 1958. Pp. 99–111.

Kernberg, Otto. *Borderline Conditions and Pathological Narcissism.* New York: Jason Aronson, 1975.

———. *Object-Relations Theory and Clinical Psychoanalysis.* New York: Ja-son Aronson, 1976.

———. "Psychoanalytic Psychotherapy with Borderline Adolescents."

In Sherman Feinstein and Peter L. Giovacchini, eds., *Adolescent Psychiatry.* Vol. VII. Chicago: University of Chicago Press, 1979. Pp. 294–321.

——. *Severe Personality Disorders.* New Haven, Conn.: Yale University Press, 1984.

Kilgore, Laura C. "Effect of Early Childhood Sexual Abuse on Self and Ego Development." *Social Casework: The Journal of Contemporary Social Work,* 69 (April 1988):224–30.

Kinsey, Alfred. *Sexual Behavior in the Human Male.* London and Philadelphia: Saunders, 1948.

Klein, George. "The Ego in Psychoanalysis: A Concept in Search of Identity." *Psychoanalytic Review* 56 (1970):511–25.

Klein, Melanie. *Contributions to Psychoanalysis, 1921–1945.* London: Hogarth Press, 1948.

Knight, Robert A. "Borderline States." *The Bulletin of the Menninger Clinic,* 17 (1953):1–12.

Kohlberg, Lawrence. "A Cognitive-Developmental Analysis of Children's Sex-Role Concepts and Attitudes." In E. E. Macoby, ed., *The Development of Sex-Differences.* Stanford, Calif.: Stanford University Press. Pp. 83–173.

Kohut, Heinz. *The Analysis of the Self.* New York: International Universities Press, 1971.

——. *The Restoration of the Self.* New York: International Universities Press, 1977.

——. *How Does Analysis Cure?* Chicago: University of Chicago Press, 1984.

Kris, Ernst. "On Preconscious Mental Processes: Regression in the Service of the Ego." In *Psychoanalytic Explorations in Art.* New York: International Universities Press, 1952. Pp. 303–26.

Kroeber, Theodore C. "The Coping Functions of Ego Mechanisms." In Robert F. White, ed., *The Study of Lives.* New York: Atherton Press, 1963. Pp. 179–98.

Kroll, Jerome. *The Challenge of the Borderline Patient.* New York: Norton, 1988.

——. *PTSD/Borderlines in Therapy.* New York: W. W. Norton, 1993.

Kutchins, Herb, and Stuart A. Kirk. "The Business of Diagnosis: DSM-III and Clinical Social Work. *Social Work,* 33 (May-June 1988):215–20.

Lang, Judith. "Beyond Polarization: The Holistic Approach to Family Practice." *Social Casework: The Journal of Contemporary Social Work,* 63 (September 1982):394–401.

Laughlin, H. P. *The Ego and Its Defenses.* 2d Ed. New York: Jason Aronson, 1979.

Lax, Ruth F. Sheldon Bach; and J. Alexis Burland. *Rapprochement.* New York: Jason Aronson, 1980.

Lazare, Aaron. "Hidden Conceptual Models in Clinical Psychiatry." *The New England Journal of Medicine*, 288 (February 1973):345–51.

Lazarus, Richard S. *Psychological Stress and the Coping Process*. New York: McGraw-Hill, 1966.

Lee, Judith A. B. "Promoting Competence in Children and Youth." In Anthony N. Maluccio, ed. *Promoting Competence in Clients: A New/Old Approach to Social Work Practice*. New York: Free Press, 1981. Pp. 236–63.

———, and Susan J. Rosenthal. "Working with Victims of Violent Assault." *Social Casework: The Journal of Contemporary Social Work*, 64 (December 1983):593–601.

Le Masters, Edgar. "Parenthood as Crisis." *Marriage and Family Living*, 19 (April 1957). Reprinted in Howard J. Parad, ed., *Crisis Intervention: Selected Readings*. New York: Family Service Association of America, 1965. Pp. 111–17.

Lerner, Harriet E. "The Hysterical Personality: A 'Woman's Disease'." In Elizabeth Howell and Marjorie Bayes, eds., *Women and Mental Health*. New York: Basic Books, 1981. Pp. 196–206.

Levinson, Daniel J. *The Seasons of a Man's Life*. New York: Alfred A. Knopf, 1978.

Levinson, Valerie R., and Shulamith L. Ashenberg Straussner. "Social Workers as 'Enablers' in the Treatment of Alcoholics." *Social Casework*, 59 (January 1978):14–20.

Levy, Michael S. "The Disease Controversy and Psychotherapy with Alcoholics." *Journal of Psychoactive Drugs*, 24 (July-September 1992):251–56.

Levy, Rona L. "Overview of Single-Case Experiments." In Aaron Rosenblatt and Diana Waldfogel, eds., *Handbook of Clinical Social Work*. San Francisco: Jossey-Bass, 1983. Pp. 583–602.

Lewis, Jerry M. "Early Treatment Planning for Hospitalized Severe Borderline Patients." *The Psychiatric Hospital*, 13 (Fall 1982):130–36.

Lewis, Lou Ann. "The Coming-Out Process for Lesbians: Integrating a Stable Identity." *Social Work*, 29 (September-October 1984):464–69.

Lidz, Theodore. *The Person*. New York: Basic Books, 1968.

Lifschutz, Joseph E. "A Brief Review of Psychoanalytic Ego Psychology." *Social Casework*, 45 (January 1964).

Liles, Ray E., and Ann O'Brien. "Crisis Intervention and Intrafamilial Sexual Abuse." In Howard J. Parad and Libbie G. Parad, eds., *Crisis Intervention Book 2: The Practitioner's Sourcebook for Brief Therapy*. Milwaukee, Wis.: Family Service America, 1900. Pp. 119–38.

Lindemann, Erich. "Symptomatology and Management of Acute Grief." *American Journal of Psychiatry*, 10 (September 1944).

Lopez, Diego, and George S. Getzel. "Helping Gay AIDS Patients in

Crisis." *Social Casework: The Journal of Contemporary Social Work,* 65 (September 1984):387–94.

Lubove, Roy. *The Professional Altruist.* New York: Atheneum, 1971.

Lutz, Werner. "Emerging Models of Social Casework Practice." University of Connecticut. Unpublished.

Mackey, Richard A.; Mitchell B. Urek; and Susan Charkoudian. "The Relationship of Theory to Clinical Practice." *Clinical Social Work Journal,* 15 (Winter 1987):368–83.

Magura, Stephen; Cathy Casriel; Douglas S. Goldsmith; and Douglas S. Lipton. "Contracting with Clients in Methadone Treatment." *Social Casework: The Journal of Contemporary Social Work,* 68 (October 1987):485–93.

Mahler, Margaret S. "On Child Psychosis and Schizophrenia: Autistic and Symbiotic Infantile Psychosis." In *The Psychoanalytic Study of the Child.* New York: International Universities Press, 1951, 7:286–305.

———. *On Human Symbiosis and the Vicissitudes of Individuation.* New York: International Universities Press, 1968.

———. "A Study of the Separation-Individuation Process and Its Possible Application to Borderline Phenomena in the Psychoanalytic Situation." *Psychoanalytic Study of the Child.* 26 (1971):403–24.

———. "On the First Three Phases of the Separation-Individuation Process." *International Journal of Psychoanalysis,* 53 (1972):333–38.

———; Fred Pine; and Anni Bergman. *The Psychological Birth of the Human Infant.* New York: Basic Books, 1975.

Maier, Henry W. *Three Theories of Child Development.* New York: Harper & Row, 1969.

Mailick, Mildred. "The Situational Perspective in Social Work." *Social Work,* 58 (July 1977):400–412.

Maluccio, Anthony N., ed. *Promoting Competence in Clients: A New/Old Approach to Social Work Practice.* New York: Free Press, 1981.

———, and Wilma D. Marlow. "The Case for the Contract." *Social Work,* 19 (January 1974):28–36.

Malyon, Alan K. "Psychotherapeutic Implications of Internalized Homophobia in Gay Men." In John C. Gonsiorek, ed., *Homosexuality and Psychotherapy: A Practitioner's Handbook of Affirmative Models.* New York: Haworth Press, 1982. Pp. 59–70.

Marcus, Esther. "Ego Breakdown in Schizophrenia: Some Implications for Casework Treatment." *American Journal of Orthopsychiatry,* 31 (April 1961):368–87. Reprinted in Francis J. Turner, ed., *Differential Diagnosis and Treatment in Social Work.* 2d Ed. New York: Free Press, 1976. Pp. 322–40.

Markowitz, Roberta. "Dynamics and Treatment of Children of Drug and Alcohol Abusers." In Shulamith Lala Ashenburg Straussner, ed., *Clinical Work with Substance-Abusing Clients*. New York: Guilford Press, 1993. Pp. 214–32.

Martin, April. "Some Issues in the Treatment of Gay and Lesbian Patients." *Psychotherapy: Theory, Research, and Practice*, 19 (Fall 1982): 341–8.

Maslow, Abraham H. *Motivation and Personality*. New York: Harper & Row; 1954.

Masterson, James. *Treatment of the Borderline Adolescent*. New York: Wiley-Interscience, 1972.

———. *The Psychotherapy of the Borderline Adult*. New York: Brunner-Mazel, 1976.

Masterson, James F., and Donald Rinsley. "The Borderline Syndrome: the Role of the Mother in the Genesis and Psychic Structure of the Borderline Personality." *International Journal of Psychoanalysis*, 56:163–77.

Matorin, Susan, and Neal De Chillo. "Psychopharmacology: Guidelines for Social Workers." *Social Casework: The Journal of Contemporary Social Work*, 65 (December 1984):579–89.

Mayer, John, and Noel Timms. *The Client Speaks: Working Class Impressions of Casework*. New York: Atherton Press, 1970.

McFarlane, Alexander C. "Post Traumatic Stress Syndrome Revisited." In Howard J. Parad and Libbie G. Parad, eds., *Crisis Intervention Book 2: The Practitioner's Sourcebook for Brief Therapy*. Milwaukee, Wis.: Family Service America, 1990. Pp. 69–92.

McIntyre, Jeffrey R. "Family Treatment of Substance Abusers." In Shulamith Lala Ashenburg Straussner, ed., *Clinical Work with Substance-Abusing Clients*. New York: Guilford Press, 1993. Pp. 171–95.

Mechanic, David. "Social Structure and Personal Adaptation: Some Neglected Dimensions." In George V. Coelho, David A. Hamburg, and John E. Adams, eds., *Coping and Adaptation*. New York: Basic Books, 1974. Pp. 32–46.

———. *Mental Health and Social Policy*. Englewood Cliffs, N.J.: Prentice-Hall, 1980.

Meissner, W. W.; John E. Mack; and Elvin S. Semrad. "Classical Psychoanalysis." In Alfred M. Freedman, Harold I. Kaplan, and Benjamin K. Sadock, eds., *Comprehensive Textbook of Psychiatry*. 2d Ed. Vol. 1. Baltimore: Williams & Wilkins, 1975. Pp. 482–565.

Meyer, Carol H. *Social Work Practice: A Response to the Urban Crisis*. New York: Free Press, 1970.

———. *Social Work Practice: The Changing Landscape*. New York: Free Press, 1976.

———. "Issues in Clinical Social Work: In Search of a Consensus." In Phyllis Caroff, ed., *Treatment Formulations and Clinical Social Work*.

Silver Spring, Md.: National Association of Social Workers, 1982. Pp. 19–26.

Middleman, Ruth R. "The Pursuit of Competence Through Involvement in Structured Groups." In Anthony N. Maluccio, ed., *Promoting Competence in Clients: A New/Old Approach to Social Work Practice.* New York: Free Press, 1981. Pp. 185–212.

Miller, Alice. *Thou Shalt Not Be Aware: Society's Betrayal of the Child.* New York: Farrar, Straus, Giroux, 1984.

Miller, Jean Baker, ed. *Psychoanalysis and Women.* New York: Penguin Books, 1973.

Miller, Jean Baker. *Toward a New Psychology of Women.* Boston: Beacon Paperback, 1977.

Millman, Robert B. "Considerations on the Psychotherapy of the Substance Abuser. *Journal of Substance Abuse Treatment,* 3 (1986):103–9.

Mishne, Judith Marks. "The Missing System in Social Work's Application of Systems Theory." *Social Casework: The Journal of Contemporary Social Work,* 63 (November 1982):547–3.

———. *The Evolution and Application of Clinical Theory: Perspectives from Four Psychologies.* New York: Free Press, 1993.

Montijo, Jorge A. "Therapeutic Relationships with the Poor: A Puerto Rican Perspective." *Psychotherapy,* 22 (Summer 1985):436–40.

Mulinski, Paul. "Dual Diagnosis in Alcoholic Clients: Clinical Implications." *Social Casework: The Journal of Contemporary Social Work,* 70 (June 1989):333–9.

Mullen, Edward J.; James R. Dumpson; and Associates. *Evaluation of Social Intervention.* San Francisco: Jossey-Bass, 1972.

Munro, Ruth. *Schools of Psychoanalytic Thought.* New York: Holt, Rinehart, & Winston, 1955.

Murphy, Lois Barclay. "The Problem of Defense and the Concept of Coping." In E. James Anthony and Cyrille Koupernik, eds., *The Child and His Family.* New York: John Wiley & Sons, 1970. Pp. 66–86.

———, and Alice E. Moriarity. *Vulnerability, Coping, and Growth from Infancy to Adolescence.* New Haven: Yale University Press, 1976.

Murray, Henry A., and Clyde Kluckhohn. "Outline of a Conception of Personality." In C. Kluckhohn, H. A. Murray, and D. Schneider, eds., *Personality in Nature, Society, and Culture.* 2d Ed. New York: Knopf, 1953. Pp. 3–52.

Nelsen, Judith. "Treatment Issues In Schizophrenia." *Social Casework,* 56 (March 1975):143–52.

Neugarten, Bernice L. "Adult Personality: Toward a Psychology of the Life Cycle." In W. Edgar Vinacke, ed., *Readings in General Psychology.* New York: American Book, 1968. Pp. 332–43.

————, and Associates, eds. *Personality in Middle and Late Life*. New York: Atherton Press, 1964.

Norman, Elaine, and Arlene Mancuso, eds. *Women's Issues and Social Work Practice*. Itasca, Ill.: Peacock, 1980.

Nunberg, H. "The Synthetic Function of the Ego." *The International Journal of Psychoanalysis*, 7 (April 1931):123–40.

O'Neill, Margaret M. "Countertransference and Attitudes in the Context of Clinical Work with Dually Diagnosed Patients." In Joel Solomon, Sheldon Zimberg, and Edward Shollar, eds., *Dual Diagnosis: Evaluation, Treatment, Training, and Program Development*. New York: Plenum Press, 1993. Pp. 127–46.

Orbach, Susie. *Fat is a Feminist Issue*. New York: Berkley, 1978.

Orlin, Lois, and Jennifer Davis. "Assessment and Intervention with Drug and Alcohol Abusers in Psychiatric Settings." In Shulamith Lala Ashenberg Straussner, ed., *Clinical Work with Substance-Abusing Clients*. New York: Guilford Press, 1993. Pp. 50–68.

Panter, Ethel J. "Ego-Building Procedures that Foster Social Functioning." *Social Casework*, 47 (March 1966):139–45.

Pape, Patricia A. "Issues in Assessment and Intervention with Alcohol and Drug-Abusing Women." In Shulamith Lala Ashenberg Straussner, ed., *Clinical Work with Substance-Abusing Clients*. New York: Guilford Press, 1993. Pp. 251–69.

Parad, Howard J. "Brief Ego-oriented Casework with Families in Crisis." In Howard J. Parad and Roger R. Miller, eds., *Ego-oriented Casework*. New York: Family Service Association of America, 1963. Pp. 145–64.

————, ed. *Ego Psychology and Dynamic Casework*. New York: Family Service Association of America, 1958.

————, ed. *Crisis Intervention: Selected Readings*. New York: Family Service Association of America, 1965.

————, and Roger Miller, ed. *Ego-Oriented Casework*. New York: Family Service Association of America, 1963.

————, and Libbie G. Parad. "Crisis Intervention: An Introductory Overview." In Howard J. Parad and Libbie G. Parad, eds., *Crisis Intervention Book 2: The Practitioner's Sourcebook for Brief Therapy*. Milwaukee, Wis.: Family Service America, 1990. Pp. 3–68.

Parloff, Morris B. "Can Psychotherapy Research Guide the Policy Maker? A Little Knowledge May Be a Dangerous Thing." *American Psychologist*, 34 (April 1979):296–306.

Patten, Sylvia B.; Yvonne K. Gatz; Berlin Jones; and Deborah L. Thomas. "Post-traumatic Stress Disorder and the Treatment of Sexual Abuse." *Social Work*, 34 (May 1989):197–203.

Peck, Robert. "Psychological Developments in the Second Half of Life."

In William C. Sze, ed., *Human Life Cycle*. New York: Jason Aronson, 1975. Pp. 609–26.

Perlman, Helen Harris. *Social Casework: A Problem-Solving Process*. Chicago: University of Chicago Press, 1957.

———. Perspectives on Social Casework. Philadelphia: Temple University Press, 1971.

———. "Once More with Feeling." In Edward J. Mullen; James R. Dumpson; and Associates, eds., *Evaluation of Social Intervention*. San Francisco: Jossey-Bass, 1972. Pp. 191–209.

———. *Relationship*. Chicago: University of Chicago Press, 1979.

Perry, Jonathan C., and Gerald L. Klerman. "The Borderline Patient: A Comparison Analysis of Four Sets of Diagnostic Criteria." *Archives of General Psychiatry*, 35 (1978):141–50.

Piaget, Jean. *The Child's Conception of the World*. London: Routledge & Kegan Paul, 1951.

———. *The Origin of Intelligence in Children*. New York: International Universities Press, 1952.

———. *The Moral Judgment of the Child*. New York: Macmillan, 1955.

Pincus, Allen, and Anne Minahan. *Social Work Practice: Model and Method*. Itasca, Ill.: F. E. Peacock, 1973.

Pinderhughes, Elaine B. "Empowerment for Our Clients and for Ourselves." *Social Casework: The Journal of Contemporary Social Work*, 64 (June 1983):331–8.

Prozan, Charlotte Krause. *Feminist Psychoanalytic Psychotherapy*. Northvale, N.J.: Jason Aronson, 1992.

Rank, Otto. *Truth and Reality*. New York: Alfred A. Knopf, 1929.

———. *Will Therapy*. New York: Alfred A. Knopf, 1945.

———. *The Trauma of Birth*. New York: Alfred A. Knopf, 1952.

Rapaport, David. "The Autonomy of the Ego." *Bulletin of the Menninger Foundation*, 15 (1951):113–23.

———. "The Theory of Ego Autonomy: A Generalization." *Bulletin of the Menninger Foundation*, 22 (1958):3–35.

———. "An Historical Survey of Psychoanalytic Ego Psychology." *Introduction to Psychological Issues*, 1 (1959):5–17.

———. "The Structure of Psychoanalytic Theory." *Psychological Issues*, 2 (1960):39–85.

Rapoport, Lydia. "The State of Crisis: Some Theoretical Considerations." *Social Service Review*, 36 (June 1962):211–7.

———. "Crisis Intervention as a Mode of Brief Treatment." In Robert W. Roberts and Robert H. Nee, eds., *Theories of Social Casework*. Chicago: University of Chicago Press, 1970. Pp. 265–312.

Rapoport, Rhona. "Normal Crisis, Family Structure, and Mental Health." In Howard J. Parad, ed., *Crisis Intervention: Selected Read-

ings. New York: Family Service Association of America, 1965. Pp. 75–87.

Reich, Wilhelm. *Character Analysis.* New York: Orgone Institute, 1949.

Reid, William J., and Laura Epstein. *Task-centered Casework.* New York: Columbia University Press, 1972.

Reid, William J. "Developing Intervention Methods Through Experimental Designs." In Aaron Rosenblatt and Diana Waldfogel, eds., *Handbook of Clinical Social Work.* San Francisco: Jossey-Bass, 1983. Pp. 650–72.

Reiter, Laura. "Sexual Orientation, Sexual Identity, and the Question of Choice." *Clinical Social Work Journal,* 17 (Summer 1989): 138–50.

Rhodes, Sonya L. "The Personality of the Worker: An Unexplored Dimension in Treatment." *Social Casework,* 60, No. 5 (May, 1979):259–69.

Richmond, Mary L. *Social Diagnosis.* New York: Russell Sage Foundation, 1917.

Ripple, Lillian; Ernestina Alexander; and Bernice Polemis. *Motivation, Capacity and Opportunity.* Social Science Monographs. Chicago: University of Chicago Press, 1964.

Roberts, Robert W., and Robert H. Nee, eds. *Theories of Social Casework.* Chicago: University of Chicago Press, 1970.

Robinson, Jeanne B. "Clinical Treatment of Black Families: Issues and Strategies." *Social Work,* 34 (July 1989):323–9.

Robinson, Virginia P. *A Changing Psychology in Social Casework.* Chapel Hill: University of North Carolina Press, 1930.

———. *The Dynamics of Supervision Under Functional Controls.* Philadelphia: University of Pennsylvania Press, 1950.

Rockland, Lawrence. *Supportive Therapy.* New York: Basic Books, 1989.

Rogers, Carl R. *Client-centered Therapy.* Boston: Houghton-Mifflin, 1951.

———. "The Necessary and Sufficient Conditions of Therapeutic Personality Changes." *Journal of Consulting Psychology,* 21 (1957): 95–103.

Roskin, Michael. "Integration of Primary Prevention in Social Work." *Social Work,* 25 (May 1980):192–7.

Rossi, Alice. "Life Span Theories and Women's Lives." *Journal of Women in Culture and Society,* 6 (Autumn 1980).

Roth, Sallyann. "Psychotherapy with Lesbian Couples: Individual Issues, Female Socialization, and the Social Context." *Journal of Marital and Family Therapy,* 11 (March 1985):273–86.

Rowland, Jr., S. James. "Ego-Directive Psychotherapy in Limited Treatment." *Social Casework,* 56 (November 1975):343–53.

Rubin, Allen. "Practice Effectiveness: More Grounds for Optimism." *Social Work,* 30 (November-December 1985):469–76.

Ryan, Angela Shen. "Cultural Factors in Casework with Chinese-Americans." *Social Casework: The Journal of Contemporary Social Work,* 66 (June 1985):333–40.

Schafer, Roy. "Problems in Freud's Psychology of Women." In Harold P. Blum, ed., *Female Psychology.* New York: International Universities Press, 1974. Pp. 331–60.

Scharff, David E., and Jill Savege Scharff. *Object Relations Family Therapy.* New York: Jason Aronson, 1987.

———. *Object Relations Couple Therapy.* New York: Jason Aronson, 1991.

Schlossberg, Shirley B., and Richard M. Kagan. "Practice Strategies for Engaging Chronic Multi-problem Families." *Social Casework: The Journal of Contemporary Social Work,* 69 (January 1988):3–9.

Schmideberg, Melitta. "The Treatment of Psychopaths and Borderline Patients." *American Journal of Psychotherapy,* 1 (1947):45–55.

Schwartz, Mary C. "Helping the Worker With Countertransference." *Social Work,* 23, No. 3 (May 1978):204–11.

Schwartz, Robert D. "When the Therapist is Gay: Personal and Clinical Reflections." *Journal of Gay and Lesbian Psychotherapy,* 1 (1) (1989):41–53.

Segal, Hanna. *Introduction to the Work of Melanie Klein.* Second Edition. New York: Basic Books, 1974.

Seinfeld, Jeffrey. *The Bad Object.* New York: Jason Aronson, 1990.

———. *The Empty Core.* New York: Jason Aronson, 1991.

———. *Interpreting and Holding.* New York: Jason Aronson, 1993.

Selye, Hans. *The Stress of Life.* New York: McGraw-Hill, 1956.

Shapiro, Edward R. "The Psychodynamics and Developmental Psychology of the Borderline Patient: A Review of the Literature." *American Journal of Psychiatry,* 135 (November 1978):1305–14.

———; Roger L. Shapiro; John Zinner; and David Berkowitz. "The Borderline Ego and the Working Alliance: Implications for Family and Individual Treatment." *International Journal of Psychoanalysis,* 58 (1977):77–87.

———; John Zinner; Roger L. Shapiro; and David Berkowitz. "The Influence of Family Experience on Borderline Personality Development." *International Review of Psychoanalysis,* 2 (1975):399–411.

Shevrin, Howard. "The Diagnostic Process in Psychiatric Evaluation." *Bulletin of the Menninger Clinic,* 37 (September 1972):451–94.

Simcox-Reiner, Beatrice. "A Feeling of Irrelevance: The Effects of a Non-Supportive Society." *Social Casework: The Journal of Contemporary Social Work,* 60 (January 1979):3–10.

Simon, Barbara L. "The Feminization of Poverty: A Call for Primary Prevention." *Journal of Primary Prevention,* 9 (1 and 2, 1988):6–17.

Simon, Bernice K. "Diversity and Unity in the Social Work Profession." *Social Work,* 22 (September 1977):394–401.

Simon, Cassandra E.; John S. McNeil; Cynthia Franklin; and Abby Cooperman. "The Family and Schizophrenia: Toward a Psychoeducational Approach." *Families in Society*, 72 (June 1991):323–34.

Siporin, Max. "Social Treatment: A New-Old Method." *Social Casework*, 51 (July 1970):13–25.

———. "Situational Assessment and Intervention." *Social Casework*, 53 (February 1972):91–109.

Smalley, Ruth E. "The Functional Approach to Casework Practice." In Robert W. Roberts and Robert H. Nee, eds., *Theories of Social Casework*. Chicago: University of Chicago Press, 1970. Pp. 77–128.

Smith, Brewster. "Competence and Socialization." In John A. Clausen, ed., *Socialization and Society*. Boston: Little, Brown, 1968. Pp. 270–320.

Solomon, Barbara Bryant. *Black Empowerment: Social Work in Depressed Communities*. New York: Columbia University Press, 1976.

———. "Value Issues in Working with Minority Clients." In Aaron Rosenblatt and Diana Waldfogel, eds., *Handbook of Clinical Social Work*. San Francisco: Jossey-Bass, 1983. Pp. 866–87.

Spaulding, Elaine C. "The Inner World of Objects and Lesbian Development." *Journal of Analytic Social Work*, 1(2) (1993):5–31.

Spiegel, Betsy Robin. "12-Step Programs as a Treatment Modality." In Shulamith Lala Ashenberg Straussner, ed., *Clinical Work with Substance-Abusing Clients*. New York: Guilford Press, 1993. Pp. 153–70.

Spitz, René. "Hospitalization: An Inquiry into the Genesis of Psychiatric Conditions in Early Childhood." *The Psychoanalytic Study of the Child*, 1 (1945):53–74.

———. "Hospitalism: A Follow-Up Report." *The Psychoanalytic Study of the Child*, 2 (1946a):113–17.

———. "Anaclitic Depression: An Inquiry into the Genesis of Psychiatric Conditions in Childhood." *The Psychoanalytic Study of the Child*, 2 (1946b):313–42.

———. "The Smiling Response: A Contribution to the Ontogenesis of Social Relations," with the assistance of K. M. Wolf. *Genetic Psychology Monographs*, No. 34 (1946c):57–125.

———. *A Genetic Field Theory of Ego Formation: Its Implications for Pathology*. New York: International Universities Press, 1959.

———. *The First Year of Life: A Psychoanalytic Study of Normal and Deviant Development of Object Relations*. New York: International Universities Press, 1965.

Spitzer, R. L.; J. B. Williams; and A. E. Skodol. "DSM III: The Major Achievements and an Overview." *American Journal of Psychiatry*, 137 (1980):1050–54.

Stamm, Isabel. "Ego Psychology in the Emerging Theoretical Base of Social Work." In Alfred J. Kahn, ed., *Issues in American Social Work*.

New York and London: Columbia University Press, 1959. Pp. 80–109.

Star, Barbara; Carol G. Clark; Karen M. Goetz; and Linda O'Malia. "Psychosocial Aspects of Wife-Battering." In Elizabeth Howell and Marjorie Bayes, eds., *Women and Mental Health.* New York: Basic Books, 1981. Pp. 426–39.

Stein, Herman. "The Concept of the Social Environment in Social Work Practice." *Smith College Studies in Social Work,* 30, No. 3 (1960). Reprinted in Howard J. Parad and Roger R. Miller, eds., *Ego-oriented Casework.* New York: Family Service Association of America, 1962. Pp. 65–88.

Stern, Adolph. "Psychoanalytic Investigation of and Therapy in a Borderline Group of Neuroses." *Psychoanalytic Quarterly,* 7 (1938): 467–89.

Stern, Daniel. "Implications of Infant Research for Psychoanalytic Theory and Practice." *Psychiatric Update,* 2. Washington, D.C.: American Psychiatric Press, 1983.

———. *The Interpersonal World of the Infant: A View from Psychoanalysis and Developmental Psychology.* New York: Basic Books, 1985.

Stiffman, Arlene Rubin. "Physical and Sexual Abuse of Children: What, Who, and Where?" In Martin Bloom, ed., *Changing Lives: Studies in Human Development and Professional Helping.* Columbia, S.C.: University of South Carolina Press, 1992. Pp. 249–57.

Stoller, Robert. "Primary Femininity." In Harold Blum, ed., *Female Psychology: Contemporary Psychoanalytic Views.* New York: International Universities Press, 1977. Pp. 59–78.

Stone, Michael H. *The Borderline Syndromes.* New York: McGraw-Hill, 1980.

Straussner, Shulamith Lala Ashenberg. "Assessment and Treatment of Clients with Alcohol and Other Drug Abuse Problems: An Overview." In Shulamith Lala Ashenberg Straussner, ed., *Clinical Work with Substance-Abusing Clients.* New York: Guilford Press, 1993.Pp. 3–32.

Strean, Herbert S. "Casework with Ego Fragmented Parents." *Social Casework,* 49 (April 1968):222–27.

———. *Social Casework: Theories in Action.* Metuchen, N.J.: Scarecrow Press, 1971.

———. *Clinical Social Work.* New York: Free Press, 1978. Chapters 2–6.

———. "Clinical Social Work: An Evaluative Review." *Journal of Analytic Social Work,* 1(1) (1993):5–23.

Stuart, Richard. "Supportive Casework with Borderline Patients." *Social Work,* 9 (January 1964):38–44.

Sullivan, Harry Stack. *Interpersonal Theory of Psychiatry.* New York: W. W. Norton, 1953.

Symonds, Alexandra. "Phobias After Marriage: Women's Declaration of Dependence." In Elizabeth Howell and Marjorie Bayes, eds., *Women and Mental Health.* New York: Basic Books, 1981. Pp. 228–39.

Tabachnick, Norman. "Crisis and Adult Development." In Howard J. Parad and Libbie G. Parad, eds., *Crisis Intervention Book 2: The Practitioner's Sourcebook for Brief Therapy.* Milwaukee, Wis.: Family Service America, 1990. Pp. 193–208.

Taft, Jessie. "The Relation of Function to Process in Social Casework." *Journal of Social Work Process,* 1, No. 1(1937):1–18.

———. "A Conception of Growth Process Underlying Social Casework." *Social Casework,* 31 (October 1950).

Taylor, Edward H. "The Biological Basis of Schizophrenia." *Social Work,* 32 (March-April 1987):115–21.

Thomlison, Ray J. "Something Works: Evidence from Practice Effectiveness Studies." *Social Work,* 29 (January-February 1984):51–56.

Thompson, Clara. "Cultural Pressures in the Psychology of Women." In Jean Baker Miller, ed., *Psychoanalysis and Women.* New York: Brunner/Mazel, 1973. Pp. 49–64.

Toffler, Alvin. *Future shock.* New York: Random House, 1970.

Tolpin, Marian. "The Self and Its Selfobjects: A Different Baby." In Arnold Goldberg, ed., *Progress in Self Psychology,* Vol. 2. New York: Guilford Press, 1986. Pp. 115–28.

Towle, Charlotte. "Helping the Client to Use His Capacities and Resources." *Social Service Review,* 22 (December 1948).

———. *The Learner in Education for the Professions.* Chicago: University of Chicago Press, 1954.

Truax, C. B., and R. R. Carkhuff. *Toward Effective Counseling and Psychotherapy: Training and Practice.* Chicago: Aldine, 1977.

Tully, Carol. "Research on Older Lesbian Women: What is Known, What is Not Known, and How to Learn More." In N. J. Woodman, ed., *Gay and Lesbian Lifestyles: A Guide for Counseling and Education.* New York: Irvington Publishers, 1992. Pp. 235–64.

Turnbull, Joanne E. "Treatment Issues for Alcoholic Women." *Social Casework: The Journal of Contemporary Social Work,* 70 (June 1989):364–69.

Turner, Francis J., ed. *Social Work Treatment.* New York: Free Press, 1986.

———, ed. *Differential Diagnosis and Treatment in Social Work.* 2d Ed. New York: Free Press, 1976.

Turner, Susan F., and Constance Hoenk Shapiro. "Battered Women: Mourning the Death of a Relationship. *Social Work,* 31 (September-October 1986):372–77.

Tyhurst, James. "The Role of Transition States—Including Disasters in Mental Illness." *Symposium on Preventive and Social Psychiatry.* Washington, D.C.: Walter Reed Army Institute of Research, 1957. Pp. 149–67.

Vaillant, George E. *Adaptation to Life.* Boston: Little, Brown, 1977.

Valentich, Mary. "Feminism and Social Work Practice." In Francis J. Turner, ed., *Social Work Treatment.* 3d Ed. New York: Free Press, 1986. Pp. 564–89.

Van Den Bergh, Nan, and Lynn B. Cooper, "Feminist Social Work." In Ann Minahan, Ed.-in-Chief, *Encyclopedia of Social Work.* Vol. 1. 18th Ed. Silver Spring, Md.: National Association of Social Workers, 1987. Pp. 610–18.

Van der Kolk, Bessel A., ed. *Psychological Trauma.* Washington, D.C.: American Psychiatric Press, 1987.

Vaughn, Charles E., and Julien P. Leff. "The Measurement of Expressed Emotion in the Families of Psychiatric Patients." *British Journal of Social and Clinical Psychology,* 15 (June 1976):157–65.

Walsh, Froma. "Family Study 1976: 14 Borderline Cases." In Roy R. Grinker and Beatrice Werble, eds., *The Borderline Patient.* New York: Jason Aronson, 1977. Pp. 158–77.

Walsh, Joseph. "Engaging the Family of the Schizophrenic Client." *Social Casework: The Journal of Contemporary Social Work,* 70 (February 1989):106–13.

Walz, Thomas, and Victor Groze. "The Mission of Social Work Revisited: An Agenda for the 1990s." *Social Work,* 36 (November 1991):500–04.

Wasserman, Sydney L. "Ego Psychology." In Francis J. Turner, ed., *Social Work Treatment.* New York: Free Press, 1974. Pp. 42–83.

Weick, Ann; Charles Rapp; W. Patrick Sullivan; and Walter Kisthardt. "A Strengths Perspective for Social Work Practice." *Social Work,* 34 (July 1989): 350–54.

Weille, Katherine Lee H. "Reworking Developmental Theory: The Case of Lesbian Identity Formation." *Clinical Social Work Journal,* 21 (Summer 1993):151–60.

Weinberger, Jerome. "Basic Concepts in Diagnosis and Treatment of Borderline States." In Howard J. Parad, ed., *Ego Psychology and Dynamic Casework.* New York: Family Service Association of America, 1958. Pp. 111–16.

Weissman, Myrna M., and Gerald L. Klerman. "Sex Differences and the Epidemiology of Depression." In Elizabeth Howell and Marjorie Bayes, eds., *Women and Mental Health.* New York: Basic Books, 1981. Pp. 160–95.

Werner, Harold D. "Cognitive Theory." In Francis J. Turner, ed., *Social Work Treatment.* 3d Ed. New York: Free Press, 1986. Pp. 91–130.

Wheeler, Barbara R., and Elaine Walton. "Personality Disturbances of

Adult Incest Victims." *Social Casework: The Journal of Contemporary Social Work,* 68 (December 1987):597–602.

White, Robert F. "Motivation Reconsidered: The Concept of Competence." *Psychological Review,* 66 (1959):297–333.

———. "Ego and Reality in Psychoanalytic Theory." *Psychological Issues.* II (3). New York: International Universities Press, 1963.

———. *Lives in Progress* (New York: Holt, Rinehart, and Winston, 1966).

———. "Strategies of Adaptation: An Attempt at Systematic Description." In George Coelho, David A. Hamburg, and John E. Adams, eds., *Coping and Adaptation.* New York: Basic Books, 1974. Pp. 47–68.

Williams, Juanita H. *Psychology of Women.* New York: Norton, 1977.

Wilson, Melvin N. "Child Development in the Context of the Black Extended Family." *American Psychologist,* 44 (February 1989):380–85.

Winnicott, D. W. "The Depressive Position in Normal Emotional Development." *British Journal of Medical Psychology,* 28 (1955):89–100.

———. *Maturational Processes and the Facilitating Environment.* New York: International Universities Press, 1965.

Wolberg, Arlene Robbins. *Psychoanalytic Psychotherapy of the Borderline Patient.* New York: Grune & Stratton, 1982.

Wolberg, Lewis, ed. *Short-Term Psychotherapy.* New York: Grune & Stratton, 1965.

———. *Techniques of Psychotherapy.* 2 Vols. New York: Grune & Stratton, 1969.

Wolf, Ernest S. *Elements of Clinical Self Psychology.* New York: Guilford Press, 1988.

Wolman, Benjamin B., ed. *Handbook of Developmental Psychology.* Englewood Cliffs, N.J.: Prentice-Hall, 1982.

Wood, Katherine M. "The Contributions of Psychoanalysis and Ego Psychology to Social Casework." In Herbert Strean, ed., *Social Casework: Theories in Action.* Metuchen, N.J.: Scarecrow Press, 1971. Pp. 76–107.

Woodroofe, Kathleen. *From Charity to Social Work in England and the United States.* Toronto: University of Toronto Press, 1971.

Yarrow, L. J. "Separation from Parents in Early Childhood." In M. L. Hoffman and L. W. Hoffman, eds., *Review of Child Development Research.* Vol. 1. New York: Russell Sage Foundation, 1964. Pp. 89–136.

Yelaja, Shankar A. *Authority and Social Work: Concept and Use.* Toronto: University of Toronto Press, 1971.

Zelvin, Elizabeth. "Treating the Partners of Substance Abusers." In Shulamith Lala Ashenberg Straussner, ed., *Clinical Work with Substance-Abusing Clients.* New York: Guilford Press, 1993. Pp. 196–213.

Zilboorg, Gregory. "Ambulatory Schizophrenia." In Psychiatry, 4 (1941):149–55.

Zinner, John, and Edward R. Shapiro. "Splitting in Families of Borderline Adolescents." In John Mack, ed., *Borderline States in Psychiatry.*
New York: Grune & Stratton, 1974. Pp. 103–22.
Zuckerwise, Richard A. "The Chronically Mentally Ill: A Perspective
from the Firing Line." In Howard J. Parad and Libbie G. Parad, eds.,
*Crisis Intervention Book 2: The Practitioner's Sourcebook for Brief Ther-
apy.* Milwaukee, Wis.: Family Service America, 1990. Pp. 227–50.

AUTHOR INDEX

Abarbanel, G., 18, 20, 23, 242, 255n10
Abelin, E.L., 126–27
Abell, N., 45
Adams, J.E., 18, 112n10
Adler, A., 3, 13, 14
Adler, G., 13, 296, 302, 304–5, 308–9, 317
Ainsworth, M.D.S., 11, 115–16
Alexander, E., 37, 49n7
Alexander, F., 80, 228n4
Allport, G.W., 15
Ambrose, J.A., 116
Anderson, C., 273, 318
Anderson, S.C., 287n2
Arieti, S., 13
Austin, L.N., 34, 229n11

Bach, S., 139n10
Bandler, B., 34
Baptiste, D.A., Jr., 101, 253
Barnett, R.C., 107
Bartlett, H., 42
Bayes, M., 21, 255n8
Beck, A.T., 16
Beck, D.F., 199n15
Behrendt, A.E., 253
Bell, S., 11, 116
Bellak, L., 9, 13, 54, 71n1, 113
Belohlavek, N., 20, 282
Benedek, T., 18, 106, 111n5
Benjamin, J., 4, 20, 129
Berenson, B.G., 229n9
Beres, D., 9
Beresford, T., 260, 287n1
Berger, R.M., 22, 101
Bergman, A., 12, 60, 69, 116, 117, 120, 122, 124, 125–26, 138n5, 139n9
Bergman, H.C., 272
Berkowitz, D., 305, 309, 310
Berlin, S., 20

Biringen, Z., 11
Birns, B., 17
Bissell, L., 258, 264
Blake-White, J., 23, 102, 283
Blanck, G., 13, 28n5, 69, 71n3, 296, 302, 303–4, 307
Blanck, R., 13, 28n5, 69, 71n3, 199n10, 296, 302, 303–4, 307
Bloom, M., 46
Blos, P., 28n6, 127
Blow, F.C., 260, 287n1
Blum, H.P., 20
Blythe, B.J., 46
Bolman, W.M., 229n13
Boskind-Lodahl, M., 20, 254n7
Bostwick, G.J., 173, 198n7
Bowker, L.H., 18, 23, 242
Bowlby, J., 3, 11–12, 17, 116, 138nn7, 8
Boyd-Franklin, N., 21
Brandchaft, B., 304
Brekke, J., 18, 244, 255n11
Brennan, E.M., 111n6
Brenner, C., 27n1
Briar, S., x, 30, 46
Bricker-Jenkins, M., 21
Brodsky, A.M., 20
Brooks-Gunn, J., 107
Broverman, D.M., 20
Broverman, I.K., 20
Brower, K.J., 260, 287n1
Buie, D.H., 296, 302, 304–5, 308–9
Burch, B., 22, 100, 130
Burland, J.A., 139n10
Butler, R.N., 18, 104

Caputo, L., 279
Carkhuff, R.R., 229n9
Carter, E.A., 199n12
Casriel, C., 287n4

Cass, V.C., 100
Cath, S., 126
Cetingok, M., 21, 233, 254n5, 255n13
Charkoudian, S., ix
Chernus, L.A., 264, 266
Chestang, L.W., 21, 98
Chilman, C.S., 255n9
Chodorow, N., 4, 20, 128, 139n11
Clark, C.G., 20
Clarkson, F.E., 20
Cockerill, E.E., 34
Coehlo, G.V., 18, 112n10
Colarusso, C., 102, 103, 111n5
Coleman, E., 22, 98, 100, 254n17
Colgan, P., 22, 253
Collier, H.V., 233
Collins, B.G., 20, 21, 254n7
Comas–Diaz, L., 21, 98
Cooper, L.B., 253n1
Cooperman, A., 273
Cottrell, L.S., 15
Courtois, C.A., 23, 102, 242, 282
Creigs, B., 287n2

Dane, B.O., 22, 274, 278, 288n11
Davies, J.M., 23, 101
Davis, J., 260
De Chillo, N., 271
DeCrescenzo, T.A., 22, 254n3
de la Cancela, V., 21, 99
Deutsch, H., 19, 293
Devore, W., 21
Dinnerstein, D., 4, 20
Drye, R., 292
Dumpson, J.R., 40, 46
Dunkel, J., 278

Edward, J., 139n13, 319n5
Eissler, K.R., 294
Elson, M., 18, 107, 134
Emery, G., 16
Englund, D.W., 319n4
Erikson, E., 3, 9–10, 19–20, 34, 69, 88–96,
    111n3, 113
Escalona, S.K., 17, 116
Espin, O.M., 21, 98
Evans, K., 260, 287n1
Ewalt, P., 45

Fairbairn, W.R.D., 4, 24, 131–32
Falco, K.L., 22, 98, 100, 256n17
Faria, G., 20, 282
Federn, P., 13, 292
Fewell, C.H., 258, 264
Field, M.H., 32, 49n1
Finestone, S., 295
Finkelhor, D., 101
Fischer, J., 40, 46
Foote, N.N., 15
Fox, E.F., 229n13
Frank, M.G., 49n10
Franklin, C., 273
Frawley, M.G., 23, 101
Freed, A.O., 319n2
Freeman, A., 16
French, T.M., 228n4
Freud, A., 6–7, 12, 27n2, 34, 76, 77–81,
    84n1, 111n2
Freud, S., 3, 4–6, 19, 53, 66, 68, 72, 76,
    85n6
Friedan, B., 20
Friedman, R.C., 22
Friedman, R.M., 22
Fromm, E., 3, 13, 14

Garrett, A., 34, 198n4, 228n1
Gatz, Y.K., 23, 102
Gediman, H., 9, 13, 54, 71n1, 113
George, K.D., 253
Germain, C.B., xiv, 26, 42, 48, 49n4,
    165n1, 198n8
Getzel, G.S., 18, 280
Ghali, S.B., 21, 99, 247
Gilligan, C., 4, 20, 97, 128
Gitterman, A., xiv, 26, 42, 165n1, 198n8
Gladwin, T., 15, 87
Goetz, K.M., 20
Golan, N., 17, 112n11, 165n5, 198n6
Goldsmith, D.S., 287n4
Goldstein, E.G., xv, 18, 42, 43, 46, 48,
    199nn12, 14, 16, 287nn3, 6, 288n9, 296,
    316, 318, 319nn1, 3
Gonsiorek, J.C., 22, 255n15
Goodman, J.A., 229n8
Gordon, W.E., 42
Gottlieb, N., 21
Gould, R.L., 18, 104, 111n5
Greenacre, P., 138n9
Greenberg, J.R., 24

Greenson, R., 204, 228n3
Greenspan, M., 21
Grinker, R.R., 17, 292, 319n4
Grinnell, R.M., 173, 198n7
Grinspoon, l., 274, 288n10
Groze, V., 44
Gunderson, J., 292, 319n4
Guntrip, H., 4, 24, 28n7, 132, 137n1
Gutierrez, L.M., 21, 234–38, 254nn5, 6

Hamburg, D.A., 18, 112n10
Hamilton, G., 30, 31, 32, 34, 228n1
Harris, M., 272
Hartmann, H., 3, 7–9, 12, 34, 53, 66, 69
Hatfield, S., 278
Henderson, D.C., 287n2
Hendrick, I., 69
Herman, J.L., 23, 102, 282, 305
Hetrick, E.S., 22, 98, 128, 252, 256n17
Hill, R., 17
Hirayama, H., 21, 233, 254n5, 255n13
Hoch, P., 292
Hogarty, G.E., 273, 318
Hollis, F., 30, 31, 34, 49n5, 170, 172, 173,
  198nn1, 4, 228n1, 295
Holroyd, J., 20
Hooyman, N.R., 21
Horner, A.J., 114
Horney, K., 3, 5, 13, 14, 19, 111n4
Horowitz, L., 310
Howell, E., 21, 255n8
Hudson, W., 46
Hurvich, M., 9, 13, 54, 71n1, 113

Inkeles, A., 87
Iodice, J.D., 273
Isay, R.A., 22, 256n17

Jacklin, C.N., 97
Jacobson, E., 3, 12, 13, 60, 132, 137n2,
  138nn4, 5
Janis, I., 17
Jones, B., 23, 102
Jones, D.L., 21, 246
Jordan, J.V., 20, 129

Kagan, R.M., 21
Kammerman, S., 41
Kaplan, A., 20, 129
Kaplan, D., 17

Kaufman, I., 319n2
Kernberg, O., 13, 24, 84nn2, 4, 132–33,
  138n5, 228n5, 296, 302, 306–7, 319n1,
  320n6
Kerr, J., 319n4
Kilgore, L.C., 23, 102
Kirsh, B., 107
Kisthardt, W., 254n4
Klein, G., 53
Klein, M., 4, 24, 131
Klerman, G.L., 20, 241, 292
Kline, C.M., 23, 102, 283
Kluckhohn, C., 15
Knight, R.A., 13, 293, 294
Kohlberg, L., 16, 97
Kohut, H., 4, 25, 133–34, 296, 302, 304,
  308
Kravetz, D., 20
Kris, E., 3, 7, 34
Kroeber, T.C., 75–76
Kroll, J., 23, 102, 293, 305
Kyte, N.S., 173, 198n7

Lang, J., 43
Laughlin, H.P., 77, 78
Lax, R.F., 139n10
Lazare, A., 294
Lazarus, R.S., 17
Lee, J.A.B., 18, 23, 199n11, 242
Leff, J.P., 270
Lehrman, L.J., 34
Le Masters, E., 17, 18, 111n7
Lerner, H.E., 20, 254n7
Levinson, D.J., 18, 105, 111n5
Levinson, V.R., 258
Levy, M.S., 259
Levy, R.L., 46
Lewis, L.A., 22, 100, 256n17
Lidz, T., 111n2
Liles, R.E., 18
Lindemann, E., 17, 112n8
Lipton, D.S., 287n4
Lopez, D., 18, 280
Lowenstein, A., 3
Lowenstein, R.M., 7, 34
Lubove, R., 30
Lutz, W., 35

McDonnell, J.R., 45
McFarlane, A.C., 23

McGoldrick, M., 199*n*12
McIntyre, J.R., 262
Mack, J.E., 76, 84*nn*1, 5
Mackey, R.A., ix
McNeil, J.S., 273
Magura, S., 287*n*4
Mahler, M.S., 3, 12, 60, 69, 116, 117, 120,
    122, 124, 125–26, 133, 135, 138*nn*5, 6,
    139*n*9, 302, 303
Maier, H.W., 28*nn*3, 9, 111*n*3, 138*n*3
Mailick, M., 30
Maluccio, A.N., 111*n*1, 229*n*7
Malyon, A.K., 22, 254*n*3, 255*n*16
Mancuso, A., 21
Marcus, E., 287*n*7
Markowitz, R., 262
Marlow, W.D., 229*n*7
Martin, A., 22, 254*n*3, 255*n*16
Martin, D.A., 22, 98, 128, 252, 256*n*17
Maslow, A.H., 3, 14–15
Masterson, J.F., 13, 296, 302, 303, 307
Matorin, S., 271
Mayer, J., 229*n*7
Mechanic, D., 26, 109, 294, 295
Meissner, W.W., 76, 84*nn*1, 5
Meyer, C.H., xv, 30, 32, 42, 47, 49*n*6,
    165*nn*2, 3
Middleman, R.R., 199*n*11
Miller, A., 23
Miller, H., x, 30
Miller, J.B., 4, 20, 129
Miller, S.O., 22, 278, 288*n*11
Millman, R.B., 260
Minahan, A., 229*n*12
Minrath, M., 21, 98
Mishne, J.M., xv, 24, 43
Mitchell, S.A., 24
Montijo, J.A., 21
Moriarity, A.E., 17, 112*n*9, 116
Mulinski, P., 258
Mullen, E.J., 40, 46
Munro, R., 28*n*8
Murphy, L.B., 17, 75, 112*n*9, 116
Murray, H.A., 3, 15

Nee, R.H., 41, 165*n*1
Nelsen, J., 288*n*8
Nelson, M.A., 229*n*13
Nemiroff, R.A., 102, 103, 111*n*5
Neugarten, B.L., 18, 104, 106, 111*n*5

Norman, E., 21
Nunberg, H., 8

O'Brien, A., 18
O'Malia, L., 20
O'Neill, M.M., 265
Orbach, S., 241
Orlin, L., 260

Panter, E.J., 287*n*8
Pape, P.A., 20, 261
Parad, H.J., 17, 198*n*4, 199*n*12
Parad, L.G., 17
Parloff, M.B., 40, 269
Patten, S.B., 23, 102
Peck, R., 18, 105
Perlman, H.H., 37, 46, 49*nn*8, 9, 198*n*4,
    201, 207, 228*n*1
Perry, J.C., 292
Piaget, J., 3, 16, 138*n*3
Pincus, A., 229*n*12
Pinderhughes, E.B., 21, 98, 234, 254*n*5
Pine, F., 12, 60, 69, 116, 117, 120, 122,
    124, 125–26, 138*n*5, 139*n*9
Polatin, P., 292
Polemis, B., 37, 49*n*7
Prozan, C.K., 22

Rank, O., 3, 14, 33
Rapaport, D., 3, 6, 9, 34
Rapoport, L., 17, 165*n*5
Rapoport, R., 111*n*7
Rapp, C., 254*n*4
Reich, W., 7, 84*n*2
Reid, W.J., 46
Reiss, D.J., 273, 318
Reiter, L., 130
Richman, G., 18, 20, 23, 242, 255*n*10
Richmond, M.L., 30–31
Rinsley, D., 302, 303
Ripple, L., 37, 49*n*7
Roberts, R.W., 41, 165*n*1
Robinson, J.B., 21, 245, 255*n*12
Robinson, V.P., 33, 228*n*1
Rogers, C.R., 3, 14, 229*n*9
Rosenkrantz, P.S., 20
Rosenthal, S.J., 18, 23, 242
Roskin, M., 47
Rossi, A., 107
Roth, S., 252

Rowland, S.J., Jr., 317
Rubin, A., 46
Rush, J., 16
Ruskin, N., 139n13, 319n5
Ryan, A.S., 21, 245, 247

Sacks, P., 34
Schafer, R., 20
Scharff, D.E., 24
Scharff, J.S., 24
Schlossberg, S.B., 21
Schmideberg, M., 291
Schwartz, R.D., 22, 253n2
Segal, H., 131
Seinfeld, J., 24
Selye, H., 17
Semrad, E.S., 76, 84nn1, 5
Shapiro, C.H., 23
Shapiro, E.R., 305, 309, 310
Shapiro, R.L., 305, 309, 310
Shaw, B.F., 16
Shevrin, H., 295
Simcox-Reiner, B., 109
Simon, B.K., xv
Simon, B.L., 20, 240
Simon, C.E., 273
Singer, M.T., 292
Siporin, M., 30, 34
Skodol, A.E., 290, 294
Smalley, R.E., 33
Smith, B., 15, 87
Solomon, B.B., 21, 234, 236, 246, 253n1, 254n6
Spaulding, E.C., 22, 130
Spiegel, B.R., 287n5
Spiegel, J.D., 17
Spitz, R., 3, 10–11, 69, 116, 138nn7, 8
Spitzer, R.L., 290, 294
Stamm, I., 29, 34
Star, B., 20
Stern, A., 291, 294
Stern, D., 4, 25, 134–36
Stiver, I., 129
Stoller, R., 96
Stolorow, R.D., 304
Stone, M.H., 319n1
Straussner, S.L.A., 258, 261, 262
Strean, H.S., xv, 42, 43, 45, 199n13
Stuart, R., 319n2
Sullivan, H.S., 3, 14

Sullivan, J.M., 260, 287n1
Sullivan, W.P., 254n4
Surrey, J.L., 20, 129
Symonds, A., 20, 254n7

Tabachnick, N., 18
Taft, J., 33
Taylor, E.H., 269
Thomas, D.L., 23, 102
Thomlison, R.J., 46
Thompson, C., 19
Timms, N., 229n7
Toffler, A., 27
Tolpin, M., 133
Towle, C., 34
Truax, C.B., 229n9
Tully, C., 22, 101
Turnbull, J.E., 20, 287n2
Turner, F.J., xi, 41, 43
Turner, S.F., 23
Turrini, P., 139n13, 319n5
Tyhurst, J., 17

Urek, M.B., ix

Vaillant, G.E., 18, 104, 111n5
Valentich, M., 20, 21, 236, 238, 254n6
Van Den Bergh, N., 253n1
Van der Kolk, B., 23, 102, 305
Vaughn, C.E., 270
Vogel, S.R., 20

Walsh, F., 319n4
Walsh, J., 288n9
Walton, E., 23, 102, 305
Walz, T., 44
Wasserman, S.L., 39
Weick, A., 111n6, 254n4
Weille, K.L.H., 22, 129
Weinberger, J., 319n2
Weissman, M.M., 20, 241
Werble, B., 292, 319n4
Werner, H.D., 16
Wheeler, B.R., 23, 102, 305
White, R.F., 15, 16, 18, 69, 84n3, 86, 87, 103–4, 111n5
Williams, J.B., 290, 294
Williams, J.H., 96
Wilson, M.N., 21

Winnicott, D.W., 4, 24, 132
Wodarski, J.S., 273
Wolberg, A.R., 310, 319n1
Wolberg, L., 228n3
Wolf, E.S., 25
Wood, K.M., 49n3
Woodroofe, K., 30, 31

Yarrow, L.J., 116
Yelaja, S.A., 33

Zelvin, E., 262
Zilboorg, G., 292
Zinner, J., 305, 309, 310
Zuckerwise, R.A., 268, 273–74

SUBJECT INDEX

Abandonment fears of borderline
 clients, 300
Abstinence from substance abuse,
 263–64
Acculturation, impact of, 247–48
Acquired immune deficiency
 syndrome. *See* AIDS, working
 with persons with
Activist, 173
Adaptation, xiv, 7–9, 86–112. *See also*
 Ego functions; Mastery-
 competence
 adaptive regression in service of ego,
 64–65
 in adulthood, 102–10
 alloplastic and autoplastic, 8
 assessment of, case examples of,
 145–63
 client-worker relationship and
 enhancement of, 212
 ego mastery and, 87–102
 social milieu's impact on, 109–10
 stress and crisis and, impact of, 108–9
Adaptive defenses, 65, 73
Addiction. *See* Substance abusers,
 working with
Adolescence, 12, 93–94, 127–28, 305–6
Adulthood
 adaptation in, 102–10
 coping with stress and crisis in, 108–9
 growth trends in, 103–4
 life review in, 104
 life stages of, 94–95, 104–7
 life structure of, 105–6
 object relations in, 136–37
 personality change in, 103–4
 role transitions in, 106
 social clock in, 104
 social milieu's impact on, 109–10

Adult life cycle, 18
Advocate role, 173, 214, 279
Affects, regulation and control of,
 59–60, 299–300
Agency, effect on client-worker
 relationship, 210
Aggressive intervener, 173
AIDS, working with persons with, 22,
 251, 274–81
Alcohol abuse. *See* Substance abusers,
 working with
Alcoholics Anonymous, 266
Altruism, 83, 84n6
Ambulatory schizophrenia, 292
American Psychiatric Association, 22,
 23, 290, 295
Anal stage, 5, 91
Anxiety, stranger, 120
Anxiety tolerance in borderline clients,
 299
Asceticism, 83
As if personality, 293
Assessment, 143–65. *See also*
 Adaptation; Borderline
 conditions; Defenses; Ego
 functions; Object relations
 of adult survivor of sexual abuse,
 283–84
 of AIDS patient, 279
 case examples illustrating, 145–63
 client-worker relationship and, 211
 data collection for, 163–64
 focus of, 143–63
 of gays and lesbians, 249–50
 influence of ego psychology on,
 35
 intervention and, 144–45, 163–64
 of people of color, 245–47
 questions guiding, 143–44

Assessment *(cont.)*
  of substance abusers, 261–62
  of women clients, 238–39
Attachment, social, 11, 115–16
Attachment theory, 10–12
Autistic phase, 12, 118
Autistic thinking, 63
Autonomous functions, 7–8, 66–68
Autonomy, enhancement of, 212
Autonomy of the ego, 7–8, 53, 66–68
Autonomy versus shame and doubt,
      10, 88, 91–92
Average expectable environment, 8

Bargainer, 173
Behavior, social determinants of, 13–14,
      35
Behavioral contracts, 265
Behavioral modification, 41
Biculturalism, 248
Biological determinism, 19–20, 95–97
Biological model of causality for
      schizophrenia, 268–69
Biopsychosocial perspective
  in assessing AIDS patient, 279
  on schizophrenics, 270–74
  on substance abusers, 260–61, 262
Bisexual orientation, 130
Blaming the victim, 19
Blank screen, 32, 228n2
Bonding, 115–16
Borderline conditions, 289–320
  borderline personality versus
      borderline schizophrenia, 291–92
  causes of, 293, 302–6
  clinical interventions for, 309–18,
      320n6
  concept of, 290–94
  controlling regression and impulsive
      or destructive behavior in, 299,
      315–16
  developmental characteristics of,
      296–301
  family contributions to, 305–6, 309
  goals of intervention in, 309–10
  historical controversies regarding,
      291–94
  identity disturbances in, 296–97, 302
  maintaining working alliance in,
      310–16

negative transference in, dealing
      with, 312–15
  primitive defenses in, 83, 297–98, 302,
      303, 304, 305–6, 312–15
  rapprochement difficulties in,
      303
  reality testing in, 298–99
  research on distinguishing features
      of, 292–93
  treatment models for, 293–94, 306–9
  use of structure with, 315–16
British School of Object Relations,
      12–13, 24, 131–32, 137n1
Broker role, 173, 279

Caregivers of AIDS patient, working
      with, 277–78, 281
Case management for schizophrenics,
      271–72
Causal relationships, reality testing and
      understanding, 55
Character defenses. *See* Defenses
Character traits, 7, 74, 84n2
Charity Organization Society, 30
Checking-back pattern, 120
Chemical dependence. *See* Substance
      abusers, working with
Child development. *See* Adaptation;
      Defenses; Ego functions; Object
      relations; Research
Child development research, 11–12, 69,
      115–28
Childhood and Society (Erikson), 9
Childhood disorders, 11–12
Chinese-Americans, working with,
      245–46, 247
Civil rights movement, 40–41
Client need, centrality of, 201
Client strengths, enhancing, 234–35
Client-worker relationship, 200–229. *See
      also* Diverse and oppressed
      populations
  agency characteristics influencing,
      210
  in assessment, 211
  with borderline clients, 309–18
  characteristics of, 200–206
  client characteristics influencing,
      207–9
  corrective experience in, 212–13

countertransference in, 205–6, 265, 278–79
in ego-supportive intervention, 169–70
equalizing power in, 236
important values and attitudes in, 202
influence of ego psychology on, 36
management of, 214–27
positive use of, 219–21
real aspects of, 202–4
termination phase of, 225–27
transference in, 32, 204–5, 221–24, 312–15
treatment of schizophrenia and, 272
uses of, 211–14
worker characteristics influencing, 209
worker's disciplined use of self in, 201–2
working alliance in, 202–4, 205, 215, 310–16
Clinical social work, definition of, 45
Cognitive development, 16–17
Cohesive self, 134
Collaboration, client-worker relationship and, 214
Collective action, encouraging, 238
"Coming out," stages of, 100, 252
Community organization, 41
Compensation, 82–83
Competence, 15, 68–69, 87. See also Mastery-competence
Complex post-traumatic stress disorder, 282
Concrete operations, stage of, 16
Conferee, 173
Confidentiality, 202
Conflict-free ego functions, 8, 66–68
Confrontation of substance abuser, 264–65
Contracting, 215, 265
Coping capacity, 69
Coping mechanisms, 17–18, 75–76. See also Adaptation; Mastery-competence
Core self, sense of, 135
Corrective relationship, 212–13
Counselor, 280
Countertransference, 205–6, 265, 278–79

Creativity, 64
Crisis
AIDS diagnosis as, 276
developmental, 9, 88–95
importance of resolution of, 9, 88
life stage, 105–6
problem-solving skills in, 18
role transition, 106
traumatic, 108
Crisis intervention, 41
Crisis theory, 17–18
Critical periods, 11, 116
Cultural background, issues in work with people of different, 245–49
Cultural values, appreciating client's, 231–32

Data collection for assessment, 163–64
Defenses, 65, 72–85. See also Ego-modifying intervention; Ego-supportive intervention
adaptive versus maladaptive, 65, 73, 74, 188–91
of adult survivor of sexual abuse, 283
assessment of, case examples of, 145–63
concept of, 6–7, 65, 72–75
coping mechanisms versus, 75–76
definition and examples of, 76–83
expansion and refinement of, 6–7
faulty reality testing and, 55–56
origins of, 74, 84n6
primitive, in borderline clients, 83, 297–98, 302, 303, 304, 305–6, 312–15
problems in working with, 74–75
Deinstitutionalization movement, 268
Delusions, 56. See also Reality testing
Denial, 82, 277, 298
Depersonalization, 58
"Depreciated character," 98
Depression era, 33
Depression in female population, 241
Depressive position, 131
Derealization, 58
Despair, ego integrity versus, 10, 88, 95
Devaluation, 83, 298
Development. See Adaptation; Defenses; Ego functions; Object relations

Developmental reflection, 171
Developmental tasks and crises,
    mastery of, 9, 88–95
Diagnosis. *See also* Assessment
    of borderline conditions, 294–301
    clinical, 294–96
    developmental, 294
    dual diagnosis perspective, 260
    pros and cons of, 295
*Diagnostic and Statistical Manual of
    Mental Disorders: Fourth Edition
    (DSM IV)*, 295–96
*Diagnostic and Statistical Manual of
    Mental Disorders: Third Edition
    (DSM III)*, 22, 290
Diagnostic school of casework, 33,
    38
Differentiation, reality testing and,
    54–55
Differentiation subphase, 12, 118,
    120–21
Direct influence, 171
Direct practice, resurgence of, 43–45
Discharge planning, 274, 317–18
Disciplined use of self, worker's, 201–2
Discrimination, 109–10, 245, 248. *See
    also* Diverse and oppressed
    populations
Disease model of addiction, 258–59
Disengagement in adolescence, 127–28
Displacement, 81
Dissociation, 283
Distortions, 55–56, 58
Diverse and oppressed populations,
    108
    awareness of and research on, 21–22,
        47, 98–101
    ego-oriented intervention with,
        230–56
        gays and lesbians, 249–53
        general principles of, 231–38
        people of color, 245–49
        women, 238–45
Domains of relatedness, 134–36
Domestic violence, 243–45
Drives, regulation and control of, 59–60
Drug abuse. *See* Substance abusers,
    working with
Dual diagnosis perspective, 260
Dynamic theory, 9

Eating disorders in women, 241
Ecological perspective, 42–43, 198n8
Economic status of women, 240
Economic theory, 9
Educative role and techniques, 172, 214,
    279
Effectance, 87. *See also* Mastery-
    competence
Efficacy, feeling of, 87. *See also* Mastery-
    competence
Egalitarian model of therapeutic
    relationship, adoption of, 236
Ego, xi, xii
    autonomy of, 7–8, 53, 66–68
    definition of, 5–6, 53
    organizing capacity of, 8
    regression in the service of, 64–65
Ego and the Id, The (Freud), 4, 5–6, 53
Ego and the Mechanisms of Defense, The
    (Freud), 6, 76
Ego apparatuses, 8, 53
Ego assessment. *See* Assessment
Ego boundaries, 58–59, 115
Ego-building approach. *See* Ego-
    supportive intervention
Ego dystonic, 198n5
Ego-dystonic homosexuality, 22
Ego-enhancing intervention, 175–76,
    183–87. *See also* Ego-supportive
    intervention
Ego functions, xii, 53–54
    adaptation and, 8
    assessment of, case examples of,
        145–63
    in borderline clients, 302, 303
    ego strength versus ego weakness,
        70, 144
    impact on client-worker relationship,
        208–9
    major, 54–70
    schizophrenia and, 269
Ego identity. *See* Identity
Ego integrity versus despair, 10, 88, 95
Ego-maintaining intervention, 175,
    180–83. *See also* Ego-supportive
    intervention
Ego mastery, adaptation and, 87–102.
    See also Mastery-competence
    efficacy and competence, 87
    feminist critique of, 95–97

mastery of developmental tasks and crises, 88–95

oppression and diversity, effects of, 98–101

trauma and, impact of, 23, 101–2

Ego-modifying intervention, 166–99. *See also* Borderline conditions; Client-worker relationship

appropriate client populations for, 173–74

case examples of, 188–91

characteristics of, 167–74

duration of, 174

ego-supportive intervention versus, 167–74

environmental intervention in, 172–73

focus of, 168–69

goals of, 166, 187–88

nature of change in, 169

transference reactions in, 205

Ego psychology

assimilation to social work, 29, 34–39

cognitive and learning theory, 16–17

criticism of, 40–41

definition of, xi–xv

emergence of, 34–37

emphasis on competence, 15

extensions of psychoanalytic theory, 6–13

Freud's structural theory and, 4–6

historical perspectives on, 29–39

implications for service delivery and social policy, 37, 47–48

influence on social work, x, 29, 35–38

issues of use in casework, 38–39

newer areas of inquiry, 18–23

personality theories with linkages to, 24–27

problem-solving model and, 37–38

psychoanalytic. *See* Psychoanalytic ego psychology

recent trends in society and social work practice, 43–46

scope and evolution of, 3–28

self-actualization and growth motivation in, 14–15

social determinants of behavior in, 13–14, 35

social work pioneers associated with, 34

stress and crisis in, 17–18

theoretical streams within, xiii–xiv

view of human functioning in, xi, xii–xiii, 35

Ego-restorative intervention, 174–75, 177–80. *See also* Ego-supportive intervention

Ego-strengthening. *See* Ego-supportive intervention

Ego strength versus weakness, 70, 144. *See also* Ego functions

Ego-supportive intervention

appropriate client populations for, 173

case examples of, 177–87

characteristics of, 167–74

client-worker relationship in, 169–70

duration of, 174

ego-building approach to borderline clients, 307, 316–17

ego-modifying intervention versus, 167–74

environmental intervention in, 172–73

focus of, 168–69

goals of, 166, 174–76

nature of change in, 169

psychological techniques in, 170–72

transference reactions in, 204–5

Ego syntonic, 198*n*5

Eliminative mode, 91

Emergent self, sense of, 135

Empowerment, 235, 237–38

Enabler, role of, 173, 280

Engagement phase, 215–19

Environmental intervention, 172–73, 214

Environmental stress, 17, 109, 112*n*9, 259

Environmental systems, impact of, 4, 25–27, 109–10, 259

Ethnicity, working with people of different, 245–49

Euthanasia, AIDS and, 280

Expectations, client, 207–8

Exploration, description, and ventilation, 171

"False" self, 132
Family
    of AIDS patient, psychosocial impact
        on, 275–78
    borderline conditions and, 305–6,
        317–18, 320n6
    schizophrenia and, 269–70, 273
    of substance abuser, focus on, 262,
        267
Family life cycle, 192–93
Family systems theory
    casework and, 41
    ego-oriented family intervention, 191,
        192–97, 267, 273, 285–86, 317–18,
        320n6
    influence of ego psychology on, 26
Father, role of, 126–27. See also
        Adaptation; Object relations
Federation of Societies for Clinical
        Social Work, 42
Feminine Mystique, A (Friedan), 20
Feminist perspective, 4, 20, 95–97,
        128–30
Formal operations, stage of, 16
Free association, 32, 204
Freudian psychoanalytic theory. See
        Psychoanalytic theory
Functional school of casework, 33,
        38
Future Shock (Toffler), 27

Gay and lesbian liberation movement,
        21–22, 40–41
Gay and lesbian life, 99–101
    adolescence and, 128
    AIDS and, 274, 275, 277–78
    selected issues in work with, 249–53
Gender identification, 92, 96–97,
        99–100, 125
Gender-specific issues, 238–45. See also
        Women
Generativity versus stagnation, 10, 88,
        95
Genetic-developmental theory, 9
Good enough mothering, 132
Group intervention, ego-oriented, 26,
        41, 191–92, 267, 273, 286, 318
Group membership and
        individualization, balancing
        focus on, 233–34

Growth motivation, 14–15
Guilt, initiative versus, 10, 88, 92

Hallucinations, 56. See also Reality
        testing
Hatching, 120–21
Health issues of women, 240–41
HIV retrovirus, 275, 276. See also AIDS,
        working with persons with
Holding environment, therapeutic, 263,
        265–66, 284–85, 311, 318
Homophobia, 22, 98, 251–52
Homosexuality, 21–22, 99–101
    selected issues in dealing with,
        249–53
Hope, sustenance of, 212
Human life cycle
    in adulthood, 94–95, 104–7
    Eriksonian stages, 9–10, 88–95
    gay and lesbian functioning over,
        100–101
    implications for service delivery
        during, 47
    women's life cycle events and roles,
        107–8, 240

Id, 6
Idealization, 82, 84n6, 283, 298
Identification, 79–80, 84n6
    with the aggressor, 79
    with external objects, 6
    gender, 92, 96–97, 99–100, 125
    projective, 83, 298
Identity
    in borderline clients, 296–97, 302
    changes in adulthood, 94–95
    crisis resolution and, 88–89
    diffusion, 302, 306
    mastery of developmental tasks and,
        88–89
    negative, 94
    role confusion versus, 10, 88, 93–94
Identity and the Life Cycle (Erikson),
        9
Identity formation, 10
    diversity and oppression, effect on,
        98–101, 252
    stages in, 89–95, 104–7, 118–27
Immigration, impact of, 247–48
Impulse control, 59–60, 299, 315–16

Incest, 101, 281, 305. *See also* Sexual
abuse
Incorporation, 80
Incorporative mode, 90
Individuality, attainment of, 125–26
Individualization, 99, 233–34
Individual treatment, 263–66, 272
Industry versus inferiority, 10, 88, 92–93
Infancy. *See* Adaptation; Defenses; Ego
functions; Object relations
Inhibitions, Symptoms, and Anxiety
(Freud), 72
Initiative versus guilt, 10, 88, 92
Innate ego apparatuses, 8
In-patient treatment for substance
abusers, 266
Instinct theory, psychoanalytic, 68
Instinctual determinants of behavior, 5
Integrative approaches in working with
substance abusers, 260–61
Integrity versus despair and disgust,
10, 88, 95
Intellectualization, 81
Intelligence, 16–17
Internalization, 80, 84n6, 125–26
Internalized homophobia, 251–52
Internalized object relations. *See* Object
relations
Interpersonal relationships of
borderline clients, 301. *See also*
Object relations
Interpretation of dreams, 32, 204
Intersubjective relatedness, 136
Intervention. *See also* Borderline
conditions; Client-worker
relationship; Diverse and
oppressed populations; Ego-
modifying intervention; Ego-
supportive intervention; Family
systems theory; Group
intervention, ego-oriented;
Techniques of intervention
assessment and, 144–45, 163–64
influence of ego psychology on,
35–36
short-term versus long-term, 163–64
Intimacy, borderline clients' problems
with, 301
Intimacy and distantiation versus self-
absorption, 10, 88, 94

Introjection, 79
Intrusive mode, 92
Isolation, 78, 251–52

Judgment, 56–58

Knowledge explosion, 41

Language, development of, 124, 136
Latency, 92
Latent schizophrenia, 292
Learning model of addiction, 258–59
Learning theory, 16–17
Lesbian object relations, 129–30. *See also*
Gay and lesbian life
Licensing, status through, 44
Life cycle, family, 192–93. *See also*
Human life cycle
Life experiences, influence of client, 208
Life model. *See* Ecological perspective
Life review, 104
Life stages, 9–10, 88–102
Life structure, 105–6
Limit-setting strategy with substance
abusers, 265
Lobbyist, 173

Maladaptive defenses, 65, 73, 188–91
Male machismo, 99
Marasmus, 11
Mastery-competence. *See also*
Adaptation
in adulthood, 102–10
concept of, 68–69
of developmental tasks, 88–95
emphasis on, 15
influence of social milieu on, 109–10
of life stages, 105–6
of role transitions, 106
of stress and crisis, 108–9
Maternal deprivation, 11
Maximization of client choice, 236–37
Mediator role, 173, 214, 279
Medical model, 39, 40, 294
Mental health model for working with
addicts, 258
Microsystems intervention, 43
Middle age. *See* Adulthood
Mistrust, trust versus, 10, 88, 89–91
Moral development, 16, 97

Moral values, impact of, 29–30
Mother. *See* Adaptation; Object relations
Mother–child observational studies, 11–12
Mothering, good enough, 132
Motivation, 37–38, 207–8, 212
Mutual aid groups, 237–38, 281
Mutual regulation, 91–92, 135

Narcissism, primary, 118
Narcissistic disorders, 25
Narcotics Anonymous, 266
National Association of Social Workers, 42, 45
Natural support networks, 247
Need-fear dilemma of borderline clients, 305, 308
Needs
    centrality of client, 201
    innate, 15
    selfobject, 133–34, 304
Negative affects in borderline clients, 300
Neuroses, 14, 23, 204
Neutralization, 8

Object constancy, 12, 119, 125–26
Object relations, 60–62, 113–39
    in adolescence, 12, 127–28, 305
    in adulthood, 136–37
    assessment of, case examples of, 145–63
    in borderline clients, 302
    British School of Object Relations, 12–13, 24, 131–32, 137n1
    in childhood, 117–27
    concept of, 60, 113–15
    development of, 117–27
    ego development and, 10–13
    father's role in, 126–27
    feminist views on, 128–30
    Kernberg's theory of, 132–33
    object representations, 114
    self psychology and, 133–34
    self-representations, 114
    separation-individuation and, 12, 117–27
    social attachment in, 115–16
    Stern's four senses of self, 134–36

Object representations, 114
Oedipal conflict, 5, 92
Old age. *See* Adulthood
Ombudsman, 173
Omnipotent control, 83, 298
Oppression, effect of, 98–101, 248–49. *See also* Diverse and oppressed populations
Options, educating clients about, 236–37
Oral stage, 5, 90, 114
Organizational theory, 26
Organizers of the psyche, 11
Outcome studies. *See* Research

Paranoid/schizoid position, 131
Parent-child relationships. *See* Adaptation; Object relations
Pattern-dynamic reflection, 171
Peer supports, connecting clients to, 237–38
People of color, working with, 245–49, 274, 278
Personality change, 103–4, 213
Personality development, socialization of women and, 239–40
Personality disorder, borderline condition as, 291
Personality theories, 4, 24–25
Personal power, building, 235
Person-situation reflection, 171
Phallic stage, 5, 92
Phases of intervention, 36–37
    engagement phase, 215–19
    termination phase, 225–27
Political action, encouraging, 238
Political values, impact of, 29–30
Post-traumatic stress disorder (PTSD), 23, 102, 242, 282
Poverty, 109–10, 248
Power in client-worker relationship, equalizing, 236
Practice setting, effect of, 210
Practice studies, importance of, 37, 46
Practicing subphase, 12, 118–19, 121–23
Preoperational stage, 16
Primary autonomy of the ego, 8, 53, 66–68
Primary caretaker. *See* Adaptation; Object relations

Primary narcissism, 118
Primary prevention, 47
Primary process thinking, 62–63
Problem solving, xiii–xiv, 18, 37–38, 212
Projection, 78
Projective identification, 83, 298
Pseudoneurotic schizophrenia, 292
"Psychiatric Deluge," 31
Psychiatric hospitalization of
    borderline clients, 317–18
Psychic determinism, 5
Psychoanalytic ego psychology, xiii. *See
    also* Adaptation; Borderline
    conditions; Defenses; Ego
    functions; Object relations
    major contributors to, 3, 4–13
    refinements and extensions of, 44
Psychoanalytic instinct theory, 68
Psychoanalytic theory
    criticisms of, 5, 7, 9
    ego psychological roots in, 4–6
    extensions and refinements of, 6–13
    focus of, xiii
    major concepts of, 4–6, 32
    psychoanalysis and, 5, 32, 204–6,
        228*n*2
    social casework and, 31–34
    structural theory in, 4–6
Psychodynamic model of causality for
    schizophrenia, 269
Psychosexual stages, 5, 88, 90, 91, 92
Psychosis, autistic and symbiotic, 12
Psychosocial model of casework, 41
Psychosocial stages, 9, 88–95
Psychotropic drugs, use of, 267, 269,
    271, 317

Race, working with people of different,
    245–49
Racism, 93, 98, 109–10, 245, 246, 248–49.
    See also Diverse and oppressed
    populations
Rape, 241, 242–43
Rapprochement subphase, 12, 119,
    123–25, 303
Rational ego, focus on, xiii–xiv
Rationalization, 81
Reaction formation, 77
Real client-worker relationship, 202–4
Reality, sense of, 58–59

Reality testing, 54–56, 298–99
Recovery model of addiction, 258–59
Regression, 7, 64–65, 67, 78–79, 315–16
Relatedness, domains of, 134–36
Relationship issues for gay and lesbian
    couples, 252–53
Religious values, impact of, 29–30
Repression, 77
Research
    on adulthood, 104–7
    on child development, 11–12, 69,
        115–28
    on client motivation, capacity, and
        opportunity, 37–38
    on effectiveness of social casework,
        40
    practice, importance of, 37, 46
Resistance, 32, 74
Resource mobilization, 214, 237, 267–68,
    273–74
Retention mode, 91
Reversal, 80
Role confusion, 10, 88, 93–94
Role flexibility in working with AIDS
    patients, 279–80
Role model, 212–13
Role transitions, 106

Schizoid mechanisms, 132
Schizophrenia, borderline, 291–92
Schizophrenic chronically mentally ill,
    working with, 268–74
Scientific charity, 30
Seasons of life. *See* Life stages
Secondary autonomy of the ego, 8,
    67
Secondary process thinking, 63
Self, the
    cohesive, 134, 301
    "false," 132
    intervention in borderline cases with
        use of, 316
    sense of reality of, 58–59
    Stern's four phases of self
        development, 25, 134–36
    turning against, 80
    worker's disciplined use of, 201–2
Self-absorption, intimacy and
    distantiation versus, 10, 88, 94
Self-actualization, 14–15

Self-awareness, worker's exercise of,
      232–33
Self-cohesion problems of borderline
      clients, 301
Self-confidence, building, 235
Self-determination, 33, 202
Self-esteem, building, 235
Self-esteem regulation problems in
      borderline clients, 300–301
Self-help groups, use of, 266, 286
Self-in-relation theory, 129
Selfobject needs, 133–34, 304
Self psychology, 25, 133–34, 304,
      307–8
Self-representations, 114
Self-soothing problems in borderline
      clients, 300
Sensory–motor stage, 16
Separation-individuation process
   in adolescence, 12, 127–28, 305
   assessment of, case examples of,
      145–63
   in development of borderline
      conditions, 303–4, 305
   development of object constancy
      during, 119, 125–26
   father's role in, 126–27
   impact on adulthood, 136–37
   phases of, 12, 117–27
   Stern's four phases of self
      development and, 134–36
   termination phase and, 227
Service delivery and social policy,
      influence of ego psychology on,
      37, 47–48
Settlement movement, 30
Sexism. See Diverse and oppressed
      populations; Women
Sex-role stereotypes, 139n11
Sexual abuse, 241–42
   borderline disorders and childhood,
      305
   trauma of, 23, 101–2
   working with adult survivors of,
      281–86
Sexual orientation. See Homosexuality
Shame and doubt, autonomy versus,
      10, 88, 91–92
Simpson, Nicole and O.J., 244
Smiling response, 116

Social attachment, 11, 115–16. See also
      Object relations
Social casework
   assimilation and influence of ego
      psychology on, 34–39
   Charity Organization Society and, 30
   criticism of use of ego psychology in,
      39
   diagnostic versus functional schism,
      33, 38
   early pioneers in, 30–39
   importance of practice research in,
      46
   origins of, 30–31
   problem-solving model, 37–38
   proliferation of practice models in, 41
   psychoanalytic theory and, 31–34
   research on effectiveness of, 40
   social treatment and, 34
Social change, 4, 26–27. See also Social
      reform
Social clock, 104
Social determinants of behavior, 13–14,
      35
Social environment, work with, 172–73,
      214
Socialization approach, 41
Socialization of women, 239–40
Social reform, 30, 34, 39–40
Social structure, influence on identity,
      coping, and ego development,
      26–27
Social work profession. See also Social
      casework
   antagonistic trends in, 30
   Charity Organization Society, 30
   diagnostic versus functional schism,
      33, 38
   early pioneers in, 30–39
   emphasis on macrosystems
      intervention, 39–40
   emphasis on social reform, 30, 34,
      39–40
   expansion of group work and
      community organization, 41
   influence of knowledge explosion on,
      41
   origins of, 30
   phases in history of, 30–43
   polarization of, 41–43

recent trends in society and, 43–46
unification of, 42–43
Social Work Treatment (Turner), 41
Sociocultural factors, influence on
    client-worker relationship, 208
Sociopolitical context, appreciating
    impact of, 231–32
Somatization, 82
Splitting, 83, 123, 124, 283, 297–98, 302,
    304, 312–13, 315
Spouse abuse, 241, 243–45
Stagnation, generativity versus, 10, 88,
    95
Stigma, 251–52, 274–76, 278. *See also*
    Diverse and oppressed
    populations
Stimulus barrier, 65–66
Stone Center for Developmental
    Services and Studies at Wellesley
    College, 129
Stonewall rebellion (New York City,
    1969), 21
Stranger anxiety, 120
Strengths perspective, 234–35
Stress. *See also* Crisis
    assessment of, 143–63
    environmental, 17, 109, 112n9, 259
    impact on ego, 17–18
    of people of color, 245
    post–traumatic stress disorder
        (PTSD), 23, 102, 242, 282
Structural theory, 4–6, 9
Structured settings for schizophrenics,
    271
Structuring techniques, 172
Subjective self, sense of, 135–36
Sublimation, 81, 84n6
Substance abusers, working with,
    257–68
    assessment, nature of, 261–62
    clinical interventions, 263–68
    integrative approaches, 260–61
    perspectives on substance abuse,
        258–59
Suicide, AIDS and, 280
Superego, 6, 301
Superego functioning, 125
Support groups, use of, 237–38, 273–74,
    281, 286
Sustainment, 170, 171

Symbiotic phase, 12, 118, 119, 135
Symbiotic psychosis, 12
Symbolization, 16
Synthetic–integrative function, 8, 69–
    70

Techniques of intervention. *See also*
    Client-worker relationship; Ego-
    modifying intervention; Ego-
    supportive intervention; Family
    systems theory
    with borderline clients, 309–18
    environmental, 172–73, 214
    group intervention, 26, 41, 191–92,
        267, 273, 286, 318
    individual treatment, 263–66, 272
    in psychoanalysis, 5, 32, 204–6, 228n2
    psychological, 170–72
    uses of, 177–91, 193–97
Termination phase, 225–27
Therapeutic holding environment, 263,
    265–66, 284–85, 311, 318
"Therapeutic neutrality," 228n2
Therapeutic relationship. *See* Client-
    worker relationship
Thorazine, 268
Thought processes, 62–63
Timing of interventions with adult
    survivors of sexual abuse, 284
Toilet training, 91
Topographic theory, 4, 9
Transference, 32, 204–5, 221–24, 312–15
Transference neurosis, 204
Transitional objects, 120, 132
Trauma
    of adult survivors of sexual abuse,
        281–86
    impact of early childhood, 23, 101–2,
        305
    women's vulnerability to, 241–45
    working through past, 285
Trust versus mistrust, 10, 88, 89–91
Turning against the self, 80
Twelve-step programs for substance
    abuser, 266

Unconscious determinants of behavior,
    4
Undifferentiated matrix, 8
Undoing, 78

Values, client, 29–30, 208, 231–32
Verbal self, sense of, 136
Victimization. *See* Diverse and
    oppressed populations
Violence, domestic, 243–45

Wife battering, 243–45
Will, 14
Women
  in adulthood, 107–8
  eating disorders in, 241
  Erikson's views of development of,
    95–96
    feminist critique of, 96–97

lesbian, 99–101, 249–53
life cycle events and roles, 107–8,
    240
object relations and, 128–30
research on development of, 96–97
selected issues in work with, 238–45
sexually abused as children, working
    with, 241–42, 281–86
views of, 19–21
Women's liberation movement, 20,
    40–41
Working alliance, 202–4, 205, 215,
    310–16
World War I, 31